# National Symposium on Family Issues

Volume 7

**Series Editors**
Susan M. McHale
Valarie King
Jennifer Van Hook



More information about this series at http://www.springer.com/series/8381

Linda M. Burton • Dorian Burton
Susan M. McHale • Valarie King
Jennifer Van Hook
Editors

# Boys and Men in African American Families

Springer

*Editors*
Linda M. Burton
Trinity College of Arts and Science
Duke University
Durham, NC, USA

Susan M. McHale
Social Science Research Institute
The Pennsylvania State University
University Park, PA, USA

Jennifer Van Hook
Department of Sociology
The Pennsylvania State University
University Park, PA, USA

Dorian Burton
Charles Hamilton Houston Institute
for Race and Justice
Harvard University
Cambridge, MA, USA

Valarie King
Department of Sociology
The Pennsylvania State University
University Park, PA, USA

ISSN 2192-9157 ISSN 2192-9165 (electronic)
National Symposium on Family Issues
ISBN 978-3-319-82923-4 ISBN 978-3-319-43847-4 (eBook)
DOI 10.1007/978-3-319-43847-4



Printed on acid-free paper

This Springer imprint is published by Springer Nature
The registered company is Springer International Publishing AG
The registered company address is: Gewerbestrasse 11, 6330 Cham, Switzerland

*To Alan Booth 1935–2015*
*Scholar, mentor, colleague, and friend.*

# Acknowledgments

Penn State's 2015 Annual Symposium on Family Issues and this resulting volume were inspired by recent trends in the rise of mass incarceration and shootings of black men and boys in mostly urban settings in the United States. We acknowledge the sacredness of these boys' and men's lives, and we dedicate this volume to their memories and to their families with the hope that the knowledge presented here will contribute to bringing these travesties to an end. What is more, this Symposium and the 22 that came before it would have never been possible without the commitment and dedication of Dr. Alan Booth who passed away last winter. Alan launched these symposia, and his legacy provided the scholarly platform for the important work presented here. We honor him for his tireless effort to bring families center stage in the lives of all people and dedicate this volume to him as well.

The editors are also grateful to many organizations for cosponsoring the Symposium and the edited volume including Penn State's Social Science Research Institute (SSRI), Population Research Institute (PRI), Prevention Research Center, and Departments of Sociology and Criminology, Human Development and Family Studies, Psychology, Biobehavioral Health, and Anthropology; Duke University's Trinity College of Arts and Sciences; and the Charles Hamilton Houston Institute for Race and Justice at Harvard University. The editors also gratefully acknowledge essential core financial support in the form of a 5-year grant from the Eunice Kennedy Shriver National Institute of Child Health and Human Development (NICHD), R13-HD048150, as well as ongoing advice from Regina Bures at NICHD. The support of our partners enabled us to attract outstanding scholars from a range of backgrounds and disciplines from the community of researchers, practitioners, and policy makers on whom the quality of the series depends.

The efforts of many individuals went into planning the 2015 Symposium and producing this volume. Our internal advisory board, consisting of Paul Amato, Emilie Smith, Dawn Witherspoon, Greg Fosco, Rhonda Belue, Patricia Miranda, Doug Teti, Kevin Thomas, Sarah Damaske, and Mayra Bamaca, were helpful from the early stages of brainstorming for the 2015 Symposium. The editors also thank the authors who produced the chapters of this volume as well as Shawn Dove (CEO, Campaign for Black Male Achievement) and Bryant Marks (associate professor of Psychology,

Morehouse College, and director, Morehouse Male Initiative) whose presentations contributed to the success of the Symposium. In addition, we are very grateful to Dawn Witherspoon, Olivenne Skinner, Eric Baumer, and Patricia Miranda for presiding over symposium sessions and Linda Burton for providing the welcoming remarks. We also thank the administrative staff in the Population Research Institute and the Social Science Research Institute at Penn State including Sherry Yocum, Molly Heckard, Angela Jordan, Stephanie Eickstedt, and Diane Diviney. Finally, the Symposium and book would not have been possible without Carolyn Scott's organizational skills, commitment, and attention to the many details that go into developing an engaging conference and producing a scholarly volume.

Linda M. Burton
Dorian Burton
Susan M. McHale
Valarie King
Jennifer Van Hook

# Contents

# Contributors

**Britni L. Adams** Department of Sociology, University of California, Irvine, CA, USA

**Leslie B. Adams** University of North Carolina, Gillings School of Global Public Health, Chapel Hill, NC, USA

**Julie Ober Allen** Department of Health Behavior and Health Education, University of Michigan School of Public Health, Ann Arbor, MI, USA

**Shervin Assari** Department of Psychiatry and Center for Research on Ethnicity, Culture and Health, University of Michigan, Ann Arbor, MI, USA

**Bobby Austin** Neighborhood Associates Corporation, Washington, DC, USA

**Eryn Piper Block** Department of Health Policy and Management, Field School of Public health, UCLA, Los Angeles, CA, USA

**Andre Brown** University of North Carolina, Gillings School of Global Public Health, Chapel Hill, NC, USA

**Linda M. Burton** Trinity College of Arts and Sciences, Duke University, Durham, NC, USA

**Dorian Burton** Charles Hamilton Houston Institute for Race and Justice, Harvard University, Cambridge, MA, USA

**Cleopatra Howard Caldwell** Department of Health Behavior and Health Education, University of Michigan, Ann Arbor, MI, USA

**Emily K. Cornish** Center for Research on Men's Health, Vanderbilt University, Nashville, TN, USA

**Donnatesa A.L. Dean** Department of Public Health, Brown School of Social Work, Washington University in St. Louis, MO, USA

**Cheyney C. Dobson** Department of Sociology, University of Michigan, Ann Arbor, MI, USA

**Derek M. Griffith** Center for Research on Men's Health and Center for Medicine, Health, and Society, Vanderbilt University, Nashville, TN, USA

**Cecily R. Hardaway** Department of African American Studies, University of Maryland, College Park, MD, USA

**David J. Harding** Department of Sociology, University of California Berkeley, Berkeley, CA, USA

**Jennifer Van Hook** Population Research Institute, The Pennsylvania State University, University Park, PA, USA

**Truman Hudson Jr.** BMe Community, Detroit, MI, USA

**Marcus Anthony Hunter** Department of Sociology and Department of African American Studies, UCLA, Los Angeles, CA, USA

**Wade C. Jacobsen** Department of Sociology and Criminology, The Pennsylvania State University, University Park, PA, USA

**Valarie King** Department of Sociology and Criminology, The Pennsylvania State University, University Park, PA, USA

**Erin B. Lane** Department of Sociology, University of Michigan, Ann Arbor, MI, USA

**Jocelyn R. Smith Lee** Department of Psychology, The School of Social and Behavioral Science, Marist College, Poughkeepsie, NY, USA

**Na Liu** Department of Medicine, Division of Allergy, Pulmonary and Critical Care, Vanderbilt University Medical Center, Nashville, TN, USA

**Susan M. McHale** Social Science Research Institute, The Pennsylvania State University, University Park, PA, USA

**Sydika A. McKissic** Center for Research on Men's Health, Vanderbilt University, Nashville, TN, USA

**Jeffrey D. Morenoff** Population Studies Center, University of Michigan, Ann Arbor, MI, USA

**Velma McBride Murry** Department of Human and Organizational Development, Peabody College, Vanderbilt University, Nashville, TN, USA

**Kendra Opatovsky** Department of Sociology, University of Michigan, Ann Arbor, MI, USA

**Wizdom A. Powell** University of North Carolina, Gillings School of Global Public Health, Chapel Hill, NC, USA

**Jennifer Richmond** University of North Carolina, Gillings School of Global Public Health, Chapel Hill, NC, USA

**Trabian Shorters** BMe Community, Miami, FL, USA

**Sandra Susan Smith** Department of Sociology, University of California Berkeley, Berkeley, CA, USA

**Howard C. Stevenson** Applied Psychology and Human Development Division, University of Pennsylvania, Philadelphia, PA, USA

**Tamara Taggart** University of North Carolina, Gillings School of Global Public Health, Chapel Hill, NC, USA

**Kevin J.A. Thomas** Department of Sociology, The Pennsylvania State University, University Park, PA, USA

**Patrick H. Tolan** Department of Psychiatry and Neurobehavioral Sciences, University of Virginia, Charlottesville, VA, USA

**Kristin Turney** Department of Sociology, University of California, Irvine, CA, USA

**Ed-Dee G. Williams** Department of Sociology, University of Michigan, Ann Arbor, MI, USA

**Jessica Wyse** Center to Improve Veteran Involvement in Care (CIVIC), Veteran's Affairs Portland Health Care System, Portland, OR, USA

**Alford Young Jr.** Departments of Sociology and Afro-American and African Studies, University of Michigan, Ann Arbor, MI, USA

# About the Editors

**Linda Burton**, **Ph.D.**, is Dean of Trinity College of Arts and Sciences, Co-Director of the International Comparative Studies Program, and the James B. Duke Professor of Sociology at Duke University.

**Dorian Burton**, **Ed.L.D.**, is the Program Officer at the William R. Kenan, Jr. Charitable Trust in Chapel Hill, NC, and co-founder of the TandemED Initiative for Black Male Achievement and Community Improvement at Harvard University Law School's Charles Hamilton Houston Institute for Race and Justice

**Susan McHale**, **Ph.D.**, is Director of the Social Science Research Institute and Distinguished Professor of Human Development and Family Studies and Professor of Demography at The Pennsylvania State University.

**Valarie King**, **Ph.D.**, is Professor of Sociology, Demography, and Human Development and Family Studies at The Pennsylvania State University, and Director of the Family Demography Training Program at the Population Research Institute.

**Jennifer Van Hook**, **PhD.**, is Professor of Sociology and Demography and Director of the Population Research Institute at The Pennsylvania State University.

# Repairing the Breach Revisited: A Focus on Families and Black Males

**Linda M. Burton, Dorian Burton, and Bobby Austin**

How black boys and men are situated in social systems, opportunity structures, developmental contexts, and the consciousness of America were the foci of an initiative launched in the early 1990s by the W. K. Kellogg Foundation's National Task Force on African American Men and Boys. The Task Force focused its attention on "African-American men and boys who, at the time, were not a part of either the recognized economic structure… the body politic of the country… nor communit[ies] with[in] their own ethnic groups …" The Task Force's influential report, *Repairing the Breach: Key Ways to Support Family Life, Reclaim Our Streets and Rebuild Civil Society in America's Communities* (Young & Austin, 1996), recounted the realities of what, by this point in historical time, most Americans should have known: that the health and development of black boys and men are anchored in an array of environmental, social, and psychological forces. These forces, in turn, are endemic to structural and operational systems ranging from macro-level political and economic structures and influences, to those at community and family levels, and to the individual cognitions and behaviors of black males themselves. The Task Force report also recognized that violence and disaffection toward and by black men and boys were symptoms of this multi-layered system of influences.

Almost two decades after the Task Force report called national attention to the breach and offered prescriptions for its repair through dialogues at all levels, cataclysmic ruptures in the breach proliferated. The dialogues—at the societal and

L.M. Burton (✉)
Trinity College of Arts and Sciences, Duke University, Durham, NC, USA
e-mail: lburton@soc.duke.edu

D. Burton
Charles Hamilton Houston Institute for Race and Justice,
Harvard University, Cambridge, MA, USA
e-mail: dorian.burton@gmail.com

B. Austin
Neighborhood Associates Corporation, Washington, DC, USA

 
L. Burton et al. (eds.), *Boys and Men in African American Families*, National Symposium on Family Issues 7, DOI 10.1007/978-3-319-43847-4_1

local levels, among academics, policy makers, religious and grass roots organizations and black males themselves—never quite reached the level of engagement or achieved the promise that the Task Force had hoped. In their absence, ruptures persisted and led to the revival of a racism-driven discourse as well as a social reality characterized by joblessness, mass incarceration, and violence toward and among black males. This discourse often negated the assets and contributions black males have long made to American society (Alexander, 2010), and both discourse and reality further marginalized, excluded and dehumanized black males (see Stevenson, Chap. 5).

Where are the voices of black men and boys in the discourses and narratives that *Repairing the Breach* called for? Needless to say, their voices have often been muted in larger society such that many black males are visibly invisible in much the same way Ralph Ellison (1952, p. 3), over a half century ago, described the influences of racism:

> I am an invisible man. No I am not a spook like those who haunted Edgar Allan Poe; nor am I one of your Hollywood-movie ectoplasms. I am a man of substance, of flesh and bone, fiber, and liquids - - and I might even be said to possess a mind. I am invisible, understand, simply because people refuse to see me ... That invisibility to which I refer occurs because of a peculiar disposition of the eyes of those with whom I come in contact. A matter of the construction of their inner eyes, those eyes with which they look through their physical eyes upon reality.

In our work and in our personal lives, we have found these common perspectives not only disheartening, but also not fully representative of the unheralded positive realities about black men and boys that we have come to know. Thus, inspired by the core mission of *Repairing the Breach,* as co-organizers of the 2015 Penn State Annual Symposium on Family Issues that led to this volume, we explicitly chose not to emphasize the prevailing dehumanizing societal discourse on black men and boys in America. Rather our agenda was guided by asset-based paradigms that direct policy and scholarly attention to how black men and boys channel their voices and their lives through connections with family and kin. Thus the perspective we advance in this volume acknowledges resilience and opportunity as necessary parts of the discourse, with families as a key site of mitigating ruptures endemic to narratives that emphasize the visible invisibility of black men and boys. Throughout, authors highlight the adaptive capacities of black men and boys in their efforts to thrive within sectors of majority culture that have opted to dismiss them. In some chapters, authors also delineate the challenges facing black males in the US, but point to family resources and supports that foster resilience in the face of challenge. In addition, authors highlight both larger social structural forces, as well as the individual behaviors and activities of boys and men that can challenge or enhance the impact of family resilience processes on black males' lives. Authors also consider black males at different points across the life course—from boyhood and adolescence to young adulthood and mid-and later life—as they are situated within families. Together, the chapters provide an interdisciplinary view of both strengths on which to build, as well as aspects of black males' lives that require productive attention and investment from society as a whole. Most importantly, this volume anchors black boys and men inside families where we, as responsible scholars and policy-makers, can direct our attention to points of opportunity and support for efforts by black males to visibly reclaim their lives and produce their own narratives of success.

## References

Alexander, M. (2010). *The new Jim Crow*. New York: The New Press.

Ellison, R. (1952). *Invisible man*. New York: Vintage Books.

Young, A., & Austin, B. W. (Eds.). (1996). *Repairing the breach: Key ways to support family life, reclaim our streets, and rebuild civil society in America's communities*. National Task Force on African-American Men and Boys, W. K. Kellogg Foundation. http://www.wkkf.org/resource-directory/resource/2001/12/repairing-the-breach-key-ways-to-support-family-life-reclaim-our-streets-and-rebuild-civil-society

# Part I
# African American Boys and Their Families

# Adjustment and Developmental Patterns of African American Males: The Roles of Families, Communities, and Other Contexts

**Velma McBride Murry, Eryn Piper Block, and Na Liu**

African American males grow up in a society in which they are commonly stereotyped as "endangered, aggressive, angry, superhuman, subhuman, lazy, hyperactive, jailed, and paroled, on probation, lost, loveless, incorrigible, or just simply self- destructive" (Stevenson, 2003, p. 185). The relevance of these descriptors to African American males' development is the potential that these characterizations will serve as a primary lens for the establishment of their "looking glass self" (Cooley, 1998). The challenge that many African American families face is how to buffer their sons to prevent these characterizations from having long lasting consequences for their development and adjustment. The plight of African American males has been a topic of discussion not only for their families but our entire nation. Reasons for concern are warranted.

According to national statistics, the mortality rate of young African American males is the highest among all racial/ethnic youth (Miniño, 2013). Further, they are overrepresented in low school performance. Across all educational levels, from grades K-12, African American males' reading level is significantly lower than other males and females across every other racial and ethnic group. On average, 12th grade African American males read at the same level as White eight-graders. Further, they are 2.5 times more likely to be suspended from school, and slightly

V.M. Murry (✉)
Department of Human and Organizational Development,
Vanderbilt University, Peabody College, Nashville, TN, USA
e-mail: velma.m.murry@Vanderbilt.edu

E.P. Block
Department of Health Policy and Management, Field School of Public health, UCLA,
Los Angeles, CA, USA

N. Liu
Department of Medicine, Division of Allergy, Pulmonary and Critical Care,
Vanderbilt University Medical Center, Nashville, TN, USA

 
L. Burton et al. (eds.), *Boys and Men in African American Families*, National Symposium on Family Issues 7, DOI 10.1007/978-3-319-43847-4_2

over half (54 %) of African American males graduate high school, compared to 75 % of Whites and Asian American students (Stetser & Stillwell, 2014). African American males are disproportionately represented in the juvenile justice system, as one in nine African American males are incarcerated, in contrast to one in 27 Latino males, and one in 60 Caucasian males are incarcerated (U.S. Department of Justice, 2015). We are reminded, however, that….

> Behind every fact is a face. Behind every statistic is a story. Behind every catchy phrase is a young person [man] whose future will be lost if something is not done immediately to change his reality. And when it comes to young, African American men, the numbers are staggering and the reality is sobering. (Thompson, 2011, para. 1.)

Despite these risk and adversities, most African American boys are faring well and are so because of their "*Ordinary Magic.*" This magic, often referred to as resilience, emerges naturally when individuals identify ways to adapt and respond to adversity (Masten, 2014). The fact that the majority of children exposed to adversity fare well has stimulated a line of scientific inquiry into the ways in which African American families prepare their children to live in a society that frequently devalues them and their families (Coard, Wallace, Stevenson, & Brotman, 2004). It is this line of inquiry that served as the overarching framework for the current book chapter.

## Organization and Scope of this Chapter

This chapter synthesizes extant studies that have examined ways in which parenting, family processes, demographic characteristics, and geographic residence affect and influence both normative (e.g., identity development, social emotional well-being, academic aspiration, prosocial friendships) and non-normative (e.g., internalizing and externalizing behaviors, high risk behaviors, school disengagement) development of African American males from childhood to early adolescence. In addition, we provide a model to guide future preventive interventions targeting African American males and their families, present findings from our longitudinal study of pathways that forecast positive developmental outcomes of African American males as they transition from middle childhood to young adulthood. Finally, we offer recommendations of ways to advance the studies of African American males through the inclusion of families and other safe havens that have been shown to assist these males in adapting and responding to adversity.

To effectively enter an analysis of the extant literature, we selected empirical studies that targeted African American males and examined the roles that family, parents, parenting, and communities/neighborhoods play in their development and adjustment. To the extent possible, we identify ways in which these factors are interlocked with contextual processes to explain individual differences in academic outcomes, mental health, and other dimensions of adjustment, such as processes that protect youth from engaging in negative behaviors, including violence, substance/drug use, and early initiation of sexual practices. In the next section, we provide a brief description of theories and conceptual models selected to frame our chapter review.

## Selected Theoretical and Conceptual Models

We rely on several theories and conceptual frameworks that have advanced the study of human development, including systems theories and explanations that integrate and combine the multiple social–ecological systems within which an individual lives, as well as conceptual models that consider ways in which self-efficacy and motivation influence and affect individual behavior. Thus, we draw on Bronfenbrenner's ecological theory (1974, 1975, 1981, 2005) to explain ways in which African American males' lives are inextricably linked with and infused into multiple interlocking contextual systems. Individuals are not passive but active agents in their environment with capacities to influence, as well as be influenced through social interactions that are embedded in their context. It is the capacity to interact within or evoke influence on one's social environment that, according to Bronfenbrenner (2005), *makes human beings human*.

In addition, the Ecodevelopmental theory (Szapocznik & Coatsworth, 1999) and relational development systems model (Lerner, 2002; Overton, 1998) are also useful in framing our review. Both frameworks assert that development is not only influenced by social relations but also affected by multiple systems that are structurally and functionally integrated and embedded in historical and sociocultural systems, including educational, public policy, government and economic systems. Moreover, according to the Ecodevelopmental theory, to provide a complete picture of human development, both risk and protective processes need to be examined simultaneously, as factors that predict development and behaviors. Risk and protective factors and processes are interrelated and multi-determined (Schwartz, Pantin, Coatsworth, & Szapocznik, 2007). Further, Spencer et al. (1997) proposed a comprehensive model, the Phenomenological Variant of Ecological Systems theory (PVEST), to guide our understanding of African American males' development. PVEST contends that consideration should be given to the contributions of both risk and protective factors which predispose youth to varying levels of vulnerability, such as gender, racial/ethnic group, socioeconomic status, and family composition. For example, the implications of how poverty, social isolation, and race related stressors affect African American males' development may differ depending on resources available to youth. Such that, how youth respond to stressfully challenging situations may differ based on support systems and coping strategies.

Thus, there is the need to move beyond understanding the experiences of African American males from a deficit-oriented explanation to one that considers how and why African American males succeed despite adversity. Moreover, variability in African American males' development and adjustment is attributed to experiences that occur across multiple contexts, the interplay of risk and protective factors, and relational interactions in their social environment.

## Context Matters

*African American males do not grow up in a vacuum.* They are sons who resided in families, with varied backgrounds and beliefs, in neighborhoods that are homogenous and diverse, and in families with resources of varying education and economic levels and social capital. While they are not monolithic, regardless of this diversity, all African American males' lives are more likely to be affected and influenced by the experiences associated with growing up in a racialized society (Garcia Coll & Garrido, 2000; Noguera, 2003). That is, historical, social/environmental, and eco-political contexts shape and influence their development, as the vestiges of slavery and Jim Crow laws continue to affect their families' daily life experiences. In fact, racism remains a major challenge confronting African American families and constitutes a primary source of family stress (Murry, Bynum, Brody, Willert, & Stephens, 2001; Peters & Massey, 1983) as such experiences continue to stifle the life opportunities and advancements of African Americans (Murry & Liu, 2014).

Approximately one in four African Americans live in poverty (Kaiser Family Foundation, n.d.). The consequences of poverty, including deprivations of survival, health and nutrition, education, and protection from harm, can directly or indirectly affect risk vulnerability for African American males. Poverty, often described as a state, is dynamic and cascades through families to directly and indirectly impact youth development, through the emergence of poverty-related environmental stressors that are both physical (e.g., substandard housing, noise, crowding) and psychosocial (e.g., increased family conflicts, parental stress, and community violence). How do families create "ordinary magic," or resilience, (Masten, 2014) in their efforts to overcome adversities and raise healthy sons? Addressing this question will necessitate a dramatic shift in underlying theories, methodological approaches, preventive interventions, and policies.

## A Paradigm Shift

Customary approaches to studying African American families have been guided by questions about dysfunction or deficits, comparing African American families unfavorably to White families. This comparative model is often based on an assumption that *all* White families, regardless of life circumstances and socio-demographic characteristics, fare better than *all* African American families. These approaches have been criticized for producing a narrow viewpoint about African American families and restricting consideration of important issues that affect them (Berkel et al., 2009; Dilworth-Anderson, Burton, & Johnson, 1993; Murry, McNair, Myers, Chen, & Brody, 2014; Sudarkasa, 2007). Furthermore, this perspective treats all non-mainstream behaviors and their consequences as results of shortcomings in persons or families, rather than manifestations of what families do in their efforts to overcome and master circumstances that emerge as they attempt to navigate and mange their lives in challenging environments (Garcia Coll et al., 1996). One has to question the logic of perpetuating an agenda that continues to raise questions about what is wrong with black families or black males? Rather than focusing *only* on why African American males are in crisis, there also is a need to identify factors and processes that foster and promote their success. Doing so will require a paradigm shift in the research and policy agenda, as well as public dialogue about African American males.

To jumpstart this paradigm shift, we synthesize empirical studies that have focused on major areas of risk concerning African American males, namely, academic disparities, mental health, delinquency and risky behaviors. For each of these topics, we also consider protective processes, to the extent available, with specific consideration given to ways in which the individual, as well as parents/caregivers, families, and communities facilitate positive developmental outcomes. The first area of focus is an overview of studies examining academic outcomes for African American boys.

## Academic Outcomes

Research studies have consistently shown severe discrepancies in the experiences and outcomes of African American males in the public education system compared to other demographic subgroups. As early as pre-K, African American males are at risk of being "labeled" as having learning disabilities, diagnosed with attention deficit hyperactivity disorder, screened for serious emotional and behavioral disorders, and overrepresented in special education tracks. African American boys are significantly overrepresented in special education and classified as having an Emotional or Behavioral Disorder (EBD), and excluded from regular classrooms assignments, if they make up 13 % of the student population (Serpell, Hayling, Stevenson, & Kern, 2009). It is worth acknowledging that school professionals who conduct and make these screenings, diagnoses, and placement decisions, as a form of intervention, often facilitate the tracking pipeline of African American males, which have long-term consequences for these students' future development.

A consequence of tracking and social labeling is being at greater risk to receive detentions, suspensions, expulsions, and to be assigned to alternative schools or special education classes (Skiba, Michael, Nardo, & Peterson, 2002). Social labeling also spills over into student-teacher relations. According to Barbarin and Crawford (2006), teachers have lower expectations of African American males, treat them more harshly, and are more likely to single them out for bad behavior, compared to other male and female students. This emphasizes the importance of improving culturally sensitive teacher-student relationships, especially when there is racial discord between student and teacher. Further, identifying effective strategies and approaches for improving schools' capacity to increase parent-teacher-school engagement, may promote parental involvement and encourage parents to advocate for their sons' academic needs (Serpell et al., 2009).

Attention to these concerns have immediate relevance for African American males, as they are more likely to be exposed to race related hassles from teachers and school personnel (Wang & Hugley, 2012), and also report higher perceived discrimination from White classmates than their same-race female peers and Asian American and Latino classmates (Bonner II, 2010). The potential detriment of racist stereotypes and racial micro-aggressions encounters can be manifested in African American males' self-concept, including undermining their sense of academic efficacy, and compromising their sense of school bonding (Bonner II, 2010; Harper, 2009; Singer, 2005).

Confronted with a sense of "otherness" from teachers and peers, African American males may cope by developing hyper-masculine attitudes (Cunningham, Swanson, & Hayes, 2013) and disengage cognitively and physically from schools to avoid negative encounters (Murry, Berkel, Brody, Miller, & Chen, 2009). Such behaviors, including absenteeism and feelings of social isolation, may compromise future aspiration and lead to academic deterioration, high school dropout delinquency, crime, and substance use (Strange, Johnson, Showalter, & Klein, 2012). Further, negative school experiences are thought to encourage other maladaptive coping, in which educationally competent youth may camouflage their academic ability, appearing to be educationally incompetent despite having abilities to do well and succeed in school (Ogbu, 1992). This maladaptive coping behavior, characterized as academic self-presentation (Murry et al., 2009; Ogbu, 1992), may be manifested in several ways, including reluctance to take notes in class, insufficient time allocated to studying and completing class assignments, low or non-participation in campus activities, which are often met with low or failing grades (Harper, Carini, Bridges, & Hayek, 2004). These troubling findings suggest the need to identify approaches and strategies to improve the educational experiences and academic outcomes of African American males.

## Protective Influence of Parents on Academic Success

Studies of early childhood development have shown that parent–child interactions involving informal numeracy learning, such as counting and number games, improve mathematic achievement for African American boys (Baker, 2015). African American boys who have access to books at home and whose parents read to them on a regular basis demonstrate greater school readiness, as evinced by higher reading scores and successful approaches to learning (Baker, Cameron, Rimm-Kaufman, & Grissmer, 2012) when they enter first grade, compared to those without these academic socialization experiences. Moreover, other studies have found positive association between early exposure to culturally appropriate books, toys, and discussions in the home to higher levels of academic achievement among African American boys (Caughy, O'Campo, Randolph, & Nickerson, 2002).

Having positive racial identity has also been associated with academic success. Murry and colleagues (2009), for example, found positive linkages among racial identity, elevated self-esteem and academic proficiency among rural African American males. Youth, who viewed academic success as part of their ancestors' accomplishments had high academic aspirations, did better in school, and their teachers viewed them as academically competent. These positive associations were directly linked with exposure to adaptive racial/ethnic socialization. A key component of this socialization was parent's encouraging youth to be strong and to work hard, which in turn fostered a sense of empowerment as well as confidence and pride among youth (Sanders, 1997).

In addition, being raised in families where future education orientation and academic success are emphasized contributes to improved academic outcomes. Specifically, parental support, including high educational expectation and access to successful academic role models, fostered stronger school bonding and increased future orientation toward education among African American males (Kerpelman, Eryigit, & Stephens, 2008). It has been suggested that exposure to positive academic modeling affords youth with opportunities to visualize the possibilities. Further, when parents provide norms and expectations about academic performance, youth are more likely to mirror and internalize their parents' beliefs, which may reduce school truancy (Li, Feigelman, & Stanton, 2000), encourage the development of personal academic goals and expectations, and in turn, foster positive academic outcomes.

In sum, although the academic condition of African American boys has been empirically studied for many years, based on our review, a major methodological gap is the lack of rigorous theoretically grounded studies. Further, much of what is known is based on cross sectional studies, as little is known about factors that predict academic success of African American males from preschool through secondary education. The fact that the majority of studies are based on convenience samples, using self-reports from youth and teachers, may not only introduce selection and social desirability biases, but also compromise generalizability of study results.

Though it may be easier said than done, models utilized in studies focusing on African American boys should be based upon culturally relevant theories that encompass the everyday lived experiences of African American families with sons (Kerpelman & White, 2006). Doing so will allow for the identification of malleable individual and family-level factors and processes in the promotion of African American males' school performance. Finally, given the stark evidence of the importance of family in their lives, it is surprising that so few studies have included family level variables as potential mediators or moderators to understand and explain African American males' academic outcomes. It has been well documented that parents are the most proximal influencers of their children; this void leaves the field without insights about the processes through which African American males' families foster future orientation, school bonding, and academic aspiration, and more importantly may be a major missed opportunity to effectively reduce and eventually eliminate the overrepresentation of African American males in academic disparities. In addition, there is a need to develop and refine measures to capture the nuances of academic achievement, as most existing studies rely solely on teachers' and youths' self-reports. In that regard, objective measures of academic achievement such as school reported grades, standardized test scores, and measures of cognitive capacity are needed. Finally, models of family-based preventive interventions that have been shown to facilitate academic success among African American males are greatly needed. In the following section, we offer an example to guide this endeavor.

The Strong African American Families (SAAF) and Pathways to African American Success (PAAS) programs, universal family-based programs, are designed to empower parents and youth to become active agents in facilitating positive youth development. These programs have been shown to not only deter early sexual onset and the initiation and escalation of substance use but have also been efficacious in the enhancement of academic competence among youth. Specifically, Murry et al. (2009) reported that SAAF evoked increases in intervention-targeted parenting processes that fostered positive change in youth protective processes (e.g., racial pride, resistance efficacy, future orientation, self-regulation), which in turn averted conduct problems in school and increased academic aspirations among youth. These findings were further replicated in a technology-delivered program, PAAS, with more immediate programmatic effects on youth academic performance (Murry et al., 2014).

Findings from the SAAF and PAAS program illustrate the important roles that families can play in the academic success of African American males. There is a need for future research, preventive interventions, and school policies that give greater consideration to youth's and parent's/caregiver's perception of academic success and the extent to which school environment, teachers, and administrators affect their son's academic performance.

## Mental Health Functioning

Studies of African American males' mental health functioning are sparse. While anxiety symptoms and disorders have been identified as salient health issues for African American youth, research on internalizing behaviors of African American males is considered a relatively new line of inquiry (Neal-Barnett, 2004). The few available research studies have focused on the prevalence of internalizing symptoms, such as depressive disorders and anxiety disorders. Data from the Youth Risk Behavior Survey (CDC, 2010) revealed that approximately 28 % of African American adolescents reported having felt sad or hopeless almost every day for 2 or more weeks in a row. Results from studies of depression across ethnic groups are equivocal with some studies reporting higher rates among African American teens, while other studies indicate that African American youth experience less depression than their non-African American counterparts (Schraedley, Gotlib, & Hayward, 1999; Wight, Aneshensel, Botticello, & Sepúlveda, 2005). What is apparent is that racial discrimination has been implicated as an underlying cause of the variety of health and social disparities affecting African Americans.

### *Cascading Effects of Racism on African American Males' Daily Lives*

Discriminatory experiences are common in African American adolescents' daily lives (e.g., Brody et al., 2014; Seaton, Caldwell, Sellers, & Jackson, 2008). Results from a nationally representative sample of African American adolescents revealed that 87 % reported experiencing at least one discriminatory incident in the past year (Seaton et al., 2008). Further, Simons, Chen, Stewart, and Brody (2003) reported that 46 % of their sample of 900 African American early adolescents residing in rural communities had experienced racial slurs; 33 % had been excluded from an activity due to race; and 18 % indicated that they had been threatened with physical harm because they are African American. Berkel et al. (2009) noted in their interviews with African American youth that the majority had encountered devaluation incidences from peers and teachers, and males reported being frequently harassed by the police in their neighborhoods. Racial discrimination has been consistently associated with elevated levels of internalizing problems (i.e., anxiety and depression) and acting out in response to distress, including substance use problems, and affiliation with delinquent peers (Berkel et al., 2009; Brody et al., 2006; Sellers, Caldwell, Schmeelk-Cone, & Zimmerman, 2003; Sellers, Copeland-Linder, Martin, & Lewis, 2006).

Results from cross-lag analyses documented the detrimental effects of racial discrimination on African American males over time. Race related stress amplifies maladaptive coping responses, such as anger and hostility, that can not only compromise psychosocial processes but also increase one's vulnerability to early onset of chronic diseases, such as elevated blood pressure (Fredrickson et al., 2000) and fasting glucose (Shen, Countryman, Spiro, & Niaura, 2008), as well as heightened plasma lipid levels (Weidner, Sexton, McLellarn, Connor, & Matarazzo, 1987), all of which have been associated with health disparities among African Americans. In fact, Brody and colleagues (2014) found that exposure to racial discrimination was associated with elevated allostatic loads among youth as they transitioned into young adulthood. A noteworthy finding was that this path was less pronounced among males who were in emotionally supportive families.

Findings from Zimmerman, Ramirez-Valles, Zapert, and Maton (2000) offer support for the protective nature of parents for African American boys. Testing the application of the stress-buffering hypothesis on the mental health functioning of 173 urban African American adolescent males, these scholars found that parental support mediated the association between social stress and anxiety and depression. Specifically, parental support insulated their sons from the negative consequences of stress by lowering symptoms of anxiety and depression. The authors concluded that parental support is a powerful resource to neutralize the cascading effects of stress on their son's mental heath functioning. Further, these findings confirm what is apparent, that parents matter. Both instrumental and emotional support from parents have been shown to buffer adolescents from stressful life events by fostering positive self-perceptions (McCreary, Slavin, & Berry, 1996).

Such support also has been shown to protect youth from internalizing negative race-related messages that have the potential to derail their sense of self (Murry, Simons, Simons, & Gibbons, 2013). These protective parenting processes are commonly referred to as adaptive racial socialization.

## *Protective Effects of Racial Socialization*

What are the mechanisms through which racial socialization buffers African Americans from the negative consequences of racial discrimination and fosters positive development and adjustment? Optimally, African American parents' messages about race prepare children for encounters with discrimination while emphasizing pride in being African American (Coard et al., 2004; Hughes & Chen, 1997; Hughes et al., 2006). Messages designed to prepare youth for racism and discrimination may include more instructions regarding coping strategies for reducing racism-related stress, resisting power structures that create barriers, and overcoming barriers to succeed (Murry et al., 2009). African American adolescent males, for example, have reported that a major source of protection from stress related to discrimination was their mothers, who helped them problem solve and provided examples of ways to deal with the persistent harassment by the police (Berkel et al., 2009). For example, a most common socialization approach is for parents to role play with their sons on how to respond when stopped by the police, as in the following quote, "My son knows how to take a neutral stance, put hands in the air, and say, 'Yes sir', 'No sir'" (Coard et al., 2004, p. 288). This form of proactive racial socialization prepares children for the possibility of future racial discriminatory encounters with authority figures, while showing youth that parents are trustworthy and care about their futures and well-being.

McHale and colleagues (2006) contend that African American mothers and fathers employ different strategies in socializing their children about race related issues. Through the process of disaggregating mothers and fathers' *approaches to racial socialization*, these authors found that mothers were more likely to engage in conversations about African American culture and cultural heritage, in addition to discussions about preparation for racial bias with their sons, whereas fathers were more likely to focus on culture specific messages but not racial bias with their sons. The authors noted that paternal racial socialization practices were associated with reduced depression among their sons, whereas the socialization practices of their mothers evinced increased depression and reduced internal locus of control in their sons. The authors offered several plausible reasons for their findings. First, the authors conferred that because mothers have increased access, and therefore more opportunities to interact with their sons, mothers may have greater awareness of developmental issues and concerns confronting their sons. The finding that mothers were more likely to discuss racism issues with their sons, compared to fathers, may be attributed to their son's disclosing race related interactions with others, and also to mothers' grave concerns about the potential risks for their sons. African American parents, particularly those raising sons in poor urban communities, struggle every day with the reality that when their sons leave home, it is possible that they may never return (Richardson Jr, Van Brakle, & St. Vil, 2014).

While the intent of parents may be to prepare their sons to "fit into mainstream culture", African American boys are more likely to exhibit externalizing behaviors if they receive racial socialization messages from their parents that emphasize mistrust and racism (Caughy, Nettles, O'Campo, & Lohrfink, 2006). A plausible explanation for this counteractive response has been offered by Davis and Stevenson (2006). Elevated depressive symptoms, irritability, and anger among African American males, in response to racial socialization, may be manifestations of their attempt to cope. As they become aware of various obstacles that may interfere with their ability to live the American Dream, African American males may respond through the use of antagonistic and aggressive behaviors (Davis & Stevenson, 2006).

Yet, there is growing consensus that having a sense of connection to one's heritage fosters cultural assets for African Americans (Gaylord-Harden, Burrow, & Cunningham, 2012) and may serve to protect them from the negative consequences of racial discrimination. Strong racial identity has been associated with positive self-concept (Murry et al., 2005) and well-being (Seaton, Scottham, & Sellers, 2006), while negatively associated with antisocial behaviors (Brook, Zhang, Finch, & Brook, 2010). While some scholars have shown that racial identity attenuates the effects of racial discrimination on mental health outcomes (Greene & Mickelson, 2006), others have shown having high levels of ethnic identity achievement appears to escalate the negative effects of discrimination on both internalizing and externalizing behaviors. Youth who demonstrate high levels of achievement actively engaged in exploring their group membership. In that regard, as race becomes more salient, African American youth may exhibit more anger when exposed to racial discriminatory incidences.

## Behavioral Outcomes

### *Conduct Problems and Delinquency*

African American males are overrepresented in delinquency and crime statistics (U.S. Department of Justice, 2009). In 2008, African American youth accounted for 52 % of all juvenile arrests for violent crime. Self-report questionnaires indicate that African American males are more likely to endorse conduct problems and aggressive behavior. While the prevalence of overall weapon carrying was higher among Caucasian adolescents, African American males were more likely to carry a gun and affiliate with peers who have access to weapons. Weapon carrying has been associated with engagement in other risky behaviors. For example, African American males who have access to guns are more likely to use marijuana, sell drugs, and engage in physical fighting (Steinman & Zimmerman, 2003). These experiences have also been identified as potential gateways to increased risk vulnerability and behaviors that lead to exposure to criminal justice systems. Minority youth make up 39 % of the juvenile population but are 60 % of committed juveniles. The consequences of these incidences are manifested in the over representativeness of minority youth in the prison system. In fact, African American male youth are twice as likely to go to prison in their lifetime than Latino youth and four times more likely than their Caucasian male counterparts (Wagner, 2012).

## *Risky Sexual Practices, Substance and Drug Use*

Several studies revealed that being raised in families with low parental control and high warmth increased risk-engaging behaviors among African American boys. While the association between low behavioral control and risk engagement has been well-document, parental involvement and supervision, as well as the development of standards for conduct and internalized norms that guide behavior in the absence of parental or adult supervision, have been associated with delayed sexual onset among African American males and females (Murry et al., 2009; Romer et al., 1999) and in the prevention of alcohol and substance use (Brody, Stoneman, Flor, & McCrary, 1994; Kotchick, Shaffer, Miller, & Forehand, 2001). One study reported a positive association between parental warmth and early sexual initiation among African American males (Kapungu, Holmbeck, & Paikoff, 2006). While reasons for this occurrence are unclear, one plausible explanation was the need to identify more salient measures that reflect warmth in African American families, such as parental connectedness and family cohesion (Kapungu et al., 2006).

Parental support (e.g., encouragement, warmth, and reinforcement for actions) that co-occurs with behavioral control (e.g., monitoring a child's actions and whereabouts, establishing limits for a child's activities) has been associated with multiple domains of African American males development, including averting delinquent behavior, early sexual onset, and initiation and escalation of alcohol/substance use (Bean, Barber, & Crane, 2006). According to Harris, Sutherland, and Hutchinson (2013) parents' influence on African American males' sexual practices (e.g., condom use, self-efficacy, less permissive sexual attitudes, fewer sexual partners, and less unprotected sex) had greater affect when there was evidence of parent–child closeness and frequent discussion about sexual issues. While youth reported that their mothers were the primary socializers with regard to sexual communication, fathers' influence was mediated through their sons' condom use, self-efficacy, attitudes, and beliefs. This suggests the need for more insight on differential impact of mothers and fathers' on their son's development, including decisions about risk avoidance behaviors.

It has been suggested that parental involvement buffers youth from risk, including academic underperformance and sexual initiation. For example, youth whose fathers or father figures were available and involved were more likely to do well in school and more likely to delay early sexual onset and substance use, compared to youth with disengaged fathers (Bryant & Zimmerman, 2003). Having a father or father figure who offers guidance and is actively engaged in monitoring one's whereabouts increases the likelihood that boys will model desired behaviors, which dissuades them from getting sexually involved and encourages them to do well in school and to actively engage in career planning (Ramirez-Valles, Zimmerman, & Juarez, 2002).

Further, growing up in a supportive, communicative family environment, in which expectations regarding risk are clearly articulated, encourages adolescents to internalize their parents' values and norms, and avoid risky behaviors (Murry, Berkel, Brody, Gerrard, & Gibbons, 2007). Such a family climate may also create an atmosphere of trust that encourages adolescents to disclose feelings, beliefs, and experiences that have implications for positive identity development. Importantly, open communication with parents appears to reduce the likelihood that adolescents will turn to peers for information and to rely on them as role models. For example, African American youth who reported having conversations with their parents about sexually related issues were less influenced by their peers' actions and perceptions for sexual behavior, and consequently less likely to engage in sexual risk behaviors (Murry et al., 2007).

## Raising Healthy Sons in a Toxic Environment

While the majority of studies have been cross-sectional in nature, there is some evidence that neighborhood disorder and lack of social controls, that often characterize low resource communities (Ross & Mirowsky, 1999), can undermine the capacity for residents to monitor and control youth activities. Therefore, youth who live in such environments are particularly vulnerable to the influence of deviant peers (e.g., Sampson & Groves, 1989; Sampson, Raudenbush, & Earls, 1997; Shaw & McKay, 1942), providing avenues for delinquent behavior. Thus, affiliating with peers who engage in violent behaviors may serve as a gateway to community violence and, eventually, serve as a pipeline to prison or increase risk for early death. While all youth in the U.S. are exposed to violence, low income African Americans are particularly vulnerable, experiencing a disproportionate amount of violence compared to other racial minority youth (Gaylord-Harden, Cunningham, & Zelencik, 2011).

The detriment of growing up in violent, socially isolated neighborhoods has been vividly described by Roche, Ensminger, and Cherlin (2007) who note that these males are at increased risk of engaging in delinquent behavior, experiencing school related problems, and elevated risk for depression. The authors offer suggestions for ways to buffer youth from these harmful consequences, recognizing the powerful effect of parents. The capacity to perform this task can be challenging for parents, especially for African American parents and particularly for those raising sons.

> All parents ultimately realize that they cannot protect their children. Black parents confront a world almost eager with violent intent toward their offspring. They [black parents] parent while burdened with the knowledge that for a black child the price of error—real or imagined—is higher than it is for white children. (Murphy, 2015, p. 2.)

Despite having the desire to do so, how can African American parents garner the skills and capacities to protect their sons from this devastation? Recognizing that a major role of parents and families is to protect, support, and promote positive developmental outcomes for children, many African American parents are taking actions when there are potential or actual threats to their child's wellbeing and use strategies and approaches to prevent or abate situations that could forestall growth and development of their child.

Roche and colleagues (2007) found that effective strategies for parenting in toxic environments are those characterized as highly restrictive behavioral control, including punitive punishment, which facilitated positive development and adjustment. Further, when neighborhood youth were not fortunate to have engaged parents but lived in a community where other adults were available to assist them, they too were less likely to engage in antisocial behaviors.

In their investigation of urban African American families, Gorman-Smith, Henry, and Tolan (2004) found that despite growing up in violent communities, the likelihood that an African American male would engage in such behaviors was moderated by particular characteristics of their home environment. The scholars identified *exceptionally functioning families as ones* who engaged in practices that protected their sons from succumbing to gang activity. These families were viewed as exceptional because, despite raising their sons in challenging environments, they were able to foster strong emotional cohesion, create a sense of family orientation, and establish routinized family management practices that dissuaded their sons from succumbing to violence and delinquent behaviors. A critical aspect of these families' protectiveness for their sons was establishing a home environment in which family members feel emotionally close and supported (Gorman-Smith, Tolan, & Henry, 2000). This type of family environment, in combination with parents being involved, vigilant, and disciplinarians with high monitoring approaches, has the potential to affect risk protection sustainability, even when their sons are bombarded with high rates of violence (Gaylord-Harden, Zakaryan, Bernard, & Pekoc, 2015). According to Nobles (2007) being in a family where one's sense of being is legitimized through connections, attachment, validation, sense of worth, and respect, fosters a sense of security in youth that empowers them to address and respond to stressful circumstances outside of their home.

There are, in some instances, situations in which parents who are raising their children in high crime communities undertake drastic measures to protect their sons. Results from a longitudinal qualitative study of parents raising their sons in high risk, low-resource, urban communities revealed that many families use "exile parenting strategies," relocating their sons to safer spaces to improve their life chances and opportunities (Richardson Jr et al., 2014). Exile parenting strategies included temporary exile, when sons are sent away for weekends or summers to stay with relatives who live in safer locations. Families, with limited social capital (i.e., informal networks to rely on to protect their sons) use permanent exile strategies, and often resort to sending their child to juvenile justice systems to protect them from neighborhood violence. African American parents, historically, have sent their children to live with grandparents, older siblings, and fictive kin (Jarrett, 1999). This suggests the need to expand our traditional way of conceptualizing and operationalizing effective parenting. As Richardson and colleagues (2014) discovered, African American families are creating adaptive approaches and strategies to protect their sons from threats of physical violence, to save them from the streets, and more importantly to extend their life. Our current theoretical models of parenting are being challenged, and research suggests the need for new paradigms for studying families who are raising sons and daughters in toxic environments.

## *Buffering Effects of Caring Communities and Institutions*

It has been well documented that growing up in close-knit communities in which the adults use strategies to support each other (e.g. monitoring neighborhood children) has implications for encouraging positive developmental pathways for African American males (Berkel et al., 2009; Burton & Jarrett, 2000; Roche et al., 2007; Sampson et al., 1997). The experience of residing in caring communities has been conceptualized as *collective socialization*. In such communities, residents influence youths' behavior by establishing norms, expectations, values, standards, protocols, and procedures for acceptable youth behavior (Simons, Simons, Conger, & Brody, 2004). Having neighbors who are invested in the wellbeing of youth also influences the youths' own parents' behaviors. Specifically, parents who are nested in cohesive communities exhibit more positive parenting than those residing in low cohesive communities. These parental and neighborhood support systems are associated with reduced academic underachievement, aggressive tendencies, and delinquency, and encourage prosocial peer affiliation (Berkel et al., 2009).

Further, churches, an influential institution in the African American community, also have been shown to foster positive youth outcomes. Asset-based studies have shown that church involvement facilitates moral development, racial pride, healthy self-esteem, and self-efficacy and in turn increases prosocial competence, including academic success and civic engagement, among African American youth (Brody et al., 1994; Lincoln & Mamiya, 1990; Williams, 2003a). That black churches have a pivotal role in the development of youth is not surprising given that this institution has historically served as a place of refuge and support for African Americans. For African American males, the church also increases their connections to other adults with whom they can build supportive relationships. Williams (2003) characterizes the black church as "a village opportunity' to provide positive experiences for youth" (p. 27) and support for their parents. In addition, religiosity and family connectedness were identified as strong protective factors for dissuading substance use among African Americans during adolescence, with continued protection from later binge drinking during young and community residents adulthood (Stevens-Watkins & Rostosky, 2010).

In sum, parents/caregivers are significant socializing agents, transmitting attitudes, values, and norms regarding appropriate behavior and consequences for misbehavior (Jaccard, Dittus, & Gordon, 2000). However, the mechanism through which parents, or other significant adults in African American males' lives, are able to influence their behavior by promoting positive development and adjustment as they transition from childhood to young adulthood needs further exploration. In the next section, we provide a model to guide future research studies of African American males, which emphasizes the buffering effects of parents as their sons' transition from middle childhood to young adulthood.

## Longitudinal Study of Normative Positive Developmental Trajectories of African American Males'

The positive youth development model is a framework that explains the internal resources necessary for young African American males to be resilient in resource-poor settings (Lerner et al., 2005; Phelps et al., 2009). We present an example of ways to document the developmental patterns of African American males, demonstrating the cascading effects of early life experiences on later development. The overall purpose of this study was to identify and explain how salient resilient factors in African American males' environmental context contribute to the promotion of positive development. In addition, analyses of these data were used to examine the association between positive youth development and risk avoidance behaviors, as the males transitioned from middle childhood to young adulthood. Data was obtained from parents and their sons, who participated in the Family and Community Health Study (FACHS), a multisite, multiple panel study of neighborhood and family effects on health and development. Participants in this large-scale study of African American youth and their caregivers included over 889 families in Iowa and Georgia, of which only the 411 families with male youth were included in the current study. Each family included a child who was in the 5th grade at the time of recruitment (M = 10.5 years), with additional waves collected when youth were 12–13 (Wave 2), 17–18 (Wave 4), and 20–21 (Wave 5) years of age (See Murry et al., 2014 for a detailed description of study design).

Results presented in Fig. 1, illustrate that the developmental pathway to low sexual and substance use risk-engaging behaviors among rural African American males from middle childhood through young adulthood is mediated through the influence of both involved, vigilant parenting and adaptive racial socialization (race-specific parenting) on youth's future orientation ($\beta = 23$, $p < 0.01$; $\beta = 0.15$, $p < 0.05$, respectively). Future orientation was positively associated with self-regulation ($\beta = 0.17$, $p < 0.01$) during early adolescence, which in turn increased the likelihood that these males would affiliate with prosocial peers ($\beta = 0.23$, $p < 0.001$) as they transitioned from early to late adolescence. Murry and colleagues (2014) also conducted profile analyses to determine the extent to which these study factors were effective in identifying high and low risk groups, and which factors differentiate low and high risk African American males (See Table 1). Findings from these analyses revealed that high risk males were more likely to be exposed to harsh and inconsistent parenting, evinced lower self-regulation and future orientation, and were more likely to affiliate with deviant peers. Low risk boys did engage in "normative functional experimentation" but these behaviors where short-term, and the stabilization of their behavior was associated with having connections with parents who instilled in them the importance of being planful and thoughtful about their behavior (e.g., emotion management), setting goals, and forming relationships with like-minded prosocial peers. Thus, the combined influence of these two parenting strategies offers support to confirm the protective nature of African Americans parents' ability to influence the development and behavior of their sons in ways that have

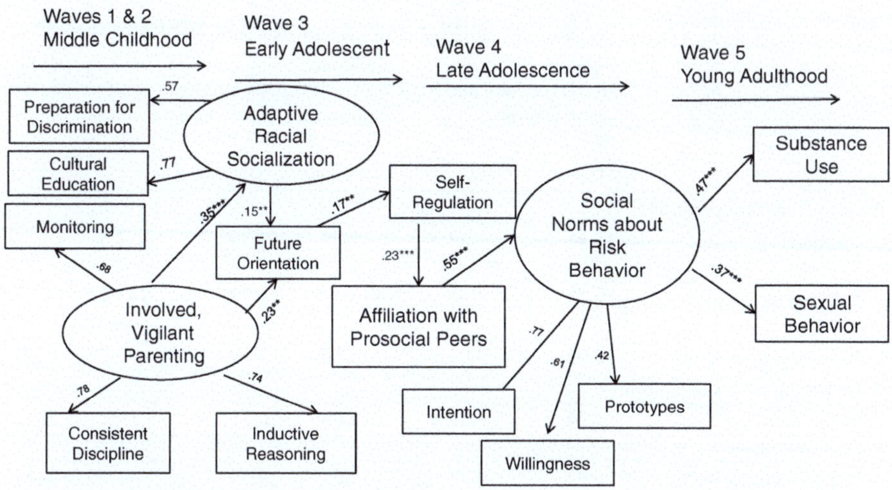


*Note.* Low risk males ($N = 331$); $X^2(121) = 209.69$, $p < .000$; comparative fit index (CFI) = .91; root mean square error of approximation (RMSEA) = .047 (.036, .058).
†Measure in previous wave controlled.
*$p < .05$; **$p < .01$; ***$p < .001$.

**Fig. 1** Standardized direct and indirect effects on behavior and adjustment

long-lasting positive effects. What these males learned from their parents during middle childhood and early adolescence continued to influence their friendship systems, norms, and values to govern and guide decision-making processes as they transitioned into young adulthood. Finally, results from our study offer support for Kassel, Wardle, and Roberts (2007) argument, which contends that, while many of the theories about African American males may make sense intuitively, most have not been empirically validated. We urge other scholars to challenge the existing scientific literatures that portray African American males as monolithic "pathological idioms tied to criminal justice systems, violence, unemployment, and disinterested in education, social mobility" (Burton & Stack, 2014, p. 178).

## Closing Remarks

African American families face major challenges raising healthy well-functioning sons. African American males are more likely to grow up in a society laced with limited prospects to achieve goals through traditional career paths, such as academics, employment, and/or family success. They may be more vulnerable to becoming involved in potentially lucrative, yet dangerous activities to compensate and overcome barriers due to lack of opportunity structures.

**Table 1** Mean scores of males self-report for risk engagement patterns by group classification

| | Class 1 High risky sex and high substance use (N=47; 12.4%) | | Class 2 Low risky sex and low substance use (N=331; 87.6%) | | t/F (p) |
|---|---|---|---|---|---|
| | Means | SD | Means | SD | |
| Involved-vigilant parenting | | | | | |
| Monitoring[a] | 13.41 | 3.87 | 15.89 | 3.30 | –4.41 (<0.001) |
| Consistent discipline[a] | 10.78 | 2.67 | 12.69 | 2.23 | –5.01 (<0.001) |
| Inductive reasoning[a] | 12.05 | 3.97 | 13.50 | 3.79 | –2.29 (0.023) |
| Adaptive racial socialization | | | | | |
| Preparation for discrimination[a] | 15.24 | 6.22 | 14.00 | 6.21 | 1.21 (0.228) |
| Cultural education[a] | 11.63 | 4.78 | 12.51 | 4.52 | –1.16 (0.248) |
| Future orientation[a] | 25.12 | 3.07 | 25.77 | 3.37 | –1.17 (0.244) |
| Self-control[b] | 30.65 | 4.75 | 33.16 | 3.75 | 12.46 (<0.001) |
| Affiliation with prosocial peers[b] | 23.32 | 2.87 | 25.64 | 3.11 | 2.96 (0.086) |
| Social norms about risk behavior | 2.41 | 2.70 | –0.32 | 2.05 | 5.94 (<0.001) |
| Intention[b] | –2.95 | 4.52 | 0.59 | 3.56 | 6.24 (0.013) |
| Willingness[b] | –3.09 | 5.31 | 0.18 | 3.16 | 14.19 (<0.001) |
| Prototypes[b] | –7.22 | 9.89 | 0.81 | 10.07 | 9.79 (0.002) |
| Substance use[a] | 9.18 | 7.13 | 6.00 | 4.70 | 3.42 (<0.001) |
| Sexual behavior[a] | 3.61 | 2.65 | 1.87 | 1.74 | 3.67 (0.001) |

[a]Independent *t*-test was used

[b]ANCOVA was used with scores of previous wave controlled

Despite the challenges associated with raising African American sons in a racialized society, many African American males fare well. They do well in school, avoid delinquent behaviors, and are not engaging in high-risk behaviors. Their ability to overcome the odds can be attributed to the protective nature of families and community, in particular, the functionality of positive social relations, and the extent to which the relational processes are reciprocal and mutually influential (Lerner, 2002; Spencer et al., 1997). We end our chapter by acknowledging that much work is needed in the field to adequately understand how African American families successfully navigate their ecological systems to raise healthy sons, whose lives are bombarded with negative messages about "who they are" and "how others think they are." There remains much to be known about African American males residing in the United States.

## Recommendations

An obvious limitation is a paucity of research studies on African American males and their families. The literature is replete with investigations of these individuals in public settings and spaces but not as members of families. Whereas there is a plethora of studies of non-African American males as members of families, the epistemological discord between studies of African American males in families creates potential difficulties in documenting how families matter to their development and adjustment. As documented in this comprehensive review, studies of African American males reflect their experiences and life patterns primarily in schools, juvenile detention centers, and as members and victims of violent communities.

Moreover, future studies of African American males *must* give greater consideration to the influence of where these males live, their family/kinship, and social and community experiences. Further, similar to the void in scientific studies of African American males, preventive intervention designed to address academic disparities and socio-emotional, behavior problems, and risky behaviors among African American males also needs to be family-based (Murry, Liu, & Bethune, 2016). Specifically, there is a need to expand the unit of analysis to include African American males and their family members. That the settings of most studies of African American males are within public institutions is puzzling. This omission, whether deliberate or unintentional, has created a perception of African American males as being "irrelevant and almost invisible in families" (cited in Burton & Stack, 2014, p. 185).

Lastly, we offer several challenges confronting researchers whose work focuses on African American males. Foremost, there is a need for more longitudinal studies to identify protective processes that forecast successful development among African American males as they transition through various developmental stages. Further, there is a need to include representative samples of African American males in order to offer a more accurate portrayal of their developmental trajectories, allowing for the disentanglement of factors that explain within group differences, such as potential mediating and moderating effects of social class, contextual factors and processes, and environmental factors. Such designs will allow for advanced studies that move beyond a social deficit racial comparison framework, wherein White males are viewed as the model that African American males should emulate.

To fully capture the "nuanced and sometimes covert rules and courses of action in families' daily lives" (Burton & Stack, 2014, p. 180) of African American males, we urge the use of mixed methods and ethnographic approaches. More longitudinal research designs are needed to identify and explore patterns of development that peak and begin to decrease as African American males transition across various developmental stages. Longitudinal designs will also make it possible to identify malleable processes and factors that can be targeted in preventive interventions designed to promote positive developmental trajectories of these youth.

Based on our review, there is urgency for the scientific community and policymakers to question what is currently known about African American males. Given the primary source and context of studies of African American males, it is not surprising that they are characterized as "endangered, aggressive, angry, superhuman, subhuman, lazy, hyperactive, jailed, and paroled, on probation, lost, loveless, incorrigible, or just simply self-destructive" (Stevenson, 2003 , p. 185). The need for greater attention to social justice begs the question: Why is there so little attention to studying issues regarding normative, positive developmental patterns of African American males? Posing such a question will increase insights on realms of competencies for African American boys and adolescents growing up in diverse contexts, including adaptive coping strategies that they and their parents developed, which have yet to be identified in research. In fact, documenting adaptive processes that promote resilience in African American families may improve the effectiveness of family-based preventive interventions designed to foster positive outcomes among African American males. To do so will require a paradigm shift with greater consideration given to examining the multidimensional aspects of African American males' lives. Further, inclusion of multiple contexts of family, community, schools, and socio-eco-political arenas is needed in the study of African American's development and adjustment. Finally, investigations of failure must be replaced by investigations of *what promotes successful development and adjustment among African American males and why*? Such information can guide and inform education public policy, and governmental and economic systems, as well as the design of culturally tailored, gender-driven preventive interventions to foster positive change.

In closing, we charge the field to give greater consideration to refining the conceptualization of African American males and to move beyond documenting the sobering statistics to confer their fatalistic future. Taking on this challenge will require the development of a comprehensive research agenda that involves all systems that touch the lives of African American males, with a focus on identifying ways to ensure that these young men have opportunities to dream and live the American Dream.

**Acknowledgements** Murry's effort on this book chapter was supported by the Lois Autrey Betts Endowment. Family and Community Health Study was funded by the National Institute of Mental Health Grant MH48165 through funding for the Center for Family Research in Rural Mental Health at Iowa State University and Center for Family Research at University of Georgia. Additional funding was provided by the National Institute on Drug Abuse, the National Institute on Alcohol Abuse and Alcoholism, and the Iowa Agricultural and Home Economics Experiment Station Project #3320.

## References

Baker, C. E. (2015). Does parent involvement and neighborhood quality matter for African American boys' kindergarten mathematics achievement? *Early Education and Development, 26*(3), 342–355.

Baker, C. E., Cameron, C. E., Rimm-Kaufman, S. E., & Grissmer, D. (2012). Family and sociodemographic predictors of school readiness among African American boys in kindergarten. *Early Education and Development, 23*(6), 833–854.

Barbarin, O., & Crawford, G. M. (2006). Acknowledging and reducing stigmatization of African American boys. *Young Children, 61*(6), 79–86.

Bean, R. A., Barber, B. K., & Crane, D. R. (2006). Parental support, behavioral control, and psychological control among African American youth: The relationships to academic grades, delinquency, and depression. *Journal of Family Issues, 27*(10), 1335–1355.

Berkel, C., Murry, V. M., Hurt, T. R., Chen, Y., Brody, G. E., Simons, R. L., et al. (2009). It takes a village: Protecting rural African American youth in the context of racism. *Journal of Youth and Adolescence, 38*, 175–188.

Bonner, F. A., II (2010). *Academically gifted African American male college students*. Santa Barbara,CA: Praeger.

Brody, G. H., Chen, Y. F., Murry, V. M., Ge, X., Simons, R. L., Gibbons, F. X., et al. (2006). Perceived discrimination and the adjustment of African American youths: A five-year longitudinal analysis with contextual moderation effects. *Child Development, 77*(5), 1170–1189.

Brody, G. H., Lei, M. K., Chae, D. H., Yu, T., Kogan, S. M., & Beach, S. R. (2014). Perceived discrimination among African American adolescents and allostatic load: A longitudinal analysis with buffering effects. *Child Development, 85*(3), 989–1002.

Brody, G., Stoneman, Z., Flor, D., & McCrary, C. (1994). Religion's role in organizing family relationships: Family process in rural, two-parent African American families. *Journal of Marriage and Family, 56*, 878–888.

Bronfenbrenner, U. (1974). Developmental research, public policy, and ecology of childhood. *Child Development, 45*, 1–5.

Bronfenbrenner, U. (1975). *The ecology of human development in retrospect and prospect*. Paper presented at the meeting of International Society for the Study of Behavioral Development, England. http://eric.ed.gov/?id=ED128387

Bronfenbrenner, U. (1981). Children and families: 1984? *Society, 18*(2), 38–41.

Bronfenbrenner, U. (Ed.). (2005). *Making human beings human: Bioecological perspectives on human development*. London: Sage.

Brook, J. S., Zhang, C., Finch, S. J., & Brook, D. W. (2010). Adolescent pathways to adult smoking: Ethnic identity, peer substance use, and antisocial behavior. *The American Journal on Addictions, 19*(2), 178–186.

Bryant, A. L., & Zimmerman, M. A. (2003). Role models and psychosocial outcomes among African American adolescents. *Journal of Adolescent Research, 18*(1), 36–67.

Burton, L. M., & Jarrett, R. L. (2000). In the mix, yet on the margins: The place of families in urban neighborhood and child development research. *Journal of Marriage and Family, 62*(4), 1114–1135.

Burton, L. M., & Stack, C. B. (2014). Breakfast at Elmo's: Adolescent boys and disruptive politics in the kinscripts narrative. In A. Garey, R. Hertz, & M. Nelson (Eds.), *Open to disruption: Time and craft in the practice of slow sociology* (pp. 174–191). Nashville, TN: Vanderbilt University Press.

Caughy, M. O., Nettles, S. M., O'Campo, P. J., & Lohrfink, K. F. (2006). Neighborhood matters: Racial socialization of African American children. *Child Development, 77*(5), 1220–1236.

Caughy, M. O., O'Campo, P. J., Randolph, S. M., & Nickerson, K. (2002). The influence of racial socialization practices on the cognitive and behavioral competence of African American preschoolers. *Child Development, 73*, 1611–1625.

Centers for Disease Control and Prevention (CDC). (2010). *Youth risk behavior surveillance – United States, 2009*. (MMWR, Surveillance Summaries, Vol. 59, No. SS5). Atlanta, GA: CDC.

Coard, S. I., Wallace, S. A., Stevenson, H. C., & Brotman, L. M. (2004). Towards culturally relevant preventive interventions: The consideration of racial socialization in parent training with African American families. *Journal of Child & Family Studies, 13*, 277–293.

Cooley, C. H. (1998). *On self and social organization*. Chicago: University of Chicago Press.

Cunningham, M., Swanson, D. P., & Hayes, D. M. (2013). School- and community-based associations to hypermasculine attitudes in African American adolescent males. *American Journal of Orthopsychiatry, 83*(2 Pt. 2), 244–251.

Davis, G. Y., & Stevenson, H. C. (2006). Racial socialization experiences and symptoms of depression among black youth. *Journal of Child and Family Studies, 15*(3), 293–307.

Dilworth-Anderson, P., Burton, L. M., & Johnson, L. B. (1993). Reframing theories for understanding race, ethnicity, and families. In P. G. Boss, W. J. Doherty, R. LaRossa, W. R. Schumm, &

S. K. Steinmetz (Eds.), *Sourcebook of family theories and methods: A contextual approach* (pp. 627–645). New York: Springer.
Fredrickson, B. L., Maynard, K. E., Helms, M. J., Haney, T. L., Siegler, I. C., & Barefoot, J. C. (2000). Hostility predicts magnitude and duration of blood pressure response to anger. *Journal of Behavioral Medicine, 23*, 229–243. doi:10.1023/A:1005596208324.
Garcia Coll, C., & Garrido, M. (2000). Minorities in the United States. In A. J. Sameroff, M. Lewis, & S. M. Miller (Eds.), *Handbook of developmental psychopathology* (2nd ed., pp. 177–195). New York: Springer.
Garcia Coll, C., Crnic, K., Lamberty, G., Wasik, B. H., Jenkins, R., Garcia, H. V., et al. (1996). An integrative model for the study of developmental competencies in minority children. *Child Development, 67*(5), 1891–1914.
Gaylord-Harden, N., Cunningham, J. A., & Zelencik, B. (2011). Effects of exposure to community violence on internalizing symptoms: Does desensitization to violence occur in African American youth? *Journal of Abnormal Child Psychology, 39*, 711–719.
Gaylord-Harden, N. K., Burrow, A. L., & Cunningham, J. A. (2012). A Cultural-asset framework for investigating successful adaptation to stress in African American youth. *Child Development Perspectives, 6*(3), 264–271.
Gaylord-Harden, N. K., Zakaryan, A., Bernard, D., & Pekoc, S. (2015). Community-level victimization and aggressive behavior in African American male adolescents: A profile analysis. *Journal of Community Psychology, 43*(4), 502–519.
Gorman-Smith, D., Henry, D. B., & Tolan, P. (2004). Exposure to community violence and violence penetration: The protective effects of family functioning. *Journal of Clinical Child and Adolescent Psychology, 33*(3), 439–449.
Gorman-Smith, D., Tolan, P. H., & Henry, D. B. (2000). A developmental–ecological model of the relation of family functioning to patterns of delinquency. *Journal of Quantitative Criminology, 16*, 169–198.
Greene, A. D., & Mickelson, R. A. (2006). Connecting pieces of the puzzle: Gender differences in black middle school students' achievement. *Journal of Negro Education, 75*, 34–48.
Harper, S. R. (2009). Niggers no more: A critical race counternarrative on black male student achievement at predominantly White colleges and universities. *International Journal of Qualitative Studies in Education, 22*(6), 697–712.
Harper, S. R., Carini, R. M., Bridges, B. K., & Hayek, J. C. (2004). Gender differences in student engagement among African American undergraduates at historically black colleges and universities. *Journal of College Student Development, 45*(3), 271–284.
Harris, A. L., Sutherland, M. A., & Hutchinson, M. K. (2013). Parental influences on sexual risk among urban African American males. *Journal of Nursing Scholarship, 45*, 141–150.
Hughes, D., & Chen, L. (1997). When and what parents tell children about race: An examination of race-related socialization among African American families. *Applied Developmental Science, 1*(4), 200–214.
Hughes, D., Rodriguez, J., Smith, E. P., Johnson, D. J., Stevenson, H. C., & Spicer, P. (2006). Parents' ethnic-racial socialization practices: A review of the research and directions for future study. *Developmental Psychology, 42*, 747–770.
Jaccard, J., Dittus, P. J., & Gordon, V. V. (2000). Parent-teen communication about premarital sex factors associated with the extent of communication. *Journal of Adolescent Research, 15*(2), 187–208.
Jarrett, R. L. (1999). Successful parenting in high-risk neighborhoods. *The Future of Children, 9*(2), 45–50.
Kaiser Family Foundation. (n.d.). *Poverty rate by race/ethnicity*. http://kff.org/other/state-indicator/poverty-rate-by-raceethnicity/. Accessed Nov 2015.
Kapungu, C. T., Holmbeck, G. N., & Paikoff, R. L. (2006). Longitudinal association between parenting practices and early sexual risk behaviors among urban African American adolescents: The moderating role of gender. *Journal of Youth and Adolescence, 35*(5), 783–794.

Kassel, J. D., Wardle, M., & Roberts, J. E. (2007). Adult attachment security and college student substance use. *Addictive Behaviors, 32*(6), 1164–1176.

Kerpelman, J. L., Eryigit, S., & Stephens, C. J. (2008). African American adolescents' future education orientation: Associations with self-efficacy, ethnic identity, and perceived parental support. *Journal of Youth and Adolescence, 37*(8), 997–1008.

Kerpelman, J., & White, L. (2006). Interpersonal identity and social capital: The importance of commitment for low income, rural, African American adolescents. *Journal of Black Psychology, 32*(2), 219–242.

Kotchick, B. A., Shaffer, A., Miller, K. S., & Forehand, R. (2001). Adolescent sexual risk behavior: A multi-system perspective. *Clinical Psychology Review, 21*(4), 493–519.

Lerner, R. M. (2002). *Concepts and theories of human development* (3rd ed.). Mahwah, NJ: Erlbaum.

Lerner, R. M., Lerner, J. V., Almerigi, J., Theokas, C., Phelps, E., Gestsdottir, S., et al. (2005). Positive youth development, participation in community youth development programs, and community contributions of fifth grade adolescents: Findings from the first wave of the 4-H Study of Positive Youth Development. *Journal of Early Adolescence, 25*(1), 17–71.

Li, X., Feigelman, S., & Stanton, B. (2000). Perceived parental monitoring and health risk behaviors among urban low-income African-American children and adolescents. *Journal of Adolescent Health, 27*(1), 43–48.

Lincoln, C. E., & Mamiya, L. H. (1990). *The black church in the African American experience.* Durham, NC: Duke University Press.

Masten, A. S. (2014). *Ordinary magic: Resilience in development.* NY: The Guildford Press.

McCreary, M. L., Slavin, L. A., & Berry, E. J. (1996). Predicting problem behavior and self-esteem among African American adolescents. *Journal of Adolescent Research, 11*(2), 216–234.

McHale, S. M., Crouter, A. C., Kim, J. Y., Burton, L. M., Davis, K. D., Dotterer, A. M., et al. (2006). Mothers' and fathers' racial socialization in African American families: Implications for youth. *Child Development, 77*(5), 1387–1402.

Miniño A. M. (2013). *Death in the United States, 2011.* (NCHS data brief, No 115). Hyattsville, MD: National Center for Health Statistics. http://www.cdc.gov/nchs/data/databriefs/db115.htm. Accessed Nov 2015.

Murphy, C. (2015). Parenting while black: Toya Graham on violence, fear and Freddie Gray. http://talkingpointsmemo.com/theslice/parenting-while-black-toya-graham-baltimore-freddie-gray. Accessed Feb 2016.

Murry, V. M., Berkel, C., Brody, G. H., Gerrard, M., & Gibbons, F. X. (2007). The strong African American families program: Longitudinal pathways to sexual risk reduction. *Journal of Adolescent Health, 41*(4), 333–342.

Murry, V. M., Berkel, C., Brody, G. H., Miller, S. J., & Chen, Y. F. (2009). Linking parental socialization to interpersonal protective processes, academic self-presentation, and expectations among rural African American youth. *Cultural Diversity and Ethnic Minority Psychology, 15*(1), 1–10.

Murry, V. M., Brody, G. H., McNair, L., Luo, Z., Gibbons, F. X., Gerrard, M., et al. (2005). Parental involvement promotes rural African American youths' self-pride and sexual self-concepts. *Journal of Marriage and Family, 67*, 627–642.

Murry, V. M., Bynum, M. S., Brody, G. H., Willert, A., & Stephens, D. (2001). African American single mothers and children in context: A review of studies on risk and resilience. *Clinical Child and Family Psychology Review, 4*(2), 133–155.

Murry, V., & Liu, N. (2014). *Are African Americans living the dream 50 years after passage of the Civil Rights Act?* Council on Contemporary Families Civil Rights online symposium. https://contemporaryfamilies.org/are-african-americans-living-the-dream/

Murry, V. M., Liu, N., & Bethune, M. C. (2016). Rural African American adolescents' development: A critical review of empirical studies and preventive intervention programs. In L. J. Crockett & G. Carlo (Eds.), *Rural ethnic minority youth and families in the United States: Theory, research, and applications* (pp. 203–225). New York: Springer.

Murry, V. M., McNair, L. D., Myers, S. S., Chen, Y. F., & Brody, G. H. (2014). Intervention induced changes in perceptions of parenting and risk opportunities among rural African American. *Journal of Child and Family Studies, 23*(2), 422–436.

Murry, V. M., Simons, R. L., Simons, L. G., & Gibbons, F. X. (2013). Contributions of family environment and parenting processes to sexual risk and substance use of rural African American males: A 4-year longitudinal analysis. *American Journal of Orthopsychiatry, 83*(2), 299–309.

Neal-Barnett, A. (2004). Orphans no more: A commentary on anxiety and African American youth. *Journal of Clinical Child and Adolescent Psychology, 33*(2), 276–278.

Nobles, W. W. (2007). African American family life: An instrument of culture. In H. P. McAdoo (Ed.), *Black families* (4th ed., pp. 69–78). Thousand Oaks, CA: Sage.

Noguera, P. A. (2003). The trouble with black boys: The role and influence of environmental and cultural factors on the academic performance of African American males. *Urban Education, 38*(4), 431–459.

Ogbu, J. U. (1992). Adaptation to minority status and impact on school success. *Theory into Practice, 31*(4), 287–295.

Overton, W. F. (1998). Developmental psychology: Philosophy, concepts, and methodology. In R. M. Lerner (Ed.), *Handbook of child psychology. Vol. 1. Theoretical models of human development* (5th ed., pp. 107–189). New York, NY: Wiley.

Öztürk, O. D. (2007). *Employment effects of minimum wages in inflexible labor markets*. Social Science Research Network. http://dx.doi.org/10.2139/ssrn.1113175. Accessed Nov 2015.

Peters, M. F., & Massey, G. (1983). Mundane extreme environmental stress in family stress theories: The case of Black families in White America. *Marriage & Family Review, 6*(1–2), 193–218.

Phelps, E., Zimmerman, S., Warren, A. E. A., Jelicic, H., von Eye, A., & Lerner, R. M. (2009). The structure and developmental course of positive youth development (PYD) in early adolescence: Implications for theory and practice. *Journal of Applied Developmental Psychology, 30*(5), 571–584.

Ramirez-Valles, J., Zimmerman, M. A., & Juarez, L. (2002). Gender differences of neighborhood and social control processes: A study of the timing of first intercourse among low-achieving urban African American youth. *Youth & Society, 33*(3), 418–441.

Richardson Jr., J. B., Van Brakle, M., & St. Vil, C. (2014). Taking boys out of the hood: Exile as a parenting strategy for African American male youth. In K. Roy & N. Jones (Eds.), Pathways to adulthood for disconnected young men in low-income communities. *New Directions for Child and Adolescent Development, 143*, 11–31.

Roche, K. M., Ensminger, M. E., & Cherlin, A. J. (2007). Variations in parenting and adolescent outcomes among African American and Latino families living in low-income, urban areas. *Journal of Family Issues, 28*, 882–909.

Romer, D., Stanton, B., Galbraith, J., Feigelman, S., Black, M. M., & Li, X. (1999). Parental influence on adolescent sexual behavior in high-poverty settings. *Archives of Pediatrics and Adolescent Medicine, 153*, 1055–1062.

Ross, C. E., & Mirowsky, J. (1999). Disorder and decay: The concept and measurement of perceived neighborhood disorder. *Urban Affairs Review, 34*(3), 412–432.

Sampson, R. J., & Groves, W. B. (1989). Community structure and crime: Testing social-disorganization theory. *American Journal of Sociology, 94*(2), 774–802.

Sampson, R. J., Raudenbush, S. W., & Earls, F. (1997). Neighborhoods and violent crime: A multilevel study of collective efficacy. *Science, 277*(5328), 918–924.

Sanders, M. G. (1997). Overcoming obstacles: Academic achievement as a response to racism and discrimination. *Journal of Negro Education, 66*(1), 83–93.

Schraedley, P. K., Gotlib, I. H., & Hayward, C. (1999). Gender differences in correlates of depressive symptoms in adolescents. *Journal of Adolescent Health, 25*(2), 98–108.

Schwartz, S. J., Pantin, H., Coatsworth, J. D., & Szapocznik, J. (2007). Addressing the challenges and opportunities for today's youth: Toward an integrative model and its implications for research and intervention. *Journal of Primary Prevention, 28*, 117–144.

Seaton, E. K., Caldwell, C. H., Sellers, R. M., & Jackson, J. S. (2008). The prevalence of perceived discrimination among African American and Caribbean black youth. *Developmental Psychology, 44*(5), 1288–1297.

Seaton, E. K., Scottham, K. M., & Sellers, R. M. (2006). The status model of racial identity development in African American adolescents: Evidence of structure, trajectories, and well-being. *Child Development, 77*(5), 1416–1426.

Sellers, R. M., Caldwell, C. H., Schmeelk-Cone, K. H., & Zimmerman, M. A. (2003). Racial identity, racial discrimination, perceived stress, and psychological distress among African American young adults. *Journal of Health and Social Behavior, 43*, 302–317.

Sellers, R. M., Copeland-Linder, N., Martin, P. P., & Lewis, R. H. (2006). Racial identity matters: The relationship between racial discrimination and psychological functioning in African American adolescents. *Journal of Research on Adolescence, 16*(2), 187–216.

Serpell, Z., Hayling, C. C., Stevenson, H., & Kern, L. (2009). Cultural considerations in the development of school-based interventions for African American adolescent boys with emotional and behavioral disorders. *The Journal of Negro Education, 78*(3), 321–332.

Shaw, C. R., & McKay, H. D. (1942). *Juvenile delinquency and urban areas: A study of rates of delinquents in relation to differential characteristics of local communities in American cities*. Chicago: University of Chicago Press.

Shen, B.-J., Countryman, A. J., Spiro, A., III, & Niaura, R. (2008). The prospective contribution of hostility characteristics to high fasting glucose levels: The moderating role of marital status. *Diabetes Care, 31*, 1293–1298. doi:10.2337/dc07-1945.

Simons, R. L., Chen, Y. F., Stewart, E. A., & Brody, G. H. (2003). Incidents of discrimination and risk for delinquency: A longitudinal test of strain theory with an African American sample. *Justice Quarterly, 20*, 501–528. doi:10.1080/07418820300095711.

Simons, L. G., Simons, R. L., Conger, R. D., & Brody, G. H. (2004). Collective socialization and child conduct problems: A multilevel analysis with an African American sample. *Youth & Society, 35*(3), 267–292.

Singer, J. N. (2005). Understanding racism through the eyes of African American male student-athletes. *Race Ethnicity and Education, 8*(4), 365–386.

Skiba, R. J., Michael, R. S., Nardo, A. C., & Peterson, R. L. (2002). The color of discipline: Sources of racial and gender disproportionality in school punishment. *The Urban Review, 34*(4), 317–342.

Spencer, M. B., Dupree, D., & Hartmann, T. (1997). A phenomenological variant of ecological systems theory (PVEST): A self-organization perspective in context. *Development and Psychopathology, 9*, 817–833.

Steinman, K. J., & Zimmerman, M. A. (2003). Episodic and persistent gun-carrying among urban African-American adolescents. *Journal of Adolescent Health, 32*(5), 356–364.

Stetser, M., & Stillwell, R. (2014). *Public high school four-year on-time graduation rates and event dropout rates: School years 2010–11 and 2011–12. First look* (NCES 2014-391). Washington, DC: U.S. Department of Education. National Center for Education Statistics. http://nces.ed.gov/pubsearch. Accessed Nov 2015.

Stevens-Watkins, D., & Rostosky, S. (2010). Binge drinking in African American males from adolescence to young adulthood: The protective influence of religiosity, family connectedness, and close friends' substance use. *Substance Use and Misuse, 45*, 435–451.

Stevenson, H. C. (2003). *Playing with anger: Teaching coping skills to African American boys through athletics and culture*. Westport, CT: Praeger.

Strange, M., Johnson, J., Showalter, D., & Klein, R. (2012). *Why rural matters 2011-12: The condition of rural education in the 50 states*. Washington, DC: Rural School and Community Trust.

Sudarkasa, N. (2007). African American female-headed households: Some neglected dimensions. In H. P. McAdoo (Ed.), *Black families* (4th ed., pp. 172–183). Thousand Oaks: Sage.

Szapocznik, J., & Coatsworth, J. D. (1999). An ecodevelopmental framework for organizing the influences on drug abuse: A developmental model of risk and protection. In M. D. Glantz & C. R. Hartel (Eds.), *Drug abuse: Origins & interventions* (pp. 331–366). Washington, DC: American Psychological Association.

Thompson, T. (2011). *Fact sheet: Outcomes for young, black men*. http://www.pbs.org/wnet/tavissmiley/tsr/too-important-to-fail/fact-sheet-outcomes-for-young-black-men/. Accessed Feb 2016.

U.S. Department of Justice. (2009). *National crime victimization survey: Criminal victimization, 2008*. (Report No. NCJ 227777). Bureau of Justice Statistics Bulletin. http://www.bjs.gov/content/pub/pdf/cv08.pdf. Accessed Nov 2015.

U.S. Department of Justice, Bureau of Justice Statistics. (2015) *Prisoners in 2014*. Retrieved from http://www.bjs.gov/content/pub/pdf/p14.pdf.

Wagner, P. (2012). *United States incarceration rates by race and ethnicity, 2010*. Prison Policy Initiative. http://www.prisonpolicy.org/graphs/raceinc.html. Accessed Feb 2016.

Wang, M. T., & Hugley, J. P. (2012). Parental racial socialization as a moderator of the effects of racial discrimination on educational success among African American adolescents. *Child Development, 83*(5), 1716–1731.

Weidner, G., Sexton, G., McLellarn, R., Connor, S. L., & Matarazzo, J. D. (1987). The role of Type A behavior and hostility in an evaluation of plasma lipids in adult women and men. *Psychosomatic Medicine, 49*(2), 136–145.

Wight, R. G., Aneshensel, C. S., Botticello, A. L., & Sepúlveda, J. E. (2005). A multilevel analysis of ethnic variation in depressive symptoms among adolescents in the United States. *Social Science & Medicine, 60*(9), 2073–2084.

Williams, D. T. (2003). *Closing the achievement gap: Rural schools. CSR Connection*. (ERIC No. 478574). http://files.eric.ed.gov/fulltext/ED478574.pdf. Accessed Nov 2015.

Williams, O. A. (2003b). Effects of faith and church on African American adolescents. *Michigan Family Review, 8*(1), 19–27.

Zimmerman, M. A., Ramirez-Valles, J., Zapert, K. M., & Maton, K. I. (2000). A longitudinal study of stress-buffering effects for urban African American male adolescents' problem behaviors and mental health. *Journal of Community Psychology, 28*(1), 17–33.

# The Adjustment and Development of African American Males: Conceptual Frameworks and Emerging Research Opportunities

**Kevin J.A. Thomas**

Significant progress has been achieved in research on the adjustment of black males in recent decades. Until recently, however, much of this progress was characterized by a fundamental misunderstanding of the contexts in which this adjustment occurs. This gap in the literature was accompanied by the limited use of culturally-appropriate models in research on black male development. Indeed, there is a long history of using white males as a reference category against which the outcomes of black males are compared. The analytical perspectives derived from this approach belie its negative consequences; among the most important is the widespread use of deficit models that frame the development of black males using a problem-centered approach that fails to capture their overall life-experiences.

Murry, Block, and Liu (Murry et al., Chap. 2) challenge the utility of deficit models as analytical perspectives useful for studying the outcomes of black males. They correctly point out that this approach shifts attention away from the fact that the majority of black males live productive lives while ignoring the salience of the critical influences that contribute towards their successes. In this sense, the authors echo the arguments of several scholars who call for a shift from the use of deficit models to an understanding of resiliency and the conditions under which black males succeed (McGee & Pearman, 2014; Terry & McGee, 2012; Valencia, 1997). Beyond their critic of the deficit approach, however, Murry and colleagues develop a theoretical model that not only emphasizes the advantages of the resiliency perspective but also highlights the benefits of a systems perspective for use in research on black male development. This perspective is central to efforts to move the boundaries of research on black males. In part, this stems from the fact that the

K.J.A. Thomas (✉)
Department of Sociology, The Pennsylvania State University,
University Park, PA, USA
e-mail: kjt11@psu.edu



L. Burton et al. (eds.), *Boys and Men in African American Families*, National Symposium on Family Issues 7, DOI 10.1007/978-3-319-43847-4_3

systems approach demonstrates the utility of understanding these development processes as products of a confluence of interrelated contextual influences.

In practical terms, the systems framework has many other advantages. First, it is an integrated approach, emphasizing the contributions of individual, family, and community-level factors to the development of black males. Moreover, it shows that although each set of factors has an independent influence on the development of black males, these influences can be better understood in terms of how they are nested within other elements of the analytical framework. Second, the utility of the systems approach spans across disciplines. It can be applied to research on educational achievement and to studies on the health and psychological development of black males. Finally, as noted by Murry and colleagues (chapter "Adjustment and Developmental Patterns of African American Males: The Roles of Families, Communities, and Other Contexts"), the framework engenders the identification of malleable targets for intervention. Thus, its contributions extend beyond the boundaries of research since it offers useful insights into the development of appropriate policies for improving the lives of black males.

## Conceptual Linkages and Future of Research on the Adjustment of Black Males

A careful reading of the description of the systems framework nevertheless raises important questions about how it can be developed to enhance its contributions toward research and policy. The need to sufficiently account for extant disparities in the experiences of black males must be considered. Other questions relate to emerging complexities in the contextual elements of the framework, including black families, communities, and institutions. In addition, there is a need for a more systematic understanding of the instrumental contributions of contexts and institutions to the adjustment of black males as well as a firmer grasp of how the interactions implied by the framework can facilitate the development of policy interventions.

Changes in children's living arrangements are among the principal influences that will affect the future development of the systems approach for understanding the adjustment of black males. Since the 1950s, black families have experienced important transformations in their structure and composition as part of larger changes in dynamics of families in the US. As part of the second demographic transition, the US has experienced a decline in the prevalence of marriage, increases in divorce and cohabitation, and significant declines in fertility (Cherlin, 2005; Teachman, Tedrow, & Crowder, 2000). Across race, these transformations have been particularly concentrated among blacks (Cherlin, 1998; Teachman et al., 2000); and as a result, black children are now less likely to live in two-parent families than they did in the past. Many of these trends are likely to remain unchanged in the near future. Future work on the determinants of adjustment among black males will therefore need to examine what these more diverse family forms imply for black male development.

Transformations in the characteristics of black families will pose specific challenges for our traditional understanding of the parental socialization of black males as a gender-differentiated process. Previous research underscores the significance of fathers for the educational socialization of their children and the unique role of mothers in the racial socialization of their sons (Lawson Bush, 2004; McHale et al., 2006). As the nature of black families changes, however, new research is needed to effectively understand what black parents do in order to adapt to these changes. Very few of these adaptations are discussed in existing research. For example, some studies argue that single-mothers adopt androgynous parenting strategies as a way of adapting to changes in family structure (Talmi, 2013). The larger picture of how parents socialize black boys in non-traditional family contexts, however, remains unclear. Indeed, we know very little about the ways in which cohabiting parents, step parents, and parents in multi-generational households contribute to the socialization of young black males.

Non-parent actors have a long history of participation in the development of black children. However, systematic analysis of the specific ways in which they foster the adjustment of black boys is limited. We know very little about how older siblings shape the developmental outcomes of young black males. Moreover, outside the immediate family, there is limited research on the instrumental ways in which extended family members and fictive kin contribute to this process. Murry and colleagues (Chap. 2) note one such contribution—that of extended family members who open up their homes to black males moving from high to low risk neighborhoods as part of the process of exile parenting. Yet, it is very likely that the instrumental contributions of non-parent actors to the development of black males are more diverse. Similarly, when knowledge on the role of fictive kin to child development processes is available (Stewart, 2007), the specific import of these roles for the adjustment of black males is usually unclear.

Research on the influence of grandparents on child development provides a key example of existing gaps in knowledge on the effects of this influence on the development of black boys. The general influence of grandparents is transmitted through care-giving and the provision of social support (Hayslip & Kaminski, 2005). Research on the specific significance of grandparent's influence for the development of black boys is, however, limited. For example, it is not clear whether grandparent's influence on the development of black boys is gendered in similar ways as the unique effects of black mothers and fathers. Yet, empirical evidence provides important clues concerning the disparate effects of these roles. Figure 1 illustrates this point by examining dropout rates among black male teenagers in non-parent households compared to the dropout rates among boys in grandmother- and grandfather-headed households. As the shown in these estimates, there are clear differences in the percentage of black boys who are dropouts across contexts. In general, dropout rates are lower among boys living with any grandparent compared to boys living in other non-parent households. Furthermore, dropout rates among black boys living with grandparents are differentiated by the sex of grandparents. Specifically, dropout rates are lower for boys who live with their grandfathers than for boys living with their grandmothers. These differences do not appear to be

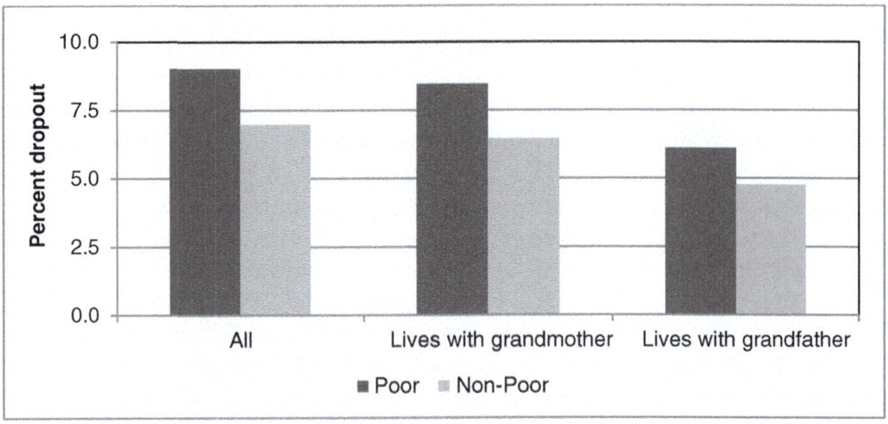


**Fig. 1** Schooling dropout among black teenage boys in non-parent household. *Data source*: 2008 to 2012 American Community Survey (ACS). https://www.census.gov/programs-surveys/acs/

explained by socioeconomic factors. Interestingly, the dropout rate of black boys living with grandfathers in poverty is similar to that of their peers living with non-poor grandmothers. These associations suggest that grandfathers make unique contributions to black male educational achievement. The specific nature of these contributions needs to be understood as it can provide key insights into how ordinary magic, as labeled by Masten (2014), is performed in grandparent families.

Other family-level changes, such as the increasing number of children living in adoptive families, create new opportunities for us to understand the racial socialization processes of black boys who do not live in traditional black family contexts. In recent decades, significant increases have been observed in the number of children living in adoptive families. Although only about 50,000 adopted children lived in the US in the mid-1940s, this number increased to approximated 2 million at the turn of the century (Kreider, 2003; Stolley, 1993). Black children are currently over-represented in the population of adopted children (Kreider & Lofquist, 2014) and these children are not always adopted by black parents. The racial composition of the population of adoptive parents in the US is very diverse (Thomas, 2016); however, what this diversity implies for the socialization of black boys generally remains unknown.

The significance of these implications can be understood by reviewing the evidence on the sex distribution of black children adopted by non-black parents. Figure 2 presents ratios of male to female adopted black children who have only-black versus non-black parents, based on data from the American Community Survey (ACS) available in the Integrated Public Use Microdata Samples (IPUMS) database (Ruggles, Genadek, Goeken, Grover, & Sobek, 2015). The estimates show that across childhood age-groups, the sex-ratio is higher among adopted black children with non-black parents compared to their peers with only-black parents. Between ages 13 and 17, for example, there are 1.26 adopted black males for every adopted black female in families with non-black parents. These distributions suggest that non-black parents who adopt black children are more likely to adopt boys rather

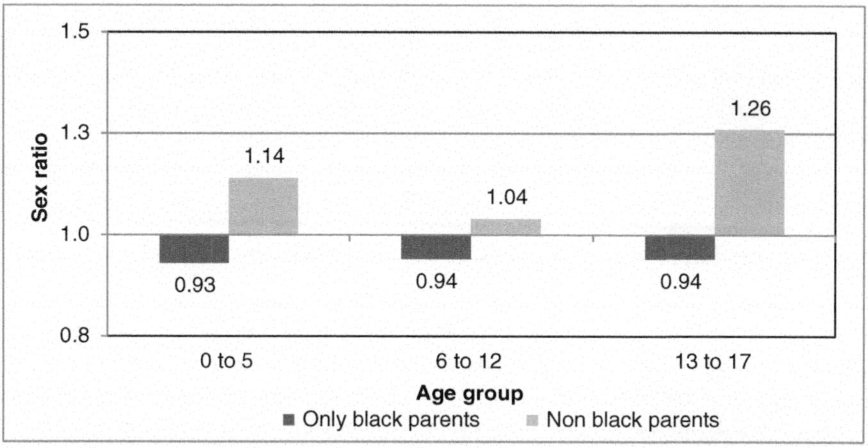


**Fig. 2** The sex ratio of male to female adopted black children with only black or non-black parents. *Data source*: 2008 to 2012 American Community Survey (ACS). https://www.census.gov/programs-surveys/acs/

than girls. Adopted black boys living in these contexts are far removed from the traditional forms of parental racial socialization typically found in black families. This does not imply that racial socialization among black boys cannot effectively occur in non-black adoptive families. However, there are significant gaps in the extant literature on the adjustment of black boys living in non-black family contexts. Addressing these gaps is important. It will require new studies that focus on investigating several critical issues including the question of how traditional racial socialization strategies used in black families can be used to promote the adjustment of adopted black boys in other racial family contexts.

Beyond the salience of adoptive families, immigration trends have potential implications for improving what we know about the determinants of development among black boys. Although the number of black immigrants in the US before 1965 was under 150,000, by 2013 the black immigrant population had increased to approximately 3.8 million (Anderson, 2015; Kent, 2007). Today, black immigrants are one of the fastest growing segments of the immigrant population and account for about 9 % of the population of blacks in the US (Anderson, 2015). This growth has been accompanied by considerable increases in the number of children living in black immigrant families (Hernandez, 2012). As these transformations occur, new opportunities are provided for examining whether extant conceptualizations of the adjustment of black males apply to the outcomes of black children in immigrant families. As existing evidence indicates, there are diverse patterns of racial socialization found in black immigrant families. Waters (2001), for example, maintains that the racial socialization of the children of black immigrants is dependent on the socioeconomic status (SES) of their families; accordingly, children in high SES immigrant families are more likely to reject the US black racial identity in favor of their immigrant ethnic identities. On the other hand, research indicates that many of the social challenges associated with racial minority status are similarly experienced by the children of black immigrants and their peers in black native families (Thomas, 2011). In addition to investigating these nuances, future studies will need to address the larger question of whether contexts influence the adjustment of black males in unique ways, conditional on their immigrant status.

## Developing Interventions Based on the Systems Model

The practical utility of the systems or adjustment model proposed by Murry and colleagues (Chap. 2) is underscored by its amenability to the development of appropriate policy interventions. The model's foundational argument of viewing the outcomes of black males as products of interconnected influences extends to the process of developing sound policy interventions. At the same time, the model helps us to understand where to intervene to improve the outcomes of black males. The simplest approach to identifying these points of intervention involves targeting interventions toward specific elements within the model. Family-level interventions, for example, could provide support to the single-parent, extended-family, and non-traditional household contexts where young black males are now increasingly found. Similarly, community-level interventions could seek to develop state and local government programs that could focus on providing safe neighborhoods in disadvantaged black communities. The systems model further points to a more complex set of interventions that could leverage opportunities found in interactions between elements of the system. These interactions could involve partnerships between families and communities or between institutions and families that help to foster resilience among black males in the early stages of the life course.

Another advantage of the adjustment model is that it helps us to understand how to intervene to improve the lives of young black males. Interventions are more likely to succeed when the growing demographic diversity of the population of young black males is taken into account. Interventions must also be developed in ways that meet the unique needs of black males living in other racial family contexts. Critical to the general process of developing interventions is the need to exploit feedback loops found between the core elements of the system. As much as it is important to develop interventions that help parents prepare their sons to interact with law enforcement institutions, it is also important to help *these institutions* prepare for interactions with black males. Careful thought should be given to how interventions are developed to help schools, churches, and other institutions contribute to the adjustment of black males. Such strategies could hold significant promise and add to the number of black males who already live productive lives.

## References


Anderson, M. (2015). A rising share of the U.S. Black population is foreign born. Pew Research Center Social and Demographic Trends. http://www.pewsocialtrends.org/2015/04/09/a-rising-share-of-the-u-s-black-population-is-foreign-born/. Accessed Dec 2015.

Cherlin, A. J. (1998). Marriage and marital dissolution among black Americans. *Journal of Comparative Family Studies, 29*(1), 147–158.

Cherlin, A. J. (2005). American marriage in the early twenty-first century. *The Future of Children, 15*(2), 33–55.

Hayslip, B., & Kaminski, P. L. (2005). Grandparents raising their grandchildren: A review of the literature and suggestions for practice. *The Gerontologist, 45*(2), 262–269.

Hernandez, D. J. (2012). Young children in black immigrant families from Africa and the Caribbean. In R. Capps & M. Fix (Eds.), *Young children of black immigrants in America: Changing flows, changing faces* (pp. 75–118). Washington, DC: Migration Policy Institute.

Kent, M. M. (2007). *Immigration and America's black population* (Vol. 62, No. 4). Washington, DC: Population Reference Bureau. http://www.prb.org/pdf07/62.4immigration.pdf. Accessed Dec 2015.

Kreider, R. M. (2003, October). *Adopted children and stepchildren: 2000. Census 2000 Special Reports*. Washington, DC: U.S. Bureau of the Census

Kreider, R. M., & Lofquist, D. A. (2014). *Adopted children and stepchildren: 2010 (P20-527)*. Washington, DC: U.S. Census Bureau.

Lawson Bush, V. (2004). How Black mothers participate in the development of manhood and masculinity: What do we know about Black mothers and their sons? *Journal of Negro Education, 73*(4), 381–391.

Masten, A. S. (2014). *Ordinary magic: Resilience in development*. New York: The Guildford Press.

McGee, E. O., & Pearman, F. A. (2014). Risk and protective factors in mathematically talented black male students: Snapshots from kindergarten through eighth grade. *Urban Education, 49*(4), 363–393.

McHale, S. M., Crouter, A. C., Kim, J. Y., Burton, L. M., Davis, K. D., Dotterer, A. M., et al. (2006). Mothers' and fathers' racial socialization in African American families: Implications for youth. *Child Development, 77*(5), 1387–1402.

Ruggles, S., Genadek, K., Goeken, R., Grover, J., & Sobek, M. (2015). *Integrated public use micro-data series: Version 6.0 [Machine-readable database]*. Minneapolis: University of Minnesota.

Stewart, P. (2007). Who is kin? Family definition and African American families. *Journal of Human Behavior in the Social Environment, 15*(2–3), 163–181.

Stolley, K. S. (1993). Statistics on adoption in the United States. *The Future of Children, 3*(1), 26–42.

Talmi, A. (2013). Gender and parenting across the lifecycle. In W. B. Wilcox & K. K. Kline (Eds.), *Gender and parenthood: Biological and social scientific perspectives* (pp. 164–190). New York: Columbia University Press.

Teachman, J. D., Tedrow, L. M., & Crowder, K. D. (2000). The changing demography of America's families. *Journal of Marriage and Family, 62*(4), 1234–1246.

Terry, C. L., Sr., & McGee, E. O. (2012). "I've come too far, I've worked too hard": Reinforcement of support structures among Black male mathematics students. *Journal of Mathematics Education at Teachers College, 3*(2), 73–84.

Thomas, K. J. (2011). Familial influences on poverty among young children in black immigrant, U.S.-born black, and nonblack immigrant families. *Demography, 48*(2), 437–460.

Thomas, K. J. (2016). Adoption, foreign-born status, and children's progress in school. *Journal of Marriage and Family, 78*(1), 75–90. doi:10.1111/jomf.12268.

Valencia, R. R. (Ed.). (1997). *The evolution of deficit thinking: Educational thought and practice*. London: Routledge.

Waters, M. C. (2001). *Black identities*. Cambridge, MA: Harvard University Press.

# Considering Risk and Resiliency Among Children of Incarcerated Parents

**Kristin Turney and Britni L. Adams**

Velma McBride Murry, Erin Block, and Na Liu (Chap. 2) draw attention to an important puzzle: How do African American boys, many of whom have a high risk of experiencing adversity, survive and thrive in childhood and adolescence? Drawing on Bronfenbrenner's (1994) ecological systems theory and Lerner's (2002) relational developmental systems model, Murry and collaborators discuss different domains—including academic outcomes, behavioral outcomes, and mental health outcomes—in which African American boys experience comparatively deleterious outcomes. The authors also use these frameworks to discuss how—despite adversities such as poverty, exposure to violence, and neighborhood disadvantage—African American boys often develop normatively. The focus is on contextual characteristics of African American families and communities to highlight how they prepare young boys to successfully face adversity. In particular, Murry and colleagues highlight the role of the family, especially parents, and other adults who can monitor, communicate, and connect with these boys to facilitate the transference of positive values related to school, future-oriented behavior, and emotional control, as well as how family members can minimize adverse reactions to hardship. The authors conclude by suggesting that current developmental theories should be revised to highlight the strategies that African American families utilize to facilitate resiliency.

We use the conceptual framework put forth by Murry and colleagues (Chap. 2) to discuss one type of adversity disproportionately experienced, not just by African American boys, but by African American children more generally: parental incarceration. Parental incarceration is an important type of adversity to consider because it is unequally distributed across the population and because existing research suggests that it can have deleterious consequences for children's academic outcomes,

K. Turney (✉) • B.L. Adams
Department of Sociology, University of California, Irvine, CA, USA
e-mail: kristin.turney@uci.edu



L. Burton et al. (eds.), *Boys and Men in African American Families*, National Symposium on Family Issues 7, DOI 10.1007/978-3-319-43847-4_4

behavioral outcomes, and health outcomes (for reviews, see Eddy & Poehlmann, 2010; Foster & Hagan, 2015; Johnson & Easterling, 2012; Murray, Farrington, & Sekol, 2012; Travis, Western, & Redburn, 2014; Wildeman, Wakefield, & Turney, 2013; Wildeman & Western, 2010). We suggest that, despite the fact that African American children are more likely than children of other race/ethnic groups to experience parental incarceration, African American children are not a monolithic group and, instead, children in this group have differential risks of being exposed to parental incarceration. We also suggest that these differential risks of being exposed to parental incarceration might shape African American children's responses to parental incarceration. In focusing on both differential risks and differential responses, we highlight how risk and resiliency, particularly among African American boys, can work in concert to produce beneficial or deleterious outcomes.

This chapter proceeds as follows: First, we describe trends in incarceration in the United States, focusing on trends in parental incarceration and on race/ethnic inequalities in these trends. Second, through an examination of population-based data from the 2011–2012 National Survey of Children's Health (NSCH) (Centers for Disease Control and Prevention National Center for Health Statistics, 2013), we describe the demographic, socioeconomic, and behavioral characteristics that shape African American boys' risks of being exposed to parental incarceration. We do this by grouping children into the following categories: children with a relatively low risk of experiencing parental incarceration, children with a relatively moderate risk of experiencing parental incarceration, and children with a relatively high risk of experiencing parental incarceration. Third, we discuss what might make African American boys resilient to parental incarceration. Finally, we discuss how risk and resiliency may jointly matter for children's well-being and conclude with suggestions for researchers, policymakers, and practitioners to help youth successfully face adversity.

## Trends in Exposure to Parental Incarceration

Incarceration rates in the United States, though recently stabilized, have increased dramatically throughout the past 4 decades (Wakefield & Uggen, 2010). In 1970, about 100 per 100,000 individuals in the population were incarcerated in *state or federal prisons*. Today, that number stands at 478 per 100,000 individuals in the population. The number stands at 623 per 100,000 individuals ages 18 and older; 904 per 100,000 men; 2805 per 100,000 African American men; and 6746 per 100,000 African American men ages 30–34 years old (Carson, 2014). These numbers, striking as they are, tell us nothing about individuals incarcerated in local jails, who comprise a substantial proportion of the incarcerated population, or individuals who have been recently released back to their families and communities.

Additionally, as the majority of inmates have children, the past 4 decades have witnessed increasing numbers of children—especially minority children and poor children—who are exposed to parental incarceration (and, in particular, paternal incarceration). Currently, about 2.6 million children nationwide have a parent in local jails, state prisons, or federal prisons (Pettit, 2012). Exposure to parental incarceration is not equally distributed across the population and is instead concentrated among minority and poor children. For example, even among the most disadvantaged White children, those whose parents dropped out of high school, parental incarceration is far from commonplace. About 7 % of these children experience paternal incarceration and 1 % experience maternal incarceration by age 14. This is in stark contrast to African American children's exposure to parental incarceration. Among African American children with parents who dropped out of high school, 50 % experience paternal incarceration, and 5 % experience maternal incarceration by age 14 (Wildeman, 2009). Taken together, these numbers suggest that, in the United States, there are children and adolescents who are especially vulnerable to parental incarceration.

## Considering Variation in Risk to Parental Incarceration Among African American Boys

It is well known that African American children, compared to their counterparts of other race/ethnic groups, are at greater risk of exposure to parental incarceration. However, it is important to understand heterogeneity within African American children. African American children (as well as children of other race/ethnic groups) have different risks of experiencing parental incarceration. Some children—based on the demographic, socioeconomic, and behavioral characteristics of their parents—have relatively low risks of experiencing parental incarceration. Other children, though, have relatively high risks of experiencing parental incarceration. We explore this heterogeneity in risk to inform resiliency among youth. We focus on African American boys, in particular, as they are the focus of this volume. This is an especially important group to study the consequences of parental incarceration, as African American children experience incarceration at much higher rates than other children (e.g., Wildeman, 2009) and there's evidence that boys experience more negative consequences of parental incarceration than do girls. Some research finds that sons of incarcerated fathers are especially vulnerable to behavioral problems, high school dropout, delinquency and criminal activity, depressive symptoms, and mortality (e.g., Haskins, 2015; Wildeman, 2010; for a review, see Foster & Hagan, 2015).

## Data

To understand the differential risks of experiencing parental incarceration among African American boys, we use data from the 2011–2012 National Survey of Children's Health (NSCH) (Centers for Disease Control and

Prevention National Center for Health Statistics, 2013). The NSCH is a cross-sectional probability sample of 95,677 non-institutionalized children ages 0–17 in the United States. The survey was conducted via telephone between February 2011 and June 2012. The sample was selected with list-assisted random-digit dialing, which was used to identify households with children ages 0–17, and was stratified by state and telephone type (landline or cell phone). Sampling weights adjust for the sampling design and survey non-response. Additional details about data collection have been described elsewhere (Centers for Disease Control and Prevention National Center for Health Statistics, 2013). The large sample size of the 2011–2012 NSCH allows for an examination of a typically difficult-to-reach population, children of incarcerated parents. The sample is large enough that it allows us to consider characteristics of African American boys, specifically (N = 4559).

## Measures

Our key measure, parental incarceration, indicates the focal child ever lived with a parent or guardian who served time in jail or prison after the child was born. This measure necessarily only captures the incarceration of a residential parent, which almost certainly underestimates parental incarceration. However, examining residential parent incarceration is especially important because prior research suggests these children suffer more deleterious consequences than their counterparts who experience the incarceration of a non-residential parent (e.g., Geller, Cooper, Garfinkel, Schwartz-Soicher, & Mincy, 2012). About 12 % of children in the analytic sample (i.e., African American boys) were exposed to the incarceration of a residential parent.

The analyses also rely on a number of demographic, socioeconomic, and behavioral characteristics. Demographically, a binary variable indicates the child's biological parents are married. Socioeconomic characteristics include the following variables, all reported by the parent respondent: parental educational attainment (less than a high school diploma, high school diploma or GED, more than high school), parent is employed, family often has difficulty getting by on its income, household member receives welfare, household member receives WIC, household income below the poverty line, and parent owns home. Behavioral characteristics include the following parent-reported variables: parent in fair or poor health, household member smokes inside the home, and neighborhood is always safe for the child. Children's adverse experiences, reported by the parent, include the following: parental divorce or separation, parental death, witness of parental abuse, witness or victim of neighborhood violence, household member has a mental health problem, and household member has a drug or alcohol problem. Finally, children's characteristics include age (ages 0–6, ages 7–12, and ages 13–17) and low birth weight.

## Analyses

We use information on demographic, socioeconomic, and behavioral characteristics to group African American boys into three groups: children with low risks of experiencing parental incarceration, children with moderate risks of experiencing parental incarceration, and children with high risks of experiencing parental incarceration. Categorizing children into these groups is a two-step process. First, we use logistic regression and all covariates described above to generate a propensity score that necessarily ranges from 0 to 1. Children with propensity scores closest to 0 have the lowest risks of experiencing parental incarceration, and children with propensity scores closest to 1 have the highest risks of experiencing parental incarceration. Second, based on their propensity scores, we group children into three similarly sized groups. Children in the lowest third of the distribution of propensity scores, those with the lowest risks of experiencing parental incarceration, have propensity scores between 0 and 0.05. Essentially, these children have between a 0 and 5 % chance of experiencing parental incarceration. Children in the middle third of the propensity score distribution, those with relatively moderate risks of experiencing parental incarceration, have propensity scores greater than 0.05 and up to and including 0.10 (or, essentially, between a 5 and 10 % chance of experiencing parental incarceration). Children in the top third of the distribution of propensity scores, those with the highest risks of experiencing parental incarceration, have propensity scores greater than 0.10 and up to and including 0.90 (or, essentially, between a 10 and 90 % chance of experiencing parental incarceration). These analyses are the first step of the heterogeneous treatment effects approach to causal inference described elsewhere (see, especially, Xie, Brand, & Jann, 2012; for an application to maternal incarceration, see Turney & Wildeman, 2015).

## Results

In Table 1, we present demographic, socioeconomic, and behavioral characteristics for children in three groups: those with a low risk of experiencing parental incarceration (28 of whom did experience parental incarceration and 1317 of whom did not experience parental incarceration), those with a moderate risk of experiencing parental incarceration (94 of whom did experience parental incarceration and 1632 of whom did not experience parental incarceration), and those with a high risk of experiencing parental incarceration (337 of whom did experience parental incarceration and 1151 of whom did not experience parental incarceration). We see striking group differences across all covariates. For example, 66.8 % of children in the low-risk group have married parents, compared to 27.6 % of children in the moderate-risk group and 10.9 % of children in the high-risk group.

**Table 1** Descriptive statistics by risk of experiencing parental incarceration, sample restricted to African American boys

| | Low risk | Moderate risk | High risk |
|---|---|---|---|
| | 0–5 % | 5–10 % | 10–90 % |
| Parent married to child's biological father | 66.8 % | 27.6 % | 10.9 % |
| Parent educational attainment | | | |
| Less than high school | 14.5 % | 23.1 % | 26.6 % |
| High school diploma or GED | 28.8 % | 39.3 % | 41.4 % |
| More than high school | 56.7 % | 37.7 % | 32.0 % |
| Parent employed | 92.2 % | 83.0 % | 66.1 % |
| Family often has difficulty getting by on its income | 0.1 % | 6.4 % | 16.3 % |
| Household member receives welfare | 0.0 % | 5.2 % | 34.4 % |
| Household member receives WIC | 5.7 % | 19.1 % | 18.8 % |
| Household income below poverty line | 1.5 % | 30.6 % | 52.1 % |
| Parent owns home | 91.5 % | 43.7 % | 29.0 % |
| Parent in fair or poor health | 4.1 % | 13.2 % | 26.0 % |
| Household member smokes inside home | 0.0 % | 5.6 % | 20.3 % |
| Neighborhood always safe for child | 60.0 % | 53.4 % | 44.5 % |
| Parental divorce or separation | 0.0 % | 16.0 % | 43.8 % |
| Parental death | 0.0 % | 5.7 % | 15.0 % |
| Witness of parental abuse | 0.0 % | 1.4 % | 23.5 % |
| Witness or victim of neighborhood violence | 0.0 % | 9.6 % | 34.0 % |
| Household member mental health problem | 1.3 % | 4.3 % | 19.4 % |
| Household member drug or alcohol problem | 0.0 % | 0.0 % | 30.0 % |
| Child age | | | |
| Ages 0–6 | 42.4 % | 38.3 % | 26.3 % |
| Ages 7–12 | 30.2 % | 32.9 % | 38.7 % |
| Ages 13–17 | 27.4 % | 28.9 % | 35.0 % |
| Child born low birth weight | 10.9 % | 14.9 % | 15.6 % |
| Parental incarceration | 28 | 94 | 337 |
| No parental incarceration | 1317 | 1632 | 1151 |

*Notes*: Analyses based on data from the 2011–2012 National Study of Children's Health (NSCH). Sample restricted to non-Hispanic Black boys (N=4559). Low-risk children have between a 0 and 5 % chance of experiencing parental incarceration, moderate-risk children have between a 5 and 10 % chance of experiencing parental incarceration, and high-risk children have between a 10 and 90 % chance of experiencing parental incarceration.

Children in the low-risk group also experience socioeconomic advantages compared to their counterparts in the other two groups. Among children in the low-risk group, 14.5 % have parents with less than a high school diploma; in the other two groups, about one-quarter of children have parents with less than a high school diploma (23.1 % in the moderate-risk group and 26.6 % in the high-risk group). Children in the low-risk group are also more likely to have employed parents

(92.2 %, compared to 83.0 % in the moderate-risk group and 66.1 % in the high-risk group). They are less likely to have parents who report difficulty getting by on their income (0.1 %, compared to 6.4 % in the moderate-risk group and 16.3 % in the high-risk group) and less likely to live in households with incomes below the poverty line (1.5 %, compared to 30.6 % of children in the moderate-risk group and 52.1 % of children in the high-risk group).

There are also vast group differences in the experience of adverse childhood events aside from parental incarceration. Children in the low-risk group, almost across the board, have experienced no adverse childhood events. However, children in the high-risk group often experienced many of these adverse childhood events. Children in this group were more likely than their counterparts to experience other forms of father absence such as parental divorce (43.8 %, compared to 0 % of children in the low-risk group and 16.0 % of children in the moderate-risk group) and parental death (15.0 %, compared to 0 % of children in the low-risk group and 5.7 % of children in the moderate-risk group). Children in this group were also more likely to witness parental abuse (23.5 %, compared to 0 % of children in the low-risk group and 1.4 % of children in the moderate-risk group) and/or witness or be the victim of neighborhood violence (34.0 %, compared to 0 % in the low-risk group and 9.6 % in the moderate-risk group). They are also more likely than their counterparts to live with a household member who has a mental health problem (19.4 %, compared to 1.3 % in the low-risk group and 4.3 % in the moderate-risk group) and/or a substance abuse problem (30.0 %, compared to 0 % in both the low- and moderate-risk groups).

Taken together, these descriptive analyses suggest that African American boys face different risks of exposure to parental incarceration based on the demographic, socioeconomic, and behavioral characteristics of their parents, with some African American boys being relatively unlikely to experience parental incarceration and other African American boys being relatively likely to experience parental incarceration. These descriptive analyses also extend prior research, the vast majority of which focuses on differences between African American children and other children, to consider the variability within African American children.

## How Variation in Risk May Structure Responses to Parental Incarceration

In response to the growing number of children exposed to parental incarceration, as well as children's unequal risks for experiencing parental incarceration, a burgeoning literature describes the intergenerational consequences of incarceration. By and large, using a variety of data and methodological techniques, this research finds that parental incarceration, especially paternal incarceration, is associated with deleterious educational, behavioral, and health outcomes in children (for reviews, see Eddy & Poehlmann, 2010; Foster & Hagan, 2015; Johnson & Easterling, 2012; Murray et al., 2012; Travis et al., 2014; Wildeman & Western, 2010; Wildeman et al., 2013). The vast majority of existing research, though, is focused on the following question:

Does parental incarceration affect children? This question is an important starting point for understanding the intergenerational consequences of incarceration. But much less research considers processes of risk and resiliency, despite strong reasons to believe that children have different risks for experiencing parental incarceration and that children may be differentially affected by parental incarceration.

This variation in risk of exposure to parental incarceration, as demonstrated above with the descriptive data, may structure children's responses to parental incarceration, as children are not equally affected by parental incarceration (Turanovic, Rodriguez, & Pratt, 2012). Although an empirical examination of how risk is associated with children's responses to parental incarceration is not possible with these cross-sectional NSCH data, existing work sheds light on this possibility. Recent research by Turney (forthcoming) uses data from the Fragile Families and Child Wellbeing study—a broadly representative sample of children born to mostly unmarried parents in urban areas (of which about three-quarters are race/ethnic minorities) that is commonly used to study the intergenerational consequences of parental incarceration—to consider the heterogeneous effects of paternal incarceration on 9-year-old children's problem behaviors and cognitive skills. (For research on the heterogeneous effects of maternal incarceration, see Turney & Wildeman, 2015.) This research finds that the variation in children's risks of experiencing paternal incarceration—with some children very unlikely to experience paternal incarceration and other children very likely to experience paternal incarceration—structures children's responses to paternal incarceration. Children with relatively low risks of exposure to paternal incarceration experience the most severe consequences stemming from this exposure. Alternatively, children with relatively high risks of exposure to paternal incarceration experience relatively few *causal* effects from the exposure. These high-risk children are resilient to the deleterious consequences of paternal incarceration. However, this resiliency should be interpreted cautiously because these children experience an array of disadvantages that may simply mute the effects of paternal incarceration (and not necessarily facilitate resiliency). Although this existing research utilizes a mostly minority sample to examine how variation in risk structures resiliency, it does not focus on African American boys specifically. We suspect the findings would hold if we were to consider only African American boys, as there is little evidence of race/ethnic differences in the effects of paternal incarceration on children's well-being (see, for example, Haskins, 2014; Turney & Haskins, 2014), but future research should investigate this possibility.

## Toward a Joint Consideration of Risk and Resiliency

Children have different risks of being exposed to parental incarceration and these risks may shape children's responses to parental incarceration. Existing research about protective interventions for youth considers the role of prosocial mentors, parental monitoring, sibling support, and parental support and warmth (Crosnoe & Elder, 2004; Li, Stanton, & Feigelman, 2000; Rutter, 1987; Werner, 1992;

Zimmerman, Bingenheimer, & Notaro, 2002). Additionally, more formally structured programs—school programs and skills training, community centers, counseling services, and religious institutions—facilitate social capital among youth (Werner, 1992; for a review, see Hawkins, Catalano, & Miller, 1992) and/or serve as an extension of family resources and monitoring (Murry & Brody, 1999). These different interventions and programs can shield youth from the negative consequences of adversity. However, given research about the intersectionality of experiences, researchers, policymakers, and practitioners may want to consider how children's resiliency to parental incarceration—and the policies and practices that foster resiliency—might depend on children's risk factors. For example, effective policies and practices geared toward children with a relatively low risk of being exposed to parental incarceration may be very different than effective policies and practices geared toward children with a relatively moderate or relatively high risk of being exposed to parental incarceration.

Children with a low risk of experiencing parental incarceration, who may experience the most deleterious consequences of parental incarceration, may benefit from a reduction in incarceration rates. For these children, it may be helpful to consider relying on criminal justice interventions other than incarceration for low-level offenders (e.g., decriminalizing possession of marijuana and other petty offenses). These children may also benefit from family interventions, as evidence suggests that parental incarceration may be a critical turning point in the life course of these youth. This group might benefit from monetary resources that aid in the transition to parental incarceration or from resources that help family members left behind establish new functional routines for youth. For example, affordable childcare may become critical for parents who depended on their partner's income before incarceration. Moreover, parents left behind may need help navigating their new roles as both mothers and fathers (in terms of providing both support and discipline to their children) and, in the absence of other familial support, their new roles in managing all aspects of households (e.g., bill paying, grocery shopping, transportation). Finally, these families might benefit from additional resources to navigate the criminal justice system for visits, phone calls, and court dates, as well as mental health resources to assist in coping with the uncertainty with this system.

Children with a high risk of experiencing parental incarceration may also benefit from reduced incarceration rates and the support services described above, but these children may need additional resources that facilitate resiliency. These children have already experienced so much adversity and instability that parental incarceration is generally not destabilizing; therefore, protective strategies might be more centered on their daily lives rather than parental incarceration itself. For example, interventions might include finding these children a stable home with economic resources and emotional support. Interventions could also consider integrating children into kinship care with supplemental income and encouraging prosocial influences (e.g., parental warmth and monitoring). These children might also benefit from exile strategies, through prosocial placements (rather than through the juvenile justice system) that remove them from their environments and place them with caregivers who can provide the intensive parenting and love needed to connect with them (Howes & Spieker, 2008).

## Conclusions

Although African Americans are disproportionately exposed to incarceration in the United States, and African American youth are disproportionately exposed to parental incarceration, this group is diverse in demographic, socioeconomic, and behavioral characteristics that shape their exposure to parental incarceration. Using data from the 2011–2012 National Survey of Children's Health (NSCH), we show that African American boys with a high risk of experiencing parental incarceration are also more likely to experience parental divorce and/or death, witness parental abuse, witness or be the victim of neighborhood crime, and be living in poverty. These same experiences are relatively rare among African American boys with a low risk of experiencing parental incarceration. We discuss how resiliency may vary among a seemingly homogenous group. Therefore, programs and policies created to help youth successfully engage with adversity should consider their diverse life circumstances and environments to provide more appropriate resources across the variation of risk. Future research on youth resiliency should continue to explore the link between differential risks and differential responses to understand variations in how youth are resilient despite the formidable challenges they face.

**Acknowledgements** This research was supported by a grant from the Foundation for Child Development to Kristin Turney. The authors are grateful to the Data Resource Center for Child and adolescent Health, Child and Adolescent Health Measurement Initiative for providing the 2011–2012 National Survey of Children's Health.

## References

Bronfenbrenner, U. (1994). Ecological models of human development. In *International encyclopedia of education* (Vol. 3, 2nd ed.). Oxford, England: Elsevier. (Reprinted in M. Gauvain & M. Cole (Eds.), *Readings on the development of children* (2nd ed., pp. 37–43). NY: Freeman).

Carson, E. A. (2014). *Prisoners in 2013 (NCJ 247282)*. Washington, DC: U.S. Department of Justice, Bureau of Justice Statistics.

Centers for Disease Control and Prevention National Center for Health Statistics. (2013, March). *State and local area integrated telephone survey. 2011–2012 National survey of children's health (Frequently asked questions)*. Retrieved from http://www.cdc.gov/nchs/slaits/nsch.htm

Crosnoe, R., & Elder, G. H. (2004). Family dynamics, supportive relationships, and educational resilience during adolescence. *Journal of Family Issues, 25*(5), 571–602.

Eddy, J. M., & Poehlmann, J. (2010). *Children of incarcerated parents: A handbook for researchers and practitioners*. Washington, DC: Urban Institute Press.

Foster, H., & Hagan, J. (2015). Punishment regimes and the multilevel effects of parental incarceration: Intergenerational, intersectional, and interinstitutional models of social inequality and exclusion. *Annual Review of Sociology, 41*(1), 135–158.

Geller, A., Cooper, C. E., Garfinkel, I., Schwartz-Soicher, O., & Mincy, R. B. (2012). Beyond absenteeism: Father incarceration and child development. *Demography, 49*(1), 49–76.

Haskins, A. (2014). Unintended consequences: Effects of paternal incarceration on child school readiness and later special education placement. *Sociological Science, 1*(1), 141–158.

Haskins, A. R. (2015). Paternal incarceration and child-reported behavioral functioning at age 9. *Social Science Research, 52*, 18–33.

Hawkins, J. D., Catalano, R. F., & Miller, J. Y. (1992). Risk and protective factors for alcohol and other drug problems in adolescence and early adulthood: Implications for substance abuse prevention. *Psychological Bulletin, 112*(1), 64–105.

Howes, C., & Spieker, S. (2008). Attachment relationships in the context of multiple caregivers. In J. Cassidy & P. R. Shaver (Eds.), *Handbook of attachment: Theory, research, and clinical applications* (pp. 317–332). New York: Guilford Press.

Johnson, E. I., & Easterling, B. (2012). Understanding unique effects of parental incarceration on children: Challenges, progress, and recommendation. *Journal of Marriage and Family, 74*(2), 342–356.

Lerner, R. M. (2002). *Concepts and theories of human development* (3rd ed.). Mahwah, NJ: Erlbaum.

Li, X., Stanton, B., & Feigelman, S. (2000). Impact of perceived parental monitoring on adolescent risk behavior over 4 years. *Journal of Adolescent Health, 27*(1), 49–56.

Murray, J., Farrington, D. P., & Sekol, I. (2012). Children's antisocial behavior, mental health, drug use, and educational performance after parental incarceration: A systematic review and meta-analysis. *Psychological Bulletin, 138*(2), 175–210.

Murry, V. M., & Brody, G. H. (1999). Self-regulation and self-worth of black children reared in economically stressed, rural, single-mother-headed families: The contribution of risk and protective factors. *Journal of Family Issues, 20*(4), 458–484.

Pettit, B. (2012). *Invisible men: Mass incarceration and the myth of black progress*. New York: Russell Sage Foundation.

Rutter, M. (1987). Psychosocial resilience and protective mechanisms. *American Journal of Orthopsychiatry, 57*(3), 316–331.

Travis, J., Western, B., & Redburn, S. (2014). *The growth of incarceration in the United States: Exploring causes and consequences*. Washington, DC: The National Academies Press.

Turanovic, J. J., Rodriguez, N., & Pratt, T. C. (2012). The collateral consequences of incarceration revisited: A qualitative analysis of the effects of caregivers of children of incarcerated parents. *Criminology, 50*(4), 913–959.

Turney, K. (in press). The unequal consequences of incarceration for children. *Demography*.

Turney, K., & Haskins, A. R. (2014). Falling behind? Children's early grade retention after paternal incarceration. *Sociology of Education, 87*(4), 241–258.

Turney, K., & Wildeman, C. (2015). Detrimental for some? The heterogeneous effects of maternal incarceration on child well-being. *Criminology & Public Policy, 14*(1), 125–156.

Wakefield, S., & Uggen, C. (2010). Incarceration and stratification. *Annual Review of Sociology, 36*, 387–406.

Werner, E. E. (1992). The children of Kauai: Resiliency and recovery in adolescence and adulthood. *Journal of Adolescent Health, 13*(4), 262–268.

Wildeman, C. (2009). Parental imprisonment, the prison boom, and the concentration of childhood disadvantage. *Demography, 46*(2), 265–280.

Wildeman, C. (2010). Paternal incarceration and children's physically aggressive behaviors: Evidence from the Fragile Families and Child Wellbeing Study. *Social Forces, 89*(1), 285–309.

Wildeman, C., Wakefield, S., & Turney, K. (2013). Misidentifying the effects of parental imprisonment? A comment on Johnson and Easterling (2012). *Journal of Marriage and Family, 75*(1), 252–258.

Wildeman, C., & Western, B. (2010). Incarceration in Fragile Families. *The Future of Children, 20*(2), 157–177.

Xie, Y., Brand, J. E., & Jann, B. (2012). Estimating heterogeneous treatment effects with observational data. *Sociological Methodology, 42*(1), 314–347.

Zimmerman, M. A., Bingenheimer, J. B., & Notaro, P. C. (2002). Natural mentors and adolescent resiliency: A study with urban youth. *American Journal of Community Psychology, 30*(2), 221–243.

# Part II
# Family Influences in Adolescence and Young Adulthood

# Dueling Narratives: Racial Socialization and Literacy as Triggers for Re-Humanizing African American Boys, Young Men, and Their Families

**Howard C. Stevenson**

While the recent notoriety of police shootings of black people have been playing on media outlets across the nation, these public assaults have left some numb and scared, some angry and revolutionary, and others apathetic and hostile towards the plight of black life experiences. The recent drama joins the decades of past dramas in which anyone with a gun can declare hunting season on black and brown bodies, voice, or presence. Consequently, I find it impossible to write a chapter on pathways to black manhood without considering how this elephant of a tragedy is not infrequent or inopportune, but socialized, predictable and post-racial (Anderson & Stevenson, 2015). This tragedy is graphic and opaque, shocking but not surprising. While these predictable post-racial assaults loom large in our hearts, minds, and souls enough to propel our most intense protest mechanisms, the voices of the assaulted are virtually silenced in the research literature on how black families cope across the lifespan. Perhaps the most troubling elements in watching our nation's finest beat down our country's least is that many of these tragedies involve black male children and youth. What can we say or do about those boys who get snatched while on those pathways or who don't see the "Bridge is out" sign along the way?

The life chances of black boys and men on many health indicators are so compromised that we take for granted that it's the contexts surrounding them that are risky, not their personhood or basic humanity. While we cannot turn a blind eye toward the data on health disparities, somehow the statistical comparison of black males to others becomes in and of itself a mechanism or lens of disparity-making. Like watching the visual examples of police shootings and black youth harassment, it's painful that the evidence of this inhumanity is in and of itself debilitating and

H.C. Stevenson (✉)
Applied Psychology and Human Development Division, University of Pennsylvania, Philadelphia, PA, USA
e-mail: howards@gse.upenn.edu



L. Burton et al. (eds.), *Boys and Men in African American Families*, National Symposium on Family Issues 7, DOI 10.1007/978-3-319-43847-4_5

traumatic. The very visual evidence of the tragedy contributes to the trauma of how maybe black lives really do *not* matter. But the absence of a frame in the research literature on black males that puts these tragedies into a humanity perspective is equally traumatic. In this chapter, I propose non-traditional influences on black male well-being and social interaction through a meta-lens of how the hidden narratives about their humanity directs the research we review, the questions we research, and the inhumanity we do not question or research.

## Excavating Dehumanization: Racial Disparity or Dignity Management in Black Male Research

Starting a research endeavor about the role of black families in the lives of black male youth seems challenging as we begin with a review of the literature and frankly, has always left me wanting. The missing piece that contributes to that angst and hesitation is that black male life experiences of humanity rejection remain peripheral within that canon. There is a surreal reaction to beginning a discussion of black male strengths and challenges with information about their compromised life chances compared to other racial or gender groups. It is, to some, a necessary first step in order to set a context for the future of problem-solving and/or strengths-based study of black families and black males, but it remains disconcerting.

Still, the challenge in integrating past research is that often, most articles in mainstream research journals fail to consider fully one very basic conceptual frame about black male socialization, coping, and health- and that is the forgetting of historic and contemporary racial dehumanization (Stevenson, 2014; Stevenson & Talley, 2016); or as I have labeled it elsewhere, "expendable black humanity." This guiding dehumanization frame excavates an underlying but persistent narrative of what black males and families must consciously or unconsciously deal with daily—being black means coping with unpredictable racial rejection. So, I'm uneasy at beginning another chapter, article, research project, or program development venture without confronting this narrative.

I believe it is imperative to raise a fundamental and partial explanation of why black manhood development from infancy to young adulthood has been misunderstood and constitutes a unique developmental trajectory. It has to do with the persistent invalidation of the humanity of black boys and youth. Research on the fears of racial conflict from neuroscience and social interaction studies have revealed that primitive emotional fears, self-preservation, microaggressions, and rage reactions toward black people defy rational understandings of misperception and brutality towards black children, youth and young adults (Eberhardt, 2005; Kwate & Meyer, 2011; Todd, Thiem, & Neel, 2016). But the power of what Goff et al. (2014) describes as dehumanization provides partial explanation as to why many racial encounters between authority figures and black boys and young men can go awry and become murderous. Ironically, racial dehumanization framing offers a unique opportunity to examine the efficacy of racial socialization-infused interventions. Why? Because if racial socialization and literacy interventions can increase racial negotiation skills and decrease the stress of face-to-face dehumanizing encounters toward black people, fewer threat-based tragedies may occur (Stevenson, 2014).

By not confronting this historic endorsement of expendable black humanity, any writing about "novel" approaches for black male improvement seems futile. Futile, because there is an addictive post-racial socialization in the public racial discourse which is designed to ignore, deny, and pretend not only that historical racial disenfranchisement is over, but that any attention to it is un-American and a racist distortion of our contemporary reality (Anderson & Stevenson, 2015). Writing about new models also seems painful because it constitutes feigning blindness toward seeing the obvious elephant question in every room that black males enter or leave, from cradle to grave. That question is a wretched and timeless but unanswerable Du Boisian query behind which lies a dehumanizing narrative regarding Black people's existence—"How does it feel to be a problem?" (DuBois, 1903).

So if that dehumanizing question lurks behind a seemingly appropriate question of "What is novel about family and community influences on black male development and striving?" then we have lost before we begin to fight the problem at hand. Which narrative do we tackle first, the plight of black male coping along developmental pathways or the plight of the pathways? Without a narrative reconstruction, how can we ethically address the question of black manhood striving?

So by posing these narratives as at war with each other, a reconstruction of sorts begins. This reconstruction requires a chronicling of how risky pathways obscure buried land mines of racial dehumanization for black boys, men, and their families (Brown, 2011a, 2011b). In essence, through illumination of the racial dehumanization narrative in research and by critiquing the lens through which we view the positionality of black male experiences, a countering of that narrative is also beginning. Black male humanity should not be on trial, not be problematic, and not be viewed as risky or at risk, but it is. Even attempts to connect historical and contemporary contexts that surround and explain black male development and striving are distorted as excuses (APA, 2008). In a review of articles on students of color in the top ten educational journals, Stevenson and Talley (2016) found that only 15% included a theoretical rationale, measurement, or interpretive analysis of findings sensitive to the racialized life experiences of the participants.

How central are racial politics in the health disparities and life experiences of black males? How can researchers ignore racial rejection and it's effects on the lives of black males as race-status group comparisons continue to be analyzed? The absence of a racial lens may best address these questions and represent a more pressing disparity of racial literacy. This is not to suggest that non-racial aspects of black male striving toward manhood are irrelevant research endeavors. Instead, I propose that researchers often avoid the more sensitive racial risk and protective frames because we don't know how, are too threatened to ask how, and thus rarely search for why we must engage these frames.

## Race vs Racial: A Racial Literacy Lens

Racial literacy is here defined as the ability to read, recast, and resolve racially stressful encounters that are conceptual, physical, emotional, social, and societal (Stevenson, 2014). By confronting the conscious or unconscious avoidance of expendable black humanity in conceptual, methodological and programmatic research, researchers might move toward the development of a narrative of racial re-humanization in the study of black families and boys. Future research might develop novel theories, methods, and programs to enhance black male well-being and the roles families may play in that well-being.

## Rejection Cycle of Individual and System Threats Explain Black Health Disparities

Black male youth underachievement in schools and exposure to violence are significant negative pathway barriers driven by a perfect storm of mutually reciprocal individual- and system-level threat reactions. Black males are more likely than their white peers to attend and be expelled from under-resourced schools. They are also more likely to experience less supportive relationships with teachers, who often hold lower success expectations, and to witness or experience violent encounters in schools and neighborhoods (Office of Civil Rights, 2014). To protect themselves from the stress and trauma of these rejections of their intellectual and motivational capacity, some black males adopt retaliatory coping strategies of disengagement from learning experiences. Simultaneously, educators struggle with how to engage and improve black male youth achievement. Many school climates are rejecting of black male youth style, attitude, and movement. In response to black male coping struggles, authority figure and school system use of disproportionate suspensions and expulsions (Office of Civil Rights, 2014) have led to greater out-of-class time for black youth than for their white and Hispanic peers. Reciprocally negative rejecting and disengaged individual- and system-level threat interactions between black males and authority figures from school, health, and justice systems can undermine healthy outcomes and partially explain black male youth racial health and academic disparities (Thomas & Stevenson, 2009).

### *Individual Threat Factors*

Several racial and gender risk and protective psychological factors contribute to black youth's appraisal of classrooms, playgrounds, and public thoroughfares as stressful. The factors include the sensitivity to adult and peer racial and gender rejection, stereotype threat, and racial microaggressions. Racial Microaggressions are brief, verbal, behavioral, and environmental indignities that communicate racial insults (Huynh, 2012). System threats are ways adults in societal institutions (police, educators, and health providers) misjudge black youth as dangerous and requiring control rather than support interventions.

*Rejection sensitivity* occurs when youth have angry or anxious expectations of rejection and overreact to it. There are gendered and racialized forms of rejection. Peer and teacher critiques of black males as inferior along academic and masculinity lines have been traced to retaliatory reactions of aggression, withdrawal, helplessness, and depression (Kistner, David, & White, 2003; Thomas et al., 2012). Rejection sensitivity and hostile attribution bias explains youth interpersonal conflict, depression, and anxiety (Ayduk et al., 2000; Downey, Bonica, & Rincón, 1999; Downey & Feldman, 1996; Feldman & Downey, 1994) as well as the maintenance of aggression in youth through peer acceptance and exclusion (Coie, Dodge, Terry, & Wright, 1991; Dishion, Patterson, Stoolmiller, & Skinner, 1991; Dodge, Price, Bachorowski, & Newman, 1990; Kupersmidt, Griesler, DeRosier, Patterson, & Davis, 1995; Laird, Jordan, Dodge, Pettit, & Bates, 2001; Crick & Dodge, 1996). Still, contextual realities should alter how much researchers generalize these concepts to black males who live in dangerous neighborhoods, where the attribution of hostility may not be biased or inaccurate and where violence retaliation is occasionally protective (Stevenson, 2004). Ironically, under-reacting to racial or gender rejection can be just as problematic to health and coping (Stevenson, 2014).

As such, the *sensitivity to racial and gendered rejection* triggers hypermasculinity reactions within contexts of manhood challenges and can interfere with peer bonding (Cassidy & Stevenson, 2005; Mendoza-Denton, Downey, Purdie, & Davis, 2002). During recreation activities on playgrounds, gender stereotyped challenges of athletic prowess and unaddressed competition anxiety are prevalent (Martens, Burton, Vealey, Bump, & Smith, 1990; Martens, Vealey, & Burton, 1995). Many black males fear becoming targets of humiliation and may use bravado and hypermasculinity as protective coping options (Cassidy & Stevenson, 2005; Spencer, Fegley, Harpalani, & Seaton, 2004). While bravado can resolve immediate gender challenges, it masks deeper stress mismanagement, overload, and hypervulnerability (Spencer et al., 2004, 2006; Stevenson, 2003, 2014). Fortunately, black males respond well to supportive interventions that reduce the stress of peer and teacher rejections (Spencer et al., 2004; Stevenson, 2003).

*Stereotype threat* and *stigma internalization* explains how some black students perceive classrooms as racially and intellectually threatening (Crocker, Major, & Steele, 1998; Gray-Little & Carels, 1997; Tatum, 1997) and believe adults view their academic potential through the lens of intellectual inferiority (Brown & Jones, 2004; Kellow & Jones, 2008; Steele & Aronson, 1995; Sue, Capodilupo, & Holder, 2008). These threats are debilitating to black individuals' sense of self, societal acceptance, and health (Blascovich, Spencer, Quinn, & Steele, 2001; Cokley, 2002; Devine, 1989; Goffman, 1963; Steele, 1999; Stevenson, Davis, Carter, & Elliott, 2003). Through disidentification and withdrawal from academics, many black youth remain less practiced in basic study habits (Crosnoe, Cavanagh, & Elder, 2003; Steinberg, Dornbusch, & Brown, 1992; Walton & Cohen, 2007).

*The negative effects of subtle racial microaggressions* include depression and somatic symptoms (Huynh, 2012; Huynh & Gillen-O'Neel, 2013), severe psychological consequences (Clark, Anderson, Clark, & Williams, 1999; Solorzano, Ceja, & Yosso, 2000; Sue et al., 2007) for ethnic minority persons (Schwartz & Meyer, 2010), but also explain black student underachievement and school belonging problems (Arrington, Hall, & Stevenson, 2003; Arrington & Stevenson, 2006; Mattison & Aber, 2007; Spencer et al., 2006; Sue et al., 2008; Weinstein, 2002), conduct problems (Brody et al., 2006), emotional and academic well-being issues (Fisher, Wallace, & Fenton, 2000; Greene, Way, & Pahl, 2006; Rosenbloom & Way, 2004; Simons et al., 2002; Sue et al., 2008) and emotional distress (Brown & Jones, 2004; Smalls, White, Tabbye, Chavous, & Sellers, 2007). The effects of racial microaggression even compromise the physical and mental health of black parents (Taylor, Washington, Artinian, & Lichtenberg, 2007). Jones, Peddie, Gilrane, King, and Gray (2013) found that subtle racial rejections are as equally powerful as overt rejections in producing negative psychological health consequences. The link between racial microaggressions and negative psychological outcomes is explained by excessive mental fatigue from constant appraisal of subtle ambiguous and denied racial insults (Noh, Kaspar, & Wickrama, 2007; Tran & Lee, 2014).

In summary, negotiating rejection sensitivity, stereotype threat, and racial microaggression experiences are racially stressful. Racial stress is defined as the experience of being emotionally overtaxed by racial matters. While perceived racial discrimination frequency of black youth in schools is related to racial discrimination stress, *racial stress* is a better predictor of health and academic outcomes (Nyborg & Curry, 2003; Seaton & Douglass, 2014).

## System Threat Appraisals and Rejection of Black Youth

*Negative Teacher Expectations, Misinterpretations, and Fearful Interactions with Black Students*. Teacher expectations of black student underperformance and lack of teaching intensity contribute to student rejection sensitivity (Chang & Sue, 2003; Decker, Dona, & Christenson, 2007; Downey & Pribesh, 2004; Murray, 1996). Authority figure competence is compromised by teacher stress (Yoon, 2002), underexposure to training in multicultural education (Cho & DeCastro-Ambrosetti, 2005; Jennings, 2007), believing in stereotypes (Oates, 2003), preservice inexperience (Bakari, 2003), cloaked hostility, favorability bias toward white students (Casteel, 1998; Saft & Pianta, 2001; Word, Zanna, & Cooper, 1974), and visceral fear reactions in the presence of blacks (Blascovich, Mendes, Hunter, Lickel, & Kowai-Bell, 2001).

Some adult educational and mental health professionals over-react to black and Latino individuals' behavioral and cultural style expressions (e.g., horseplay, bravado, being loud) (Boykin et al., 2005; Neal, McCray, Webb-Johnson, & Bridgest, 2003; Skiba, Michael, Nardo, & Peterson, 2002; Stevenson, Winn, Walker-Barnes,

& Coard, 2005), even as these style expressions are linked to academic achievement for black males (Irving & Hudley, 2008). These *overreactions* are visible in stereotypic expectations of dangerousness, underachievement, and special education needs (Eberhardt, Goff, Purdie, & Davies, 2004).

*School systems' overreactions* to black student disengagement are manifested in disproportionate police surveillance within school settings, school discipline, zero tolerance policies, referral to special education, suspension and expulsion, and arrests (Advancement Project, 2005; Alexander, 2010; Ferguson, 2003; Gregory & Weinstein, 2008; McCarthy & Hoge, 1987; Skiba et al., in press; Skiba, Peterson, & Williams, 1997; Skiba & Williams, 2014; Wu, Pink, Crain, & Moles, 1982). Despite the absence of evidence that black males disproportionately misbehave more than their white peers, they are suspended and expelled more harshly and frequently from pre-school through secondary education (Gilliam, 2005; Schott Foundation for Early Education, 2015; Skiba & Williams, 2014). Black students (16 %) are suspended and expelled at three times the rate of white students (6 %) (Hoffman, Llagas, & Snyder, 2003). Among those suspended and expelled black students, 20 % are boys and 12 % are girls. Students of color with disabilities are highest among this group to be suspended. While blacks make up 18 % of students in preschool, they account for 42 % of students with an out-of-school suspension and 48 % of students with multiple out-of-school suspensions.

These discipline strategies contribute to unsafe school climates and less supportive teacher-student relationships, which undermine minority student achievement (Cornell, Allen, & Fan, 2012; Cornell, Gregory, & Fan, 2011; Gregory, Cornell, & Fan, 2011; Mattison & Aber, 2007). The quality of teacher-student relationships has been found to mediate negative school climate (Meehan, Hughes, & Cavell, 2003).

Racial disparities and rejections do not occur only at the institutional level. They also occur at levels of individual and interpersonal functioning. Despite studies that describe systemic health and achievement gaps, research on the effects of daily face-to-face (FTF) and in-the-moment (ITM) stereotyped rejections or racial microaggressions is increasing and may more efficiently explain youth short- and long-term functioning. Still, there is little research on how youth may learn to cope with face-to-face racial slights (Stevenson, 2014).

A summary of individual and system threat reactions to black male strivings suggest their pathways to manhood are fraught with instances of dehumanization. Specifically,

a. Unsupportive authority figure relationships with black males occur due to mutual difficulty with negotiating the stress of interpersonal face-to-face and in-the-moment conflicts/encounters that are often racialized and gendered.
b. Research has demonstrated that there are unique racial perceptions and dynamics that interfere with the development of healthy affirming relationships.
c. Unique racial risk and protective factors and encounters exist for black males that do not exist for other racial and gendered groups.

d. Black males are unprepared to manage the stress of racial and gendered micro-aggressions in school and public contexts and ineffectively cope with societal rejections they face.
e. Authority figures are ill-prepared to manage the helplessness and anxiety of educating and protecting black boys as evidenced by unjust discipline approaches, lower educator expectations and stereotyping, and lower quality teachers and teacher-student relationships.
f. Despite the life-threatening consequences of these racial encounters, the more prevalent problem is that black males are not receiving the full measure and access to quality learning, health, and justice opportunities.
g. Stressful FTF racial encounters present both crisis and opportunity to improve the quality of relationships between authority figures and black youth. FTF experiences are more proximal than systemic racism approaches can remedy on behalf of black male youth behavioral and academic conflicts in school, justice, and health settings.

## Black Male Narrative Reform: Racial Socialization as Critical Consciousness for Buffering Racial Rejection

Narrative reform regarding the dehumanization of black male promise and potential has to involve facing the realities of both internalized individual racial threats as well as systemic-level racial threats to black manhood (Brown, 2011a, 2011b; Fultz & Brown, 2008; Stevenson, 2003, 2014). This reform should include novel approaches to black male progress and success in schools, neighborhoods, and employment that reduce the negative effects of both non-racialized and racialized individual (racial stress, stereotype threat, rejection sensitivity, and discrimination) and systemic (misinterpretation and fears of black males, unnecessary arrest and incarceration, and overexposure to less qualified teachers, low teacher academic expectations, and less supportive relationships with teachers) threat factors.

### *The Role of Non-Racial Individual and Systemic Interventions for Black Males*

While disrupting this negative racialized and gendered cycle of relational disengagement has the potential to alter health and academic trajectories of black males in schools, few interventions directly address specific racial/gender risk and protective factors. Most school-based interventions do not use racially competent research frames (theory, measures, analyses) that are sensitive to racial and gendered risk (microaggressions) and protective (socialization) factors to address black male underachievement and maladaptive coping. However, non-racial and universal approaches do not target unique racial life stressors of black males and assume a one-size fits all policy. This raises the question of whether racial vs non-racial interventions matter in the promotion of positive racial and non-racial outcomes for black males.

Evidenced-based treatments (EBT) are challenged by low participation rates of ethnic minorities and community mental health providers (Kataoka, Zhang, & Wells, 2002; Weisz, Sandler, Durlak, & Anton, 2005), low transfer of EBT lab-based experiments to community-based clinical and practice contexts (Baumann et al., 2015; Sholomskas et al., 2005), low sensitivity to the depth of cultural experiences of ethnic minority populations (Bernal, Jiménez-Chafey, & Domenech Rodríguez, 2009; Zayas & Rojas-Flores, 2002), and a lack of treatment effects for black youth (Fain, Greathouse, Turner, & Weinberg, 2014).

Even if EBTs include persons of color as participants, the treatments rarely integrate conceptual frameworks, research methods, and therapeutic interventions that prepare for or influence the racially-specific health risk and protective factors of African American youth (Spencer et al., 2006). Griner and Smith (2006) state that interventions that specifically target racial/ethnic groups are four times more effective than interventions that target mixed racial/ethnic samples. Interventions that target client-native languages are two times more effective than English-only interventions. These critiques have prompted the call for more cultural adaptation of EBTs with families and youth of color (Baumann et al., 2015; Domenech Rodríguez & Bernal, 2012). Despite the lack of clarity on how well EBTs address racial disparities in health and education, there are promising non-racial interventions to minimize raced achievement and discipline gaps.

## General Self-Affirmation Reduces Achievement Gaps

Self-affirmation has emerged as one social psychological strategy to reduce the effects of stereotype threat by providing students with positive self-reflections prior to engagement in stressful academic performance tasks (Cohen, Garcia, Purdie-Vaughns, Apfel, & Brzustoski, 2009). The rationale is that affirming one's potential and capabilities reduces the stress from threat-based racial stereotypes, thus mitigating their negative impact on achievement performance. Cohen, Garcia, Apfel, and Master (2006) found that a self-affirmation intervention improved intellectual achievement of low, moderate, and high performing black students and showed a 40 % reduction in racial achievement gap (mean grade point scores). A 2-year follow-up of this study found that these achievement gains for black students, especially underperforming black students, persisted (Cohen et al., 2009).

Current self-affirmation approaches assume a one-time intervention impact at the beginning of the evaluation of impact (Cohen et al., 2009; Dee, 2015) with potential recursive properties by connecting to teacher-driven or system-driven reinforcements and reciprocal feedback loops (Cohen et al., 2006; Purdie-Vaughns et al., 2009; Yeager, Walton, & Cohen, 2013). While general self-affirmation holds promise for black male youth achievement, it does not address a racialized set of life experiences that include in-the-moment face-to-face (FTF) racial rejections.

**Disproportionate Suspension and Expulsion Can be Reduced**

While the misinterpretations of black youth exist among authority professionals, novel approaches to change school structures and climates can reduce disproportionate expulsion rates for black students (Gregory et al., 2011). Through policies and practices, schools embody both remediation and exacerbation of racial discrimination stress (Gregory et al., 2011; Seaton & Douglass, 2014; Skiba et al., 2015).

## *Racial Socialization, Parenting, and Physical Activity for Disrupting Negative Trajectories*

While racial stress may explain conflicts between black students and authority figures, youth who make accurate threat appraisals and practice racial coping strategies can cope more effectively with rejection (Thomas, Coard, Stevenson, Bentley, & Zamel, 2009). Some disengagement from schooling can be protective if students positively reappraise the stress of learning and then re-engage (Nussbaum & Steele, 2007). Finding key points in the life trajectories of black males to disrupt negative expectations and rejection experiences for black males bodes well for improving their health and academic outcomes. Though many black youth disproportionately experience violence exposure, victimization, and academic disengagement (Becker & Luthar, 2002; Griffin, 2002; Hoffman et al., 2003; Jencks & Phillips, 1998; Noguera, 2003), the benefits of *racial socialization, parental engagement, physical activity and positive reappraisal* strategies can reduce emotional barriers that enhance youth social vulnerability in risky contexts (Bailey & Bradbury-Bailey, 2006; Bailey & Paisley, 2004; Stevenson, 2003, 2014; Watts, Abdul-Adil, & Pratt, 2002).

## *Racial Socialization*

Racial socialization has been identified as a compensatory or protective factor for African American youth and families in mediating youth racial stress (Stevenson & Arrington, 2009), behavioral functioning (Rodriguez, Cavaleri, Bannon, & McKay, 2008), academic underachievement (Neblett, Smalls, Ford, Nguyen, & Sellers, 2009), and parental and children's use of mental health services (Bannon, Cavaleri, Rodriguez, & McKay, 2008). Past research on racial socialization reveals several advancements in understanding racial/ethnic childrearing and identity development. First, parents from different racial groups parent according to the dangers and supports facing their children. Second, cultural heritage and style permeate child-rearing practices in ways that are rarely captured in universal parenting intervention programs (Stevenson et al., 2005). Third, not just parents, but educators also racially socialize in ways that inhibit and promote black youth well-being (Bentley-Edwards & Stevenson, 2016; Lesane-Brown, Brown, Caldwell, & Sellers, 2005). While many types of racial/ethnic socialization measures have been developed by an array of child development researchers (Bentley-Edwards & Stevenson, 2016; Hughes & Chen, 1997; Lesane-Brown et al., 2005; Stevenson, 1994; Stevenson, Cameron, Herrero-Taylor & Davis, 2002) to verify the prevalence, intensity, and sophistication of the construct for different ethnic and racial groups, these tend to focus on past or legacy experiences. This early descriptive work justified racial socialization as a protective construct related to positive achievement, well-being, and social engagement outcomes for preschoolers, adolescents and adults (Hughes et al., 2006).

Benefits of racial socialization include greater emotional well-being and self-regulation (Burton, Winn, Stevenson, & Clark, 2004; Liddle, Jackson-Gilfort, & Marvel, 2006; Watts et al., 2002), conflict engagement coping and racial self-efficacy (Lightsey & Barnes, 2007; Scott, 2003), positive academic outcomes (Banerjee, Harrell, & Johnson, 2011; Bowman & Howard, 1985; Neblett, Phillip, Cogburn, & Sellers, 2006) and anger management in black youth (Stevenson, Reed, Bodison, & Bishop, 1997; Stevenson et al., 1997). For adults, legacy racial socialization is linked to improved parenting (Coard, Wallace, Stevenson, & Brotma, 2004; McKay, Atkins, Hawkins, Brown, & Lynn, 2003), positive teacher perceptions of black youth (Thomas et al., 2009), and reduced distress (Bynum, Burton, & Best, 2007). Despite these benefits, most legacy forms of racial socialization follow hit-and-miss or "hope-and-pray" frames. Future work must move beyond the recounting of past racial socialization messages and practices to teach the *best* racial socialization skills.

## The Role of Parents/Mentors in Reducing Emotional Distress

Recent research highlights the powerful connection between quality teacher-student relationships and children's learning (Anhert et al., 2012, Hughes, Wu, Kwok, Villarreal, & Johnson, 2012). Teacher-student and parent/mentor-student relationship quality promote black student achievement (Darch, Miao, & Shippen, 2004; Hurd & Sellers, 2013; Meehan et al., 2003; Slaughter-Defoe, Stevenson, Arrington, & Johnson, 2011; Whitney, Hendricker, & Offitt, 2011), lower rejection sensitivity, depression, and anxiety (McDonald, Bowker, Rubin, Laursen, & Duchene, 2010), and protection from racial discrimination (Cooper, Brown, Metzger, Clinton, & Guthrie, 2013). Most racial socialization research on parental racial messages show negligible impact on psychological distress (Bynum et al., 2007). Still, professionals and parents become overwhelmed by youth emotional struggles and can benefit from racial literacy training (Stevenson, 2014). One racialized parenting intervention has undergone rigorous randomized control trial investigation and been found to significantly improve parent and child outcomes (Coard, Foy-Watson, Zimmer, & Wallace, 2007).

## *The Benefits of Physical Activity (PA)*

Due to funding deficits, urban school districts have cut recess and sports which decreases access to the health benefits of physical activity: youth self-regulation, concentration, motivation, emotional well-being, weight control, and stress reduction (Biddle & Mutrie, 2007; Gordon-Larsen, McMurray, & Popkin, 2000; Lewis et al., 1993; Martens et al., 1990; Pelligrini & Bjorkland, 1997). Physical activity is also linked to improved grades, standardized test scores, and classroom behavior (Ardoy et al., 2014; Carlson et al., 2008; Castelli, Hillman, Buck, & Erwin, 2007; Coe, Pivarnik, Womack, Reeves, & Malina, 2006). Sadly, only 42 % of children aged 6–11 and 8 % of teens aged 12–19 get 60 min of daily exercise (Troiano et al., 2008).

## *From Socialization to Literacy: Teaching Males to Reappraise Racially Stressful Interactions*

One catalyst element in racial socialization, parenting engagement, and the use of physical activity approaches is their potential to teach positive reappraisal skills that can help youth reappraise systemic racial rejections and individual threat reactions. The Preventing Long-term Anger & Aggression in Youth (PLAAY) intervention is in the early stages of development but has demonstrated promise in measuring and targeting the amelioration of unique racialized life challenges of black male youth (Stevenson, 2003, 2014). PLAAY uses intervention strategies of cognitive restructuring, mindfulness, journaling, in-the-moment observation, debating, and role-playing through the vehicles of group therapy, and physical activity through basketball to motivate youth to persist through FTF conflicts. Research on the use of behavioral scripting in teaching racial coping has yielded positive outcomes in reducing the psychological pressure of racial interactions (Avery, Richeson, Hebl, & Ambady, 2009; Blascovich, Spencer, et al., 2001; Towles-Schwen & Fazio, 2003). PLAAY uses this knowledge to prepare parents, teachers, and natural mentors to practice and teach racial, gender, and behavioral coping skills of frustration tolerance, retaliation restraint, and racial and gender assertiveness to black youth.

PLAAY is designed to bring a racial literacy focus in order to positively influence youth stress and coping and integrate racial socialization skills as intentional rather than serendipitous. The protective aspects of racial socialization-infused interventions is in helping black youth and families to reduce the threat level of racial, gender, and general stressful encounters (Bentley-Edwards, Adams-Bass, & Stevenson, 2009); that is, to engage in positive reappraisal or recasting (Folkman, 2008; Folkman & Moskowitz, 2000). PLAAY alerts students to the effects of authority and institutional racial stress reactions and teaches them to outmaneuver, not overreact to these realities.

Racial literacy includes racial coping skills-building and asks "What racial coping skills are core in preparing youth for future racially stressful encounters?" (Stevenson, 2014). Racial literacy emphasizes (1) affirming racial conflict coping beliefs (self-efficacy) and (2) practicing racial coping skills repeatedly (mastery). Given that self-efficacy is unique to the behavior, best modeled by teachers/parents/mentors (Wang & Eccles, 2012), and is influential in reducing stress and increasing prosocial and retaliation restraint behaviors (Bandura, Caprara, Barbaranelli, Pastorelli, & Regalia, 2001; Bandura, Pastorelli, Barbaranelli, & Caprara, 1999; Solberg & Villarreal, 1997), we expect PLAAY to increase racial, interpersonal, and academic coping self-efficacy in facing conflicts.

Getting black male youth to restrain retaliation, re-engage relationships, and persist at academic tasks when rejected by peers, parents, or teachers through positive stress reappraisal are key goals of PLAAY. Recast theory proposes that individuals can modify a racially stressful moment to be less overwhelming. Black boys participating in PLAAY showed lower rejection sensitivity compared to a control group with group communalism and peer modeling as the salient mechanisms Davis et al. (2003). Teaching skills of countering stereotypes lead to performance approach strategies, ethnic group bonding, and discrimination preparedness (Kellow & Jones, 2008; Pinel, 1999; Stevenson, 2003).

## PLAAY Intervention Outcomes: Racial Literacy Meets Physical Activity

In one trial, PLAAY was conducted in an alternative juvenile discipline school and targeted black male students (Stevenson, 2003). The school attendance rates increased from 62 to 69 % while average unexcused absences decreased from 38 to 26 % during that time. Suspensions dropped from 328 to 117 (Family Resource Trend Report, 2000). The principal and district truancy statistician identified the PLAAY project as the primary reason for those improvements. Over 4 years, the PLAAY project studied the behaviors of 280 youth. A smaller subgroup of about 90 underwent random assignment to PLAAY ($n=50$) and control groups ($n=40$). Treatment integrity and fidelity were accomplished on the PLAAY components (Davis, Zamel, Hall, Espin, & Williams, 2003).

At post-test, PLAAY students scored significantly lower than control students in rejection sensitivity, rejection feelings, and anxious expectations (Davis et al., 2003). Using pre-test scores as covariates in a MANCOVA (Wilks' Lambda$=0.534$, $F=7.48$, $p<0.0001$, $eta^2=0.10$), there were significant effects for angry rejection reactivity ($F=7.63$, $p<0.01$; $eta^2=0.10$), rejection feelings ($F=10.10$, $p<0.002$; $eta^2=0.13$), anxious rejection sensitivity ($F=19.43$, $p<0.0001$; $eta^2=0.23$), angry rejection sensitivity ($F=24.21$, $p<0.0001$; $eta^2=0.27$), and angry feelings ($F=3.73$, $p<0.05$; $eta^2=0.05$). Results provided mixed support for hypotheses of lower rejection sensitivity for PLAAY students. When experiencing interpersonal conflict in classrooms, playgrounds, and neighborhoods, PLAAY students reported significantly higher anger feelings, but lower rejection feelings and lower angry reactions to rejection compared to control group students. PLAAY students identified and expressed their feelings better than the control students.

Teacher ratings of maladjustment (ASCA) were added to the model. Several three-way mixed (2×2×2) anovas were conducted on 3 levels of rejection sensitivity (RS anger, RS anxiety, and angry psychological reactions) with time as the within-subjects variable (pretest and posttest of rejection sensitivity), while intervention (PLAAY vs. Control) and overactive and underactive behavioral adjustment (Positive or Poor) served as the between-subjects variables. Overactive Behavioral Difficulties included attention-deficit hyperactive, oppositional-defiant, impulsive aggressive, provocative-aggressive syndromes while Underactive Behavioral Difficulties included Diffident and Avoidant syndromes. The significant findings for angry rejection reactions occurred for positively and poorly adjusted boys in delinquency (Wilks lambda = 0.963, $F = 4.11$, $p < 0.05$, $Eta^2 = 0.037$), and attention-deficit behaviors (Wilks lambda = 0.842, $F = 20.04$, $p < 0.0001$; $Eta^2 = 0.158$). PLAAY students with poor delinquency and attention-deficit adjustment scores showed significantly lower angry psychological reactions to rejection at post-test compared to the control group (Davis et al., 2003).

Since this trial, the PLAAY model has been applied by training middle and high school girls, parents as emotional coaches during physical activity, and black barbers as counselors of young black men between the ages of 18–24. African American barbers are natural healers and were trained to provide violence retaliation restraint and unsafe sex risk reduction skills to 700 black young men struggling with these issues (Jemmott, Stevenson, Jemmott, & Coleman, 2016).

## The Stalking Talk: What to Say to My Trayvon

As compelling as it is to disrupt the interaction between individual- and system-level threats in order to reduce black male vulnerability across the lifespan, none of it tells us directly what parents should say to their children in the face of that drama (Stevenson & Jones, 2015). In theory or idea, racial socialization is effortless. In real-time with our children, those conversations are awkward. Despite 2½ decades of research knowledge, racial literacy intervention development, and black male parenting experience, on one fateful night I found myself helpless as to what to say to my 8 year old son. When Julian spontaneously asked me to explain why a grown self-appointed neighborhood watchman would shoot an unarmed teenage black boy while he was walking home from a convenience store holding only skittles and a can of ice tea, I stuttered. After one stutter too many, I decided to audiotape it. After the acquittal trial of George Zimmerman, Julian was awestruck watching on CNN the parents of Trayvon Martin express their sadness about the verdict.

On behalf of awkward parenting anywhere, and to be filed under the category of "What should a black parent tell his black son when he is being racially stalked while coming home?" I share with you our conversation on that night.

*Julian's words are in non-bold type and Dad's (Howard's) are in bold type. Other people's names have been omitted.*

[After and while watching Trayvon Martin's parents discuss their disappointment about the not guilty verdict in the George Zimmerman trial, Julian ponders aloud the absurdity of how a black boy can be shot for walking home from a 7-11 convenience store.]

It's sad. "We don't care. You're not our kind."

It's like. "We're better than you …"

**Yes**

"and there's nothing you can do about that. And if you scare me or something like that, I will shoot you because I'm scared of you."

**Exactly. And the problem is that because of bad images on TV, the way that people are trained and raised, when they grow up, they're raised to be scared of black boys & black people.**

**And it's not right. It's not fair, but you know it's one thing to be scared. People get scared all the time but it's wrong to take that fear and say it's ok to kill somebody or hurt somebody.**

**And I don't like the idea--and that's why Daddy gets mad about it sometimes and that's also why Mommy and Daddy want to teach you so that if anybody is following you that you need to know how to talk to them and to stand up for yourself, yet not under-react or over-react. Do you know what under-react means? Like it means like you pretend that nothing's happening.**

Yeah, yeah.

**What's that mean?**

Like you know--something's happened but pretending, "Oh, it's fine."

**Yeah**

But over-reacting is like yelling and saying, "OH MY GOD!" I-I-I-I…it's just like you're panicking.

**Yes, exactly and—and partly that's because even with cops, some cops who are not, umm, and all cops are not bad. Most cops know exactly what they're doing. Some cops might be--**

**—and have been caught being afraid of African American boys- and then try to be difficult or rough with them and treat them as if they're doing something wrong.**

And after, you know what? After umm, Trayvon Martin--you know what?

**What?**

Those people, Oh, my God…a group of policemen…we don't know if maybe the guy disrespected the police, but the police came & started hitting him.

**When?**

It was on the news, on the news? A while ago, a while ago? I don't know, it's just maybe they hit him for like, no reason.

**Right**

Or--something--they start--they start hitting the guy. They pushed him on the car and start hitting him like.

**With their batons?**

Yes, with their batons, yeah.

**Yeah, that might be in one of those older pictures. But I think Daddy wants you to remember to first to be respectful with anybody and if you think it's gonna be dangerous, then it's ok to ask for help. Yell out for help. But initially, you wanna treat everybody right. You always do. I notice that. But if somebody's stalking you—**

It's not the same for everyone else--.

It's not always the same, no. You gotta be careful--

Yeah because people can disrespect you--

**Exactly**

--and think that you're, eh, "You don't--you don't look---you don't--look like you're…" It's like they're saying that "You don't look right, so I have the right to disrespect you."

**Yeah, and that's what we call, we call that racism. That some people, a lot of people unfortunately, will look at a boy, who like Trayvon or like you, with a hoodie on and see that maybe you, and believe that something, you're gonna do wrong. Instead of, other people who wear hoodies, they don't look at--at them the same way and that's wrong. And that's why Daddy wants you to be safe and that's why-**

So you mean like- when you said 'other people'–like, like If Trayvon was a white, --umm, that he wouldn't be disrespected that bad.

**We don't believe he would be disrespected like that, no. Not in that neighborhood where Trayvon went and I think sometimes—**

I think I heard on the news that he was in a white neighborhood.

**Yeah, well he was in his neighborhood. He was in the neighborhood where he lives; On his way home, going home. So, in a way, it's not even wrong going through someone else's neighborhood--if you are not doing anything.**

**Umm, but the other thing is true that even black people can look at other black people as if there is something wrong with them and other boys, and that's just as--that's a problem too. We're just as concerned as if anybody says "I'm better than you."**

Really?

And Dad, I need to stop you there.

**What?**

So remember when we were at that-- me- and- _____ invited me over at the swimming pool with _____?

**Yes**

And ____?

**Yes**

Mommy told me that there was a guy disrespecting us and there were like two guys and they were like "What?"

**Yes**

"What are you doing?"—like—"What…?" They were looking at us like, "Wh-What are you doing here?"

And then they're like, "I thought this place was white people only."

**Is that what he said?**

Well, I don't--he really looked like that.

**No, he had a look. I don't think he said that, according to Mommy.**

No, it looked like. It probably looked like he said, "Huh"--"What are these guys doing here?

**Yeah, he had that disposition, that attitude and…You were the only persons of color there, you and _____, and Mommy and Ms. _____. So, what else could it be? Makes you wonder, "Why is he saying that?" and uh, I just want you to know that that's somebody else's problem, That's not your problem. That's their problem.**

**Don't you ever think that you are less than somebody else. No matter how people treat you. If they treat you bad, it means they don't know how to treat people right. You understand that? Don't you start thinking, "There's something wrong with me." Or, um, "I must be bad." NO! That ain't got nothing to do with somebody else…accusing you.**

**They're wrong. They're misguided. They're messed up in the head, not you. And that was the problem with George Zimmerman. His parents didn't teach him how to deal with his emotions--**

Or maybe they did but he did the wrong choice.

**Well it's possible they could have talked to him, but I don't think so…The way they talked about their son…they think that-**

Wait a minute, George Zimmerman, you mean?

**Parents, yeah…**

Yeah, what did they say about him?

**Well, I think they basically felt that he was justified to follow and stalk**

What the?

**Yeah, I think that's wrong.**

That's--one minute-- so they're saying he has the right to follow a black kid, get in a fight with him, and shoot him!!?

**Well, I don't think they're saying that he had a right to. I think they felt because he was scared of him, that he had a right to shoot him. They do not in any way see what was wrong in what Trayvon Martin did. I mean what George Zimmerman did.**

What George Zimmerman did. Well that's wrong.

**Their parents must be so, so, so sad.**

**We don't want you to think that you can't go places. Daddy's going to be behind you 100 %. You got good friends. We're gonna make sure that you ain't gonna be anywhere that you are not safe. We're going to be with you.**

**But just in case…this doesn't happen a lot, but just in case. Right? I did the same thing with Bryan. I gave him the same talk. We call this the "Stalking Talk."**

**If anybody tries to bother my child…mmm, mmm, mmm.**

What will happen?

**Well, they better run.**

Because what??

**I'm gonna get 'em.**

See?

**I'm gonna get 'em.**

Really?

**Oh yeah.**

Well, then they're gonna get you because they might have weapons or something.

**Well, YOU KNOW WHAT, I'm gonna call police too, like I should. But I feel like I wanna get 'em. But you can't. YOU GOT--you right—you got—you right--- you can't just—you can't just go chasing people.**

They can be armed; they can be armed.

**Yeah, you right, you right. Yeaaahhhh, you right. I feel like I wanna go…**

Plus they could be an army or something.

**I know--I feel like I wanna go get 'em, messing with my son. I don't like that.**

ummmmm

**But they can be—but aaaa--you right. You gotta be careful. And um, you gotta--gotta be careful. You never know what some crazy people will think about you.**

**Just as long as you believe you are beautiful like Daddy believes you're beautiful and handsome, and Mommy believes that you are beautiful and handsome and smart. And you deserve to be on this planet just as happy and beautiful, as smart as you want to be. You can do anything you want, baby.**

**That's what my mommy used to say to me. "You can do--be anything you want". Anything. Even when people try to hurt you. Even if they don't like you, just brush 'em off and keep on movin'.**

## Summary and Implications for Policy on Black Male Mental Health

There are significant gaps in the literature around racially specific risk and protective factors for black males in safely navigating the pathways to manhood. Racial socialization and literacy are proposed as novel approaches to conceptualize, measure, and analyze black male strivings in the creation of non-traditional interventions.

Several dilemmas have been raised. One is the race vs. racial dilemma that questions whether quality non-dehumanizing research compares black males to other biologically classified static race groups or instead compares these groups through a "racial" lens where lived experiences lead to deeper within-group diversity theorizing. Secondly, while the role of risk and protective factors in the mental health functioning of youth and families is a rubric whose time remains stable in the research literature, what's missing is the microscopic attention to the racial interactions and conflicts that surround risk and protection for the contexts, and not the humanity of black male youth and families. Thus, a universal understanding of risk and protection becomes less fitting. Creating reliable measures of racial risk and protective mediators and outcomes assumes that there are unique ways that racial politics moderate healthy development. Certainly, comparison research designs allow for researchers to understand how different racial groups respond differently to generic racially-neutral family and youth coping measures. But measures that capture how black parents' fears of racial profiling of, and sanctioned state violence against, black children are rarely constructed.

Third, one relevant protective factor that appreciates the racial politics embedded in black youth and family social interaction is racial socialization. Racial socialization includes a set of normative childrearing coping and communication approaches in families to illuminate the racial dangers families perceive to undermine or enhance their children's emotional, psychological and physical safety and well-being. These protective, affirmative, and corrective practices of child-rearing include parental delivery and youth receptivity of knowledge, attitudes, and skills about behaving and processing what to say and do during racially stressful and supportive encounters. These practices range from how to greet members of racial in- and out-groups to how to speak directly or indirectly within predominantly white social or academic environments, to how to positively reappraise stress, emotionally self-regulate, and disclose experiences of racial conflict and interaction.

While racial socialization has been defined often as intentional messages that parents deliver and children receive, it also includes indirect, unintentional or serendipitous communications. The affirmation aspects of racial socialization processes are particularly salient given the persistence of racial rejection and assault experiences that black youth and adults experience in school, neighborhood, and public contexts. Without a way to psychologically and interpersonally renounce the rejections of racial hostility in daily social encounters, these racial microaggressions will undermine emotional processes that are foundational to self-care and healthy daily functioning (Sue et al., 2008).

While not considered a traditional African American family practice, implicit and explicit racial socialization in both verbal and nonverbal forms have been occurring in black families through humor and wit, writing and poetry, music and dance, and politics and protests for centuries. It has been our cataloguing of racial socialization processes in the last 3 decades that has vaulted this "traditional" child-rearing practice from an atheoretical construct worthy of description to a mediating protective factor that triggers positive health outcomes for children and youth. In recent intervention research using black urban barbershops, (have reliably trained black male barbers to provide direct unsafe sex and retaliation violence risk reduction skills in face-to-face partner and stranger relationships to black males aged 18–24, while they are cutting their hair (Brawner et al., 2013; Jemmott et al., 2016). These engagements become demonstrations of racial socialization with specific therapeutic elements of affection, protection, and correction surrounded by the mechanism of black cultural style and passion.

So reconstructing the narrative of deficit-laden experiences of black family child-rearing represents a different research direction than the traditional comparison research approaches. The focus of black family strengths and challenges must be specifically identified through systematic measurement development and assessment. White comparison participants become the standard of healthy or normative lived experiences without measures of lived racial experiences whether intended by research investigators or not. This is true because we know that families and youth of color differ not only in their coping with racial conflicts and microaggressions, but also in their awareness of these daily or weekly interactions.

It can be said that parents parent according to the fears they have of the specific challenges and rejections their children will face. It is hard to imagine parenting of black male's research excluding measurement of parental racial fears regarding racial profiling. This measurement is also bracketed by framing racial socialization processes as depth of attitudes, frequency of communication, parent delivery (what parents say they say to children) or adolescent receptivity (what youth say they received from parents), content-focused (racial pride and bias preparation) or problem-solving situational skills-focused (what you should do during a racial encounter) and race/ethnic generic (belonging to my group) or race/ethnic specific (tell black youth why black history and culture matters in their self-esteem). Not only measurement, but the theoretical rationale for the development and inclusion of racialized conceptualization, measurement, and interpretation of black family child-rearing practices is missing in the extant literature.

Future black family research must study the proximal nature of racialized risk and protective factors of black male youth and young adults because they daily face rejections generated from racial fears directly related to their blackness and maleness. Proxy variables of "ethnic identity" are too vague and imprecise to capture this reality. The publicized media recordings of police shootings and brutality of black people over the last several years have heightened a nagging and wretched truth in my work on racial socialization intervention.

I cannot reconcile that few if any of our evidenced based programs would be equipped to effectively problem solve the trauma generated from the experiences of Eric Gardner, Tamir Rice, Sandra Bland, Trayvon Martin, and numerous others. The video-taped recorded versions of these state-sanctioned assaults on black children and young adults are a drop in the bucket compared to the ones where no physical camera or psychological lens exists. To say that our research remains distal by not developing interventions and programs that address this racial trauma is only geometrically problematized by the fact that even videotaping of these events is intensely questioned as inauthentic, thus denying what black people experience.

Perhaps there is hope in the work of "wise interventions" that shows that by affirming the smartness and competence of all students before and while they are engaging in academic tasks of schooling, the racial differences in GPA and achievement between minority and white students are minimized and in some cases erased (Sherman, Bunyan, Creswell, & Jaremka, 2009). The same process of affirmation has been found to help students of color to appreciate critical feedback as helpful rather than demeaning (Yeager et al., 2013). While there is recent evidence that affirmation does not always work to erase the achievement gap (Dee, 2015), it mostly remains promising as an agent of changing racial differences, without targeting the specific racial threat dynamics of the achievement process.

Given that a "racial trauma/dehumanization/coping" lens toward understanding black family influences via racial socialization on black manhood is rarely utilized in research studies, and the measurement to track the prevalence, intensity, and coping of racial trauma/dehumanization is lacking, where do we begin?

In this review of literature on black male functioning, several questions arise. Should we and can we as researchers effectively evaluate research on black boys and men without distinguishing "raced" and "racial" lenses? Can we develop measures that appreciate and capture the breadth, frequency, and intensity of daily racialized risk and protective experiences? Are racial vs non-racial stress and coping factors equally capable of distinguishing health, academic, and relational outcomes among black males? By not attending to racial dehumanization in our theory conceptualization, measurement selection, and results interpretation in studies of black youth, are we simply reifying discriminatory distal and deficit frames of black male youth potential, coping, and achievement?

Black males travel across the expanse of a lifetime battling within themselves between swallowing the dehumanization narrative as just the way life is or defying the odds. They should not have to shrink themselves just to get an education. Before our young men can run from the internalized oppression of the black male expendability narrative and run into the open arms of the caring and critically conscious parents and professionals, teachers and trainers, aunties and ancestors from the village we have always dreamt of, they must walk.

Before our children can walk out of stores and neighborhoods as customers and residents rather than suspects, or walk into colleges and universities as students articulating and walk out as graduates matriculating, they must crawl.

Long after our little boys crawl, they will play in sandboxes with hidden land mines of psychological dehumanization questioning their innocence and their play as developmentally inappropriate. To date, no existing evidenced-based intervention has a direct response to this peculiar traumatization. Nevertheless, our boys will eventually ask us all, parents and researchers alike, "Why when I walk down the street, people treat me like a snake?" We cannot respond with blindness.

## References


Advancement Project. (2005). *Education on lockdown: The schoolhouse to jailhouse track.* Washington, DC: Advancement Project. Retrieved from http://www.advancementproject.org/resources/entry/education-on-lockdown-the-schoolhouse-to-jailhouse-track.

Ahnert, L., Harwardt-Heinecke, E., Kappler, G., Eckstein-Madry, T., & Milatz, A. (2012). Student–teacher relationships and classroom in first grade: How do they relate to students' stress regulation?. *Attachment & Human Development, 14*(3), 249–263.

Alexander, M. (2010). *The new Jim Crow: Mass incarceration in the age of colorblindness*. New York: The New Press.

American Psychological Association. (2008). *Resilience in African American children and adolescents: A vision for optimal development.* APA Task Force on Resilience and Strength in Black Children and Adolescents. Washington, DC: American Psychological Association. http://www.apa.org/pi/families/resources/task-force/resilience-af-am.aspx. Accessed Sept 2015.

Anderson, R. & Stevenson, H. C. (2015). *Post-racial socialization: Putting the cart way before the horse.* (Technical Report 001). University of Pennsylvania: Racial Empowerment Collaborative.

Ardoy, D. N., Fernández-Rodríguez, J. M., Jiménez-Pavón, D., Castillo, R., Ruiz, J. R., & Ortega, F. B. (2014). A physical education trial improves adolescents' cognitive performance and academic achievement: The EDUFIT study. *Scandinavian Journal of Medicine & Science in Sports, 24*(1), 52–61. Retrieved from http://www.ncbi.nlm.nih.gov/pubmed/23826633.

Arrington, E. G., & Stevenson, H. C. (2006). *Final report for the Success of African American Students (SAAS) in Independent Schools project.* Philadelphia: University of Pennsylvania Graduate School of Education. http://repository.upenn.edu/gse_pubs/23/.

Arrington, E. G., Hall, D. M., & Stevenson, H. C. (2003). The success of African-American students in independent schools. *Independent School, 62*(4), 10–19.

Avery, D. R., Richeson, J. A., Hebl, M. R., & Ambady, N. (2009). It does not have to be uncomfortable: The role of behavioral scripts in Black–White interracial interactions. *Journal of Applied Psychology, 94*(6), 1382–1393.

Ayduk, O., Mendoza-Denton, R., Mischel, W., Downey, G., Peake, P. K., & Rogriguez, M. (2000). Regulating the interpersonal self: Strategic self-regulation for coping with rejection sensitivity. *Journal of Personality and Social Psychology, 79*(5), 776–792.

Bailey, D. F., & Bradbury-Bailey, M. E. (2006). Promoting achievement for African American males through group work. *The Journal for Specialists in Group Work, 32*(1), 83–96.

Bailey, D. F., & Paisley, P. O. (2004). Developing and nurturing excellence in African American male adolescents. *Journal of Counseling & Development, 82*(1), 10–17.

Bakari, R. (2003). Pre-service teachers' attitudes toward teaching African American students: Contemporary research. *Urban Education, 38*(6), 640–654.

Bandura, A., Caprara, G. V., Barbaranelli, C., Pastorelli, C., & Regalia, C. (2001). Sociocognitive self-regulatory mechanisms governing transgressive behavior. *Journal of Personality and Social Psychology, 80*, 125–135.

Bandura, A., Pastorelli, C., Barbaranelli, C., & Caprara, G. V. (1999). Self-efficacy pathways to childhood depression. *Journal of Personality and Social Psychology, 76*, 258–269.

Banerjee, M., Harrell, Z. A., & Johnson, D. J. (2011). Racial/ethnic socialization and parental involvement in education as predictors of cognitive ability and achievement in African American children. *Journal of youth and adolescence, 40*(5), 595–605.

Bannon, W. M., Jr., Cavaleri, M. A., Rodriguez, J., & McKay, M. M. (2008). The effect of racial socialization on urban African American use of child mental health services. *Social Work in Mental Health, 6*(4), 9–29.

Baumann, A. A., Powell, B. J., Kohl, P. L., Tabak, R. G., Penalba, V., Proctor, E. K., et al. (2015). Cultural adaptation and implementation of evidence-based parent-training: A systematic review and critique of guiding evidence. *Children and Youth Services Review, 53*, 113–120.

Becker, B. E., & Luthar, S. S. (2002). Social-emotional factors affecting achievement outcomes among disadvantaged students: Closing the achievement gap. *Educational Psychologist, 37*(4), 197–214.

Bentley-Edwards, K., & Stevenson, H. C. (2016). The multidimensionality of racial/ethnic socialization: Scale construction for the cultural and racial experiences of socialization (CARES). *Journal of Child and Family Studies, 25*(1), 96–108. http://link.springer.com/article/10.1007%2Fs10826-015-0214-7.

Bentley-Edwards, K. L., Adams-Bass, V. N., & Stevenson, H. C. (2009). Racial socialization: Roots, processes and outcomes. In H. Neville, B. Tynes, & S. Utsey (Eds.), *Handbook of African American psychology* (pp. 255–267). Thousand Oaks: Sage Publications.

Bernal, G., Jiménez-Chafey, M. I., & Domenech Rodríguez, M. M. (2009). Cultural adaptation of treatments: A resource for considering culture in evidence-based practice. *Professional Psychology: Research and Practice, 40*(4), 361–368.

Biddle, S. J. H., & Mutrie, N. (2007). *Psychology of physical activity: Determinants, well-being, and interventions* (2nd ed.). London: Routledge.

Blascovich, J., Mendes, W. B., Hunter, S. B., Lickel, B., & Kowai-Bell, N. (2001). Perceiver threat in social interactions with stigmatized others. *Journal of Personality and Social Psychology, 80*(2), 253–267.

Blascovich, J., Spencer, S. J., Quinn, D., & Steele, C. (2001). African-Americans and high blood pressure: The role of stereotype threat. *Psychological Science, 12*, 225–229.

Bowman, P., & Howard, C. (1985). Race related socialization, motivation, and academic achievement: A study of black youths in three-generation families. *Journal of American Academy of Child Psychiatry, 24*(2), 134–141.

Boykin, A. W., Albury, A., Tyler, K. M., Hurley, E. A., Bailey, C. T., & Miller, O. A. (2005). Culture-based perceptions of academic achievement among low-income elementary students. *Cultural Diversity & Ethnic Minority Psychology, 11*(4), 339–350.

Brawner, B. M., Baker, J. L., Stewart, J., Davis, Z. M., Cedarbaum, J., & Jemmott, L. S. (2013). "The black man's country club": Assessing the feasibility of an HIV risk-reduction program for young heterosexual African American men in barbershops. *Family Community Health, 36*(2), 109–118.

Brody, G. H., Chen, Y. F., Murry, V. B., Ge, X., Simons, R. L., Gibbons, F. X., et al. (2006). Perceived discrimination and the adjustment of African American youths: A five-year longitudinal analysis with contextual moderation effects. *Child Development, 77*(5), 1170–1189.

Brown, A. L. (2011a). Racialised subjectivities: A critical examination of ethnography on black males in the USA, 1960s to early 2000s. *Ethnography and Education, 6*(1), 45–60. doi:10.1080/17457823.2011.553078.

Brown, A. L. (2011b). Same old stories: The black male in social science and educational literature, 1930s to the present. *Teachers College Record, 9*(113), 2047–2079.

Brown, W. T., & Jones, J. M. (2004). The substance of things hoped for: A study of the future orientation, minority status perceptions, academic engagement, and academic performance of black high school students. *Journal of Black Psychology, 30*(2), 248–273.

Burton, L. M., Winn, D.-M., Stevenson, H. C., & Clark, S. L. (2004). Working with African American clients: Considering the "homeplace" in marriage and family therapy practices. *Journal of Marital & Family Therapy, 30*(4), 397–410.

Bynum, M. S., Burton, E. T., & Best, C. (2007). Racism experiences and psychological distress in African American freshman: Is racial socialization a buffer? *Cultural Diversity and Ethnic Minority Psychology, 13*(1), 64–71.

Carlson, S. A., Fulton, J. E., Lee, S. M., Maynard, L. M., Brown, D. R., Kohl, H. W., III, et al. (2008). Physical education and academic achievement in elementary school: Data from the Early Childhood Longitudinal Study. *American Journal of Public Health, 98*(4), 721–727.

Cassidy, E. F., & Stevenson, H. C. (2005). They wear the mask: Hypermasculinity and hypervulnerability among African American males in an urban remedial disciplinary school context. *Journal of Aggression, Maltreatment and Trauma, 11*(4), 53–74.

Casteel, C. A. (1998). Teacher-student interactions and race in integrated classrooms. *Journal of Educational Research, 92*(2), 115–120.

Castelli, D. M., Hillman, C. H., Buck, S. M., & Erwin, H. E. (2007). Physical fitness and academic achievement in third-and fifth-grade students. *Journal of Sport and Exercise Psychology, 29*(2), 239–252.

Chang, D. F., & Sue, S. (2003). The effects of race and problem type on teachers' assessments of student behavior. *Journal of Consulting and Clinical Psychology, 71*(2), 235–242.

Cho, G., & DeCastro-Ambrosetti, D. (2005). Is ignorance bliss? Pre-service teachers' attitudes toward multicultural education. *The High School Journal, 89*(2), 24–28.

Clark, R., Anderson, N. R., Clark, V. R., & Williams, D. R. (1999). Racism as stressor for African Americans: A biopsychosocial model. *American Psychologist, 54*(10), 805–816.

Coard, S. I., Foy-Watson, S., Zimmer, C., & Wallace, A. (2007). Considering culturally relevant parenting practices in intervention development and adaptation: A randomized control trial of the Black Parenting Strengths and Strategies (BPSS) program. *The Counseling Psychologist, 35*, 797–820.

Coard, S. I., Wallace, S. A., Stevenson, H. C., & Brotma, L. M. (2004). Towards culturally relevant preventive interventions: The consideration of racial socialization in parent training with African American families. *Journal of Child and Family Studies, 13*(3), 277–293.

Coe, D. P., Pivarnik, J. M., Womack, C. J., Reeves, M. J., & Malina, R. M. (2006). Effect of physical education and activity levels on academic achievement in children. *Medicine and Science in Sports and Exercise, 38*(8), 1515–1519.

Cohen, G. L., Garcia, J., Apfel, N., & Master, A. (2006). Reducing the racial achievement gap: A social-psychological intervention. *Science, 313*(5791), 1307–1310.

Cohen, G. L., Garcia, J., Purdie-Vaughns, V., Apfel, N., & Brzustoski, P. (2009). Recursive processes in self-affirmation: Intervening to close the minority achievement gap. *Science, 324*(5925), 400–403.

Coie, J. D., Dodge, K. A., Terry, R., & Wright, V. (1991). The role of aggression in peer relations: An analysis of aggression episodes in boys' play groups. *Child Development, 62*(4), 812–826.

Cokley, K. (2002). Ethnicity, gender and academic self-concept: A preliminary examination of academic disidentification and implications for psychologists. *Cultural Diversity & Ethnic Minority Psychology, 8*(4), 378–388.

Cooper, S. M., Brown, C., Metzger, I., Clinton, Y., & Guthrie, B. (2013). Racial discrimination and African American adolescents' adjustment: Gender variation in family and community social support, promotive and protective factors. *Journal of Child and Family Studies, 22*(1), 15–29.

Cornell, D., Allen, K., & Fan, X. (2012). A randomized controlled study of the Virginia Student Threat Assessment Guidelines in grades K-12. *School Psychology Review, 41*, 100–115.

Cornell, D., Gregory, A., & Fan, X. (2011). Reductions in long-term suspensions following adoption of the Virginia Student Threat Assessment Guidelines. *Bulletin of the National Association of Secondary School Principals, 95*, 175–194.

Crick, N. R., & Dodge, K. A. (1996). Social information-processing mechanisms on reactive and proactive aggression. *Child Development, 67*(3), 993–1002.

Crocker, J., Major, B., & Steele, C. (1998). Social stigma. In D. T. Gilbert, S. T. Fiske, & G. Lindzey (Eds.), *Handbook of social psychology* (4th ed., Vols. 1 & 2, pp. 504–553). New York, NY: McGraw-Hill.

Crosnoe, R., Cavanagh, S., & Elder, G. H., Jr. (2003). Adolescent friendships as academic resources: The intersection of friendship, race, and school disadvantage. *Sociological Perspectives, 46*(3), 331–352.

Darch, C., Miao, Y., & Shippen, P. (2004). A model for involving parents of children with learning and behavior problems in the school. *Preventing School Failure, 48*, 24–34.

Davis, G. Y., Zamel, P. C., Hall, D., Espin, E., & Williams, V. R. (2003). Life after PLAAY: Alumni group and rites of passage empowerment. In H. C. Stevenson (Ed.) *Playing with anger: Teaching coping skills to African American boys through athletics and culture* (pp. 169–182). Westport, CT: Praeger.

Decker, D. M., Dona, D. P., & Christenson, S. L. (2007). Behaviorally at-risk African American students: The importance of student-teacher relationships for student outcomes. *Journal of School Psychology, 45*, 83–109.

Dee, T. S. (2015). Social identity and achievement gaps: Evidence from an affirmation intervention. *Journal of Research on Educational Effectiveness, 8*(2), 149–168.

Devine, P. G. (1989). Stereotypes and prejudice: Their automatic and controlled components. *Journal of Personality and Social Psychology, 56*(1), 5–18.

Dishion, T. J., Patterson, G. R., Stoolmiller, M., & Skinner, M. L. (1991). Family, school, and behavioral antecedents to early adolescent involvement with antisocial peers. *Developmental Psychology, 27*(1), 172–180.

Dodge, K. A., Coie, J. D., Pettit, G. S., Price, J. M. (1990). Peer status and aggression in boys' groups: Developmental and contextual analyses. *Child Development, 61*(5), 1289–1309.

Domenech Rodríguez, M. M., & Bernal, G. (2012). Frameworks, models, and guidelines for cultural adaptation. In G. Bernal & M. M. Domenech Rodríguez (Eds.), *Cultural adaptations: Tools for evidence-based practice with diverse populations* (pp. 23–44). Washington, DC: American Psychological Association.

Downey, D. B., & Pribesh, S. (2004). When race matters: Teachers' evaluations of students' classroom behavior. *Sociology of Education, 77*, 267–282.

Downey, G., Bonica, C., & Rincón, C. (1999). Rejection sensitivity and adolescent romantic relationships. In W. Furman, B. B. Brown, & C. Feiring (Eds.), *The development of romantic relationships in adolescence* (pp. 148–174). Cambridge: Cambridge University Press.

Downey, G., & Feldman, S. I. (1996). Implications of rejection sensitivity for intimate relationships. *Journal of Personality and Social Psychology, 70*(6), 1327–1343.

DuBois, W. E. B. (1903). *The souls of black folk*. Chicago: A.C. McClurg & Co.

Eberhardt, J. L. (2005). Imaging race. *American Psychologist, 60*(2), 181–190.

Eberhardt, J. L., Goff, P. A., Purdie, V. J., & Davies, P. G. (2004). Seeing black: Race, crime, and visual processing. *Journal of Personality and Social Psychology, 87*(6), 876–893.

Fain, T., Greathouse, S. M., Turner, S. F., & Weinberg, H. D. (2014). Effectiveness of multisystemic therapy for minority youth: Outcomes over 8 years in Los Angeles County. *Journal of Juvenile Justice, 3*(2), 24–37.

Family Resource Trend Report. (2000). Philadelphia, PA: Philadelphia Unified School District.

Feldman, S., & Downey, G. (1994). Rejection sensitivity as a mediator of the impact of childhood exposure to family violence on adult attachment behavior. *Development and Psychopathology, 6*, 231–247.

Ferguson, R. F. (2003). Teachers' perceptions and expectations and the Black-White test score gap. *Urban Education, 38*(4), 460–507.

Fisher, C. B., Wallace, S. A., & Fenton, R. E. (2000). Discrimination distress during adolescence. *Journal of Youth and Adolescence, 29*, 679–695.

Folkman, S. (2008). The case for positive emotions in the stress process. *Anxiety, Stress & Coping: An International Journal, 21*(1), 3–14.

Folkman, S., & Moskowitz, J. T. (2000). Stress, positive emotion, and coping. *Current Directions in Psychological Science, 9*(4), 115–118.

Fultz, M., & Brown, A. (2008). Historical perspectives on African American males as subjects of education policy. *American Behavioral Scientist, 51*(7), 854–871.

Gilliam, W. S. (2005). *Pre-kindergarteners left behind: Expulsion rates in state pre-kindergarten systems*. Foundation for Child Development. FDC Policy Brief Series No. 3. http://challengingbehavior.fmhi.usf.edu/explore/policy_docs/prek_expulsion.pdf. Accessed Sept 2015.

Goff, P. A., Jackson, M. C., Di Leone, B. A. L., Culotta, C. M., & DiTomasso, N. A. (2014). The essence of innocence: Consequences of dehumanizing black children. *Journal of Personality & Social Psychology, 106*(4), 526–545.

Goffman, E. (1963). *Stigma: Notes on the management of spoiled identity*. New York: Simon and Schuster.

Gordon-Larsen, P., McMurray, R. G., & Popkin, B. M. (2000). Determinants of adolescent physical activity and inactivity patterns. *Pediatrics, 105*(6), e83.

Gray-Little, B., & Carels, R. A. (1997). The effects of racial dissonance on academic self-esteem and achievement in elementary, junior high, and high school students. *Journal of Research on Adolescence, 7*(2), 109–132.

Greene, M. L., Way, N., & Pahl, K. (2006). Trajectories of perceived adult and peer discrimination among Black, Latino, and Asian American adolescents: patterns and psychological correlates. *Developmental psychology, 42*(2), 218.

Gregory, A., Cornell, D., & Fan, X. (2011). The relationship of school structure and support to suspension rates for black and white high school students. *American Educational Research Journal, 48*, 904–934.

Gregory, A., & Weinstein, R. S. (2008). The discipline gap and African Americans: Defiance or cooperation in the high school classroom. *Journal of School Psychology, 46*(4), 455–475.

Griffin, B. W. (2002). Academic disidentification, race, and high school dropouts. *The High School Journal, 85*(4), 71–81.

Griner, D., & Smith, T. B. (2006). Culturally adapted mental health intervention: A meta-analytic review. *Psychotherapy: Theory, Research, Practice, Training, 43*(4), 531–548.

Hoffman, K., Llagas, C., & Snyder, T. D. (2003). *Status and trends in the education of blacks,* (NCES 2003–034). Washington, DC: U.S. Department of Education, National Center for Education Statistics. http://nces.ed.gov/pubs2003/2003034.pdf.

Hughes, D., & Chen, L. (1997). When and what parents tell children about race: An examination of race-related socialization among African American families. *Applied Developmental Science, 1*(4), 200–214.

Hughes, D., Rodriguez, J., Smith, E. P., Johnson, D. J., Stevenson, H. C., & Spicer, P. (2006). Parents' ethnic-racial socialization practices: A review of research and directions for future study. *Developmental Psychology, 42*(5), 747–770.

Hughes, J. N., Wu, J. Y., Kwok, O. M., Villarreal, V., & Johnson, A. Y. (2012). Indirect effects of child reports of teacher-student relationship on achievement. *Journal of Educational Psychology, 104*(2), 350–365.

Hurd, N. M., & Sellers, R. M. (2013). Black adolescents' relationships with natural mentors: Associations with academic engagement via social and emotional development. *Cultural Diversity and Ethnic Minority Psychology, 19*(1), 76–85.

Huynh, V. W. (2012). Ethnic microaggressions and the depressive and somatic symptoms of Latino and Asian American adolescents. *Journal of Youth and Adolescence, 41*(7), 831–846.

Huynh, V. W., & Gillen-O'Neel, C. (2013). Discrimination and sleep: The protective role of school belonging. *Youth & Society*. doi:10.1177/0044118X13506720.

Irving, M. A., & Hudley, C. (2008). Cultural identification and academic achievement among African American males. *Journal of Advanced Academics, 19*(4), 676–698.

Jemmott, L.S., Stevenson, H. C., Jemmott, J., & Coleman, C. (2016). *Shape-Up Project: Building better brothers through safe sex and violence retaliation risk reduction in black barbershops.* Manuscript submitted for publication to *Journal of Men and Masculinities*.

Jencks, C., & Phillips, M. (1998). America's next achievement test: Closing the black-white test score gap. *American Prospect, 40*, 44–53. http://prospect.org/article/americas-next-achievement-test.

Jennings, T. (2007). Addressing diversity in US teacher preparation programs: A survey of elementary and secondary programs' priorities and challenges from across the United States of America. *Teaching and Teacher Education: An International Journal of Research and Studies, 23*(8), 1258–1271.

Jones, K. P., Peddie, C. I., Gilrane, V. L., King, E. B., & Gray, A. L. (2013). Not so subtle: A meta-analytic investigation of the correlates of subtle and overt discrimination. *Journal of Management*. Advance online publication. http://dx.doi.org/10.1177/0149206313506466.

Kataoka, S. H., Zhang, L., & Wells, K. B. (2002). Unmet need for mental health care among US children: Variation by ethnicity and insurance status. *American Journal of Psychiatry, 159*(9), 1548–1555.

Kellow, J. T., & Jones, B. D. (2008). The effects of stereotypes on the achievement gap: Reexamining the academic performance of African American high school students. *Journal of Black Psychology, 34*(1), 94–120.

Kistner, J. A., David, C. F., & White, B. A. (2003). Ethnic and sex differences in children's depressive symptoms: Mediating effects of perceived and actual competence. *Journal of Clinical Child and Adolescent Psychology, 32*(3), 341–350.

Kupersmidt, J. B., Griesler, P. C., DeRosier, M. E., Patterson, C. J., & Davis, P. W. (1995). Childhood aggression and peer relations in the context of family and neighborhood factors. *Child Development, 66*(2), 360–375.

Kwate, N. O. A., & Meyer, I. H. (2011). On sticks and stones and broken bones. *Du Bois Review: Social Science Research on Race, 8*(1), 191–198.

Laird, R. D., Jordan, K. Y., Dodge, K. A., Pettit, G. S., & Bates, J. E. (2001). Peer rejection in childhood, involvement with antisocial peers in early adolescence, and the development of externalizing behavior problems. *Development and Psychopathology, 13*(02), 337–354.

Lesane-Brown, C., Brown, T. N., Caldwell, C. H., & Sellers, R. M. (2005). The comprehensive race socialization inventory. *Journal of Black Studies, 36*(2), 163–190.

Lewis, C. E., Raczynski, J. M., Heath, G. W., Levinson, R., Hilyer, J. C., Jr., & Cutter, G. R. (1993). Promoting physical activity in low-income African-American communities: The PARR project. *Ethnicity & disease, 3*(2), 106–118.

Liddle, H. A., Jackson-Gilfort, A., & Marvel, F. A. (2006). An empirically supported and culturally specific engagement and intervention strategy for African American adolescent males. *American Journal of Orthopsychiatry, 76*(2), 215–225.

Lightsey, O. R., Jr., & Barnes, P. W. (2007). Discrimination, attributional tendencies, generalized self-efficacy, and assertiveness as predictors of psychological distress among African Americans. *Journal of Black Psychology, 33*(1), 27–50.

Martens, R., Burton, D., Vealey, R. S., Bump, L. A., & Smith, D. E. (1990). Development and validation of the Competitive State Anxiety Inventory - 2. In R. Martens, R. S. Vealey, & D. Burton (Eds.), *Competitive anxiety in sport* (pp. 117–190). Champaign, IL: Human Kinetics Books.

Martens, R., Vealey, R. S., & Burton, D. (1995). *Competitive anxiety in sport.* Champaign, IL: Human Kinetics Books.

Mattison, E., & Aber, M. S. (2007). Closing the achievement gap: The association of racial climate with achievement and behavioral outcomes. *American Journal of Community Psychology, 40*(1–2), 1–12.

McCarthy, J. D., & Hoge, D. R. (1987). The social construction of school punishment: Racial disadvantage out of universalistic process. *Social Forces, 65*(4), 1101–1120.

McDonald, K. L., Bowker, J. C., Rubin, K. H., Laursen, B., & Duchene, M. S. (2010). Interactions between rejection sensitivity and supportive relationships in the prediction of adolescents' internalizing difficulties. *Journal of Youth and Adolescence, 39*(5), 563–574.

McKay, M. M., Atkins, M. S., Hawkins, T., Brown, C., & Lynn, C. J. (2003). Inner-city African American parental involvement in children's schooling: Racial socialization and social support from the parent community. *American Journal of Community Psychology, 32*(1/2), 107–114.

Meehan, B. T., Hughes, J. N., & Cavell, T. A. (2003). Teacher–student relationships as compensatory resources for aggressive children. *Child Development, 74*(4), 1145–1157.

Mendoza-Denton, R., Downey, G., Purdie, V., & Davis, A. (2002). Sensitivity to status-based rejection: Implications for African-American students' college experience. *Journal of Personality and Social Psychology, 83*(4), 896–918.

Murray, C. B. (1996). Estimating achievement performance: A confirmation bias. *Journal of Black Psychology, 22*(1), 67–85.

Neal, L. V. I., McCray, A. D., Webb-Johnson, G., & Bridgest, S. T. (2003). The effects of African American movement styles on teachers' perceptions and reactions. *Journal of Special Education, 37*(1), 49–57.

Neblett, E. W., Phillip, C. L., Cogburn, C. D., & Sellers, R. M. (2006). African American adolescents' discrimination experiences and academic achievement: Racial socialization as a

cultural compensatory and protective factor. *Journal of Black Psychology, 32*, 199–218. doi:10.1177/0095798406287072.
Neblett, E. W., Smalls, C. P., Ford, K. R., Nguyen, H. X., & Sellers, R. M. (2009). Racial socialization and racial identity: African American parents' messages about race as precursors to identity. *Journal of Youth and Adolescence, 38*, 189–203.
Noguera, P. A. (2003). The trouble with Black boys: The role and influence of environmental and cultural factors on the academic performance of African American males. *Urban Education, 38*(4), 431–459.
Noh, S., Kaspar, V., & Wickrama, K. A. S. (2007). Overt and subtle racial discrimination and mental health: Preliminary findings for Korean immigrants. *American Journal of Public Health, 97*, 1269–1274. doi:10.2105/AJPH.2005.085316.
Nussbaum, A. D., & Steele, C. M. (2007). Situational disengagement and persistence in the face of adversity. *Journal of Experimental Social Psychology, 43*(1), 127–134.
Nyborg, V. M., & Curry, J. F. (2003). The impact of perceived racism: Psychological symptoms among African American boys. *Journal of Clinical Child and Adolescent Psychology, 32*(2), 258–266.
Oates, G. L. S. C. (2003). Teacher-student racial congruence, teacher perceptions, and test performance. *Social Science Quarterly, 84*(3), 508–525.
Pellegrini, A. D., & Bjorklund, D. F. (1997). The role of recess in children's cognitive performance. *Educational Psychologist, 32*(1), 35–40.
Pinel, E. C. (1999). Stigma consciousness: The psychological legacy of social stereotypes. *Journal of Personality and Social Psychology, 76*(1), 114–128.
Purdie-Vaughns, V., Cohen, G. L., Garcia, J., Sumner, R., Cook, J. C., & Apfel, N. H. (2009). *Improving minority academic performance: How a values-affirmation intervention works.* Teachers College Record. http://www.tcrecord.org/content.asp?contentid=15774. Accessed Sept. 2015.
Rodriguez, J., Cavaleri, M. A., Bannon, W. M., & McKay, M. M. (2008). An introduction to parenting and mental health services utilization among African American families: The role of racial socialization. *Social Work in Mental Health, 6*(4), 1–8.
Rosenbloom, S. R., & Way, N. (2004). Experiences of discrimination among African American, Asian American, and Latino adolescents in an urban high school. *Youth & Society, 35*(4), 420–451.
Saft, E. W., & Pianta, R. C. (2001). Teachers' perceptions of their relationships with students: Effects of child age, gender, and ethnicity of teachers and children. *School Psychology Quarterly, 16*(2), 125–141.
Schott Foundation for Early Education. (2015). *Black Lives Matter: The Schott 50 State Report on Public Education and Black Males.* http://www.blackboysreport.org/2015-black-boys-report.pdf Accessed Sept 2015.
Schwartz, S., & Meyer, I. H. (2010). Mental health disparities research: The impact of within and between group analyses on tests of social stress hypotheses. *Social Science & Medicine, 70*(8), 1111–1118.
Scott, L. D., Jr. (2003). The relation of racial identity and racial socialization to coping with discrimination among African American adolescents. *Journal of Black Studies, 33*(4), 520–538.
Seaton, E. K., & Douglass, S. (2014). School diversity and racial discrimination among African-American adolescents. *Cultural Diversity and Ethnic Minority Psychology, 20*(2), 156–165.
Sherman, D. K., Bunyan, D. P., Creswell, J. D., & Jaremka, L. M. (2009). Psychological vulnerability and stress: The effects of self-affirmation on sympathetic nervous system responses to naturalistic stressors. *Health Psychology, 28*(5), 554.
Sholomskas, D. E., Syracuse-Siewert, G., Rounsaville, B. J., Ball, S. A., Nuro, K. F., & Carroll, K. M. (2005). We don't train in vain: A dissemination trial of three strategies of training clinicians in cognitive-behavioral therapy. *Journal of Consulting and Clinical Psychology, 73*(1), 106–115.
Simons, R. L., Murray, V., McLoyd, V., Lin, K. H., Cutrona, C., & Conger, R. D. (2002). Discrimination, crime, ethnic identity, and parenting as correlates of depressive symptoms among African American children: A multilevel analysis. *Development and Psychopathology, 14*(2), 371–393.

Skiba, R. J., Chung, C.-G., Trachok, M., Baker, T., Sheya, A., & Hughes, R. L. (2015). Where should we intervene How infractions, students, and schools all contribute to out-of-school suspension. In D. J. Losen (Ed.), *Closing the school discipline gap: Research for policymakers*. New York: Teachers College Press.

Skiba, R. J., Horner, R. H., Chung, C.-G., Rausch, M. K., May, S. L., & Tobin, T. (2011). Race is not neutral: A national investigation of African American and Latino disproportionality in school discipline. *School Psychology Review, 40*(1), 85–107.

Skiba, R. J., Michael, R. S., Nardo, A. C., & Peterson, R. L. (2002). The color of discipline: Sources of racial and gender disproportionality in school punishment. *Urban Review, 34*(4), 317–342.

Skiba, R. J., Peterson, R. L., & Williams, T. (1997). Office referrals and suspension: Disciplinary intervention in middle schools. *Education & Treatment of Children, 20*(3), 295–315.

Skiba, R. J. & Williams, N. T. (2014). *Are black kids worse? Myths and facts about racial differences in behavior* (Supplementary Paper I), The Equity Project at Indiana University, Center for Evaluation and Education Policy. http://www.indiana.edu/~atlantic/wp-content/uploads/2014/03/African-American-Differential-Behavior_031214.pdf.

Slaughter-Defoe, D. T., Stevenson, H. C., Arrington, E. G., & Johnson, D. J. (2011). *Black educational choice in a climate of school reform: Assessing the private and public alternatives to traditional K-12 public schools*. Santa Barbara, CA: Praeger.

Smalls, C., White, R., Tabbye, C., Chavous, T., & Sellers, R. (2007). Racial ideological beliefs and racial discrimination experiences as predictors of academic engagement among African American adolescents. *Journal of Black Psychology, 33*(3), 299–330.

Solberg, V. S., & Villarreal, P. (1997). Examination of self-efficacy, social support, and stress as predictors of psychological and physical distress among Hispanic college students. *Hispanic Journal of Behavioral Science, 19*(2), 182–201.

Solorzano, D., Ceja, M., & Yosso, T. (2000). Critical race theory, racial microaggressions, and campus racial climate: The experiences of African American college students. *Journal of Negro Education, 69*(1/2)60–73.

Spencer, M. B., Fegley, S., Harpalani, V., & Seaton, G. (2004). Understanding hypermasculinity in context: A theory-driven analysis of urban adolescent males' coping responses. *Research in Human Development, 1*(4), 229–257.

Spencer, M. B., Harpalani, V., Cassidy, E., Jacobs, C. Y., Donde, S., & Goss, T. N. (2006). Understanding vulnerability and resilience from a normative developmental perspective: Implications for racially and ethnically diverse youth. In D. Cicchetti & D. J. Cohen (Eds.), *Developmental psychopathology: Vol. 1. Theory and method* (2nd ed., pp. 627–672). Hoboken, NJ: Wiley.

Steele, C. M. (1999). The psychology of self-affirmation: Sustaining the integrity of the self. In R. F. Baumeister (Ed.), *The self in social psychology* (pp. 372–390). Philadelphia, PA: Psychology Press/Taylor & Francis.

Steele, C. M., & Aronson, J. (1995). Stereotype threat and the intellectual test performance of African Americans. *Journal of Personality and Social Psychology, 69*(5), 797–811.

Steinberg, L., Dornbusch, S. M., & Brown, B. B. (1992). Ethnic differences in adolescent achievement: An ecological perspective. *American Psychologist, 47*(6), 723–729.

Stevenson, H. C. (1994). Validation of the scale of racial socialization for African American adolescents: Steps toward multidimensionality. *Journal of Black Psychology, 20*(4), 445–468.

Stevenson, H. C. (2003). *Playing with anger: Teaching coping skills to African American boys through athletics and culture*. Westport, CT: Praeger.

Stevenson, H. C. (2004). Boys in men's clothing: Racial socialization and neighborhood safety as buffers to hypervulnerability in African American adolescent males. In N. Way & J. Y. Chu (Eds.), *Adolescent boys: Exploring diverse cultures of boyhood* (pp. 59–77). New York: New York University Press.

Stevenson, H. C. (2014). *Promoting racial literacy in schools: Differences that make a difference*. New York: Teachers College Press.

Stevenson, H. C., & Arrington, E. G. (2009). Racial-ethnic socialization mediates perceived racism and the racial identity of African American adolescents. *Cultural Diversity and Ethnic Minority Psychology, 15*(2), 125–136.

Stevenson, H. C., Cameron, R., Herrero-Taylor, T., & Davis, G. Y. (2002). Development of the teenage experience of racial socialization scale: Correlates of race-related socialization from the perspective of black youth. *Journal of Black Psychology, 28*, 84–106.

Stevenson, H. C., Davis, G. Y., Carter, R., & Elliott, S. (2003). Why black males need cultural socialization. In H. C. Stevenson (Ed.), *Playing with anger: Teaching coping skills to African American boys through athletics and culture*. Westport, CT: Praeger.

Stevenson, H. C., & Jones, K. M. (2015). What if my Trayvon came home? Teaching a wretched truth about breathing while black. In K. Fasching-Varner & N. Hartlep (Eds.), *The assault on communities of color*. New York: Rowman & Littlefield.

Stevenson, H. C., Reed, J., Bodison, P., & Bishop, A. (1997). Racism stress management: Racial social beliefs and the experience of depression and anger in African American youth. *Youth & Society, 29*(2), 197–222.

Stevenson, H. C. & Talley, L. (2016). *Clarifying our racial lens: Framing racial analysis and measurement in educational research on students of color*. Paper presented at the American Educational Research Association Conference, Washington, DC.

Stevenson, H. C., Winn, D.-M., Walker-Barnes, C., & Coard, S. I. (2005). Style matters: Toward a culturally relevant framework for interventions with African American families. In V. C. McLoyd, N. E. Hill, & K. A. Dodge (Eds.), *African American family life: Ecological and cultural diversity* (pp. 311–334). New York: Guilford Press.

Sue, D. W., Capodilupo, C. M., & Holder, A. M. B. (2008). Racial microaggressions in the life experience of black Americans. *Professional Psychology: Research and Practice, 39*, 329–336.

Sue, D. W., Capodilupo, C. M., Torino, G. C., Bucceri, J. M., Holder, A. M. B., Nadal, K. L., et al. (2007). Racial microaggressions in everyday life: Implications for clinical practice. *American Psychologist, 62*, 271–286. doi:10.1037/0003-066X.62.4.271.

Tatum, B. D. (1997). Why are all the Black kids sitting together in the cafeteria? In *And other conversations about race*. New York: Basic Books.

Taylor, J. Y., Washington, O. G., Artinian, N. T., & Lichtenberg, P. (2007). Parental stress among African American parents and grandparents. *Issues in Mental Health Nursing, 28*(4), 373–387.

Thomas, A. J., Carey, D., Prewitt, K.-R., Romero, E., Richards, M., & Velsor-Friedrich, B. (2012). African American youth and exposure to community violence: Supporting change from the inside. *Journal for Social Action in Counseling and Psychology, 4*(1), 54–68.

Thomas, D. E., Coard, S. I., Stevenson, H. C., Bentley, K., & Zamel, P. (2009). Racial and emotional factors predicting teachers' perceptions of classroom behavioral maladjustment for urban African American male youth. *Psychology in the Schools, 46*(2), 184–196.

Thomas, D., & Stevenson, H. C. (2009). Gender risks and education: The particular classroom challenges of urban, low-income African American boys. *Review of Research in Education, 33*, 160–180.

Todd, A. R., Thiem, K. C., & Neel, R. (2016). Does seeing faces of young black boys facilitate the identification of threatening stimuli? *Psychological Science, 27*, 384–393.

Towles-Schwen, T., & Fazio, R. H. (2003). Choosing social situations: The relation between automatically activated racial attitudes and anticipated comfort interacting with African Americans. *Personality and Social Psychology Bulletin, 29*(2), 170–182.

Tran, A. G. T., & Lee, R. M. (2014). You speak English well! Asian Americans' reactions to an exceptionalizing stereotype. *Journal of Counseling Psychology, 61*(3), 484–490.

Troiano, R. P., Berrigan, D., Dodd, K. W., Masse, L. C., Tilert, T., & McDowell, M. (2008). Physical activity in the United States measured by accelerometer. *Medicine and Science in Sports and Exercise, 40*(1), 181–188.

U.S. Department of Education Office for Civil Rights (2014, March). *Civil rights data collection. Data snapshot: School discipline*. (Issue Brief No. 1). Washington, DC. http://ocrdata.ed.gov/Downloads/CRDC-School-Discipline-Snapshot.pdf.

Walton, G. M., & Cohen, G. L. (2007). A question of belonging: Race, social fit, and achievement. *Journal of Personality and Social Psychology, 92*(1), 82–96.
Wang, M. T., & Eccles, J. S. (2012). Social support matters: Longitudinal effects of social support on three dimensions of school engagement from middle to high school. *Child Development, 83*(3), 877–895.
Watts, R. J., Abdul-Adil, J. K., & Pratt, T. (2002). Enhancing critical consciousness in young African American men: A psychoeducational approach. *Psychology of Men & Masculinity, 3*(1), 41–50.
Weinstein, R. S. (2002). *Reaching higher: The power of expectations in schooling*. Cambridge, MA: Harvard University Press.
Weisz, J. R., Sandler, I. N., Durlak, J. A., & Anton, B. S. (2005). Promoting and protecting youth mental health through evidence-based prevention and treatment. *American Psychologist, 60*(6), 628–648.
Whitney, S. D., Hendricker, E. N., & Offitt, C. A. (2011). Moderating factors of natural mentoring relationships, problem behaviors, and emotional well-being. *Mentoring and Tutoring: Partnership in Learning, 19*(1), 83–105.
Word, C. O., Zanna, M. P., & Cooper, J. (1974). The nonverbal mediation of self-fulfilling prophecies in interracial interaction. *Journal of Experimental Social Psychology, 10*(2), 109–120.
Wu, S. C., Pink, W., Crain, R. L., & Moles, O. (1982). Student suspension: A critical reappraisal. *Urban Review, 14*(4), 245–303.
Yeager, D., Walton, G., & Cohen, G. L. (2013). Addressing achievement gaps with psychological interventions. *Phi Delta Kappan, 94*(5), 62–65.
Yoon, J. S. (2002). Teacher characteristics as predictors of teacher-student relationships: Stress, negative affect, and self-efficacy. *Social Behavior and Personality, 30*(5), 485–494.
Zayas, L. H., & Rojas-Flores, L. (2002). Learning from Latino parents: Combining etic and emic approaches to designing interventions. In J. M. Contreras, K. A. Kerns, & A. M. Neal-Barnett (Eds.), *Latino children and families in the United States: Current research and future directions* (pp. 233–249). Westport, CT: Praeger.

# A Trauma-Informed Approach to Affirming the Humanity of African American Boys and Supporting Healthy Transitions to Manhood

**Jocelyn R. Smith Lee**

> We declare our right on this earth **to be a man, to be a human being, to be respected as a human being, to be given the rights of a human being in this society, on this earth, in this day,** which we intend to bring into existence by any means necessary.—Malcolm X

In 1964, Malcolm X delivered a speech at the founding rally of the Organization for Afro-American Unity that would infamously become known as his "By any means necessary" speech (BlackPast.org, n.d.). Central in Malcolm X's message was a demand that black people in the United States be ascribed the right to be acknowledged as human beings and given the full rights and respect therein. Fifty-three years later, we find ourselves situated in the middle of a similar national discourse where through hashtag, protest, and die-in, diverse Americans led by young, black grassroots leaders are challenging what Howard Stevenson (Chap. 5) describes as *expendable black humanity* (p. 56), and declaring that "Black Lives Matter."

Beginning in childhood, boys and men in African American families must daily negotiate the narrative of black male dehumanization that implicitly operates across systems including education, healthcare, and criminal justice (Goff, Jackson, Lewis Di Leone, Culotta, & DiTomasso, 2014; Haslam, 2006). Although recent research examining implicit bias in criminal justice, for example, is beginning to investigate how the dehumanization of black males is predictive of the use of excessive force and inequitable sentencing (Eberhardt, Goff, Purdie, & Davies, 2004; Goff, Eberhardt, Williams, & Jackson, 2008), Stevenson offers a broader critique of the research community for its widespread failure to acknowledge "the persistent invalidation of the humanity of black boys and men" (Chap. 5 p. 56). Stevenson further challenges the research community for avoiding the application of this racial lens in research, intervention, and practice with African American families. He argues for

J.R. Smith Lee (✉)
Department of Psychology, The School of Social and Behavioral Science, Marist College, Poughkeepsie, NY, USA
e-mail: jocelyn.smithlee@marist.edu



L. Burton et al. (eds.), *Boys and Men in African American Families*, National Symposium on Family Issues 7, DOI 10.1007/978-3-319-43847-4_6

the development of a narrative of racial re-humanization in the study of black boys and their families and points to racial socialization and racial literacy lenses as key resources and strategies in this effort. At the same time, Stevenson notes the limitations of even these evidence-based interventions to address the inherent trauma experienced by black boys and their families as a result of their racialized lived experiences. It is to this end that I suggest coupling a trauma-informed perspective (SAMHSA, 2015) with a racial literacy lens toward the development of a framework that affirms the humanity of boys in African American families and supports healthy transitions to manhood.

## Affirming the Humanity of Black Males: A Trauma-Informed Approach

Trauma-informed care is an approach to engaging people that recognizes the presence of trauma symptoms and histories and acknowledges the role that trauma has played in the lives of individuals, families, and cultural groups (SAMSHA, 2015). It also operates from an understanding of the vulnerabilities or triggers of trauma survivors as to avoid re-traumatization and offer support.

According to the Substance Abuse and Mental Health Services Administration (SAMSHA, 2015) a system that applies a trauma-informed approach:

1. *Realizes* the widespread impact of trauma and understands potential paths for recovery
2. *Recognizes* the signs and symptoms of trauma in individuals, families, clients, staff, and others involved with a system
3. *Responds* by fully integrating knowledge about trauma into policies, procedures, and practices
4. Seeks to actively *Resist* re-traumatization

A trauma-informed approach also involves viewing trauma through an ecological and cultural lens and recognizing that context plays a significant role in both the prevalence of trauma exposure and shaping how individuals perceive and process traumatic events (SAMHSA, 2014). At the individual level it affirms a person's traumatic experiences as real and responds with systems-level changes that seek to avoid harm and promote healing.

As it relates to research, policy and practice with boys and men in African American families, applying a trauma-informed approach gives us a lens through which we can make explicit the pervasive narrative of black male dehumanization. As suggested by Stevenson (Chap. 5), having frameworks that allow us to acknowledge the historic (e.g. Emmett Till, Age 14, 1955, Mississippi) and contemporary (e.g. Tamir Rice, Age 12, 2014, Ohio) racial tragedies experienced by black boys, young men, and their families from a humanity perspective is critical to the development of research, policy, and prevention practice that supports healthy pathways to manhood.

A trauma-informed approach also offers us tools that can shift the pathologizing narrative about black boys and men that cast them as dangerous and deviant to one that affirms their humanity. We begin to accomplish this narrative reconstruction, in part, by changing the questions we ask in our research, policy, and practice with black males. Instead of asking black boys and men "What's wrong with you?" (Bloom, 1997; Rich, 2009), a contemporary variant of the DuBoisian question, "How does it feel to be a problem?", a trauma-informed approach pushes us to ask black boys and men, "What's happened to you?" (Rich, Corbin, Bloom, Evans, & Wilson, 2009). In doing so, we begin to see black boys and men as people not as problems; to see risky places, not risky people; and to respond to the needs of black males with compassion, not contempt or condemnation. Only then are we positioned to engage in meaningful scientific inquiry that will help unpack the lived experiences of black boys and men; make explicit their humanity within the public sphere; recognize their vulnerability to pain; and, hear, see, and address the invisible wounds of trauma (Mollica, 2009) many black boys may carry with them into adulthood. This is critically important, as trauma research indicates traumatic experiences in early life are predictive of mental, behavioral, physical, and relational health outcomes in adolescence and later adulthood (Felitti, 2002; Rich et al., 2009). Therefore, identifying and addressing the traumas experienced by black males can help support healthy transitions into and beyond adulthood for this group (Smith, 2015).

## Acknowledging and Conceptualizing Trauma in the Lives of Black Boys and Men

Black youth, particularly those residing in economically disadvantaged urban contexts, are disproportionately vulnerable to lifetime exposures to trauma (Rich et al., 2009; Smith, 2015; Wade, Shea, Rubin, & Wood, 2014). In studies examining the prevalence of trauma, black youth were more likely than white youth to have experienced singular incidences of trauma, and they were also more likely to experience multiple traumatic exposures (Costello, Erkanli, Fairbank, & Angold, 2002). Direct (experiencing) and indirect (witnessing) exposures to violence remain central experiences of trauma among boys of color (Adams, 2010). Previous research has established exposure to neighborhood violence as predictive of adverse mental health outcomes including anxiety, depressive symptoms, and posttraumatic stress symptoms (Bell & Jenkins, 1991; Fitzpatrick, 1993; Garbarino, 1995, 1999; Jenkins, Wang, & Turner, 2009; Johnson, 2010; Rich, 2009; Smith & Patton, 2016).

Chronic exposure to community violence simultaneously places black boys at disproportionate risk for experiencing the traumatic loss of a loved one to violence and becoming homicide survivors (Finkelhor, Ormrod, Turner, & Hamby, 2005; Smith, 2015). Homicide is a leading cause of death for black youth and black males in the United States (CDC, 2015). Homicide is a persistent health disparity maintained by structural inequities (e.g. poverty, residential segregation, educational inequities, unequal employment structures, discrimination, racism) (Eitle, D'Alessio,

& Stolzenberg, 2006; LaVeist, 2005). The likelihood that black youth will have someone close to them murdered is 7.8 times that for white youth (Finkelhor et al., 2005), and previous research evidences significant mental and behavioral health consequences (e.g. PTSD, substance abuse) for surviving loved ones of homicide victims (Hertz, Prothrow-Stith, & Chery, 2005; Smith, 2015; Smith & Patton, 2016; Zinzow, Rheingold, Hawkins, Saunders, & Kilpatrick, 2009).

In my own ethnographic work with 40 black male homicide survivors (ages 18–24) in Baltimore, young men reported experiencing an average of three homicide deaths of friends or family members across the life course (Smith, 2015). Experiences of traumatic loss were most prevalent in adolescence with participants reporting a clustering of homicide deaths during this developmental period. One young man, Antwon (age 18) reported experiencing the deaths of four close friends during his 17th year of life. However, the systems serving black boys and men often fail to recognize the prevalence of traumatic exposure and violent victimization among this population (Sered, 2015). This is in part due to narrow conceptualizations of trauma that have not been inclusive of the daily experiences of black males and their families.

Trauma is broadly defined as experiences or situations that: (1) are emotionally painful and distressing; (2) may overwhelm an individual's ability to cope, producing a sense of powerlessness; and (3) have lasting adverse effects on the individual's functioning and physical, social, emotional, or spiritual well-being (Rich et al., 2009; SAMHSA, 2012; van der Kolk, Roth, Pelcovitz, Sunday, & Spinazzola, 2005). Given the historical legacy of racial oppression in the United States, researchers have worked to expand this definition to include more subtle yet chronic experiences of adversity (e.g. racism, discrimination, poverty, incarceration, etc.) into conceptualizations of trauma (Rich et al., 2009). Young black men living in low-income urban communities may be disproportionately vulnerable to these forms of chronic adversity as they are often the targets of racial profiling, discriminatory hiring practices/unemployment, and policing (Pager, 2005; Pager, Western, & Bonikowski, 2009).

Scholars are also working to incorporate cultural considerations into their understanding of trauma. As described by Sharpe (2008), historical and collective experiences of trauma experienced by groups of people are referred to as cultural trauma (see Alexander, Eyerman, Giesen, Smelser, & Sztompka, 2001). For African Americans, experiences of cultural trauma include slavery, Jim Crow, lynching, and the enduring legacies of racism, discrimination, and marginalization. These experiences, situated in the collective memory and history of the African American community, echo across generations, informing and influencing the cultural and individual identities of African Americans and shaping their interactions with the world (Eyerman, 2001; Sharpe, 2008). In this way, cultural trauma is a contextual contributor to the practice of racial socialization among African American families (Bentley, Adams, & Stevenson, 2009; Neblett, Smalls, Ford, Nguyen, & Sellers, 2009). Yet, the historical experience of oppression can compound contemporary incidents of trauma experienced by black boys and men given their persistent marginalization. A trauma-informed approach gives us the theoretical tools to incorporate these understandings in our research, policy, and practice with boys and men in African American families.

Racial trauma is conceptualized as physical and psychological symptoms that people of color often experience after exposure to particularly stressful experiences of racism (Bryant-Davis & Ocampo, 2005; Carter, 2007; Helms, Nicolas, & Green, 2012; Jernigan et al., 2015). These exposures to racism can be personal, such as when one is the direct recipient of a racist comment or discriminatory behavior; or these exposures can be indirect, such as when one sees or learns about another racial minority being the target of a racist act (Jernigan & Henderson-Daniel, 2011). From the death of Michael Brown (age 18) in Ferguson, MO, to the beating of University of Virginia student, Martese Johnson (age 20), visible and often lethal violence enacted upon black lives, often black boys and men, by state authorities, has made indirect exposures to racism via news and social media a persistent aspect of daily life in America for the last several years. In fact, it was the 2010 murder of Trayvon Martin (age 18) in Sanford, Florida that gave birth to the Black Lives Matter movement.

Carter and Sant-Barket (2015) suggest racist encounters including police racial violence (Song Richardson, 2015) can result in Race-Based Traumatic Stress among African Americans, a unique form of psychological injury that produces emotional pain, anger, and anxiety as well as symptoms similar to PTSD, including intrusion, arousal, and avoidance (Carter, 2007). Continued research is needed to understand how these contemporary direct and indirect exposures to racial trauma impact the physical and psychosocial well-being of black boys and men, particularly in response to police profiling and brutality. Coupling Carter and Sant-Barket's (2015) Race-Based Traumatic Stress framework with Stevenson's (2014) racial literacy training could create unique opportunities to help boys and men in African American families manage the pain and rejection of racial trauma and dehumanization.

## An Integrated Approach to Affirming Humanity: Trauma-Informed PLAAY

A trauma-informed approach to research and intervention with boys and men in African American families positions us to recognize the life course and racialized traumas they experience. It also challenges us to resist retraumatization by incorporating this knowledge into our research, polices, and practices. For systems like law-enforcement, this might mean rigorous training of police officers to increase cultural competence and reduce racial bias. For black boys, it may mean interventions like Stevenson's Preventing Long-term Anger and Aggression in Youth (PLAAY) (Stevenson, 2014). This racial literacy intervention is designed to help black males "read, recast, and resolve racial stress" (Stevenson, Chap. 5, p. 58). For black families, it may include strategies such as racial socialization (Brown & Tylka, 2011; Stevenson, 1995, 1997; Stevenson & Arrington, 2009), which helps to foster the development of racial identity and buffer against the deleterious consequences of racist encounters.

The integration of trauma-informed, racial socialization, and racial literacy lenses into a theoretical framework may yield powerful results for the health and well-being of black boys and their families. The integration of these frameworks has the potential to equip black boys and young men with a unique coping skill set to protect against the internalization of racism, resist externalizations of racial stress and anger that could place them in danger (e.g. interactions with law enforcement), and identify healthy ways to process pain and trauma. At the same time, this integrated approach could train parents and adults across settings (e.g. youth serving organizations, schools, etc.) to identify trauma symptoms and to "teach racial, gender, and behavioral coping skills … to black youth" (Stevenson, Chap. 5, p. 66). Altogether, this framework would offer boys and young men in African American families resources to process the pain of racial trauma, cope with racialized encounters, and resist dehumanizing narratives. Future research and theorizing is needed to test the effectiveness of this integrated approach for addressing the complexity of traumas experienced by boys and men in African American families and for affirming the humanity of this group.

## References

Adams, E. J. (2010). *Healing invisible wounds: Why investing in trauma-informed care for children makes sense*. Washington, DC: Justice Policy Institute.

Alexander, J., Eyerman, R., Giesen, B., Smelser, N., & Sztompka, P. (2001). *Cultural trauma theory and applications*. Berkeley: University of California Press.

Bell, C. C., & Jenkins, E. J. (1991). Children and traumatic stress. *Journal of Health Care for the Poor and Underserved, 2*, 175–185.

Bentley, K. L., Adams, V. N., & Stevenson, H. C. (2009). Racial socialization: Roots, processes and outcomes. In H. Neville, B. Tynes, & S. Utsey (Eds.), *Handbook of African American psychology* (pp. 255–267). Thousand Oaks, CA: Sage Publications.

BlackPast.org. (n.d.). *(1964) Malcolm X's speech at the founding rally of the Organization of Afro-American Unity*. Retrieved October 2015, from http://www.blackpast.org/1964-malcolm-x-s-speech-founding-rally-organization-afro-american-unity#sthash.UpypCBRc.dpuf

Bloom, S. (1997). *Creating sanctuary: Toward the evolution of sane societies*. New York: Routledge.

Brown, D. L., & Tylka, T. L. (2011). Racial discrimination and resilience in African American young adults: Examining racial socialization as a moderator. *Journal of Black Psychology, 37*(3), 259–285.

Bryant-Davis, T., & Ocampo, C. (2005). Racist incident-based trauma. *Counseling Psychologist, 33*(4), 479–500.

Carter, R. T. (2007). Racism and psychological and emotional injury: Recognizing and assessing race-based traumatic stress. *Counseling Psychologist, 35*(1), 13–105.

Carter, R. T., & Sant-Barket, S. M. (2015). Assessment of the impact of racial discrimination and racism: How to use the race-based traumatic stress symptom scale in practice. *Traumatology, 21*(1), 32–39.

Centers for Disease Control and Prevention. (2015). *Leading causes of death by age group, black males-United States, 2010*. Retrieved December 2015, from http://www.cdc.gov/men/lcod/2010/lcodblackmales2010.pdf

Costello, E. J., Erkanli, A., Fairbank, J. A., & Angold, A. (2002). The prevalence of potentially traumatic events in childhood and adolescence. *Journal of Traumatic Stress, 15*(2), 99–112.

Eberhardt, J. L., Goff, P. A., Purdie, V. J., & Davies, P. G. (2004). Seeing black: Race, crime, and visual processing. *Journal of Personality and Social Psychology, 87*, 876–893.

Eitle, D., D'Alessio, S. J., & Stolzenberg, L. (2006). Economic segregation, race, and homicide. *Social Science Quarterly, 87*, 638–657.

Eyerman, R. (2001). *Cultural trauma: Slavery and the formation of African American identity*. New York: Cambridge University Press.

Felitti, V. J. (2002). The relationship of adverse childhood experiences to adult health: Turning gold into lead. *Zeitschrift für Psychosomatische Medizin und Psychotherapie, 48*, 359–369. Retrieved from http://www.ncbi.nlm.nih.gov/pubmed/12407494

Finkelhor, D., Ormrod, R. K., Turner, H., & Hamby, S. L. (2005). The victimization of children and youth: A comprehensive national survey. *Child Maltreatment, 10*(1), 5–25.

Fitzpatrick, K. M. (1993). Exposure to violence and presence of depression among low-income, African American youth. *Journal of Consulting and Clinical Psychology, 61*(3), 528–531.

Garbarino, J. (1995). *Raising children in a socially toxic environment*. San Francisco, CA: Jossey-Bass.

Garbarino, J. (1999). *Lost boys: Why our sons turn violent and how we can save them*. New York: Anchor Books.

Goff, P. A., Eberhardt, J. L., Williams, M. J., & Jackson, M. C. (2008). Not yet human: Implicit knowledge, historical dehumanization, and contemporary consequences. *Journal of Personality and Social Psychology, 94*(2), 292–306.

Goff, P. A., Jackson, M. C., Lewis Di Leone, B. A., Culotta, C. M., & DiTomasso, N. A. (2014). The essence of innocence: Consequences of dehumanizing black children. *Journal of Personality and Social Psychology, 106*(4), 526–545.

Haslam, N. (2006). Dehumanization: An integrative review. *Personality and Social Psychology Review, 10*(3), 252–264.

Helms, J. E., Nicolas, G., & Green, C. E. (2012). Racism and ethnoviolence as trauma: Enhancing professional and research training. *Traumatology, 18*(1), 65–74.

Hertz, M. F., Prothrow-Stith, D., & Chery, C. (2005). Homicide survivors: Research and practice implications. *American Journal of Preventive Medicine, 29*(5), 288–295.

Jenkins, E., Wang, E., & Turner, L. (2009). Traumatic events involving friends and family members in a sample of African American early adolescents. *American Journal of Orthopsychiatry, 79*(3), 398–406. doi:10.1037/a0016659.

Jernigan, M. M., Green, C. E., Pérez-Gualdrón, L., Liu, M., Henze, K. T., Chen, C., et al. (2015). *#racialtraumaisreal*. Institution for the Study and Promotion of Race and Culture. Retrieved October 2015, from http://www.bc.edu/content/dam/files/schools/lsoe_sites/isprc/pdf/racialtraumaisrealManuscript.pdf

Jernigan, M. M., & Henderson-Daniel, J. (2011). Racial trauma in the lives of Black children and adolescents: Challenges and clinical implications. *Journal of Child & Adolescent Trauma, 4*, 123–141.

Johnson, W. E. (2010). From shortys to old heads: Contemporary social trajectories of African American males across the life course. In W. E. Johnson (Ed.), *Social work with African American males*. New York: Oxford University Press.

LaVeist, T. A. (2005). *Minority populations and health: An introduction to health disparities in the United States*. San Francisco, CA: Jossey-Bass.

Mollica, R. F. (2009). *Healing invisible wounds: Paths to hope and recovery in a violent world*. Nashville, TN: Vanderbilt University Press.

Neblett, E. W., Smalls, C. P., Ford, K. R., Nguyen, H. X., & Sellers, R. M. (2009). Racial socialization and racial identity: African American parents' messages about race as precursors to identity. *Journal of Youth and Adolescence, 38*, 189–203.

Pager, D. (2005). Walking the talk: What employers say versus what they do. *American Sociological Review, 70*(3), 355–380.

Pager, D., Western, B., & Bonikowski, B. (2009). Discrimination in a low wage labor market: A field experiment. *American Sociological Review, 74*(5), 777–799.

Rich, J. A. (2009). *Wrong place, wrong time: Trauma and violence in the lives of African American men*. Baltimore: Johns Hopkins University Press.

Rich, J., Corbin, T., Bloom, S., Evans, S., & Wilson, A. (2009). *Healing the hurt: Approaches to the health of boys and young men of color*. The California Endowment Fund. Retrieved August 2010, from http://www.calendow.org/uploadedFiles/Publications/BMOC/Drexel%20-%20Healing%20the%20Hurt%20-%20Full%20Report.pdf

Sered, D. (2015). *Young men of color and the other side of harm: Addressing disparities in our responses to violence*. New York: Vera Institute of Justice. Retrieved February 2016, from http://www.vera.org/sites/default/files/resources/downloads/men-of-color-as-victims-of-violence-v3.pdf

Sharpe, T. (2008). Sources of support for African-American family members of homicide victims. *Journal of Ethnic & Cultural Diversity in Social Work, 17*(2), 197–216. doi:10.1080/15313200801947231.

Smith, J. R. (2015). Unequal burdens of loss: Examining the frequency and timing of homicide deaths experienced by young black men across the life course. *American Journal of Public Health, 105*(S3), S483–S490. doi:10.2105/AJPH.2014.302535. http://ajph.aphapublications.org/doi/abs/10.2105/AJPH.2014.302535.

Smith, J. R., & Patton, D. U. (2016). Posttraumatic stress symptoms in context: Examining trauma responses to violent exposure and homicide death among Black males in urban neighborhoods. *American Journal of Orthopsychiatry*. doi:10.1037/ort0000101. Advanced online publication.

Song Richardson, L. (2015). Police racial violence: Lessons learned from Social Psychology. *Fordham Law Review, 83*(6), 2961–2976.

Stevenson, H. C. (1995). The relationship of racial socialization and racial identity in African American adolescents. *Journal of Black Psychology, 21*(1), 49–70.

Stevenson, H. C. (1997). Managing anger: Protective, proactive, or adaptive racial socialization identity profiles and African-American manhood development. *Journal of Prevention & Intervention in the Community, 16*(1–2), 35–61.

Stevenson, H. C. (2014). *Promoting racial literacy in schools: Differences that make a difference*. New York: Teachers College Press.

Stevenson, H. C., & Arrington, E. G. (2009). Racial/ethnic socialization mediates perceived racism and identity experiences of African American students. *Cultural Diversity and Ethnic Mental Health, 15*(2), 125–136.

Substance Abuse and Mental Health Services Administration (SAMSHA). (2012). *Trauma definition*. Retrieved October 2014, from http://www.samhsa.gov/traumajustice/traumadefinition/definition.aspx

Substance Abuse and Mental Health Services Administration (SAMSHA). (2014). *Trauma-informed care in behavioral health services*. Treatment Improvement Protocol. TIP 57. HHS Publication No. (SMA) 13-4801. Rockville, MD: Substance Abuse and Mental Health Services. Retrieved October 2015, from http://store.samhsa.gov/shin/content/SMA14-4816/SMA14-4816.pdf

Substance Abuse and Mental Health Services Administration (SAMSHA). (2015). *Trauma-informed approach*. Retrieved December 2015, from http://www.samhsa.gov/nctic/trauma-interventions

van der Kolk, B. A., Roth, S., Pelcovitz, D., Sunday, S., & Spinazzola, J. (2005). Disorders of extreme stress: The empirical foundation of a complex adaptation to trauma. *Journal of Traumatic Stress, 18*(5), 389–399. doi:10.1002/jts.20047.

Wade, R., Jr., Shea, J. A., Rubin, D., & Wood, J. (2014). Adverse childhood experiences of low-income urban youth. *Pediatrics, 134*, e13–e20. doi:10.1542/peds.2013-2475.

Zinzow, H. M., Rheingold, A. A., Hawkins, A. O., Saunders, B. E., & Kilpatrick, D. G. (2009). Losing a loved one to homicide: Prevalence and mental health correlates in a national sample of young adults. *Journal of Traumatic Stress, 22*(1), 20–27. doi:10.1002/jts.

# Humanizing Developmental Science to Promote Positive Development of Young Men of Color

**Patrick H. Tolan**

Stevenson (Chap. 5) provides a compelling scientific framing of critical issues toward articulating a humanized narrative for understanding, supporting, and facilitating successful development of boys of color. He provides a thoughtful examination of the existing literature and enriches it with personal reflections. He exposes the absence of a humane-oriented frame for understanding how young men of color develop well and emphasizes that they do so while facing ongoing and substantial threats to their health and well-being, as well as to their mortality. Stevenson brings into relief what should already be prominent for us as scientists and as fellow humans: the need for a frame that acknowledges the singular developmental course and set of circumstances that characterize the lives of these men in our country at this time. Stevenson goes further and suggests important opportunities for constructing and applying that frame and provides multiple examples of how the required work is not exotic but rather is an empathic perspective arising through sound application of good methodology. We are reminded that typicality is an important developmental science interest and should be as much a priority for this population as any other. He identifies opportunities to conduct research and scientifically evaluated interventions that acknowledge the proliferation of successes that characterize the vast majority of experiences of young men of color, as well as the harm caused when we implicitly subscribe to the misrepresentation that it is most critical to understand their elevated risk in order to understand and aid their development. Utilizing multiple lines of evidence, Stevenson carefully argues for an alternative, humane correction to our practical and scientific narratives about the socialization pathways and threats to success affecting so many of these young men.

P.H. Tolan (✉)
Department of Psychiatry and Neurobehavioral Sciences, University of Virginia, Charlottesville, VA, USA
e-mail: pht6t@virginia.edu



L. Burton et al. (eds.), *Boys and Men in African American Families*, National Symposium on Family Issues 7, DOI 10.1007/978-3-319-43847-4_7

The purpose of this chapter is to bring my perspective as a developmental scientist, who has an ecological orientation, and react to Stevenson's persuasive argument, with the goal of augmenting suggestions he provides. These include theoretical and methodological principles and opportunities for pursuing excellent developmental research and sounder action to move from this impoverished and deficient state of understanding of young men of color to an empathic one.

## Humanizing Intervention Evaluation

Stevenson (Chap. 5) reports on effects of a set of empirically tested interventions, including examples from his own work. However, he does so in a manner that raises two important issues regarding scientific evaluation and experimental tests of interventions. This requires us to examine what we want to learn from conducting experimental tests and intervention evaluations, whether they are promoting healthy development, preventing risk development, and problematic outcomes, or treating, remediating, or managing resulting problems in functioning.

The first issue is to what extent we should judge effectiveness by primarily functional outcomes. At first glance, it seems obvious that interventions that (a) promote mental health, (b) prevent engagement in criminal behavior, or (c) help reduce or control post-traumatic stress disorder symptoms should be favored. These criteria of significant change in successful development and reduced problems in functioning should be the main concern. However, as Stevenson (Chap. 5) and others note elsewhere, there is a need to more carefully consider how those outcomes are achieved. Specifically, to what extent do program activities and content reflect appreciation for the life circumstances, capabilities, struggles, and the larger political forces that are determining stress, risk exposure, and self-understanding, thought to be the means to promoting effective development (Watts, Diemer, & Voigt, 2011)? Given that the prevailing orientation is to evaluate interventions apart from recognition of the sociopolitical context, there is high probability that much of what may be identified as working (having statistically significant effects), if examined through a cultural and political lens, has only marginal or superficial impact and remains dehumanizing of young men of color (Mistry & Dutta, 2015). This is because the participants are seen as victims who need social welfare, or they are seen as potential threats who need to be directed away from trouble, rather than as fellow humans with particular struggles, extensive competencies, and who are deserving of interventions that validate and guide from an authentic and empowering relationship. As Stevenson (Chap. 5) notes, there are several promising mechanisms of developmental influence which can be used to refocus interventions. They might also be valuable for evaluating effects of interventions beyond basic prevalence changes in problems. These mechanisms include agency and self affirmations, racial socialization and identity approaches, and those that are oriented around the threats and strains faced by boys of color in our educational, health care, child welfare, and police/juvenile justice systems. If the interventions are intended to enhance development or provide the foundation for capabilities to flourish, then it seems that evaluations need to go beyond noting statistical differences in functioning indicators in order to show how these outcomes rest on respectful, affirming, agency-supporting engagement of youth.

The second humanizing intervention study and evaluation issue Stevenson (Chap. 5) brings into focus is the need to consider racial socialization as a central framework in attempts to understand and affect development of young men of color. This question can be understood as two foci within his chapter. First, he suggests the need for more recognition of racial socialization as innervating development of these young men and includes the example of his own experience talking with his son about how to handle racial discrimination and overt hostility.

Stevenson (Chap. 5) suggests that racial socialization means more than training youth how to avoid, withstand, and overcome racially based threats, insults, and harm. Rather, it must also include helping youth develop an understanding of racial issues that is affirming and informing about race in their lives. This includes explicit support and skills training for a nuanced affirming identify. In other words, interventions need to be built from within the developmental situation and attendant to the converging systems of influence on young men of color. Consequently, racial socialization/literacy is a major feature in program organization and ethos. This goes well beyond cultural adaptation of programs found to have effects with other populations.

Stevenson (Chap. 5) also identifies the importance of influencing the adults and systems in the lives of these young men as important foci for racial socialization. Teachers, police, and others should be engaged in acknowledging and changing dehumanizing, alienating, and oppressive assumptions they hold about young men of color. While skills for managing these negative experiences are needed, in order to have substantial impact, we need to create humane interventions and recognize where responsibility for changing injustices lie. If we are to enable parents, teachers, police, and others who so critically affect the lives of these young men, the racial socialization interventions must aim beyond young men of color to these influencers. In fact, it may be that interventions that promote agency about racial socialization from within a framework of humanizing concern for boys of color may have substantial benefits that typical sensitivity training or admonishments against prejudice may not.

## Rehumanizing Developmental Pathways Research Narratives

Rehumanizing intervention effects studies and evaluations is an important message in Stevenson's call. A related one is to attune the narrative or themes characterizing our studies of development, particularly in relation to young men of color. This is poignantly represented in Stevenson's (Chap. 5) exchange with his son, as they both struggle to cope with tragedy-producing prejudices to manage fear, bolster confidence, and learn personal responsibility. Turning to technical challenges, Stevenson identifies several tasks including creating reliable and valid measures that can inform a shifted narrative centered around risk and protective factors of importance: capability, challenge, agency, oppression, perseverance and transcendence, and practical safety in a hostile world. He appropriately identifies topics, constructs, and pathway characterizations needed to move away from generic models of risk. As can be noted in this coverage, in most risk models there is at most, a brief reference to racial discrimination. Also, these models are heavily deficit-focused in explaining developmental variation. Stevenson outlines alternative frameworks that characterize how families and youth of color try to make their lives work well within a racialized understanding of development (with attending variations in what is meant by "making life work well"). Several valuable examples of topics and even developmental themes and courses are provided. For example, it is suggested that parenting black males should incorporate racial socialization with a historical and sociological basis for discriminatory threats. It should simultaneously help explain necessary coping responses, Stevenson posits, yet also be informed by adolescent receptivity to parental direction and authority. Another example is how parenting can bolster pride and confidence, provide practical guidance, properly externalize the basis for these challenges, and acknowledge threats, such as racial profiling and hostile or alienating orientation from teachers, police, and others.

One issue of importance for scientific progress in understanding and facilitating positive development of young men of color (and of other groups as well) is how to relate the distinctions and similarities of development of groups. Is it best to form distinct streams of understanding focused within specific social classes, ethnic groups, or cultural orientations that can then be abstracted into more general developmental principles? Or still, in order to explain variation, should the approach be to seek more general or universal experiences, socialization influences, and pathways of development, viewing differences in opportunity, threats, types of stress and strain and supports and coping efficacy, and alignment of influencing systems (Williams, Tolan, Durkee, Amir, & Anderson, 2012)? These are not simply questions of sensitivity, but also affect realities such as what studies are funded, how different scientific activities and findings are related and organized for significance, and how scientists share understanding and work in conjunction toward meaningful progress. Perhaps most importantly, this question seems to be one that helps keep culturally informed and minority focused studies apart from fundamental developmental research (Williams et al., 2012). For example, while Stevenson (Chap. 5) focuses on black male youth, much of what he notes is arguably applicable to men of color as well. Similarly, much of the literature has not been framed with intention to speak about a specific group within a specific socio-ecological niche but to focus as an example of more general influences. Should specific understanding of race or ethnic groups (or other culturally important distinctions such as religion) necessitate distinguishing specific narratives, measures, pathways, and literature? Clearly, the answer is not to simply reduce distinctions to variations around a singular set of experiences, developmental influences, or person-environment alignment, but there are good reasons for differences and a need for discourse about how variation should be framed and how distinction and sameness/continuity should be influencing study. This is an ongoing issue, one that is not readily approached in our field, let alone likely to reach resolve soon. However, the issue is one that merits more attention and direct discussion as it can hamper understanding and the ability to aid development of young men of color as well as others.

Closely related to this issue and prominent in Stevenson's chapter, is the value of intersectionality in framing developmental studies and narratives about development (Cole, 2009). An important consideration when determining how distinct the narratives/models should be for African-American young men is how valuable is it to view this narrative as the intersection of race, gender, and age. To what extent is it more fruitful to unpack, multi-dimensionalize, and apply the current narratives and Stevenson's humanizing alternatives? Is it more informative, useful, and impactful if we focus instead on the singularity of this group's situation, issues, needs, and outcomes? How is the information provided here and the focus on young men of color enhanced if the issues affecting women of color are juxtaposed and seen as similar in many ways? Might such a framework reduce the distinctions of development of young men of color to simply that of many groups with variations in privilege, power, oppression, and developmental pathways? How might the intersection of social class and race enable a more humanizing and insightful understanding of young men of color? Or would this obfuscate the issue by painting the challenges outlined by Stevenson as related to relative economic standing, and therefore a variant on those affecting others of similar income levels? One advantage of applying an intersectional framework is that the approach permits relating the specific to the general in a more direct way and seems to be less susceptible to presumptions about what identity bases are most important. Another advantage of an intersectional framework is its usefulness for combating the privileged experience of some ethnic groups (e.g. white western Europeans), genders (males), and those with wealth as healthy, typical, or protypical. Might intersectionality promote humanizing developmental narratives by shifting from a privileged intersection to one of more equity?

## Humanizing the Developmental Scientist

Stevenson (Chap. 5) has provided another important contribution along with pointing to the need for humanizing intervention and developmental studies. He provides an eloquent example of the person of the scientist as present *and* as a positive presence in the scientific discourse. When I read his chapter and began formulating my comments, my first tendency was to agree with Stevenson on the view that focusing on person and close relationship levels is misdirecting. It can be compared to tinkering with the deckchairs when what is required is attending to how the sails are set and what leaks might be causing the ship to sink. He voiced concern that I have toiled with over decades. That is, does adhering to a stress-coping-support approach to resilience, risk, and successful development in trying to understand and provide some potentially useful interventions for families raising children within the inner-city lead to focusing on just managing injustices (Tolan, Guerra, & Montaini-Klovdahl, 1997)? Is the "more stress" framework for understanding the issues of development actually distracting, or is it being co-opted and failing to focus on important catalysts of development? By bringing a personal voice into a broad critical analysis, Stevenson reminds us that each of us need to be cognizant of our socio-politico-legal reality in relation to the enormous potential for harm that is allowed because the victims are African-American males. Moreover, when one considers within the pervasive, perhaps primary theme in the historical record of Europeans' tendency to wage war, colonize, and enslave indigenous people, all in the name of cultural superiority (civilizing), usually ignoring more base motives of greed, it seems compelling to stay focused at the societal organization level. This is a matter of political action and policy implementation with hopes of future generations living by different rules and laws, experiencing diversity first hand as an enriching commonplace aspect of life, and holding equity as a cherished value. And, as a developmental scientist, perhaps I should not turn to my skills and disciplinary practices as a scientist, but instead work in service of others more skilled in helping to destroy racism, reduce inequities, and promote justice. Perhaps what I should do is say to my economist, lawyer, and politician friends who see developmental science as not useful for progress with these problems, "You are right about what is needed and how change can occur. How can I help you?"

We might conclude that elegant research, even grand intervention studies, will not have much substantive impact. We might theorize that operationalization and theoretical refinements will not shift the stories represented in Stevenson's chapter. However, I think this is not the case. There are some key contributions that can come from developmental science. In part, this is because I see no signs that our society is going to transform any time soon nor realize the social and political shifts that would erase the particular threats and pathway issues that Stevenson outlines.

## *Producing Knowledge About How and Why Most Men of Color Succeed*

Demographic and developmental psychology studies document that while facing more risks and higher morbidity and mortality rates than other groups in our society, most young men of color develop successfully as denoted by indicators of personal relationships and life satisfaction, occupational and income benchmarks, and health indicators (Toldson & Morton, 2012). This does not mean one is ignoring the disproportionality of exposure to risk and harmful effects, nor does it mean ignoring the rates of incarceration, school failure, and unemployment that are elevated for this group. It means, with consideration, that we must seek information about how the majority of these young men succeed by personal and societal standards. How might such information inform understanding, action, and policy? The current, almost singular focus, on documenting disparities and explanations of elevated risk distracts us from many promising actions and better understanding. What might this shift in focus tell us, and how could those results act as a humanized counter narrative?

There can be debate around whether this focus is best approached as a resilience story or if it mainly provides an understanding of typicality of development and critical components of health for this population (as well as enriching our narrow understanding of typicality and health in other populations). Nevertheless, this is a crucial contribution that may best come from developmental scientists.

## *Shifting Intervention Framing from "Undoing" Risk to Promoting Effective Development*

A second contribution that developmental scientists can make, even if the critical influences are macro and beyond our usual focus of study, is to help shift how interventions are formulated. Currently, the prevailing approach is to document risk factors, or those characteristics statistically related to greater probability of a problem (outcome of interest), and create interventions to reduce that risk factor (or provide compensatory skills). Consequently, disproportionality will be decreased. However, this approach presumes that by studying how problems arise we know what will prevent or correct them. This approach has been predominant in justice seeking and in psychopathology intervention approaches for many years. Instead, there may be more informative approaches for identifying circumstances, supports, skills, strengths, and microsystem features related to positive development, to lower the typical morbidity, and to increase success based on social functioning and health benchmarks. There is a growing roster of prevention and social and emotional promotion programs that have empirically shown to reduce risk and have positive developmental effects. The components and the processes that comprise these interventions are very promising bases for shifting intervention design from undoing risk to promoting effective development.

## *Producing Scientific Results to Humanize Developmental Science About Young Men of Color*

Often there is no empirical basis for linking what explains problems and what should be done to address them. This may be a presumption that is not correct. Moreover, it seems shortsighted to overlook how development is successful or what circumstances, opportunities, supports, capabilities, skills and experiences characterize those who do not have problematic outcomes. How might an analysis of what goes well, inform interventions which promote positive development? For example, knowledge that implicit bias affects teacher and police reactions tells us little about how to remove that burden from the developmental challenges of boys of color and their families. What might we do if instead we studied what helps teachers and police to be unbiased in perception and actions?

Specifically, I suggest a concerted effort to obtain and produce sound knowledge about several topics:

- How changing demographics and diversity in our society are likely to affect developmental narratives, pathways, and identities, and how these in turn might promote values of diversity and equity.
- International approaches to understanding group differences, inequities, and typicality to help enrich narratives and the kinds of populations used to describe and define typicality, healthy development, and relative stress and resources.
- Changing roles of men, male identity, and inequalities and how the concurrent shifts in these are intersecting in relation to development of young men of color.
- Shifting age related population trends and how these affect the relative salience of traditional and more modern values, practices, and mores.
- Under what circumstances and with what practices are impositions of inequality in justice, education, health care, and social life minimized?
- Which legal and regulatory policies produce reduced or minimal inequities? How do practices that enact such policies affect inequities? What are examples or predictors of low injustice, inequity, and discrimination (or even the absence of such)?

## Conclusion

Somewhere between naiveté and cynicism is a pathway of important work and improved thinking that can rehumanize our understanding of young men of color. It is one that can shift the all too common narrative that focuses too much on simply coping with injustice and uncontrollable harm. As Stevenson (Chap. 5) outlines and argues cogently, this path depends on reconnecting understanding of young men of color to responsibility and care for them through reflection and action that shifts how we developmental scientists organize and focus our studies. Among the guiding lights he provides are challenges to the way we organize and focus interventions, how we evaluate them as effective, what developmental narrative frames our studies, and how we emphasize connection, caring, and capability over alienation, rejection, and failure as central to our studies and their purpose. Moreover, his chapter brings into relief important and very controversial (and often under-considered) issues of how much we should view boys of color as a population distinct from others who share some demographic characteristics and how typicality and variation are to be understood as part of a coherent developmental science.

## References

Cole, E. M. (2009). Intersectionality and research in psychology. *American Psychologist, 64*, 170–180.

Mistry, J., & Dutta, R. (2015). Human development and culture: Conceptual and methodological issues. In W. F. Overton & P. C. Molenaar (Eds.), *Handbook of child psychology and developmental science: Volume 1: Theory and method* (7th ed., pp. 369–407). Hoboken, NJ: Wiley.

Tolan, P. H., Guerra, N. G., & Montaini-Klovdahl, L. (1997). Staying out of harm's way: Coping and the development of inner-city children. In S. A. Wolchik & I. N. Sandler (Eds.), *Handbook of children's coping: Linking theory and intervention* (pp. 453–479). New York: Plenum Press.

Toldson, I. A., & Morton, J. (2012). Black people don't read: The definitive guide to dismantling stereotypes and negative statistical claims about Black Americans. *Amazon's CreateSpace*.

Watts, R. J., Diemer, M. A., & Voigt, A. M. (2011). Critical consciousness: Current status and future directions. *New Directions for Child and Adolescent Development, 134*, 43–57.

Williams, J. L., Tolan, P. H., Durkee, M. I., Amir, G. F., & Anderson, R. E. (2012). Integrating racial and ethnic identity research into developmental understanding of adolescents. *Child Development Perspectives, 6*(3), 304–311.

# Part III
# Role of Families in the Well-Being of African American Men

# Families, Prisoner Reentry, and Reintegration

**David J. Harding, Jeffrey D. Morenoff, Cheyney C. Dobson, Erin B. Lane, Kendra Opatovsky, Ed-Dee G. Williams, and Jessica Wyse**

## Introduction

Since the mid-1970s the United States has experienced an enormous rise in incarceration. Whereas in 1975 the population in jails and prisons on any given day was roughly 400,000 people, by 2003 this number had increased more than fivefold to 2.1 million people (Western, 2006). Although the upward trend in incarceration has begun to level off in the last few years, the number of individuals in state and federal prisons was over 1.6 million at the end of 2009 (West, Sabol, & Greenman, 2010). Compared to other nations and compared to earlier periods in US history, current incarceration rates are unprecedented (Raphael & Stoll, 2009), leading to what some have termed the era of mass imprisonment (Garland, 2001; Mauer & Chesney-Lind, 2002).

---

The original version of this chapter was revised. An erratum to this chapter can be found at DOI 10.1007/978-3-319-43847-4_17

D.J. Harding (✉)
Department of Sociology, University of California Berkeley, Berkeley, CA, USA
e-mail: dharding@berkeley.edu

J.D. Morenoff
Population Studies Center, University of Michigan, Ann Arbor, MI, USA

C.C. Dobson • K. Opatovsky
Department of Sociology, University of Michigan, Ann Arbor, MI, USA

E.B. Lane
Department of Sociology, University of Michigan, Ann Arbor, MI, USA

E.-D.G. Williams
School of Social Work and Department of Sociology, University of Michigan, Ann Arbor, MI, USA

J. Wyse
Center to Improve Veteran Involvement in Care (CIVIC), Veteran's Affairs Portland Healthcare System, Portland, OR, USA



L. Burton et al. (eds.), *Boys and Men in African American Families*, National Symposium on Family Issues 7, DOI 10.1007/978-3-319-43847-4_8

The rise in incarceration has been disproportionately experienced by minorities, particularly young black men, and those with low levels of education. One in nine African-American men age 20–34 is in prison on any given day (Pew Center on the States, 2008), and among those with less than a high school degree the number is approximately one in three (Western, 2006). Over half of African-American men with less than a high school degree go to prison at some time in their lives (Pettit & Western, 2004). Declining labor force participation by young African-American men during the late 1990s, when a strong economy pulled other low-skill workers into the labor market, has been attributed to incarceration and its effects (Holzer, Offner, & Sorensen, 2005). Alexander (2010), Wacquant (2001), and others have argued that the prison system now plays the same role in racial domination and exclusion as slavery, Jim Crow, and the ghetto did in previous historical periods, separating African-Americans from whites, tainting blacks with a mark of inferiority, and providing a source of cheap and exploited labor. According to this framework, the black ghetto and the penitentiary are linked, both by high rates of movement between poor black neighborhoods and prisons and by their common symbolic status as locations of exclusion, stigma, and social control.

An extensive research literature suggests that incarceration has exacerbated already existing racial and socioeconomic inequalities by making those who are already disadvantaged even more so (for a review, see Wakefield & Uggen, 2010). Released prisoners are disadvantaged educationally, economically, and socially (Visher & Travis, 2003). The flow of people into and out of prisons has contributed to increasing inequality in recent decades, primarily by reducing opportunities for employment and lowering wages among former prisoners, but also by decreasing the prevalence of two-parent families (Western, 2006). The stigma of serving time in prison is the strongest force identified thus far driving these effects (Holzer, Raphael, & Stoll, 2004, 2007; Pager, 2007; Pager, Western, & Bonikowski, 2009). As a result, the families that are most impacted by incarceration are faced with reintegrating individuals who often have poor prospects for employment.

Because almost all prisoners are eventually released, "mass incarceration" has in turn produced a steep rise in the number of individuals reentering society and undergoing the process of social and economic reintegration (Travis, 2005). Over 700,000 individuals are now released from state and federal prisons each year (West et al., 2010). As a result, the prison boom was accompanied by an even larger boom in community corrections. The number of individuals on parole and probation increased dramatically, and one in 31 American adults is either on probation, parole, or in prison or jail on any given day. Moreover, racial and class disparities similar to those for incarceration are also evident for community corrections supervision (Pew Center on the States, 2009). As Wacquant (2001) notes, the carceral state now extends further into the community via probation and parole supervision than it did a few decades ago.

Black former prisoners face particular challenges in reentry and reintegration. The stigma of incarceration in the labor market is especially strong for blacks, who are doubly disadvantaged by both their race and their criminal record (Pager, 2003). Black former prisoners are more likely to return to more disadvantaged neighborhoods where crime and violence are more common and unemployment rates are higher (Harding, Morenoff, & Herbert, 2013; Massoglia, Firebaugh, & Warner, 2013). As we document below, black former prisoners are more disadvantaged when it comes to work experience and education and have spent more time in prison than their white counterparts. Prior research has also shown that blacks are typically excluded from social networks that lead to blue collar jobs (Royster, 2003), and young black men often face harsh treatment in various parts of the criminal justice system (Rios, 2011).

The effects of incarceration are felt not just by the individuals who go to prison but by their families as well. As we discuss later, a nascent literature on the consequences of incarceration for the families of prisoners documents economic, social, and health effects of having a family member incarcerated. Yet the same families who experience such effects *during* prison also play a primary role in assisting their loved ones in the process of reintegration *after* prison. In this chapter, we explore the role of family, broadly defined, in prisoner reintegration. More specifically, we attempt to understand what kinds of family supports, obligations, and conflicts enhance or hinder reentry and reintegration after prison.

We view reintegration as a process that unfolds over time—often in fits and starts—in which an individual gradually establishes social ties to friends and family and comes to participate in social institutions such as the labor market, educational and health care institutions, religious organizations, civic participation, and community life more generally. Desistance from crime and avoidance of drug and alcohol abuse are critical foundations for prisoner reintegration, but they do not constitute reintegration on their own. Reintegration involves first finding ways to meet basic material needs for food and housing and, ideally, expands to encompass economic stability and mobility and becoming a full participant in social, economic, political, and cultural life of one's family, community, and nation. In this chapter we examine the initial stages of reintegration, focusing on early markers of stability and economic reintegration as well as avoidance of crime and substance abuse.

To understand the role of families in the process of reintegration, we draw upon analyses of two data sources. One is a statistical analysis of the associations between family context (as measured by household composition or type of institutional housing) and four outcomes (residential stability, employment, arrests, and substance use), using administrative data on a sample of individuals paroled in Michigan in 2003 and followed over time. The other is a qualitative analysis of prospective, longitudinal in-depth interviews with 22 individuals released from prisons in Michigan in 2007–2008 and followed for up to 3 years. These data provide two very different but complementary windows into how and why families enhance or hinder reintegration. The statistical analysis investigates the role of living in different family contexts as well as living in institutional settings for reintegration outcomes. The qualitative analysis provides insight on the processes and mechanisms through which family relationships, broadly defined, affect prisoner reintegration.

## Families and Incarceration: During and After Prison

### *Complexity and Fluidity in Defining Family and Home*

As we consider the role of families in prisoner reintegration, we define family broadly, to include not just parents, siblings, and romantic partners but also more distant relatives and non-blood relations that nonetheless serve the same social and economic functions as family members. This reflects the reality of the diversity of meanings of family and home among former prisoners. For example, the first residences where Michigan parolees lived after prison, based on our administrative data, include living with parents (33.6 %), with spouses or partners (11.4 %), siblings or cousins (11.2 %), with other family members from a generation older than the parolee (6.3 %), living alone (6.0 %), with an acquaintance or friend (2.9 %), and with an adult child or younger relative (1.3 %). This private, non-institutional housing only accounts for about three quarters of first residences. The remainder move into institutional housing when they leave prison, either because they cannot find anyone willing to take them in, or because such residences are required by the parole board. These residences include criminal justice institutions similar to halfway houses (13.1 %), hotels (5.2 %), homeless shelters (3.3 %), and substance abuse or mental health treatment programs (3.6 %). Finally, a further aspect of family life after prison is that only a quarter of parolees in our data return to the same residential address where they lived before prison. Although in some cases their families have moved while they were in prison, former prisoners are often negotiating new places in households rather than returning to familiar households.

Even these numbers understate the diversity and fluidity of family life after prison. Qualitative work by Braman (2004) and Leverentz (2014), for example, shows that extended and non-nuclear families are common, and that there is a great deal of flux in household composition. Indeed, the median former prisoner in our Michigan data moves residences two and half times per year in the first 2 years after release (Harding et al., 2013). By any standard, this is a remarkable level of residential instability. Some of this residential mobility is surely positive—moves from institutional or group housing to live with family, or moves to better housing or better neighborhoods as former prisoners find work. Yet, this figure also suggests the fragility of living arrangements, and that integration into a household takes considerable time for many former prisoners. Our estimates indicate that about a quarter of this residential instability is generated by the criminal justice system in the form of short-term custody for parole violations (Harding et al., 2013).

### *Effects of Incarceration on Family Members*

Family reintegration after prison cannot be understood without considering the period of incarceration and how it is experienced by both prisoners and their family members. Prior research on families and incarceration has focused mainly on the impact of the incarceration of parents (mostly fathers) on children and their mothers (e.g. Harris & Miller, 2003). One set of consequences is economic. Half of fathers in prison were the primary breadwinner in the family before their incarceration (Wakefield & Wildeman, 2013). The incarceration of a parent can also interfere with the non-incarcerated partner's economic stability, increasing the risk that the partner will become unemployed, experience housing insecurity, and receive public assistance (National Research Council of the National Academies, 2014; Wakefield & Wildeman, 2013). Families must deal with these economic hardships while also supporting their incarcerated loved one (Braman, 2004; Comfort, 2007). Additional expenses include commissary accounts, care packages, and the cost of prison phone calls and visits (Grinstead, Faigekes, Bancroft, & Zack, 2001).

The incarceration of a father also has profound health and developmental consequences for children. Mothers experience greater depression and anxiety when the father of their children goes to prison (Wildeman, Schnittker, & Turney, 2012) and exhibit more neglect and harsh parenting (Turney, 2014c). The incarceration of a father can trigger feelings of shame and embarrassment in children and erode trust between children and fathers (National Research Council of the National Academies, 2014). Paternal incarceration is also associated with higher rates of learning disabilities, attention deficit disorder, behavioral or conduct problems, developmental delays, and speech or language problems (Haskins, 2015; Turney, 2014b, 2015b; Wildeman & Turney, 2014). Children of incarcerated fathers enter school less prepared to learn, are more likely to be placed in special education, and are more likely to be held back (Haskins, 2014; Turney & Haskins, 2014). On the other hand, the incarceration of a father with a severe substance addiction or pattern of violent behavior can benefit children (National Research Council of the National Academies, 2014). Another key finding is that incarceration tends to lead to reduced contact between fathers and children after release. Much of this reduction can be explained by the dissolution of relationships between mothers and the incarcerated fathers (Turney, 2015a) and the formation of new romantic relationships for the mothers (Turney & Wildeman, 2013). In addition, paternal incarceration leads to less child contact with paternal but not maternal grandparents (Turney, 2014a).

## *Family Relationships During Incarceration*

For many prisoners, incarceration has a profound effect on their social ties, to both family and non-family. In our qualitative data, we see a significant drop-off in social ties to non-family members and a corresponding increase in the intensity and importance of familial relationships that do survive incarceration. Prisoners look forward to release with optimism but also trepidation. They want to make a new life for themselves, and they know that family support will be critical. At the same time, they worry that rebuilding and maintaining those relationships will be challenging, especially given the ways they have disappointed their families in the past. As one of our subjects put it just days before his release, "In prison I can't disappoint anyone. Out there I can."

This intensification of family ties can lead to real changes in relationship behaviors during prison. In her ethnography of the partners of men incarcerated at San Quentin, Comfort (2007) documents an increase in communication and emotional responsiveness among male prisoners. Moreover, Comfort (2007) and Braman (2004) show how family members support their incarcerated relatives both economically and emotionally, and also play a role in preparing them for release. Family members provide a link to the outside world, brokering relationships with social services, educational programs, and sometimes employers in preparation for release.

Although much is made of the physical deprivations of prison life and the threat of violence that prisoners face, our qualitative data also show that separation from family produces at least as much suffering among prisoners. Mostly cut off from regular direct contact, prisoners yearn for information about their loved ones and experience stress over missing important life events. In prison, for example, letters from loved ones written on paper—a seemingly lost art form—become prized possessions, tangible symbols of connections. As one of our subjects explained, "Mail is everything when you're in the joint, when the officer passed me my mail. There ain't no worse feeling than when he just walks right past your bunk."

## Conceptual Framework: Family Effects on Reentry and Reintegration

Our conceptual framework draws from and expands upon our prior work on romantic relationships and desistance from crime after prison (Wyse, Harding, & Morenoff, 2014), which drew on criminological theories of desistance, primarily social control theory augmented with strain theory and social support theory. In Sampson and Laub's (1993) influential formulation of social control theory, marriage is viewed as a key source of informal social control for criminally involved men. We start from this conceptual origin by discussing the key tenets of social control theory, particularly as it relates to marriage, the primary family relationship to which it has been applied. Because marriage rates among the justice-system-involved population are extremely low in our contemporary period, we describe how the theory can be broadened to understand the role of families more generally in post-prison reintegration. We develop a typology of potential processes and mechanisms through which families may affect prisoner reintegration by drawing on additional theoretical frameworks and concepts.

### *Informal Social Control, Marriage, and Desistance*

One of the most influential theories for research on prisoner reentry is Sampson and Laub's account of how informal social control changes over a person's life course (Laub & Sampson, 2003; Sampson & Laub, 1993). This framework emphasizes the importance of social bonds—particularly those resulting from marriage, employment, and military service—in deterring criminality and encouraging desistance (Laub, Nagin, & Sampson, 1998; Laub & Sampson, 2003; Sampson, Laub, & Wimer, 2006). These bonds can be strengthened by key life events, so-called "turning points" that potentially increase informal social control by altering daily routines and stabilizing pro-social roles. Other accounts emphasize changes that former offenders experience in their personal identities or self-concepts (Maruna, 2001) as another key factor influencing informal social control. The theoretical importance of informal social control has generated considerable scholarship on the role that romantic relationships play in desistance from crime. The formation of high quality marital relationships is understood to be one of the key potential "turning points" in desisting from crime (Bersani, Laub, & Nieuwbeerta, 2009; King, Massoglia, & MacMillan, 2007, Laub & Sampson, 2003; Sampson et al., 2006; Sampson & Laub, 1993; Warr, 1998).

While marriage is increasingly rare among criminal offenders and returning prisoner (Giordano, Cernkovich, & Rudolph, 2002; Western, 2006), it is nonetheless important to consider the theoretical arguments for why marriage may promote informal social control and encourage desistance (Sampson et al., 2006), as the protective pathways may be present in other familial relationships as well. First, marriage increases the potential cost of crime because criminal activity may threaten the bond of attachment and lead to its dissolution (Hirschi, 1969; Sampson & Laub, 1993). Second, marriage may keep ex-offenders away from situations and social relationships that present criminal opportunities and influence, propositions that are also consistent with routine activities theory and differential association theory (Cohen & Felson, 1979; Osgood, Wilson, O'Malley, Bachman, & Johnston, 1996; Warr, 1998). Such changes can have a particularly strong dampening effect on crime for men, who otherwise would be more likely to either associate with criminal peers or put themselves in places and situations that present greater criminal opportunities. Third, marriage provides structure and supervision, particularly when the partner expects the offender to have a legitimate job, contribute income, and support the household, and to avoid activities that might threaten the family's economic stability. Fourth, marriage can provide both partners with identities that are inconsistent with criminal behavior. Marriage may change the way people see themselves, their responsibilities, and their relationships with others, strengthening the ability of conventional norms to govern behavior, lest criminal activity conflict with role expectations, such as that of the provider.

A broader limitation of informal social control theory as it has been applied to studying prisoner reentry is that it focuses attention on life events that strengthen social bonds—such as marriage, enlisting in the military, and steady employment—that are relatively rare in this population and thus do not provide very much analytical leverage for understanding what helps or hinders efforts to desist from crime in the contemporary period. Former prisoners have a very difficult time getting jobs, and even the fortunate ones who find jobs have a difficult time holding on to them (National Research Council of the National Academies, 2014). Military service is closed to most convicted felons, and marriage is rare in this subpopulation (Greenfeld & Snell, 1999; Western, 2006). Thus, we argue that it is important for research on post-prison experiences of ex-offenders to consider a wider set of social relationships, social contexts, and institutions to understand the contemporary experience of prisoner reentry and reintegration. Here we focus on family contexts, relationships, and roles.

## *Toward a Conceptual Framework for Families and Reintegration*

We draw on the theoretical concepts discussed thus far, augmented with other criminological theories, to develop a typology of processes and mechanisms through which families may affect reintegration outcomes like those we examine in this chapter. Table 1 lists the family processes that we argue are most critical to prisoner reintegration and categorizes them based on the theoretical pathways through which they are connected to reintegration outcomes: material circumstances, informal social control, or emotional support/stress. Within each category, we identify

**Table 1** Theoretical mechanisms through which family relationships may affect prisoner reintegration

| Mechanisms through which family relationships may affect prisoner reintegration | Direction of influence on residential stability | Direction of influence on desistance | Direction of influence on employment | Theoretical traditions |
|---|---|---|---|---|
| *Material circumstances* | | | | |
| Instrumental support | + | + | + | Control theory, strain theory |
| Role strain | – | – | + | Strain theory |
| *Informal social control* | | | | |
| Monitoring/supervision | ? | + | + | Control theory, differential association, routine activities |
| Coercion/negative social control | ? | – | – | Strain theory, differential social support and coercion |
| *Emotional supports and stressors* | | | | |
| Expressive support | + | + | + | Control theory, strain theory, social support theory |
| Relationship stress | – | – | – | Control theory, strain |

*Source*: Adapted from Wyse et al. (2014)

processes that create both positive and negative influences on the main reintegration outcomes in our study: residential mobility, desistance/recidivism, and employment. It is important to note that most, if not all, relationships generate a mix of positive and negative influences on reintegration. For example, even the most emotionally supportive relationship can at times create emotional stress, and the provision of material supports for an extended period of time may be critical to material survival but also may generate role strain, especially for men whose conventional role within the family has been economic provider. In other words, this is a typology of processes, not a typology of relationships. How a relationship with a family member or a role in a household influences reintegration will ultimately depend on the characteristics of the family member, the nature of the relationship, and the characteristics of the former prisoner. We expect that gender will be one particularly salient characteristic, given the continued importance of gender for family roles.

**Material Resources** Instrumental support is defined as "the use of the relationship as a means to a goal" (Lin, 1986). Family relationships can be a source of instrumental support by providing material aid (such as money or housing), or advice and guidance toward achieving specific goals. Such support can be crucial for former prisoners who enter the community often with little more than the clothes on their backs, yet require housing as well as transportation, food and spending money almost immediately. Our prior qualitative analysis of how former prisoners make ends meet after prison shows that economic security and stability was impossible without familial support. Moreover, all of our subjects who achieved some form of upward social mobility did so primarily through the assistance of family members, who helped them to secure stable jobs that provided a toehold in the formal labor market and opportunities for upward mobility (Harding, Wyse, Dobson, & Morenoff, 2014).

Housing is a key form of material support provided by families. Formerly incarcerated persons face a unique set of obstacles to finding and maintaining secure and stable housing, including prejudice and discrimination against those with a criminal record, legal barriers, and hurdles stemming from the direct involvement of the criminal justice system in the lives of former prisoners (e.g. restrictions on where one can live and who one can live with, custodial sanctions for parole violations). Housing insecurity and homelessness have important consequences for returning prisoners. Some researchers have argued that secure housing is the most pressing, immediate, short-term need for returning prisoners (Lutze, Rosky, & Hamilton, 2014; Metraux & Culhane, 2004; Roman & Travis, 2006;), and parole officials cite housing as the biggest need for parolees (Petersilia, 2003). Moreover, stable housing may be the foundation upon which other aspects of reintegration rely (Bradley, Oliver, Richardson, & Slayter, 2001): it can be difficult for returning prisoners to find and maintain stable employment, maintain family connections, receive physical and mental health care, and avoid substance use without stable housing (Lutze et al., 2014).

However, reliance on others for material support may also have negative consequences, especially among male returning prisoners, because these situations may lead to role strain. Role strain occurs when an individual is unable to fulfill the expectations of a given role or when role expectations compete with one another (Agnew, 1992;

Ganem & Agnew, 2007). Failure at the provider role through conventional means may lead to criminal activity as an alternative way to fulfill these responsibilities. Role strain may be especially challenging when coupled with difficulties finding employment and contributing to the household over the long term. Moreover, the stress of role strain may lead to substance abuse, which can in turn lead to re-offending. One way to cope with role strain is to exit the role, which in this case would mean leaving the household or breaking off family relationships that lead to role strain, which would also create more residential instability.

**Informal Social Control** A pillar of Sampson and Laub's (1993) age-graded theory of informal social control is that close social bonds help people monitor and supervise one another to enforce mutual obligations and restraints. Although the literature emphasizes the capacity of spouses as agents of social control, similar processes are common in other family relationships, such as parent-child, grandparent-grandchild, or even child-parent relationships. The risk of breaking important social bonds may motivate former prisoners to avoid substance abuse and criminal behavior and encourage pro-social behavior such as searching for employment. Moreover, family relationships provide important forms of identity and prosocial roles for individuals who face otherwise spoiled identities. These identities and roles are symbolically important to those who face challenges achieving other forms of social status such as employment or education. Inhabiting the role of spouse or parent provides the opportunity for symbolic affirmation and reinforcement of post-prison identities, especially when other potentially affirming roles—such as successful workers or students—are unattainable. As we will see below, due to the high rate of health problems and disability in the families of our subjects, caregiving roles were common for former prisoners to take on in order to find a place for themselves in their families and households.

Although the restrictions and restraints that family members impose can often benefit returning prisoners in their reintegration efforts, in other circumstances, family members may channel such influence to encourage or coerce one another into remaining active in crime, substance use, or other forms of antisocial behavior (Colvin, Cullen, & Vander Ven, 2002). Coercion can thus be viewed as the negative counterpart to the protective effects of family-based social control. Moreover, family members may actively or passively approve of criminal behavior when it provides benefits to them (such as money for the household or access to drugs). Family relationships can put individuals at risk for domestic violence and other forms of emotional or physical abuse, all of which can interfere with other aspects of reintegration, such as residential stability, employment, and community involvement.

**Emotional Dynamics** Although much of the theoretical and empirical focus of the literature on relationships and desistance has focused on the ways in which romantic partnership affects patterns of social interaction and routine activities, other family members can also play critical roles in providing emotional support and buffering returning prisoners from stressful life events that could otherwise trigger violence, substance use, or rash decision-making (Cohen, 2004; Cullen, 1994; Umberson, Chen, House, Hopkins, & Slaten, 1996). Such support may be particularly important in this population, given the emotional challenges posed by imprisonment. Men in our qualitative data felt they had to present a tough, emotionally-distant demeanor in order to stay safe, while women felt isolated and lonely. Upon release, former prisoners face a period of emotional upheaval, as their high expectations for themselves and their loved ones often meet harsh realities. We observed many instances in which family members provided a sympathetic ear, affirmation, and confidence-boosts in an otherwise lonely time, though this was substantially more common for male offenders than for females. These relationships often replaced more harmful alternatives for dealing with stress and emotional problems, such as substance use or criminally-involved peers.

Yet, just as family relationships can provide support, they can also bring new sources of stress, such as conflict and disagreement. Although strain theory suggests that the strain resulting from social relationships can lead to crime (Agnew, 1992), there remains very little research detailing the connection between relationship stress and crime, let alone other aspects of reintegration. The stress created by conflict within family relationships may also trigger drug and alcohol use. Because staying sober is one of the greatest challenges of reentry for many former prisoners, avoiding stressful relationships can be one way to protect against potential relapse. Leverentz (2014) shows how the competing demands of family relationships or family roles and addiction recovery programs—which often emphasize independence and staying away from relationships that may be "triggers" for use—can lead to addiction relapse and re-offending.

## Data and Methods

### *Quantitative Analysis*

Our quantitative data come from detailed administrative records—compiled in collaboration with the Michigan Department of Corrections (MDOC)—on a cohort of 11,064 Michigan prisoners who were placed on parole in Michigan during 2003. Over 90% of Michigan's released prisoners are put on parole, one of the higher conditional release rates among American states. Our analyses in this chapter are based on a randomly selected one-third sample ($n=3681$) of this population on which we collected more detailed data on post-prison living arrangements by coding narrative case notes that parole agents update regularly on each parolee. We coded the location and living arrangements at every known residence where the person lived while on parole or under custody until their discharge from parole, death, or end of the observation period on August 19, 2009. The median length of observation was roughly 5 years (1845 days). For more information on our sampling framework, data collection and cleaning, reliability and validity of residential data recorded by parole agents, and matching of records with other administrative data on employment and arrests, see our prior work (Harding et al., 2013; Herbert, Morenoff, & Harding, 2015; Morenoff & Harding, 2011).

Our measures of family relationships in the quantitative data are limited to an individual's living arrangements during the observation. The term "living arrangements" commonly refers to whether an individual lives alone or with another person (or persons) and how the individual is related to others in the household (Statistics Canada, 2015). We follow this convention but also expand it to include non-household living arrangements such as sleeping on the street or residing in a homeless shelter, hotel or motel, residential treatment programs, health care facility, or correctional facility (e.g., jail, prison, correctional center). In addition, since previous research has found that returning prisoners who move back to pre-prison neighborhoods after prison are more likely to recidivate (Kirk, 2009), we also measure whether a person returns to the same residence where he/she lived prior to prison (for the prison spell that ended in 2003).

Our analysis focuses on the impact of living arrangements on four outcomes: residential moves, finding employment in the formal labor market (as captured by the Michigan unemployment insurance system), being arrested by the police (as recorded by local police departments and compiled by the Michigan State Police), and testing positive for alcohol or drugs while on parole (as recorded by the Michigan Department of Corrections). The variables used to measure each of the outcomes are described in Appendix, Table 6. We used discrete-time event-history models for repeated events to analyze the duration of *episodes* related to each outcome. We define an episode as a continuous period during which an individual is at risk of experiencing the outcome (Herbert et al., 2015; Steele, 2008). In our analysis of residential mobility, we estimated event history models with logistic regression. To model the other outcomes—employment, arrest, and testing positive for substance use—we used multinomial logistic regression to allow for the specification of competing risks (see Table 6 for details). The competing risks in these models are being returned to prison or dying while on parole, which we collapsed into a single category due to the rarity of death on parole. In the analysis of residential mobility we do not have competing risks because being returned to prison counts as a residential move. For a more extensive analysis of residential mobility that looks at competing risks by type of move, see Herbert et al. (2015). Since the coefficients from multinomial models can be difficult to interpret, we instead present marginal effects, calculated as the change in the probability of the outcome associated with a categorical change in the independent variable (compared to the reference category). We stratified all models by race (black vs. non-black) to examine whether the associations between living arrangements and reintegration-related outcomes vary by race. We also examined possible gender interactions, but due to the small proportion of women in our sample, we did not have the statistical power to reliably detect such interactions and do not report them here. We are confident, however, that the results below apply to men, the primary focus of this volume.

In the interest of parsimony, we present only the results from three types of independent variables (the full model results are presented in the Appendix). The first is living arrangements, which we categorized as follows: living with parents (the reference group), with a romantic partner, with other family members, alone or with others, on the streets or in a homeless shelter, in a hotel or motel, in a facility for substance use treatment or health care, in a jail or corrections center, in a prison, or in a residence that was not recorded by the parole agent. We measure living arrangements at the beginning of a given time period but also control for one's cumulative experience in different living arrangements during the observation period in an effort to isolate the effects of current living arrangements. (In the residential mobility analysis, living arrangements are measured at the start of the current residential episode. Every time a person's living arrangements change, a new episode begins.) Second, we estimate the effects of returning "home" with a time-varying indicator of whether the parolee was living at the same residence where he/she lived before going to prison. Third, we examine the connections between outcome events by using lagged measure of each outcome (e.g., residential mobility, employment, arrest, and testing positive for substance use) to predict other outcomes. For example, we model residential moves as an outcome but also use the number of residential moves in the prior time period to predict employment, arrest, and testing positive for substance use. Our models also include a large set of control variables. These include measures of background characteristics (measured at the time the person was admitted to prison for the spell that ended with parole in 2003), including gender, age at parole, marital status, number of dependents, education, mental illness, history of substance abuse, time (in years) served in prison for the spell that ended with parole in 2003, the number of prior prison sentences a person had, type of offense (related to the sampled prison spell), whether the parolee was a sex offender, and whether the person was employed at all in the year before going to prison.

## Qualitative Data

Our qualitative data come from longitudinal in-depth unstructured interviews that probe the social, economic, and cultural processes related to prisoner reintegration. The sample of 15 male and seven female interview subjects was selected from Michigan Department of Corrections' (MDOC) administrative records based on their expected release date (those who would be released within 2 months of the baseline interview) and release county (four counties in Southeast Michigan). In this chapter we focus on the experiences of the male subjects. We intentionally chose to study a small number of subjects intensively over a relatively long period of time for three reasons. First, a longitudinal design is necessary due to the rapidly changing nature of the lives of released prisoners. Former prisoners' experiences immediately after release may be very different from their experiences months and years later. Second, a longer follow-up allows for the observation of outcomes that take time to develop. Third, frequent interviews are required to capture the processes driving change over time as well as to increase subject retention in this hard to study population. For further information on data collection procedures, subject retention, interview timing, attrition, and subject characteristics, see our prior work with these data (Harding et al., 2014; Wyse et al., 2014).

Because statistical representativeness across multiple subject characteristics is impossible in a study with a small sample size, we instead pursued a purposive sampling strategy common in qualitative research. Our goal in selecting subjects was to ensure racial and gender diversity, diversity of local geographic context, and diversity of services and supervision provided by MDOC. Accordingly, the sample was stratified by gender, race (white vs. black), reentry county (urban vs. suburban), whether the subject was supposed to receive services from the Michigan Prisoner Reentry Initiative, which was not fully implemented at the time, and whether the subject was going to be released without parole supervision. Within these categories, potential subjects available at the time of recruitment were selected at random. This sampling strategy ensures that theoretically important categories are present and therefore that conclusions drawn are not particular to the largest group of former prisoners in the population (minority males released to central cities). As a result, our sample is not representative of the population of former prisoners released in Michigan during this time period.

Interviews covered a diverse array of topics, both researcher and subject driven, but focused on the subject's community context, family roles and relationships, criminal activities and experiences, labor market activity, life in prison, service use, and health and well-being, including drug and alcohol abuse. Initial in-prison interviews were roughly 90 min, while follow-up interviews usually lasted 1–2 h. Our research design captures subjects both directly before release and during the first 2–3 years after release, a critical period for desistance and reintegration (National Research Council of the National Academies, 2007).

We began our analysis by systematically reading through all interview field notes and transcripts and coding all residences and significant social relationships (whether easily identified as family or non-family or not) for each individual for the entire period of observation. For each residence, we coded many different factors, including time in the residence, locations, type of residence, who else was living in the household, the subject's roles in the household and feeling of security and stability in the household, instances of conflict and social support, and why they entered and exited the residence. For each social relationship, we coded how the subject described the relationship, how and when the relationship started and/or stopped, levels and instances of trust, social support, conflict, frequency of interaction, and stability in the relationship, and geographic proximity. We then coded for each subject all instances of the processes discussed in the conceptual framework above and shown in Table 1 (instrumental support, role strain, informal social control, negative social control or coercion, emotional support, and emotional stress), how they unfolded, and whether and how they were linked to specific reintegration outcomes, including substance use and criminal behavior, residential mobility, employment, educational opportunities, and relationships with others. Finally, we paid specific attention to caregiving activities and the health problems and care needs of subjects and their families, documenting all such caregiving and care receiving and the ways in which such activities related to family and household roles as well as reintegration outcomes.

## Results

### *Quantitative Analyses*

Summary statistics on baseline characteristics of the sample for the quantitative analysis are presented in Table 2. Black parolees tend to be more socioeconomically disadvantaged, with lower levels of education and lower employment rates prior to

**Table 2** Summary Statistics on Baseline Characteristics by Race

| | Black (n = 1960) | | Non-Black (n = 1727) | |
|---|---|---|---|---|
| Variables | Mean | (SD) | Mean | (SD) |
| Age | 35.00 | (9.94) | 35.66 | (9.46)* |
| Female | 0.08 | (0.01) | 0.07 | (0.01) |
| Education | | | | |
| 8 years or less | 0.07 | (0.01) | 0.08 | (0.01) |
| Some high school | 0.40 | (0.01) | 0.29 | (0.01)*** |
| GED | 0.29 | (0.01) | 0.33 | (0.01)** |
| High school graduate | 0.18 | (0.01) | 0.22 | (0.01)** |
| Some college or more | 0.05 | (0.01) | 0.07 | (0.01)* |
| Employed in year prior to prison | 0.12 | (0.01) | 0.17 | (0.01)*** |
| Marital status | | | | |
| Never married | 0.73 | (0.01) | 0.59 | (0.01)*** |
| Married | 0.12 | (0.01) | 0.13 | (0.01) |
| Divorced or separated | 0.15 | (0.01) | 0.27 | (0.01)*** |
| Widowed, common law, unknown | 0.01 | (0.00) | 0.01 | (0.00) |
| One or more dependents | 0.66 | (0.01) | 0.53 | (0.01)*** |
| Known mental illness | 0.14 | (0.01) | 0.29 | (0.01)*** |
| Years in prison for sampled spell | 3.13 | (3.29) | 2.64 | (2.72)*** |
| #Prior prison spells | | | | |
| 0 | 0.43 | (0.01) | 0.53 | (0.01)*** |
| 1 | 0.27 | (0.01) | 0.24 | (0.01) |
| 2 or 3 | 0.22 | (0.01) | 0.18 | (0.01)** |
| 4 or more | 0.08 | (0.01) | 0.04 | (0.00)*** |
| Type of offense | | | | |
| Assaultive offense | 0.29 | (0.01) | 0.27 | (0.01) |
| Drug offense | 0.38 | (0.01) | 0.12 | (0.01) |
| Other offense | 0.33 | (0.01) | 0.61 | (0.01) |
| Sex offender | 0.06 | (0.01) | 0.10 | (0.01) |
| Substance abuse history | | | | |
| None | 0.51 | (0.01) | 0.52 | (0.01) |
| Alcohol only | 0.03 | (0.00) | 0.06 | (0.01)*** |
| THC only | 0.11 | (0.01) | 0.04 | (0.00)*** |
| Hard drugs only | 0.06 | (0.01) | 0.04 | (0.00)*** |
| Alcohol and THC | 0.05 | (0.01) | 0.07 | (0.01)* |
| Hard drugs and alcohol/THC | 0.25 | (0.01) | 0.27 | (0.01) |

Test of difference in proportions/means between blacks and non-blacks: ***$p<0.001$; **$p<0.01$; *$p<0.05$

prison than non-blacks. Although there were no group differences in the proportion married, blacks were more likely to have never been married, while non-blacks were more likely to have been divorced or separated. Blacks, on average, served more time in prison for the sampled spell and had more prior prison spells than non-blacks. Blacks were more likely to be serving time for a drug offense and to have a history of using cannabis (THC) or hard drugs, but they were less likely to be mentally ill, be convicted of a sexual offense, and have a history of alcohol use.

Next, we consider the key time-varying characteristics in our analysis. Table 3 shows the percentage of days during the observation period that black and non-black parolees spent in different living arrangements and other time-varying states. On average, parolees spent more time living with their parents than in any other private living arrangement, although blacks spent significantly less time with parents than non-blacks. Blacks spent a larger share of time living with "other family," which includes (in descending order of frequency) living with a sibling, aunt or uncle, grandparent, cousin, child, relative of a romantic partner (current or former), or unidentified family member; whereas non-blacks spent more time living alone or with people unrelated to them. This suggests that black parolees experience somewhat more complex family forms than non-blacks. Although the fraction of time spent homeless or living in transient hotels/motels was relatively small and similar for blacks and non-blacks, the average parolee still spent roughly 3 % of his/her time in these unstable and precarious arrangements. Parolees spent larger shares of time in living arrangements that were unknown to the parole agent (or at least not recorded in the case notes), often when an absconding warrant had been issued, and

**Table 3** Percentage of observation time spent in types of residences by race

| | Black (n = 1960) | | Non-Black (n = 1727) | |
|---|---|---|---|---|
| Variables | Mean | (SD) | Mean | (SD) |
| Living arrangements | | | | |
| Parent | 22.95 | (32.63) | 26.08 | (33.29)** |
| Partner | 13.89 | (25.99) | 14.57 | (26.94) |
| Other family | 17.79 | (28.19) | 12.63 | (25.01)*** |
| Alone or with other | 8.36 | (19.88) | 14.62 | (25.29)*** |
| Hotel/motel | 1.32 | (7.34) | 1.74 | (7.78) |
| Mission/shelter/homeless | 1.24 | (5.95) | 1.54 | (7.11) |
| Receiving treatment/care | 2.67 | (6.75) | 3.04 | (7.76) |
| Correctional centers and other non-sanction institutions | 2.23 | (8.17) | 2.39 | (8.71) |
| Jail/intermediate sanction | 8.18 | (9.86) | 7.87 | (10.41) |
| Unknown | 11.50 | (17.93) | 6.01 | (11.95)*** |
| Prison | 9.85 | (14.09) | 9.52 | (14.77) |
| Living at pre-prison address | 17.70 | (30.92) | 18.15 | (31.02) |
| Absconding | 7.95 | (15.19) | 3.54 | (9.36)*** |

Test of difference in means between blacks and non-blacks: ***$p<0.001$; **$p<0.01$; *$p<0.05$

black parolees spent significantly more time in unknown living arrangements and more time absconding than non-blacks. Both groups spent substantial portions of time in institutional living arrangements, largely due to the "revolving door" between parole and custody. Together, prison, jail, and correctional centers accounted for roughly 20 % of the average parolee's time, or one in 5 days.

Frequencies for the outcomes are presented in Table 4. Residential moves were quite common for both groups. For example, 4.6 % of black parolees moved in an average week, which means that the average black parolee moved once every 21.7 weeks. The overall rate of moving for non-blacks was similar. However, blacks were more likely than non-blacks to experience a forced move for an intermediate sanction (incarceration in a jail or correctional center) and they were more likely to abscond; while non-black parolees were more likely to move to new private residences. These results suggest a larger role for the criminal justice system in residential mobility among blacks. Blacks were also less likely to be employed, more likely to be arrested, more likely to be tested for substance use, and more likely to have a positive result when tested. Note that for both black and non-black parolees, rates of finding formal employment when unemployed were very low.

Results from the discrete-time event history models are reported in Table 5. The first two columns of results show the marginal effects of the key independent variables on the hazard of moving in a given week (the probability of moving in the current week among those who did not move in prior weeks). There are several significant

**Table 4** Summary statistics on outcomes by race

| | Blacks | | Non-Blacks | | |
|---|---|---|---|---|---|
| Outcome | % | *Person-period obs*[a] | % | *Person-period obs* | Chi-square[b] |
| Any move | 4.60 | *275,574* | 4.85 | *213,101* | 15.54*** |
| Type of move | | | | | |
| To new private residence | 24.20 | *275,574* | 35.42 | *213,101* | 429.51*** |
| To homelessness | 1.95 | | 2.72 | | |
| To treatment/care | 11.69 | | 9.96 | | |
| To jail/intermediate sanction | 38.74 | | 32.54 | | |
| To prison | 10.58 | | 10.33 | | |
| To absconding | 12.85 | | 9.03 | | |
| Employed | 9.30 | *14,596* | 14.35 | *10,698* | 147.23*** |
| Arrested | 3.60 | *68,293* | 2.64 | *56,786* | 104.40*** |
| Substance use tests | | | | | |
| Tested vs. Not Tested | 34.37 | *36,288* | 32.88 | *30,836* | 215.69*** |
| Positive vs. Negative | 18.12 | | 11.26 | | |

***p<0.001; **p<0.01; *p<0.05

[a]The time periods are *weeks* for residential moves, *calendar quarters* for employment, and *months* for arrests and substance use tests

[b]Chi-square test of association between race and outcome

**Table 5** Marginal effects from discrete-time event-history models of moving, being employed, being arrested, and testing positive for substance use

| | Residential move (in week) | | Employment (in calendar quarter) | | Arrest (in month) | | Positive vs. negative substance abuse test (in month) | |
|---|---|---|---|---|---|---|---|---|
| | Blacks | Non-Blacks | Blacks | Non-Blacks | Blacks | Non-Blacks | Blacks | Non-Blacks |
| *Status at start of current time period* | | | | | | | | |
| Living arrangement (ref = parents) | | | | | | | | |
| Partner | 0.002 | –0.002 | 0.028** | –0.016 | –0.004 | 0.004 | –0.001 | 0.000 |
| Other family | 0.008*** | 0.011*** | 0.002 | 0.002 | –0.005 | –0.010** | 0.004 | 0.009 |
| Alone or with other | 0.006* | 0.008** | 0.001 | –0.019 | 0.011 | –0.002 | 0.002 | 0.000 |
| Hotel/motel | 0.018 | 0.040*** | –0.013 | –0.002 | 0.033 | 0.011 | 0.005 | –0.001 |
| Mission/shelter/homeless | 0.019*** | 0.054*** | 0.017 | 0.013 | 0.001 | 0.000 | –0.003 | –0.011 |
| Receiving treatment/care | | | 0.048* | –0.019 | –0.023*** | –0.016*** | –0.039*** | –0.025*** |
| Correctional centers and other non-sanction institutions | | | –0.009 | –0.072*** | –0.030*** | –0.011 | –0.012 | –0.019*** |
| Jail/intermediate sanction | | | –0.039*** | –0.062*** | –0.016** | –0.017*** | | |
| Unknown | –0.001 | 0.007** | –0.009 | –0.111 | 0.013 | –0.028*** | –0.010 | –0.035*** |
| Absconding | | | –0.054*** | –0.114*** | 0.038 | 0.201*** | | |
| Living at pre-prison address | –0.004* | –0.004* | –0.002 | 0.001 | –0.006* | –0.001 | –0.002 | 0.003 |
| *Events in last time period*[a] | | | | | | | | |
| #Moves to new residence | | | 0.001 | –0.002 | 0.037*** | 0.027*** | 0.027*** | 0.016*** |
| Employed[b] | –0.012*** | –0.009*** | | | –0.008** | 0.003 | –0.004 | 0.001 |
| #Arrests | 0.007*** | 0.011*** | –0.003 | –0.007 | | | –0.027 | –0.018 |

| | Blacks | Non-Blacks | Blacks | Non-Blacks | Blacks | Non-Blacks | Blacks | Non-Blacks |
|---|---|---|---|---|---|---|---|---|
| Substance abuse tests (ref = no positive test) | | | | | | | | |
| Not tested | 0.007 | –0.002 | –0.019*** | 0.007 | 0.002 | 0.002 | | |
| One positive test | 0.023*** | 0.027*** | –0.022** | 0.021 | –0.001 | –0.002 | | |
| Two positive tests | 0.033*** | 0.043*** | –0.028* | –0.032 | –0.011 | –0.007 | | |
| Three or more positive tests | 0.088*** | 0.026 | –0.024 | –0.047 | 0.017 | 0.020 | | |
| *Person-period observations* | *275,574* | *213,101* | *14,596* | *10,698* | *24,672* | *23,474* | *25,918* | *24,447* |

***p<0.001; **p<0.01; *p<0.05

[a]In the case of residential moves, these variables capture events that occurred in the month prior to the start of the current residential episode

[b]Refers to employment status in the last calendar quarter that ended prior to the start of the current episode

associations between a parolee's living arrangement at the start of a residential episode and episode duration. The hazard of moving was lowest among those living with parents (the reference group) or romantic partners. The hazard of moving was significantly higher for those in other types of private living arrangements. The magnitude of these effects can be better understood by contextualizing them against the group-specific baseline hazards for moving reported in Table 4. For example, for blacks, living with other family increases the hazard of moving by 0.008 points, which implies a shift from the average episode length of 21.74 weeks (derived from the baseline hazard in Table 2) to 18.54 weeks, or a reduction in the residential episode by approximately 3.18 weeks. This effect was higher for non-blacks, shaving approximately 3.85 weeks off the duration of an average residential episode. Living alone or with others (besides family or partners) also increased the hazard of moving for both groups. Being homeless was, not surprisingly, the most unstable living arrangement, reducing the length of an average episode by 6.29 weeks for blacks and 10.85 weeks for non-blacks. Living in a hotel or motel was also very unstable for non-blacks but did not significantly change the hazard of moving for blacks. In other words, when black parolees moved to a hotel or motel, they were likely to spend a longer time there compared to non-black parolees, a difference that is statistically significant.

There were also other significant predictors of moving. Returning to live at one's pre-prison residence was associated with longer episode durations (i.e., lower hazards of moving) for both groups. The duration of a residential episode was also related to events that occurred prior to the start of the episode. Those who had been arrested or tested positive for substance use in the month prior to the start of the episode were likely to experience more residential instability (shorter episode duration), whereas episode duration was longer among those who were employed in the prior quarter.

Next we consider the results from models of employment, where positive marginal effects on the "hazard" of becoming employed also indicate shorter durations of unemployment spells. Although there were few significant differences in the duration of unemployment spells across the different types of private living arrangements, one important exception was that for blacks, living with a romantic partner was associated with shorter unemployment spells. The marginal effect of living with a romantic partner on employment for blacks (0.028) implies a shift in the duration of the average unemployment episode from 10.76 quarters (derived from the baseline hazard of 0.093 in Table 2) to 8.27 quarters, or a 2.5 quarter reduction in the length of an average unemployment spell. Supplemental analyses (not shown) show that this association is entirely driven by male parolees. Most of the institutional living arrangements were associated with significantly lower probability of finding employment for both groups. The marginal effects of being incarcerated in a jail or correctional center at the beginning of the current calendar quarter are especially large, translating into increases in unemployment spells of 7.77 quarters for blacks and 5.30 quarters for non-blacks. Absconding dramatically reduced the probability of being formally employed, which is not surprising given the practice of "system avoidance" among those who are trying to avoid detection from an arm of the criminal justice system (Brayne, 2014; Goffman, 2014). Testing positive for substance use also reduced the probability of finding employment, although this relationship was only significant among blacks.

Finally, we consider arrest and testing positive for substance use. There were few significant differences among private living arrangements in the hazard of being arrested or testing positive. However, parolees living in institutional settings that provide high levels of supervision—such as residential treatment facilities, correctional centers and jails—were at lower risk of being arrested and testing positive. Returning "home" to one's pre-prison address reduced the hazard of arrest, but only for blacks, and it was not significantly related to the hazard of testing positive for substance use. Thus, we find no evidence to support claims that returning home can increase the risk of recidivism or relapse. To the contrary, we found that returning home was protective against arrest for blacks, among whom the marginal effect (–0.006) was equivalent to prolonging the average time to arrest from 33.45 months (derived from the baseline hazard of 0.036 in Table 4) to 38.93 months, or an additional 5.64 months. On the other hand, residential instability—as captured by the number of moves to a new residence in the month prior to the start of a new episode—was associated with increases in the hazards of arrest and testing positive. In sum, although the type of family living arrangements *per se* does not appear to be consequential for arrests and substance use tests, residential stability is associated with more positive outcomes in these domains.

## *Qualitative Analyses*

Whereas our quantitative analyses focus on the associations between different types of family and non-family living arrangements and reintegration outcomes, our qualitative analyses focus on social interactions and exchanges with family members, providing an alternative window into the role of family in prisoner reintegration. We organize our presentation of results around the conceptual framework discussed earlier and shown in Table 1, first discussing material circumstances, then informal social control, and then emotional dynamics. We note that the same family relationship or household can generate multiple, even conflicting, processes related to prisoner reintegration. Indeed in the examples below, we will often see our subjects facing a trade-off between material support, particularly basic needs like housing and food, and more negative features that come from maintaining a relationship with or living with a particular family member, such as role strain, emotional stress, or opportunities for crime or drug use. A related caveat is that the distinctions between categories in our conceptual framework can become blurry when applied to a specific case. For example, the line between informal social control and emotional support, though conceptually distinct, can become blurry if the same subject's experiences are viewed through multiple lenses.

Throughout this discussion we highlight a significant cross-cutting theme that emerged from our analysis: the prevalence of caregiving, care work for compensation, and health problems among the family members of our subjects. Our subjects engaged in various caretaking roles and responsibilities, ranging from routine household chores such as cooking and cleaning to acting as a full-time caretaker for a disabled adult and child. Indeed, caregiving and care work often proved to be the most straightforward way for our subjects to find meaningful roles and responsibilities in their new households, given their difficulties in the labor market. Eight out of the 22 subjects assumed some sort of primary caretaker role, either for an adult (three) or a child (five). An additional five engaged in some other sort of "care work" that provided monetary or in-kind compensation during their time in the study. An additional seven participants had household members with some kind of health problem, disability or substance abuse problem, and nearly all of the subjects had health issues of their own, ranging from addiction to epilepsy to diabetes to depression. As we will see below, these caretaking responsibilities proved to be meaningful and fulfilling for most of our subjects, but many also found themselves juggling their own needs with those of household members, leading to a great deal of stress. We saw no clear racial or gender distinctions in care work, caregiving, or the experience of living with a family member with health-related challenges (but our small non-random sample precludes any sort of statistical analysis or strong conclusions in this regard). Yet, as we will see below, care work and caregiving often had different implications for men and women. These roles seemed to be a source of stress and frustration for the men, who realized that they are in these arrangements because they do not have full-time employment.

**Material Circumstances** By far the most common support provided by family members and romantic partners was direct provision of material resources, or what we term instrumental support. Most commonly this came in the form of providing food and shelter, both immediately after release and for many but not all, in the longer term. All but four of the 15 male subjects lived with family or romantic partners immediately after their release, including romantic partners (4); parents (6); and siblings (1). Only one male subject (Lamar) remained independent throughout the study period (living with a brother only during the first week after his release). We view these patterns as consistent with the quantitative results above that show the importance of living with family members, particularly parents and romantic partners, for residential stability and avoiding homelessness. Family members also provided many other forms of material assistance, including transportation to look for work, parole meetings, treatment programs, and school, gifts of clothing, contributing to savings toward independent housing, assistance with job applications, and paying off legal fees and other debts.

Often such instrumental support came in exchange for caregiving of various forms, as time and effort were typically the only resources that subjects had to contribute to the household, particularly in the early period after release. In other cases, such caregiving was directly compensated care work for family members who offered financial support in exchange for services such as cleaning and other household chores, babysitting, or caring for adults with serious health problems. In some case, such care work actually became a form of informal employment. For example, Henry, a 52-year old African-American man who was incarcerated for auto theft, moved in with his fiancé (who was disabled and had a colostomy bag), her 11-year old daughter, and her 18-year-old son (who had cerebral palsy and received disability benefits).

Although Henry found a few days of informal work as a handyman, he spent most of the study period in and out of jail and struggled to contribute to the household. He hoped to become certified by the state to provide state-paid care for his fiancé's son, but in the end he provided care for free, saving his fiancé $150 a week.

For a small number of subjects, families were able to provide instrumental support that went beyond helping to meet basic needs such as food, housing, and transportation to assistance with finding more stable jobs and building careers. Only more advantaged families were able to provide such assistance, which included loaning or gifting significant amounts of money to help study participants cover the costs of schooling or job training, and leveraging their own social networks to help their loved one secure a job that could provide stable employment with a living wage and prospects for upward mobility. One example is James, a black male in his mid-twenties, who served a probation sentence on a narcotics charge and later went to prison for operating a motor vehicle while intoxicated, which led to an accident that killed his cousin who was one of the passengers. Both prior to and after his prison sentence, James relied heavily on social support, primarily from his mother but also from siblings and extended family. A chief source of support was the housing and transportation provided by his mother, who was on disability, and eventually a romantic partner with whom he later lived and split rent. Moreover, unlike many of our subjects, James received support in establishing a career as a barber. Prior to release, James stated that he had tentative plans to go to barber school. Multiple family members served as role models for this career path, including a brother, a stepbrother, and cousins who were all barbers (including one cousin who owned a barbershop). Further, James reported that his brother provided advice on this career, and his sister payed for his barber apprentice permit and financial aid application fees to help him attend barber school.

While James struggled to find any work during the study period outside of barbering (receiving no guidance in this job-seeking), he started informally engaging in barbering at his mother's house and then transitioned to working at a barbershop 2 months after his release. Not long after, he began barber school, but he quickly dropped out to work more hours to earn more money, saying he intended to continue his formal training in the future. He returned to work at the barbershop where he had originally started and built up a clientele. Not long after, he moved in with his girlfriend. Through the instrumental support he received from his family, James was able to gain and maintain stable employment that then helped him to become economically independent. Sadly, James was killed in a home invasion only 9 months later. A few other men were able to more directly leverage family members' social networks and economic resources to help them find and sustain more stable and higher-paying employment, but the majority of our subjects did not have social support that could help them to this degree.

While instrumental support from family was essential for meeting basic needs for food and housing, it also created role strain, particularly for our male subjects, who envisioned playing the role of provider for their families after their release. The challenges of finding work after prison, particularly for black men (Pager, 2003), made fulfilling a traditional male role in the household impossible for most of the men. Such role strain had consequences for their feelings of security in the household and their desistance from crime. Consider David, a white 28-year-old with a history of breaking and entering to support his drug habit. A few days after he was paroled, he left his drug treatment program early and failed to contact his parole officer—an act of absconding. Unable to stay with his mother or other family members for fear that authorities would find him, David was taken in by his former girlfriend Loretta, the mother of his child, and they soon resumed a relationship. They lived in a low-income housing complex with their daughter and Loretta's two other children. To get by, they relied entirely on Loretta's public benefits, including rent vouchers and food stamps. Over time, David became increasingly stressed about not bringing any income into the household. At his first post-release interview, 4 weeks after release, he explained that he even considered limiting his own eating because he was not contributing income: "I wasn't eating for a minute … I felt like I was taking out of the children's mouth; that's not my food." Still, David continued living with his girlfriend, who bought him not only food but also cigarettes and beer. After he was returned to prison David explained that the strain of living off his girlfriend's largesse was one of the main factors that led him to resume criminal activity. He had noticed that one of his girlfriend's neighbors often left her apartment for weeks at a time. Just weeks after our interview, David burglarized the neighbor's apartment after a night of drinking. He explained that the main reason he committed the crime was that he could not continue living in the household without contributing financially. He had planned to pawn the stolen goods to help with household expenses, but police arrived the next morning.

It would seem that, for David, his role as a father and romantic partner in the household initiated a particular role expectation that served more as a motivation for criminal involvement than a protective factor. We observed other men in our sample like David, who described their inability to fulfill the provider role as motivation for income-generating criminal actions. Moreover, several men who were later arrested for criminal offenses, such as car theft, had in previous interviews expressed considerable discomfort with being unable to contribute. Such role strain can be understood as closely linked to traditional gender norms dictating that men should provide material resources for their family—the breadwinner role. Such role strain often manifested itself in unpredictable ways. For example, some single men in our sample cited their inability to fulfill the role of breadwinner as a reason for avoiding romantic relationships, while others appeared to limit their contact with children when they were unable to help provide for the child. Instances of role strain were most common among men living with romantic partners and children. We did not observe the same degree of role strain among study participants living with their parents, nor did we see it among our female subjects, as they could adopt caregiver roles in the family without violating conventional gender norms.

In some instances, even the men in our study were able to deflect or diminish potential role strain by substituting the caregiving role for the breadwinning role when they struggled to find employment. Although such men still viewed their household roles as far from ideal, their caregiving helped them reconcile their identity as a family member with their challenges securing stable employment. Several of the men described their completion of household chores, such as repairs and yard work, as an economic contribution to the household, thus viewing the household as a place where they engaged in work, even though they were unemployed.

Consider Randall, an African-American man in his late thirties who had been in prison for drug dealing, car theft, and firearm possession. Randall faced very bleak employment prospects. He had a long list of felonies, lacked a high school degree, had no recent work experience, and was living in an area of Detroit where there were few jobs to be had. Randall did not obtain stable employment until nearly 3 years after his release from prison. During this time, Randall pieced together informal labor and engaged in various forms of caretaking work in different households where he lived. For example, not long after his release, he moved in with his brother, sister-in-law, and their two teenage sons. Unable to find a job, Randall contributed his food stamp benefits to the household, did odd jobs for other family members, and briefly sold marijuana to generate a small income. This was not an ideal situation for Randall. Unemployed, he felt badly about his dependence on his family. "It feels like I'm taking food out they [the kids'] mouth when I'm eating in the house, and I ain't working. But all she wants me to do, basically, is keep the house clean." Randall thus helped around the house and contributed his food stamp benefits to the household, expecting that his brother would eventually connect him to a job. This job prospect fell through, however, leading to a rift in the relationship that was also related to his brother's drinking and accompanying verbal aggression. Two months later, Randall was kicked out, feeling used by his family, who had spent his monthly food stamp allotment. He then faced a prolonged period of unstable housing, including squatting in an abandoned house during the dead of winter, until eventually landing in a more permanent living arrangement with his chronically unemployed stepsister and her father, a retired blue collar worker whom Randall referred to as an uncle. Despite finding a place to live, Randall was still unable to find work and he never quite felt secure with his place in the household, especially after his stepsister's brother retuned from prison to live in the household as well. On multiple occasions Randall packed his bags to leave, only to have his "uncle" insist that he was welcome to stay. Randall eventually came to understand his role through his household labor:

> [My stepsister's brother] had a talk with me one day, and I told him flat out, "I don't feel comfortable being here, that's why I always leave because I feel like I can't help around this house as far as contributing food or money or anything." And he like, "My dad ain't asking for much, he just wants you to do something around here. You can keep the house clean, anything, he'll appreciate that." And I be having the house clean, every morning, I get up. He's like, "Treat this like you treated your own cell when you was locked up." I keep the whole house smelling fresh.

As this example illustrates, such caregiving roles could be a source of considerable stress, anxiety and/or frustration for men, especially those caught in undesirable living arrangements because they did not have full-time employment. Rather than a new identity that helps compensate for lack of employment, caregiving roles can serve as a constant reminder of such perceived failures. Randall repeatedly expressed his anxiety over not having a job, and being so dependent on his uncle:

> One night about two weeks ago I told [my stepsister] I didn't feel comfortable being here, I keep throwing that in their face because I feel I ain't doing nothing. And I told her I ain't

feel that [her father] wanted me there. Then she takes me back like, "He ain't mad at you. He said he like that you ain't out there just running the streets and that you take care of your business." I fixed the room up, and it's been good ever since. Then I don't ask her for nothing because I feel I don't have to ask for nothing, he's already doing the best he can for me.

Despite reassurances from his uncle that he was fulfilling his household role, Randall continued to feel conflicted about his dependency on his uncle and hesitant to ask for further support. At the same time, his ability to engage in care work (i.e. fixing the room up) helped assuage these insecurities, and he lived with his uncle and stepsister for over a year, only leaving to form a new household with his fiancé and her son in the suburbs.

Particularly masculine forms of caregiving and care work helped lessen the role strain that other men felt when their contributions came from more feminized care work, such as the house cleaning exemplified by Randall. A contrasting example comes from Geoffrey, a 45-year-old white man who began using cocaine when he was a teenager but nonetheless also had a fairly successful career as a plumber and home remodeler. When we met him, Geoffrey was completing his fourth term in prison, this time for cashing a stolen check. Geoffrey left prison eager to begin plumbing work again and ostensibly confident that his drug-using days were behind him. He moved in with a girlfriend and her daughter. When Geoffrey could not find formal work as a plumber, he spent his time working around the house, repairing problems that had accumulated while he was in prison. When asked about his monetary contributions to the household shortly after release, he explained:

I help her out … I don't pay the bills, she does. She pays all the bills. But like I take care of other things. I buy food. I keep the house maintenance-wise, everything, it doesn't matter what it is, I do it.

For example, Geoffrey replaced the front steps on the house and paid to have his girlfriend's car fixed. Not long after, Geoffrey turned to working informally doing short-term jobs for friends and acquaintances at relatively low wages or for in-kind exchange. After breaking up with the girlfriend and moving out, Geoffrey continued this form of care work in exchange for places to live, sometimes for only a few days but also for several months at a time.

Another form of role strain can occur when caregiving and care work interferes with meetings one's own needs. In these situations, our subjects were torn between the roles they developed for themselves in the family after release (and the desire to assist family members in need) and their own long-term well-being. For example, caregiving interfered with the time and energy they had for meeting parole requirements (such as mandatory programming) and searching for employment. Consider Damian, a 71 year old African-American man from Detroit. While Damian was still in prison, his adult stepson pled for him to move in with him and his mother (Damian's ex-wife), because she had suffered multiple strokes, and they were struggling financially. Damian had his own health problems, including glaucoma, high blood pressure, hypertension, and "a bad back." In addition, he was a heavy drug user before prison. Although he moved in to help his ex-wife and his stepson, he ended up frustrated and feeling taken advantage of. "They're relying on me at this point. But it's hard for me to get my thing together when I'm dealing with their things more so than mine." He explained that he believes his ex-wife is faking her ailments and that he is being taken advantage of to help with the rent. Damian was paying their portion of the rent for their section-8 subsidized-housing with his Social Security income. His relationship with his stepson, who suffers from bipolar disorder, became increasingly stressful also. Damian was arrested and put in jail after borrowing his son's car (which he drives without a license) which turned out to be stolen. When he returned home from jail, he found his ex-wife and son using drugs heavily and worried that their drug use was a threat to his sobriety. At this point, Damian's household responsibilities proved overwhelming and he felt they were interfering with rebuilding his life after prison, so he moved out and into a shelter for former prisoners. "Right now, it's all about me," he explained. "Until I get me straight." Damian felt relieved to be free of his caretaking responsibilities, and—despite his unstable housing situation—looked forward to re-starting his music career, buying a house, and completing parole.

**Informal Social Control** Another possible role for families in reintegration is direct monitoring or supervision of the behavior of their loved one returning home from prison. Such monitoring may encourage positive behaviors, such as complying with parole requirements, looking for work, or enrolling in school or training programs, or it may discourage negative behaviors such as involvement in crime or substance abuse. Similarly, relationships with family members, especially co-residential relationships, may structure a former prisoner's time so as to avoid people and places that might encourage crime or substance use. In short, relationships may change routine activities, and time with family members can displace time spent with others or doing other things. Although we did not observe this phenomenon in the experiences of our subjects as much as we expected, an example from James, discussed earlier, illustrates the concepts.

Close to a year after his release, James moved with his girlfriend of 10 months and her four children to a residence in a new neighborhood, which he thought would help him stay out of trouble. Beyond feeling more secure in his new neighborhood, James also reported that living with his girlfriend kept him out of trouble: "I won't do nothing stupid because all I do is go to work and come straight home … I got somebody to come home to I can say is mine; ain't nobody else[s]." His girlfriend provided him with transportation to work and kept him busy outside of work. When he did go out, it was generally with her to do things like shoot pool or go to a movie.

James' girlfriend not only helped structure his time, but she also provided informal social control, stopping him from going out and getting into trouble. He describes an example of how she shaped his behavior:

> The other night, my friend wanted to go to this little bar down here, and she didn't want to go. She was with me. I didn't go. So we left. Then what happened? Somebody got killed. Three people … Yeah, I probably would have got in trouble. Because I was the popular kid in school and we right around in the same neighborhood, so you know it's going to be people still around here, we used to go to school [with].

Although James credited his girlfriend with helping him to stay out of trouble and maintain employment, he also occasionally chaffed at this informal social control, attributing it to unreasonable suspicion of cheating, jealousy and a lack of trust. In a sentiment echoed by other men, James explained: "I get stressed sometimes. You know how women get jealous. Sometimes she don't trust me … [Some women] think you want to go out and cheat." Still, James viewed his girlfriend positively and, notably, reported no substance use or criminal activity during the study period.

Why was effective monitoring from family and romantic partners less common than theory might lead us to expect? One reason is that family members and partners were often ill equipped to provide such monitoring or supervision, a function of their own health and substance abuse problems as well as other responsibilities such as caring for children or other family members. In fact, we saw many family members and romantic partners either passively accepting substance abuse or crime, or in some cases actively enabling it (as we discuss further below). Christopher's relationship with his romantic partner provides an example of passive acceptance. Christopher, a white male in his late thirties with no children, has been in and out of prison in a 7 year period, mostly for drug-related offenses. At the time of his release, Christopher reported that staying free from prison for a year would be "unbelievable." Upon release, Christopher initially experienced significant housing instability, rotating between shelters, 3/4 houses, and homelessness, and struggled mightily with his addiction. However, 7 months after his release, he met and moved in with a woman whom he eventually married and remained with throughout the duration of the study period. During this time, Christopher's wife provided critical support including not only housing, but also assistance with transportation and employment and a "humongous" amount of emotional support, as Christopher put it.

However, his wife also struggled with her role in his substance abuse, and she herself suffered from substance abuse in the past. (They met in a substance abuse recovery group.) While Christopher reported in interviews that he would be in prison without her, he also thought she was "an enabler because she doesn't put her foot down." This appears to be reflected in her behavior: Soon after they began their relationship she picked up Christopher from a drug house during a serious relapse with crack cocaine; she let Christopher drive her car even when he was intoxicated; she housed a few different individuals who used substances (including both crack and alcohol) while he was living with her; and she continued to support Christopher throughout his relapses. While Christopher achieved an 8-month period of sobriety, which he described as motivated by his wife and a baby they had together a year after his release, he otherwise continued to abuse substances throughout the study period and engaged in further criminal behavior that ultimately resulted in a new prison sentence. The only time he described his wife as directly intervening in his use was in his final interview in prison when he recounted how prior to his incarceration she tried to remove the plates from their car to stop him from driving and kicked him out of the house. While Christopher recognized the difficulty of intervening in his abuse, he noted that he wished she had given him an ultimatum to go into detox or move out. Whether his wife, or anyone else, could have effectively prevented Christopher from relapsing and committing the robbery that led to his re-incarceration is impossible to say, but their experiences illustrate the challenges of monitoring and supervising former prisoners.

A more common form of informal social control from family relationships was the motivation that maintaining the relationship provided. Returning to substance use or criminal activity might jeopardize the relationship, or at the very least, result in further prolonged separation from loved ones. DeAngelo is a 27-year old African-American who was concluding his second stint in prison when we began our study. During childhood, his family lived in poverty, they moved frequently, and his mother dated a series of abusive men. His first prison sentence was a 3-year term at age 21 for breaking and entering an unoccupied building; he explained that he and his brother, who had been homeless, were seeking a place to sleep. At 26, a third drunk driving conviction landed him in prison again. During this prison bit, DeAngelo was diagnosed with severe depression, bipolar disorder, and acute anxiety, and realized that these conditions had been exacerbated by his alcoholism. When he was paroled, DeAngelo's 19-year-old girlfriend picked him up from prison, and he moved in with her and her mother. DeAngelo explained how his first relationship after prison functioned to control his behavior:

> My girl and her mom, she's been more of a mother to me than my mother ever have. And they just good people. They never judge me because of my past. They never looked at me and perceived me as a hoodlum or a thug … She just been there for me, and I never had that before. So, it feels good. *And I really can't let them down.*

In the same interview DeAngelo suggested that this love and support made him less likely to engage in criminal behavior in the future because he had more to lose were he to resume criminal activity.

Children can provide a similar motivation. Indeed, among those subjects who had children, almost all mentioned in their pre-release interviews that rebuilding their relationships with their children and being a better parent were key motivators for staying out of prison. Christopher, described earlier, attributed a turn towards sobriety as motivated in part by his newly born son. He explained that he can stand in the liquor aisle at the local grocery store and, "I think of the baby, and you weigh the two and there's not even a scale to weight it." DeAngelo, who obtained custody of his son during the study period, viewed his role as a father as an important motivator for getting his life together.

> I look at it like this now. Now that I've got my son … it's not even really about me no more. It is, like a mental sense and an emotional sense, it's about him. I've got to get everything in order for him. Because if I ain't right, he can't be right. I've got to be able to provide financially … He deserves to have a positive role model in his life

The informal social control provided by family relationships was unfortunately not always so positive, a phenomenon we refer to as coercion and negative social control. In such cases family members either presented opportunities for criminal behavior and substance abuse or directly participated in such behaviors with our subjects. Outright coercion by romantic partners was limited to our female subjects, while the men in our sample were more likely to have family members who encouraged their involvement in criminal activity. Recall Randall, whom we discussed earlier as an example of role strain from a caregiving role in the household. In the past, Randall had committed crimes with one of his brothers, and upon his release, that brother and other family members presented him with opportunities to engage in crime again. When Randall did some odd jobs for a cousin in the hopes of making some extra spending money, that cousin paid him in marijuana and told him to sell it. A different brother, with whom he lived for a few months immediately after his release, demanded a cut of the marijuana for his own personal use in exchange for living in his house and provided the opportunity to sell marijuana to friends for whom he cut hair on the weekends. Another brief foray into drug selling was prompted by another cousin, who enlisted Randall to help him sell heroin. Randall did so for a week and then quit.

**Emotional Dynamics** As suggested by some of the subject experiences we have already discussed, a third key aspect of family relationships is their emotional context and character. Given the loss of non-family social ties and the intensification of family relationships that we observed during our subjects' time in prison, it is not surprising that they relied heavily and primarily on their family members and romantic partners for emotional support in the challenging and stressful period after release. One can think of this emotional support as a form of caregiving provided by family, often replacing more harmful alternatives for dealing with stress and emotional problems, such as substance use. In many cases, such emotional support proved to be an important buffer against relapse or an encouragement to persevere in a previously unsuccessful job search.

The men in our sample tended to receive this type of emotional support from romantic partners. Consider 27-year-old Jake, who was released from his second term in prison after serving 3 years for drunken driving. Once Jake was paroled, he began a romantic relationship with Anna, a friend of his sister with whom he had corresponded in prison. Soon Jake came to rely on Anna emotionally. In our first post-prison interview, he explained that the drinking problem that originally landed him in prison had been triggered by his relationship with his ex-wife, who had cheated on him. Jake valued sharing emotionally with Anna, and was able to talk through the continuing difficulties he experienced interacting with his ex-wife, with whom he has two children:

> That's one of the things me and her are good at. We discuss everything and anything … Past relationships aren't a topic that we can't discuss … which is good for me. I talk to her about every time my ex comes over.

This support has been critical for Jake, who feels his drinking is triggered by emotional stress. When asked by the interviewer, what are the biggest triggers for alcohol or drugs, Jake responded:

> When I get off of work I feel entitlement to drink because I just worked for the day, you know. I'm not a very angry person but I know anger will drive me to drink very quickly. When I get upset, emotions, past relationships are a good trigger for me. Top five probably deal with my ex-wife, the relationship I'm in, how I'm dealing with my family has a lot to do with relationships, my communication with people. But it's almost like my emotions and keeping that in check.

To counteract this urge to drink at night, Jake made a practice of calling Anna right after work. Meanwhile, Anna faced her own struggle with addiction. When Jake first started the relationship, he viewed their shared experience with addiction and incarceration as a plus: She understood what he was going through and recognized the signs and triggers that might presage a relapse. Several months into their relationship, Anna suffered a relapse, and the relationship then became more threatening to Jake's sobriety than emotionally supportive, so he ended it.

Family relationships can also create stress, such as when they become conflictual, when family members or partners have substance abuse or other health problems, or when the demands of the relationship feel overwhelming. Being in a relationship requires emotional work, and focusing on romantic partners might mean former prisoners have fewer emotional resources to expend on their own recovery and reintegration. Moreover, when family relationships turn from supportive to stressful, this can sometimes induce returning prisoners to turn to drugs and alcohol as a coping mechanism. In cases where this leads to a sustained relapse, the drug and/or alcohol use can threaten efforts to desist. Stressful, conflict-laden relationships are the negative analogue to the emotionally supportive relationships we discussed above, and illustrate how the effects of relationships differ based on the characteristics of the relationship.

The connection between relationship stress from romantic partners and recidivism was more pronounced among our female participants, but our male subjects also experienced difficulties due to relationship stress. Recall that Jake described his current relationship as the primary emotional support system he had for maintaining sobriety, but also explained that the continuing stress of interactions with former partners could trigger a relapse. Other men echoed Jake's concern with stressors from prior relationships and their connection to drug and alcohol abuse. For example, DeAngelo traced the roots of his alcoholism, a significant contributor to the crimes that led to his incarceration, to a particularly painful ending to his marriage:

> I was devastated. Like how could you accept these vows knowing that you was this kinda person, knowing that you can't live up to what these vows are saying? I think that's when I really start drinking. I've always drank, but I think that's when I really started drinking. But like I was just hurt. Man, I felt just like mistreated, like I just felt like something that you just don't even care about, something you throw out. I couldn't feel so low.

After the disintegration of this relationship, DeAngelo began drinking heavily. Over the next few years his drinking accelerated and he was arrested 3 times for driving while intoxicated. For many of our male subjects, the desire to maintain relationships with children from prior relationships forced them to interact with women with whom they had long, often troubled, histories, and led to stressful interactions.

Another possible consequence of relationship stress is residential instability. When family relationships or household roles become too stressful, a response may be to leave the household in order to escape the stress. For example, recall Damian, the 71-year old former musician discussed above, for whom caregiving proved so stressful and disruptive to his own goals that he moved out of the household that included his ex-wife and his son, even though the move left him homeless.

Family health problems were also significant sources of stress for our subjects, leading in some cases to relapse or criminal behavior. Consider again Randall, who tried to cope with his role strain by providing household labor. Eleven months after his release, Randall began a romantic relationship with a woman he met at a job assistance program. She suffered from a severe drug addiction and dropped out of college. Despite the challenges that both of them faced, Randall viewed the relationship as mutually supportive and considered asking her to marry him. "I think it'd help both of us … With her, keep her mind straight, and me, keep me from running the streets … Keep my mind right. Keep me focused." Randall and his girlfriend got engaged, and his new fiancé became pregnant. Randall was looking forward to a new life with his fiancé and their baby. His new role would motivate him to stop drinking and find a job.

> I told [my fiancé] that this is basically the deal I made with myself. That as soon as my baby got here I was gonna stop [drinking]. 'Cause I was just gonna be there a hundred percent. And then by me getting a job the same time, that would've cut [the drinking] all the way down, 'cause I wouldn't have had time to do nothing, 'cause I'm the type, I'll work all day.

For the first time since his release, Randall received job offers, one from a fast food restaurant and one from a light manufacturing plant. Randall felt a new sense of optimism after 2 years of daily struggle. But only a few days later, his fiancé experienced a difficult labor, and the baby girl died in neonatal intensive care just days after she was born. Randall worried that his fiancé's pain from the complications of labor coupled with the emotional loss would prompt her to relapse. He turned down the job offers and struggled to care for her as best he could. Randall himself began to suffer from severe depression and suicidal ideations due to his own grief. He dealt with the loss the only way he knew how. "I really been drinking now since my baby passed … I drink like a pint, a fifth or something like that [every day]."

## Discussion and Conclusion

### *Summary of Key Findings*

We found in both the quantitative and qualitative analyses that families have complex and countervailing effects on reintegration outcomes. Our statistical analysis focused on how different types of living arrangements are associated with markers of post-prison reintegration. We found that familial living arrangements played a critical role in providing residential stability after prison, which we view as foundational for reintegration in other domains and for desisting from crime and substance abuse. For both blacks and non-blacks, living with a parent or romantic partner greatly reduced the probability of moving relative to other private living arrangements. Residential stability, in turn, was negatively associated with arrests and substance abuse, although it was not associated with finding employment. Living in a private residence, in comparison to living in an institutional setting, was generally positively associated with finding employment. However, institutional living arrangements were associated with lower risks of arrest and testing positive for substance use, findings we interpret as resulting from the greater formal social control experienced in institutional residences. For blacks, living with a romantic partner increased the probability of employment, which is consistent with a theoretical framework emphasizing informal social control provided by romantic partners, particularly the role of romantic partners in motivating positive behaviors.

Our qualitative analysis focused on the role that family members and romantic partners play in prisoner reintegration. The influence of family depends heavily on the operation of traditional gender norms, the characteristics of family members, the characteristics of former prisoners, and the nature of the relationships and households in question. The most important and consistent role that families play in reintegration is meeting the basic material needs of former prisoners, particularly food and housing but also transportation and other forms of material assistance. Some families are able to provide even greater support, leveraging their economic and social resources to help their loved ones revive or establish career trajectories that lead to long-term stable employment and eventual economic independence. Family members can also be a key source of informal social control, through monitoring and supervising behavior, structuring routine activities, and providing motivation. These functions help former prisoners avoid negative behaviors such as substance abuse and crime and encourage more positive behaviors such as employment, schooling, and developing pro-social roles as parents, partners, or other caregiving roles. We suspect that the positive association between living with a romantic partner and finding employment, which we observed among blacks in the quantitative analysis, may be driven by such informal social control mechanisms. A third positive role for family members is providing emotional support, helping former prisoners weather the challenges of prisoner reentry and avoid falling back on old ways of dealing with stress and conflict, typically substance abuse. Women often played such roles. Our male subjects received emotional support from their romantic partners and, to a lesser degree, from female family members such as mothers.

However, the material support that families provided often led to role strain, especially for men returning home from prison who envisioned themselves as stepping into provider roles. Given the incredible challenges former prisoners face in the formal labor market, few of our male subjects were able to effectively play this provider role. Sometimes they replaced this provider role with more of a caregiving or care work role, but this challenged conventional male gender roles, and in some cases such caregiving proved overwhelming, conflicting with the other requirements of parole and post-prison reintegration. This role strain led in some cases to engagement in criminal behavior to make money, to relapse due to stress, or to residential instability (exiting the household to avoid role strain). Family relationships can also carry other sources of stress, such as interpersonal conflict or difficult caregiving burdens. A final type of negative influence can come from family members who themselves are engaged in substance use or crime and thus provide opportunities and inducements (sometimes resorting to coercion) for former prisoners to do so as well.

We can understand many of these processes through the lens of caregiving, care work, and more generally, health and health problems among both former prisoners and their families. Caregiving is, after all, a central part of family life. Many of our subjects, both men and women, established places for themselves in households or families through caregiving activities and care work. Given the traditional conception of caregiving and care work as feminine, these roles often worked better for our female subjects than our male subjects, for whom caregiving and to a lesser degree care work were sources of role strain. However, both men and women experienced the stresses of intensive caregiving. Moreover, former prisoners themselves required care from family members and romantic partners, given their pre-existing health and substance abuse problems and their meager social and economic resources.

Thus far we have said little about racial differences in the role of families in prisoner reintegration. This is because we saw few racial differences in either our qualitative or quantitative analyses, but that is a direct result of our focus in this chapter on dynamics *internal* to the family. In our quantitative analyses, both blacks and whites benefited from living with family in terms of residential stability, for example. In our qualitative analyses, both black and white men experienced role strain when they could not play the provider role and benefitted from the emotional support of romantic partners, for instance. Similarly, both blacks and whites with children drew motivation from their roles as parents. Yet, we do believe race plays a structural role in prisoner reintegration, largely by structuring the larger context within which families and former prisoners live and work, as revealed by the prior literature discussed above. Black families that receive former prisoners on average have fewer resources than the families of white former prisoners and live in poorer neighborhoods with higher rates of crime that are further from jobs and more heavily policed. Moreover, blacks have less work experience and lower levels of education and are more stigmatized by a felony record in the labor market, making it even more difficult for them to find work after release, and more likely to be harshly treated by the criminal justice system. Thus, we see in the administrative data that blacks are less likely to find employment, slightly more likely to be tested for substances while on parole, more likely to test positive, and more likely to abscond, to be arrested, put in a custodial sanction, or re-incarcerated. Non-blacks are more likely to move between private residences and more likely to be homeless. This suggests that differences in reintegration outcomes by race are more likely to be generated by family structural positions and circumstances external to the family than to racial differences in internal family dynamics.

## Implications for Future Research

One implication of our findings is that the successful reintegration of former prisoners will depend heavily on the family resources and other social supports to which they have access. This hypothesis deserves further investigation, and more work needs to be done to understand the dimensions of family reintegration that matter most and the processes or mechanisms through which they have their effects. In particular, our qualitative analysis suggest that future data collection on former prisoners and their families must include measures of the characteristics, experiences, and histories of the family members and romantic partners with whom former prisoners are interacting and/or living. Given the considerable health problems experienced by both the former prisoners and their family members and romantic partners that we document in our qualitative data, including physical health problems and addiction and other mental health problems, data collection should include health characteristics. Also important will be the nature of the relationships that former prisoners have with their family members and the different roles that former prisoners play in households as well as the resources of their family members and romantic partners.

Second, research thus far on these collateral consequences has focused mainly on the children of incarcerated fathers and the romantic partners of incarcerated men, with some additional attention on the children of incarcerated mothers. However, both our administrative and qualitative data on the families receiving former prisoners show that these collateral consequences may be felt by many others, from parents to siblings to grandparents. Braman's (2004) ethnographic work suggests that other family members are also heavily impacted by incarceration, reentry, and the challenges of reintegrating released prisoners. We have yet to fully investigate the full scope of the collateral consequences on incarceration and reentry for families.

## *Implications for Policy and Practice*

We close by considering what we can do to ease the transition back home for prisoners and their families and improve reintegration. Although many possible interventions hold promise for improving reintegration—including shorter prison sentences, alternatives to incarceration, better access to substance abuse treatment and medical care more generally, and better job training and educational opportunities, we focus here on policies directly related to families. First, we can do more to facilitate family contact during incarceration and reduce its costs. The current system includes prisons located far from urban areas, strict limitations and hassles on visitors, and exorbitant costs of phone calls. This system is designed to serve the interests of the overburdened corrections bureaucracy rather than facilitate the reintegration of prisoners after release. Surely information technology could be better leveraged to increase contact and communication with family during prison, and virtual visitation is now being offered on a limited basis in some states, including Pennsylvania and Oregon. There is also some evidence (Bales & Mears, 2008; Derkzen, Gobeil, & Gileno, 2009) that inmates who receive more frequent visits are less likely to recidivate later. One of these studies (Bales & Mears, 2008) also found that the timing of visits was important—visits closer to inmates' release from prison being more strongly associated with desistance—suggesting that visits are useful not only for maintaining family ties while in prison, but also for helping prisoners to prepare for release and reintegration.

Another way that correctional facilities could help build more positive ties between prisoners and their families is through parenting education programs for fathers and mothers. Although there is evidence that such programs can help inmates interact more with their children and change attitudes toward parenting, the connection between these programs and post-prison outcomes has not yet received sufficient study. The What Works in Reentry Clearinghouse (Council of State Governments

Justice Center, 2015) recently identified 20 studies of parenting education programs for incarcerated parents, but none met their criteria for rigor.

We can also do more to allow prisoners to assist family members while they are incarcerated as a way to build reciprocal exchange. Braman (2004) suggests, for example, that material support, however minor, has symbolic value for both families and prisoners, potentially increasing or at least maintaining the strength of family bonds. The question of prison labor is a tricky one, but work in prison at fair wages that could be directed to supporting family on the outside might have both economic and social benefits for prisoner reintegration.

Another pathway to the same goal would be to remove barriers to public benefits and receipt of social services among former prisoners. These barriers not only represent a form of secondary punishment of the ex-offender, but this is also a punishment that is visited upon their families, who end up stepping in to fill the gap. In the past, formerly incarcerated people have also been excluded from public housing, leading some who lacked other housing options to live with their family in public housing but remain off the lease, thus placing their family at risk of eviction. In 2011, U.S. Department of Housing and Urban Development Secretary Shaun Donovan (2011) wrote a letter to Public Housing Agency Directors encouraging them to be more flexible and reasonable with their admissions policies for formerly incarcerated people. Since then, some local housing authorities have launched initiatives to help people with criminal histories access federally subsidized housing and to make the screening process more holistic so that applicants with conviction histories can be evaluated on a range of criteria (Vera Institute of Justice, Center on Sentencing and Corrections, 2015).

A related point is that the burden of reintegrating prisoners falls mostly on their families, and these are often families that are ill-equipped to bear this burden. For instance, families often end up paying some or all of former prisoners' supervision fees, court fees, fines, and restitution. Moreover, in our own data we saw numerous instances of public benefits intended to support certain family members, particularly children, the elderly, and the disabled, being stretched to cover the needs of former prisoners. Social services, whether targeted at the reentry population or the poor more generally, do not seem to be doing much to alleviate this burden. We can think of this as a further collateral consequence of mass incarceration and mass reentry and an abdication of state responsibility for individuals on community supervision. As Comfort (2007) has argued, families are taking on social work and social welfare functions that in prior times would have been the responsibility of parole officers, who are now primarily tasked with monitoring and controlling an unprecedented reentry population.

**Acknowledgments** This research was supported by the Office of the Vice President for Research, Rackham Graduate School, Department of Sociology, Joint Ph.D. Program in Sociology and Public Policy, National Poverty Center, University of Michigan Center for Local, State, and Urban Policy, the Russell Sage Foundation, the National Institute of Justice (2008-IJ-CX-0018), the National Science Foundation (SES-1061018, SES- 1060708), and the Eunice Kennedy Shriver National Institute of Child Health and Human Development (1R21HD060160 01A1) and by center grants from the Eunice Kennedy Shriver National Institute of Child Health and Human

**Table 6** Description of outcomes and episodes for discrete-time event-history analysis

| Outcome/categories | Source | Units of time | Episodes |
|---|---|---|---|
| *Residential mobility*<br>*Any move*<br>No move (reference)<br>Moved | Michigan Department of Corrections: parole agent case notes | Weeks (measured in 7-day intervals from start of first episode) | A new episode begins when (a) the person was released from prison during the prior week or (b) the person begins the week in a non-institutional residence that is different from the place where the person was living at the start of the prior week. An episode cannot start when a person is incarcerated or is in a residential facility receiving treatment or care. An episode ends when a person moves to a new residence (either private or institutional), absconds, is discharged from parole, moves out of state, dies, or reaches the end of the observation period without an event |
| *Employment*<br>Not employed (reference)<br>Employed<br>Returned to prison or died | Michigan Unemployment Insurance Agency records | Calendar quarters | A new episode begins when (a) the person was released from prison during the prior quarter or (b) the person was employed during the prior quarter but unemployed in the current quarter. An episode ends if the person becomes employed after being unemployed in the prior quarter, is returned to prison, moves out of state, is discharged from parole, dies, reaches the end of the observation period without an event. A new episode cannot begin if a person is currently in prison or already been discharged from parole |
| *Arrest*<br>Not arrested (reference)<br>Arrested<br>Returned to prison or died | Michigan State Police records | Months (measured in 30-day intervals from start of first episode) | A new episode begins when (a) the person was released from prison during the prior month or (b) the person was arrested in the prior month. An episode ends when a person is arrested, is discharged from parole, moves out of state, dies, or reaches the end of the observation period without an event. A new episode cannot begin if a person is currently in prison or already been discharged from parole |
| *Substance use*<br>Not tested<br>Tested positive<br>Tested negative (reference)<br>Returned to prison or died | Michigan Department of Corrections: substance abuse test records | Months (measured in 30-day intervals from start of first episode) | A new episode begins when (a) the person was released from prison during the prior month or (b) the person tested positive for substance use during the prior month. An episode ends when a person tests positive for substance use, is discharged from parole, moves out of state, dies, or reaches the end of the observation period without an event. A new episode cannot begin if a person is currently in prison or already been discharged from parole |

Development to the Population Studies Centers at the University of Michigan (R24 HD041028) and at UC Berkeley (R24 HD073964), and by the National Institute on Aging to the Population Studies Centers at the University of Michigan (T32 AG000221). We thank Charley Chilcote and Paulette Hatchett at the Michigan Department of Corrections for facilitating access to the data and for advice on the research design. We thank Steve Heeringa and Zeina Mneimneh for advice on the sample design. Brenda Hurless, Bianca Espinoza, Andrea Garber, Jonah Siegal, Jay Borchert, Amy Cooter, Jane Rochmes, Claire Herbert, Jon Tshiamala, Katie Harwood, Elizabeth Sinclair, Carmen Gutierrez, Joanna Wu, Clara Rucker, Michelle Hartzog, Tyrell Connor, Madie Lupei, Elena Kaltsas, Brandon Cory, and Elizabeth Johnston provided excellent research assistance.

# Appendix

See Tables 6, 7, 8, 9, and 10.

**Table 7** Multinomial logit event history models of residential moves

| | Black | | Non-Black | |
|---|---|---|---|---|
| Number of observations (person weeks) | 275,574 | | 213,101 | |
| Log pseudolikelihood | 47,342.958 | | −37,940.558 | |
| Pseudo $R^2$ | 0.0798 | | 0.0819 | |
| | Residential move during episode | | | |
| | *Black* | | *Non-Black* | |
| Variables | Coef. | (SE) | Coef. | (SE) |
| *Measures of time* | | | | |
| Episode number | 0.005 | (0.011) | −0.003 | (0.013) |
| Episode number$^2$ | 0.000 | (0.001) | 0.001 | (0.001) |
| Episode number$^3$ | 0.000 | (0.000) | 0.000 | (0.000) |
| Interval number | −0.049 | (0.002) | −0.057 | (0.003) |
| Interval number$^2$ | 0.001 | (0.000) | 0.001 | (0.000) |
| Interval number$^3$ | 0.000 | (0.000) | 0.000 | (0.000) |
| Interval number$^4$ | 0.000 | (0.000) | 0.000 | (0.000) |
| *Living arrangement at beginning of week (ref=parents)* | | | | |
| Romantic partner | 0.051 | (0.056) | −0.043 | (0.062) |
| Other family | 0.183 | (0.055) | 0.251 | (0.069) |
| Other private | 0.147 | (0.059) | 0.194 | (0.062) |
| Hotel/motel | 0.380 | (0.174) | 0.736 | (0.131) |
| Mission/shelter/homeless | 0.397 | (0.108) | 0.910 | (0.107) |
| Unknown | −0.015 | (0.049) | 0.153 | (0.056) |

(continued)

**Table 7** (continued)

| | Black | | Non-Black | |
|---|---|---|---|---|
| *Non-private living arrangements during previous week* | | | | |
| Treatment/care | 0.122 | (0.041) | 0.133 | (0.045) |
| Intermediate sanction | 0.169 | (0.028) | 0.124 | (0.033) |
| Prison | –0.341 | (0.051) | –0.413 | (0.056) |
| Absconding | 0.230 | (0.115) | 0.592 | (0.137) |
| None (first episode since 2003 release) | 0.064 | (0.039) | 0.000 | (0.045) |
| *Proportion of days since 2003 release in each living arrangement* | | | | |
| Parent | 0.002 | (0.001) | 0.004 | (0.001) |
| Romantic partner | 0.002 | (0.001) | 0.002 | (0.001) |
| Other family | 0.001 | (0.001) | 0.003 | (0.001) |
| Other private | 0.001 | (0.001) | 0.002 | (0.001) |
| Receiving treatment/care | 0.024 | (0.003) | 0.022 | (0.003) |
| Hotel/motel | 0.011 | (0.002) | 0.011 | (0.002) |
| Mission/shelter/homeless | 0.010 | (0.002) | 0.007 | (0.002) |
| Correctional institution not used for sanction | 0.027 | (0.004) | 0.019 | (0.003) |
| Jail/correctional center | 0.020 | (0.002) | 0.018 | (0.002) |
| Prison | 0.007 | (0.001) | 0.008 | (0.001) |
| Living at pre-prison address | –0.095 | (0.040) | –0.094 | (0.041) |
| Any employment in current quarter | –0.273 | (0.030) | –0.193 | (0.030) |
| Number of arrests in month | 0.162 | (0.050) | 0.249 | (0.059) |
| *Substance use test outcomes in previous month (ref=tested negative)* | | | | |
| Not tested | 0.169 | (0.092) | –0.057 | (0.102) |
| One positive test | 0.470 | (0.036) | 0.495 | (0.051) |
| Two positive tests | 0.625 | (0.082) | 0.730 | (0.122) |
| Three or more positive tests | 1.263 | (0.172) | 0.495 | (0.243) |
| Cumulative proportion of quarters employed since 2003 release | 0.000 | (0.001) | 0.000 | (0.001) |
| Cumulative arrest rate per week since 2003 release | 0.006 | (0.008) | –0.005 | (0.009) |
| Female | 0.083 | (0.094) | 0.005 | (0.067) |
| Has any dependants | 0.032 | (0.030) | 0.011 | (0.032) |
| Female × has any dependants | –0.154 | (0.108) | 0.074 | (0.105) |
| Age (centered at 18) | –0.013 | (0.013) | –0.011 | (0.012) |
| $Age^2$ | 0.001 | (0.001) | 0.000 | (0.001) |
| $Age^3$ | 0.000 | (0.000) | 0.000 | (0.000) |
| *Marital status (ref=single)* | | | | |
| Married | 0.076 | (0.044) | –0.001 | (0.063) |
| Divorced or separated | 0.112 | (0.040) | 0.023 | (0.040) |
| Widowed, unknown, or common law | 0.161 | (0.140) | –0.053 | (0.106) |

(continued)

**Table 7** (continued)

| | Black | | Non-Black | |
|---|---|---|---|---|
| *Education (ref=0–8 years)* | | | | |
| 9–11 years of education | −0.148 | (0.055) | −0.103 | (0.058) |
| GED | −0.069 | (0.057) | −0.074 | (0.057) |
| 12 years of education | −0.164 | (0.063) | −0.153 | (0.064) |
| 13–19 years of education | −0.108 | (0.087) | −0.177 | (0.083) |
| Unknown | −0.182 | (0.139) | −0.103 | (0.136) |
| Known mental illness status | 0.160 | (0.039) | −0.011 | (0.034) |
| Flag for missing metal illness status | −0.056 | (0.081) | 0.168 | (0.219) |
| *Substance abuse history (ref=none)* | | | | |
| Alcohol only | −0.138 | (0.077) | −0.039 | (0.070) |
| THC only | −0.165 | (0.041) | 0.000 | (0.066) |
| Hard drugs only | 0.048 | (0.054) | 0.100 | (0.063) |
| Alcohol + THC | −0.106 | (0.054) | −0.124 | (0.057) |
| Hard drugs + alcohol/THC | 0.101 | (0.033) | 0.046 | (0.036) |
| *Offense type (ref=non-assaultive)* | | | | |
| Drug offense | −0.107 | (0.030) | −0.108 | (0.057) |
| Assaultive offense | −0.016 | (0.037) | −0.085 | (0.039) |
| Sex offender | 0.101 | (0.066) | 0.052 | (0.058) |
| Duration of prison spell prior to 2003 release (years) | −0.016 | (0.008) | −0.007 | (0.012) |
| *Prison Prefix (ref=prefix A)* | | | | |
| B | 0.143 | (0.033) | 0.166 | (0.037) |
| C or D | 0.242 | (0.039) | 0.309 | (0.044) |
| E or above | 0.189 | (0.057) | 0.308 | (0.077) |
| Living in private residence prior to incarceration | −0.044 | (0.043) | 0.015 | (0.047) |
| Any history of homelessness in pre-prison data | −0.005 | (0.075) | 0.105 | (0.074) |
| Employed during 1 year prior to incarceration | −0.047 | (0.049) | −0.069 | (0.046) |
| Employment history prior to incarceration unknown | −0.052 | (0.067) | 0.013 | (0.087) |
| Constant | −2.779 | (0.119) | −2.779 | (0.136) |

**Table 8** Multinomial logit event history models of arrests

| | Black | | Non-Black | | | | | |
|---|---|---|---|---|---|---|---|---|
| Number of observations (person months) | 24,672 | | 23,474 | | | | | |
| Log pseudolikelihood | −3939.07 | | −3241.52 | | | | | |
| Pseudo R2 | 0.2212 | | 0.2398 | | | | | |
| | Arrested (possibly imprisoned) | | | | Imprisoned without arrest | | | |
| | Black | | Non-Black | | Black | | Non-Black | |
| Variables | Coef. | (SE) | Coef. | (SE) | Coef. | (SE) | Coef. | (SE) |
| *Measures of time* | | | | | | | | |
| Episode number | 1.038 | (0.163) | 0.997 | (0.208) | 1.211 | (0.234) | 0.521 | (0.367) |
| Episode number^2 | −0.292 | (0.073) | −0.161 | (0.059) | −0.315 | (0.082) | −0.293 | (0.175) |
| Interval number | −0.012 | (0.012) | 0.009 | (0.015) | 0.006 | (0.020) | −0.033 | (0.025) |
| Interval number^2 | −0.003 | (0.001) | −0.001 | (0.001) | 0.002 | (0.001) | 0.001 | (0.001) |
| Interval number^3 | 0.000 | (0.000) | 0.000 | (0.000) | 0.000 | (0.000) | 0.000 | (0.000) |
| Interval number^4 | 0.000 | (0.000) | 0.000 | (0.000) | 0.000 | (0.000) | 0.000 | (0.000) |
| *Living arrangement (ref=parents)* | | | | | | | | |
| Romantic partner | −0.142 | (0.153) | 0.154 | (0.161) | 0.167 | (0.283) | −0.096 | (0.259) |
| Other family | −0.166 | (0.142) | −0.544 | (0.197) | −0.073 | (0.260) | −0.240 | (0.279) |
| Other private | 0.333 | (0.164) | −0.078 | (0.168) | 0.249 | (0.288) | −0.138 | (0.252) |
| Receiving treatment/care | −1.277 | (0.340) | −1.049 | (0.319) | −0.877 | (0.480) | −0.509 | (0.421) |
| Hotel/motel | 0.801 | (0.466) | 0.390 | (0.429) | −0.339 | (0.734) | −0.288 | (0.923) |
| Mission/shelter/homeless | 0.025 | (0.441) | −0.044 | (0.630) | −0.290 | (0.899) | −0.781 | (0.779) |
| Correctional institution not used for sanction | −2.266 | (0.474) | −0.576 | (0.447) | −1.816 | (0.700) | −0.330 | (0.569) |
| Jail/correctional center | −0.427 | (0.279) | −0.849 | (0.316) | 2.203 | (0.271) | 1.451 | (0.269) |
| Unknown | 0.339 | (1.677) | −6.666 | (7.649) | −20.228 | (6.707) | −19.590 | (7.475) |
| Absconding | 1.079 | (0.696) | 2.809 | (0.261) | 2.177 | (0.455) | −20.047 | (1.051) |

(continued)

**Table 8** (continued)

| | Black | | Non-Black | | | | | |
|---|---|---|---|---|---|---|---|---|
| Female | −0.237 | (0.344) | −0.258 | (0.353) | −0.468 | (0.544) | −0.337 | (0.511) |
| Has any dependants | −0.002 | (0.091) | 0.070 | (0.108) | −0.208 | (0.151) | −0.092 | (0.167) |
| Female × has any dependants | −0.088 | (0.392) | −0.274 | (0.422) | 0.211 | (0.636) | 0.593 | (0.609) |
| Age (centered at 18) | −0.061 | (0.018) | −0.007 | (0.019) | −0.048 | (0.033) | −0.023 | (0.027) |
| Age^2 | 0.000 | (0.000) | −0.001 | (0.001) | 0.000 | (0.001) | 0.000 | (0.001) |
| *Marital status* (*ref=single*) | | | | | | | | |
| Married | −0.111 | (0.150) | −0.416 | (0.178) | −0.190 | (0.244) | −0.306 | (0.278) |
| Divorced or separated | −0.002 | (0.152) | −0.165 | (0.146) | −0.002 | (0.240) | −0.016 | (0.210) |
| Widowed, unknown, or common law | 0.425 | (0.447) | 0.387 | (0.463) | −14.487 | (0.774) | 1.116 | (0.434) |
| *Education* (*ref=0–8 years*) | | | | | | | | |
| 9–11 years of education | −0.050 | (0.160) | −0.098 | (0.186) | 0.211 | (0.273) | 0.397 | (0.286) |
| GED | −0.023 | (0.166) | 0.181 | (0.178) | −0.038 | (0.287) | 0.337 | (0.290) |
| 12 years of education | −0.031 | (0.183) | −0.166 | (0.194) | 0.254 | (0.314) | 0.075 | (0.306) |
| 13–19 years of education | −0.013 | (0.228) | −0.167 | (0.277) | −0.224 | (0.437) | 0.441 | (0.354) |
| Unknown | −0.182 | (0.299) | 0.322 | (0.418) | 0.480 | (0.652) | −0.275 | (0.838) |
| Employed during 1 year prior to incarceration | −0.338 | (0.151) | −0.100 | (0.139) | 0.110 | (0.217) | 0.017 | (0.206) |
| Employment history prior to incarceration unknown | 0.202 | (0.190) | 0.159 | (0.250) | 0.286 | (0.335) | −0.438 | (0.385) |
| *Substance abuse history* (*ref=none*) | | | | | | | | |
| Alcohol only | 0.165 | (0.221) | 0.383 | (0.185) | 0.188 | (0.443) | 0.763 | (0.286) |
| THC only | 0.439 | (0.131) | 0.058 | (0.254) | 0.111 | (0.228) | 0.510 | (0.317) |
| Hard drugs only | 0.627 | (0.178) | 0.250 | (0.283) | 0.444 | (0.280) | 0.374 | (0.379) |
| Alcohol + THC | 0.227 | (0.182) | 0.621 | (0.151) | 0.182 | (0.326) | 0.686 | (0.241) |

| | | | | | | | | |
|---|---|---|---|---|---|---|---|---|
| Hard drugs + alcohol/THC | 0.540 | (0.108) | 0.149 | (0.116) | 0.230 | (0.187) | 0.560 | (0.170) |
| *Offense type (ref=non-assaultive)* | | | | | | | | |
| Drug offense | −0.178 | (0.097) | −0.119 | (0.161) | −0.140 | (0.175) | 0.093 | (0.246) |
| Assaultive offense | −0.039 | (0.117) | −0.056 | (0.119) | −0.036 | (0.193) | 0.060 | (0.173) |
| Sex offender | 0.089 | (0.162) | −0.027 | (0.171) | 0.754 | (0.226) | 0.736 | (0.198) |
| Duration of prison spell prior to 2003 release (years) | −0.047 | (0.024) | −0.039 | (0.028) | −0.016 | (0.041) | 0.035 | (0.041) |
| *Prison prefix (ref=prefix A)* | | | | | | | | |
| B | 0.372 | (0.104) | 0.703 | (0.113) | 0.477 | (0.174) | 0.361 | (0.176) |
| C or D | 0.812 | (0.122) | 0.684 | (0.142) | 0.787 | (0.223) | 0.234 | (0.216) |
| E or above | 0.986 | (0.201) | 1.776 | (0.268) | 1.253 | (0.306) | 1.213 | (0.339) |
| Living at pre-prison address | −0.218 | (0.105) | −0.019 | (0.123) | 0.055 | (0.188) | 0.202 | (0.186) |
| *Cumulative number of years spent in each living arrangement after 2003 release* | | | | | | | | |
| Parent | 0.000 | (0.000) | 0.000 | (0.000) | 0.000 | (0.001) | 0.000 | (0.001) |
| Romantic partner | 0.000 | (0.000) | −0.001 | (0.001) | 0.000 | (0.001) | 0.000 | (0.001) |
| Other family | 0.000 | (0.000) | 0.001 | (0.000) | 0.000 | (0.001) | 0.001 | (0.001) |
| Other private | −0.001 | (0.000) | 0.000 | (0.000) | 0.000 | (0.001) | 0.000 | (0.001) |
| Receiving treatment/care | −0.001 | (0.002) | 0.001 | (0.002) | 0.001 | (0.002) | 0.001 | (0.002) |
| Hotel/motel | 0.000 | (0.002) | 0.001 | (0.002) | 0.002 | (0.001) | −0.004 | (0.003) |
| Mission/shelter/homeless | 0.001 | (0.002) | −0.002 | (0.002) | 0.002 | (0.002) | 0.001 | (0.002) |
| Correctional institution not used for sanction | 0.002 | (0.001) | 0.000 | (0.002) | 0.000 | (0.003) | 0.003 | (0.001) |
| Jail/correctional center | −0.001 | (0.002) | −0.001 | (0.002) | −0.003 | (0.003) | 0.000 | (0.002) |
| Unknown | 0.001 | (0.001) | 0.010 | (0.006) | 0.006 | (0.005) | −0.042 | (0.034) |
| Absconding | −0.002 | (0.002) | −0.005 | (0.004) | −0.002 | (0.002) | 0.001 | (0.003) |

(continued)

**Table 8** (continued)

| | Black | | Non-Black | | | | | |
|---|---|---|---|---|---|---|---|---|
| *Substance use test outcomes in previous month (ref=tested negative)* | | | | | | | | |
| Not tested | 0.108 | (0.086) | 0.111 | (0.107) | 0.397 | (0.155) | 0.096 | (0.148) |
| One positive test | –0.044 | (0.163) | –0.119 | (0.229) | 0.147 | (0.286) | –0.184 | (0.322) |
| Two positive tests | –0.564 | (0.581) | –0.484 | (0.695) | –0.979 | (1.307) | –1.069 | (0.886) |
| Three or more positive tests | 0.608 | (0.616) | 0.814 | (0.750) | 1.387 | (0.871) | 1.134 | (0.776) |
| Number of arrests in month | 1.431 | (0.064) | 1.377 | (0.069) | 1.505 | (0.096) | 1.543 | (0.080) |
| Cumulative arrest rate per year since 2003 release | –0.078 | (0.011) | –0.046 | (0.013) | –0.068 | (0.016) | –0.027 | (0.017) |
| Any employment in current quarter | –0.313 | (0.105) | 0.107 | (0.115) | –0.257 | (0.199) | –0.246 | (0.173) |
| Cumulative proportion of quarters employed since 2003 release | 0.002 | (0.001) | –0.003 | (0.001) | 0.001 | (0.003) | 0.005 | (0.002) |
| Constant | –3.102 | (0.276) | –3.978 | (0.302) | –5.376 | (0.446) | –6.096 | (0.481) |

**Table 9** Multinomial logit event history models of substance use tests (reference outcome is negative test)

| | Black | Non-Black | | | | | | | | | | |
|---|---|---|---|---|---|---|---|---|---|---|---|---|
| Number of observations (person months) | 25,918 | 24,447 | | | | | | | | | | |
| Log pseudolikelihood | −22,217 | −19,015 | | | | | | | | | | |
| Pseudo R2 | 0.0808 | 0.0814 | | | | | | | | | | |
| | Positive test | | | | Continued without test | | | | Returned to prison | | | |
| | *Black* | | *Non-Black* | | *Black* | | *Non-Black* | | *Black* | | *Non-Black* | |
| | Coef. | (SE) | Coef. | (SE) | Coef. | (SE) | Coef. | (SE) | Coef. | (SE) | Coef. | (SE) |
| *Measures of time* | | | | | | | | | | | | |
| Episode number | 0.324 | (0.042) | 0.341 | (0.049) | −0.011 | (0.044) | −0.194 | (0.052) | 0.238 | (0.068) | 0.138 | (0.084) |
| Episode number^2 | −0.012 | (0.008) | −0.017 | (0.006) | 0.003 | (0.004) | 0.021 | (0.006) | −0.038 | (0.021) | −0.014 | (0.016) |
| Interval number | −0.055 | (0.011) | −0.046 | (0.014) | 0.050 | (0.009) | 0.047 | (0.009) | 0.068 | (0.017) | 0.036 | (0.021) |
| Interval number^2 | 0.005 | (0.001) | 0.002 | (0.002) | −0.001 | (0.001) | 0.000 | (0.001) | −0.006 | (0.002) | −0.005 | (0.002) |
| Interval number^3 | 0.000 | (0.000) | 0.000 | (0.000) | 0.000 | (0.000) | 0.000 | (0.000) | 0.000 | (0.000) | 0.000 | (0.000) |
| Interval number^4 | 0.000 | (0.000) | 0.000 | (0.000) | 0.000 | (0.000) | 0.000 | (0.000) | 0.000 | (0.000) | 0.000 | (0.000) |
| *Living Arrangement (ref=parents)* | | | | | | | | | | | | |
| Romantic partner | −0.086 | (0.119) | −0.018 | (0.181) | −0.115 | (0.112) | −0.034 | (0.124) | 0.176 | (0.219) | −0.055 | (0.208) |
| Other family | −0.009 | (0.101) | 0.173 | (0.156) | −0.107 | (0.104) | −0.132 | (0.129) | −0.179 | (0.197) | −0.367 | (0.229) |
| Other private | 0.164 | (0.129) | −0.077 | (0.166) | 0.194 | (0.122) | −0.149 | (0.124) | 0.469 | (0.245) | −0.169 | (0.230) |
| Receiving treatment/care | −0.909 | (0.208) | −1.423 | (0.299) | 0.120 | (0.157) | −0.024 | (0.164) | −1.035 | (0.432) | −0.722 | (0.359) |
| Hotel/motel | −0.080 | (0.277) | 0.028 | (0.400) | −0.308 | (0.208) | 0.032 | (0.255) | 0.179 | (0.564) | 0.645 | (0.468) |
| Mission/shelter/homeless | −0.275 | (0.297) | −0.503 | (0.459) | −0.396 | (0.214) | −0.080 | (0.277) | −0.253 | (0.657) | −2.411 | (1.141) |
| Correctional institution not used for sanction | −0.478 | (0.230) | −0.912 | (0.376) | −0.374 | (0.167) | −0.077 | (0.211) | −1.996 | (0.744) | 0.096 | (0.453) |

(continued)

**Table 9** (continued)

| | Black | Non-Black | | | | | | | | | | |
|---|---|---|---|---|---|---|---|---|---|---|---|---|
| Unknown | –0.481 | (0.694) | 0.036 | (1.523) | –0.557 | (0.458) | 15.282 | (0.667) | 0.322 | (2.038) | 11.201 | (6.995) |
| Female | 0.344 | (0.293) | 0.189 | (0.304) | 0.927 | (0.365) | 0.866 | (0.277) | 0.511 | (0.544) | 0.578 | (0.420) |
| Has any dependants | 0.018 | (0.079) | 0.001 | (0.113) | 0.136 | (0.086) | –0.103 | (0.099) | 0.118 | (0.137) | 0.014 | (0.140) |
| Female × has any dependants | –0.295 | (0.321) | –0.304 | (0.372) | –0.643 | (0.403) | –0.579 | (0.348) | –0.966 | (0.641) | –0.293 | (0.513) |
| Age (centered at 18) | –0.001 | (0.014) | 0.050 | (0.018) | 0.000 | (0.017) | 0.030 | (0.015) | –0.087 | (0.027) | –0.012 | (0.023) |
| Age^2 | 0.000 | (0.000) | –0.001 | (0.000) | 0.000 | (0.000) | –0.001 | (0.000) | 0.001 | (0.001) | 0.000 | (0.001) |
| *Marital status* (*ref=single*) | | | | | | | | | | | | |
| Married | –0.058 | (0.119) | –0.405 | (0.186) | 0.039 | (0.135) | –0.292 | (0.145) | 0.034 | (0.210) | –0.644 | (0.241) |
| Divorced or separated | –0.220 | (0.114) | –0.198 | (0.129) | –0.178 | (0.127) | –0.064 | (0.115) | –0.067 | (0.211) | –0.042 | (0.179) |
| Widowed, unknown, or common law | 0.132 | (0.350) | 0.259 | (0.363) | –0.245 | (0.470) | –0.710 | (0.389) | –0.182 | (0.672) | 0.111 | (0.472) |
| *Education* (*ref*=0–8 *years*) | | | | | | | | | | | | |
| 9–11 years of education | 0.075 | (0.135) | –0.189 | (0.177) | 0.324 | (0.163) | 0.025 | (0.162) | 0.120 | (0.232) | 0.642 | (0.293) |
| GED | 0.056 | (0.137) | –0.354 | (0.174) | 0.302 | (0.165) | 0.020 | (0.162) | 0.275 | (0.238) | 0.681 | (0.291) |
| 12 years of education | 0.056 | (0.157) | –0.466 | (0.188) | 0.535 | (0.176) | 0.000 | (0.166) | 0.473 | (0.262) | 0.568 | (0.303) |
| 13–19 years of education | –0.066 | (0.208) | –0.476 | (0.244) | 0.244 | (0.234) | 0.037 | (0.211) | –0.050 | (0.401) | 0.738 | (0.353) |
| Unknown | 0.211 | (0.289) | –0.365 | (0.340) | 0.542 | (0.327) | 0.091 | (0.397) | 0.189 | (0.560) | 0.455 | (0.744) |
| Employed during 1 year prior to incarceration | –0.075 | (0.118) | 0.135 | (0.140) | 0.034 | (0.134) | –0.087 | (0.129) | –0.073 | (0.203) | –0.013 | (0.183) |
| Employment history prior to incarceration unknown | –0.050 | (0.173) | –0.294 | (0.307) | 0.059 | (0.169) | –0.045 | (0.234) | 0.115 | (0.257) | 0.106 | (0.352) |
| *Substance abuse history* (*ref=none*) | | | | | | | | | | | | |
| Alcohol only | 0.065 | (0.255) | –0.308 | (0.220) | 0.258 | (0.256) | –0.138 | (0.183) | 0.603 | (0.317) | 0.756 | (0.255) |
| THC only | 0.408 | (0.121) | 0.035 | (0.213) | –0.004 | (0.140) | 0.055 | (0.242) | 0.298 | (0.199) | 0.408 | (0.292) |

| | | | | | | | | | | | | |
|---|---|---|---|---|---|---|---|---|---|---|---|---|
| Hard drugs only | 0.322 | (0.146) | 0.215 | (0.287) | 0.022 | (0.178) | 0.041 | (0.252) | 0.471 | (0.295) | 0.445 | (0.317) |
| Alcohol + THC | 0.336 | (0.153) | 0.298 | (0.184) | 0.233 | (0.173) | 0.207 | (0.176) | 0.298 | (0.262) | 0.778 | (0.221) |
| Hard drugs + alcohol/THC | 0.158 | (0.097) | 0.231 | (0.114) | 0.032 | (0.109) | 0.124 | (0.106) | 0.557 | (0.164) | 0.616 | (0.152) |
| *Offense type (ref = non-assaultive)* | | | | | | | | | | | | |
| Drug offense | 0.074 | (0.090) | –0.142 | (0.145) | 0.164 | (0.101) | –0.053 | (0.129) | –0.124 | (0.157) | –0.126 | (0.215) |
| Assaultive offense | –0.086 | (0.098) | –0.265 | (0.118) | –0.209 | (0.112) | –0.316 | (0.106) | –0.141 | (0.174) | 0.023 | (0.153) |
| Sex offender | 0.043 | (0.158) | –0.034 | (0.167) | –0.098 | (0.171) | 0.105 | (0.157) | 0.355 | (0.219) | 0.337 | (0.197) |
| Duration of prison spell prior to 2003 release (years) | –0.030 | (0.021) | 0.003 | (0.032) | –0.004 | (0.019) | –0.022 | (0.026) | –0.012 | (0.030) | –0.061 | (0.042) |
| *Prison prefix (ref = prefix A)* | | | | | | | | | | | | |
| B | 0.035 | (0.089) | 0.268 | (0.108) | –0.106 | (0.096) | 0.037 | (0.104) | 0.297 | (0.153) | 0.467 | (0.153) |
| C or D | 0.101 | (0.110) | 0.113 | (0.133) | 0.010 | (0.123) | 0.016 | (0.129) | 0.881 | (0.192) | 0.503 | (0.185) |
| E or above | 0.228 | (0.161) | 0.126 | (0.343) | 0.090 | (0.193) | –0.086 | (0.249) | 0.755 | (0.322) | 1.212 | (0.329) |
| Living at pre-prison address | 0.027 | (0.093) | 0.007 | (0.119) | 0.098 | (0.100) | –0.164 | (0.103) | –0.019 | (0.154) | –0.087 | (0.154) |
| *Cumulative number of quarters spent in each living arrangement after 2003 release* | | | | | | | | | | | | |
| Parent | 0.000 | (0.000) | –0.001 | (0.000) | 0.000 | (0.000) | 0.000 | (0.000) | 0.000 | (0.000) | 0.000 | (0.001) |
| Romantic partner | 0.000 | (0.000) | –0.001 | (0.001) | 0.000 | (0.000) | 0.000 | (0.000) | 0.000 | (0.001) | –0.001 | (0.001) |
| Other family | 0.000 | (0.000) | –0.001 | (0.001) | 0.000 | (0.000) | 0.000 | (0.000) | 0.001 | (0.000) | 0.001 | (0.001) |
| Other private | –0.001 | (0.000) | 0.000 | (0.001) | 0.000 | (0.000) | 0.000 | (0.000) | –0.001 | (0.001) | –0.001 | (0.001) |
| Receiving treatment/care | 0.002 | (0.001) | 0.000 | (0.002) | 0.002 | (0.001) | 0.000 | (0.002) | 0.003 | (0.002) | 0.002 | (0.002) |
| Hotel/motel | –0.001 | (0.001) | –0.002 | (0.002) | –0.002 | (0.001) | –0.001 | (0.001) | –0.002 | (0.002) | –0.005 | (0.005) |
| Mission/shelter/homeless | 0.000 | (0.001) | –0.004 | (0.002) | –0.001 | (0.001) | –0.001 | (0.002) | 0.000 | (0.002) | 0.001 | (0.002) |
| Correctional institution not used for sanction | 0.001 | (0.001) | 0.000 | (0.002) | –0.001 | (0.001) | –0.001 | (0.001) | 0.000 | (0.003) | –0.003 | (0.003) |

(continued)

**Table 9** (continued)

| | Black | Non-Black | | | | | | | | | | |
|---|---|---|---|---|---|---|---|---|---|---|---|---|
| Jail/correctional center | −0.011 | (0.003) | −0.001 | (0.002) | 0.000 | (0.002) | 0.002 | (0.001) | 0.000 | (0.002) | 0.004 | (0.002) |
| Unknown | 0.001 | (0.001) | 0.008 | (0.007) | 0.001 | (0.001) | 0.005 | (0.006) | 0.001 | (0.002) | 0.014 | (0.008) |
| Absconding | −0.001 | (0.002) | −0.002 | (0.003) | 0.004 | (0.002) | 0.002 | (0.002) | 0.001 | (0.003) | −0.012 | (0.006) |
| Number of arrests in month | −0.460 | (0.315) | −0.436 | (0.493) | 0.004 | (0.145) | 0.221 | (0.198) | 0.283 | (0.361) | 0.534 | (0.457) |
| Cumulative arrest rate per year since 2003 release | 0.020 | (0.064) | 0.026 | (0.096) | 0.110 | (0.055) | 0.130 | (0.078) | 0.122 | (0.060) | 0.154 | (0.079) |
| Number of residential moves in month | 0.746 | (0.052) | 0.722 | (0.066) | 0.359 | (0.033) | 0.257 | (0.034) | 1.701 | (0.071) | 1.477 | (0.069) |
| Cumulative residential move rate per year since 2003 release | −0.005 | (0.007) | −0.006 | (0.011) | −0.004 | (0.006) | −0.018 | (0.008) | −0.132 | (0.019) | −0.082 | (0.015) |
| Any employment in current quarter | −0.222 | (0.085) | −0.082 | (0.095) | −0.229 | (0.060) | −0.174 | (0.059) | −0.720 | (0.169) | −0.229 | (0.146) |
| Cumulative proportion of quarters employed since 2003 release | 0.001 | (0.001) | 0.000 | (0.001) | −0.001 | (0.001) | −0.002 | (0.001) | 0.002 | (0.002) | −0.004 | (0.002) |
| Constant | −1.938 | (0.232) | −2.071 | (0.303) | −0.004 | (0.263) | 0.332 | (0.267) | −2.568 | (0.419) | −3.431 | (0.474) |

**Table 10** Multinomial logit event history models of employment

| | Black | | Non-Black | | | | | |
|---|---|---|---|---|---|---|---|---|
| Number of observations (person quarters) | 14,596 | | 10,698 | | | | | |
| Log pseudolikelihood | –6704 | | –5924 | | | | | |
| Pseudo R2 | 0.1086 | | 0.1045 | | | | | |
| | Employed | | | | Returned to prison | | | |
| | *Black* | | *Non-Black* | | *Black* | | *Non-Black* | |
| Variables | Coef. | (SE) | Coef. | (SE) | Coef. | (SE) | Coef. | (SE) |
| *Measures of time* | | | | | | | | |
| Episode number | 1.020 | (0.249) | 0.475 | (0.200) | 0.472 | (0.276) | 0.025 | (0.276) |
| Episode number^2 | –0.151 | (0.062) | –0.084 | (0.042) | –0.062 | (0.061) | –0.064 | (0.058) |
| Interval number | 2.305 | (0.199) | 2.004 | (0.354) | 1.129 | (0.169) | 1.703 | (0.235) |
| Interval number^2 | –0.497 | (0.057) | –0.432 | (0.105) | –0.217 | (0.041) | –0.394 | (0.066) |
| Interval number^3 | 0.038 | (0.006) | 0.032 | (0.011) | 0.016 | (0.004) | 0.032 | (0.007) |
| Interval number^4 | –0.001 | (0.000) | –0.001 | (0.000) | 0.000 | (0.000) | –0.001 | (0.000) |
| *Season (ref=Jan–March)* | | | | | | | | |
| April–June | –0.232 | (0.101) | –0.384 | (0.093) | –0.054 | (0.104) | –0.017 | (0.124) |
| July–September | 0.354 | (0.088) | 0.209 | (0.081) | –0.102 | (0.104) | 0.250 | (0.117) |
| October–December | 0.481 | (0.089) | 0.453 | (0.089) | –0.140 | (0.108) | 0.014 | (0.131) |
| *Living arrangement (ref=parents)* | | | | | | | | |
| Romantic partner | 0.331 | (0.115) | –0.145 | (0.108) | 0.104 | (0.149) | –0.165 | (0.176) |
| Other family | 0.030 | (0.110) | 0.004 | (0.108) | 0.064 | (0.133) | –0.144 | (0.176) |
| Other private | 0.020 | (0.142) | –0.138 | (0.117) | 0.104 | (0.180) | 0.270 | (0.158) |
| Receiving treatment/care | 0.540 | (0.187) | –0.124 | (0.182) | 0.312 | (0.196) | 0.359 | (0.219) |
| Hotel/motel | –0.068 | (0.408) | 0.070 | (0.241) | 1.016 | (0.303) | 0.774 | (0.308) |
| Mission/shelter/homeless | 0.234 | (0.327) | 0.207 | (0.264) | 0.359 | (0.344) | 0.902 | (0.318) |

(continued)

**Table 10** (continued)

| | Black | | Non-Black | | | | | |
|---|---|---|---|---|---|---|---|---|
| Correctional institution not used for sanction | −0.127 | (0.188) | −0.786 | (0.164) | 0.021 | (0.220) | −0.990 | (0.305) |
| Jail/correctional center | −0.646 | (0.178) | −0.607 | (0.159) | −0.035 | (0.164) | −0.080 | (0.177) |
| Unknown | −0.046 | (0.377) | −1.302 | (0.535) | 0.696 | (0.257) | 0.782 | (0.357) |
| Absconding | −1.037 | (0.175) | −1.482 | (0.235) | −0.708 | (0.180) | −0.355 | (0.219) |
| County unemployment rate | −0.073 | (0.132) | 0.008 | (0.084) | 0.018 | (0.159) | −0.113 | (0.115) |
| County unemployment rate^2 | 0.002 | (0.009) | −0.003 | (0.005) | −0.004 | (0.011) | 0.006 | (0.007) |
| Female | −0.015 | (0.213) | 0.296 | (0.179) | −0.252 | (0.279) | 0.033 | (0.302) |
| Has any dependants | −0.066 | (0.071) | −0.127 | (0.069) | 0.179 | (0.087) | −0.030 | (0.099) |
| Female × has any dependants | 0.226 | (0.250) | −0.305 | (0.230) | 0.224 | (0.330) | 0.042 | (0.375) |
| Age (centered at 18) | 0.029 | (0.015) | −0.003 | (0.012) | −0.055 | (0.016) | −0.060 | (0.018) |
| Age^2 | −0.001 | (0.000) | −0.001 | (0.000) | 0.000 | (0.000) | 0.000 | (0.000) |
| *Marital status* (*ref=single*) | | | | | | | | |
| Married | 0.051 | (0.105) | 0.074 | (0.105) | −0.012 | (0.136) | −0.195 | (0.173) |
| Divorced or separated | 0.129 | (0.097) | 0.023 | (0.090) | 0.318 | (0.122) | 0.216 | (0.128) |
| Widowed, unknown, or common law | −0.099 | (0.290) | −0.281 | (0.257) | 0.256 | (0.309) | 0.473 | (0.307) |
| *Education* (*ref=0–8 years*) | | | | | | | | |
| 9–11 years of education | 0.255 | (0.130) | 0.180 | (0.126) | 0.216 | (0.154) | 0.144 | (0.177) |
| GED | 0.329 | (0.136) | 0.245 | (0.127) | 0.412 | (0.158) | 0.261 | (0.173) |
| 12 years of education | 0.577 | (0.137) | 0.244 | (0.135) | 0.210 | (0.174) | 0.064 | (0.190) |
| 13–19 years of education | 0.504 | (0.183) | 0.196 | (0.178) | 0.274 | (0.223) | 0.328 | (0.246) |
| Unknown | 0.294 | (0.299) | 0.302 | (0.309) | 0.559 | (0.374) | 0.306 | (0.329) |
| Employed during 1 year prior to incarceration | 0.280 | (0.096) | 0.191 | (0.087) | −0.034 | (0.132) | −0.061 | (0.128) |
| Employment history prior to incarceration unknown | −0.018 | (0.152) | 0.087 | (0.161) | −0.103 | (0.192) | −0.097 | (0.236) |

| | | | | | | | | |
|---|---|---|---|---|---|---|---|---|
| *Substance abuse history (ref=none)* | | | | | | | | |
| Alcohol only | 0.181 | (0.186) | 0.019 | (0.148) | 0.080 | (0.248) | 0.654 | (0.182) |
| THC only | −0.149 | (0.113) | 0.039 | (0.154) | 0.069 | (0.130) | 0.563 | (0.203) |
| Hard Drugs only | −0.100 | (0.149) | −0.471 | (0.189) | 0.473 | (0.147) | 0.142 | (0.209) |
| Alcohol + THC | −0.102 | (0.149) | 0.046 | (0.123) | 0.238 | (0.144) | 0.515 | (0.170) |
| Hard drugs + alcohol/THC | −0.058 | (0.085) | −0.038 | (0.079) | 0.518 | (0.095) | 0.581 | (0.107) |
| *Offense type (ref=non-assaultive)* | | | | | | | | |
| Drug offense | −0.045 | (0.081) | −0.035 | (0.104) | −0.372 | (0.091) | −0.142 | (0.151) |
| Assaultive offense | 0.054 | (0.092) | 0.001 | (0.078) | 0.104 | (0.106) | 0.196 | (0.112) |
| Sex offender | 0.032 | (0.148) | 0.098 | (0.113) | 0.598 | (0.136) | 0.694 | (0.149) |
| Duration of prison spell prior to 2003 release (years) | 0.052 | (0.017) | 0.018 | (0.019) | 0.021 | (0.023) | 0.043 | (0.030) |
| *Prison prefix (ref=prefix A)* | | | | | | | | |
| B | 0.128 | (0.080) | −0.178 | (0.080) | 0.812 | (0.098) | 0.979 | (0.114) |
| C or D | 0.001 | (0.099) | −0.179 | (0.099) | 1.139 | (0.115) | 1.368 | (0.127) |
| E or above | 0.040 | (0.155) | −0.212 | (0.199) | 1.201 | (0.167) | 2.042 | (0.214) |
| Living at pre-prison address | −0.037 | (0.091) | 0.017 | (0.082) | −0.129 | (0.115) | 0.040 | (0.131) |
| *Cumulative number of quarters spent in each living arrangement after 2003 release* | | | | | | | | |
| Parent | −0.064 | (0.025) | −0.075 | (0.022) | −0.038 | (0.028) | 0.040 | (0.034) |
| Romantic partner | −0.059 | (0.029) | −0.042 | (0.027) | −0.092 | (0.037) | −0.003 | (0.040) |
| Other family | −0.073 | (0.024) | −0.014 | (0.035) | −0.056 | (0.030) | 0.139 | (0.044) |
| Other private | −0.022 | (0.034) | −0.057 | (0.041) | −0.056 | (0.045) | −0.018 | (0.046) |
| Receiving treatment/care | −0.017 | (0.082) | 0.032 | (0.073) | 0.065 | (0.094) | 0.164 | (0.078) |
| Hotel/motel | −0.041 | (0.163) | −0.113 | (0.197) | 0.043 | (0.135) | −0.007 | (0.201) |
| Mission/shelter/homeless | 0.097 | (0.088) | −0.339 | (0.141) | −0.016 | (0.140) | 0.021 | (0.155) |
| Correctional institution not used for sanction | 0.006 | (0.092) | 0.221 | (0.087) | −0.189 | (0.150) | 0.281 | (0.136) |

(continued)

**Table 10** (continued)

| | Black | | Non-Black | | | | | |
|---|---|---|---|---|---|---|---|---|
| Jail/correctional center | 0.155 | (0.063) | 0.071 | (0.069) | 0.090 | (0.066) | 0.224 | (0.080) |
| Unknown | −0.266 | (0.144) | 0.108 | (0.101) | 0.049 | (0.078) | 0.125 | (0.209) |
| Absconding | −0.062 | (0.028) | −0.005 | (0.034) | −0.008 | (0.031) | 0.043 | (0.051) |
| *Substance use test outcomes in previous quarter (ref=tested negative)* | | | | | | | | |
| Not tested | −0.251 | (0.069) | 0.062 | (0.065) | −0.107 | (0.085) | −0.030 | (0.094) |
| One positive test | −0.281 | (0.121) | 0.205 | (0.132) | 0.134 | (0.130) | 0.184 | (0.175) |
| Two positive tests | −0.359 | (0.204) | −0.326 | (0.268) | 0.261 | (0.184) | 0.122 | (0.249) |
| Three or more positive tests | −0.318 | (0.285) | −0.576 | (0.416) | 0.091 | (0.275) | −0.848 | (0.569) |
| Number of arrests in calendar quarter | −0.034 | (0.171) | −0.047 | (0.215) | 0.164 | (0.132) | 0.233 | (0.212) |
| Cumulative arrest rate per quarter since 2003 release | −0.528 | (0.340) | −0.160 | (0.350) | 0.716 | (0.255) | 0.045 | (0.391) |
| Number of residential moves in calendar quarter | 0.026 | (0.037) | −0.008 | (0.033) | 0.111 | (0.029) | 0.108 | (0.030) |
| Cumulative residential move rate per year since 2003 release | −0.023 | (0.010) | −0.001 | (0.008) | 0.000 | (0.008) | 0.007 | (0.006) |
| Constant | −5.902 | (0.605) | −4.170 | (0.549) | −4.890 | (0.709) | −4.697 | (0.628) |

## References

Agnew, R. (1992). Foundation for a general strain theory of crime and delinquency. *Criminology, 30*(1), 47–87.

Alexander, M. (2010). *The new Jim Crow: Mass incarceration in the age of colorblindness.* New York: New Press.

Bales, W. D., & Mears, D. P. (2008). Inmate social ties and the transition to society: Does visitation reduce recidivism? *Journal of Research in Crime & Delinquency, 45*(3), 287–321.

Bersani, B. E., Laub, J. H., & Nieuwbeerta, P. (2009). Marriage and desistance from crime in the Netherlands: Do gender and socio-historical context matter? *Journal of Quantitative Criminology, 25*(1), 3–24.

Bradley, K. H., Oliver, R. B. M., Richardson, N. C., & Slayter, E. M. (2001). *No place like home: Housing and the ex-prisoner.* Community Resources for Justice. Retrieved from http://www.crj.org/cji/entry/publication_noplacelikehome

Braman, D. (2004). *Doing time on the outside.* Ann Arbor, MI: University of Michigan Press.

Brayne, S. (2014). Surveillance and system avoidance: Criminal justice contact and institutional attachment. *American Sociological Review, 79*(3), 367–391.

Cohen, L. E., & Felson, M. (1979). Social change and crime rate trends: A routine activity approach. *American Sociological Review, 44*(4), 588–608.

Cohen, S. (2004). Social relationships and health. *American Psychologist, 59*(8), 676–684.

Colvin, M., Cullen, F. T., & Vander Ven, T. (2002). Coercion, social support, and crime: An emerging theoretical consensus. *Criminology, 40*(1), 19–42.

Comfort, M. (2007). *Doing time together.* Chicago: University of Chicago Press.

Council of State Governments Justice Center. (2015). *What works in reentry clearinghouse.* Retrieved from https://whatworks.csgjusticecenter.org/

Cullen, F. T. (1994). Social support as an organizing concept for criminology: Presidential address to the Academy of Criminal Justice Sciences. *Justice Quarterly, 11*(4), 527–559.

Derkzen, D., Gobeil, R., & Gileno, J. (2009). *Visitation and post-release outcome among federally-sentenced offenders.* Correctional Service Canada. Retrieved from http://www.csc-scc.gc.ca/research/r205-eng.shtml

Donovan, S. (2011, June 17). *Letter to Public Housing Authority executive directors.* Retrieved from http://usich.gov/resources/uploads/asset_library/Rentry_letter_from_Donovan_to_PHAs_6-17-11.pdf

Ganem, N. M., & Agnew, R. (2007). Parenthood and adult criminal offending: The importance of relationship quality. *Journal of Criminal Justice, 35*(6), 630–643.

Garland, D. (2001). *Mass imprisonment: Social causes and consequences.* Thousand Oaks, CA: Sage.

Giordano, P. C., Cernkovich, S. A., & Rudolph, J. L. (2002). Gender, crime, and desistance: Toward a theory of cognitive transformation. *American Journal of Sociology, 107*(4), 990–1064.

Goffman, A. (2014). *On the run: Fugitive life in an American city.* Chicago: University of Chicago Press.

Greenfeld, L. A., & Snell, T. L. (1999). *Women offenders* (NCJ 175688). Bureau of Justice Statistics Special Report. Retrieved from http://www.bjs.gov/content/pub/pdf/wo.pdf

Grinstead, O., Faigekes, B., Bancroft, C., & Zack, B. (2001). The financial cost of maintaining relationships with incarcerated African-American men: Results from a survey of women prison visitors. *Journal of African-American Men, 6*(1), 59–69.

Harding, D. J., Morenoff, J. D., & Herbert, C. W. (2013). Home is hard to find: Neighborhoods, institutions, and the residential trajectories of returning prisoners. *Annals of the American Academy of Political and Social Science, 647*(1), 214–236.

Harding, D. J., Wyse, J., Dobson, C., & Morenoff, J. D. (2014). Making ends meet after prison. *Journal of Policy Analysis and Management, 33*(2), 440–470.

Harris, O., & Miller, R. R. (Eds.). (2003). *Impacts of incarceration on the African-American family.* New Brunswick, NJ: Transaction Publishers.

Haskins, A. R. (2014). Unintended consequences: Effects of paternal incarceration on child school readiness and later special education placement. *Sociological Science, 1*, 141–158.
Haskins, A. R. (2015). Paternal incarceration and child-reported behavioral functioning at age 9. *Social Science Research, 52*, 18–33.
Herbert, C. W., Morenoff, J. D., & Harding, D. J. (2015). Homelessness and housing insecurity among former prisoners. *Russell Sage Foundation Journal of the Social Sciences, 1*(2), 44–79.
Hirschi, T. (1969). *Causes of delinquency*. Berkeley: University of California Press.
Holzer, H. J., Offner, P., & Sorensen, E. (2005). What explains the continuing decline in labor force activity among young black men? *Labor History, 46*(1), 37–55.
Holzer, H. J., Raphael, S., & Stoll, M. A. (2004). Will employers hire former offenders? Employer preferences, background checks, and their determinants. In B. Western, M. E. Patillo, & D. F. Wiman (Eds.), *Imprisoning America: The social effects of mass incarceration* (pp. 205–243). New York: Russell Sage Foundation.
Holzer, H. J., Raphael, S., & Stoll, M. A. (2007). The effect of an applicant's criminal history on employer hiring decisions and screening practices: Evidence from Los Angeles. In S. D. Bushway, M. A. Stoll, & D. Weiman (Eds.), *Barriers to reentry?: The labor market for released prisoners in post-industrial America* (pp. 117–150). New York: Russell Sage Foundation.
King, R., Massoglia, M., & MacMillan, R. (2007). The context of marriage and crime: Gender, the propensity to marry, and offending in early adulthood. *Criminology, 45*(1), 33–65.
Kirk, D. S. (2009). A natural experiment on residential change and recidivism: Lessons from Hurricane Katrina. *American Sociological Review, 74*(3), 484–505.
Laub, J. H., Nagin, D. S., & Sampson, R. J. (1998). Trajectories of change in criminal offending: Good marriages and the desistance process. *American Sociological Review, 63*(2), 225–238.
Laub, J. H., & Sampson, R. J. (2003). *Shared beginnings, divergent lives: Delinquent boys to age 70*. Cambridge, MA: Harvard University Press.
Leverentz, A. (2014). *The ex-prisoner's dilemma: How women negotiate competing narratives of reentry and desistance*. New Brunswick, NJ: Rutgers University Press.
Lin, N. (1986). Conceptualizing social support. In N. Lin, A. Dean, & W. Edsel (Eds.), *Social support, life events, and depression* (pp. 17–30). Orlando, FL: Academic Press.
Lutze, F. E., Rosky, J. W., & Hamilton, Z. K. (2014). Homelessness and reentry: A multisite outcome evaluation of Washington State's Reentry Housing Program for high risk offenders. *Criminal Justice and Behavior, 41*(4), 471–491.
Maruna, S. (2001). *Making good: How ex-offenders reform and reclaim their lives*. Washington, DC: American Psychological Association.
Massoglia, M., Firebaugh, G., & Warner, C. (2013). Racial variation in the effect of incarceration on neighborhood attainment. *American Sociological Review, 78*(1), 142–165.
Mauer, M., & Chesney-Lind, M. (Eds.). (2002). *Invisible punishment: The collateral consequences of mass imprisonment*. New York: New Press.
Metraux, S., & Culhane, D. P. (2004). Homeless shelter use and reincarceration following prison release. *Criminology and Public Policy, 3*(2), 139–160.
Morenoff, J. D., & Harding, D. J. (2011). *Final technical report: Neighborhoods, recidivism, and employment among returning prisoners*. National Institute of Justice, U.S. Department of Justice. Retrieved from https://www.ncjrs.gov/pdffiles1/nij/grants/236436.pdf
National Research Council of the National Academies. (2007). *Parole, desistance from crime and community integration*. Washington, DC: National Academies Press.
National Research Council of the National Academies. (2014). *The growth of incarceration in the United States: Exploring causes and consequences*. Washington, DC: National Academies Press.
Osgood, D. W., Wilson, J. K., O'Malley, P. M., Bachman, J. G., & Johnston, L. D. (1996). Routine activities and individual deviant behavior. *American Sociological Review, 61*(4), 635–655.
Pager, D. (2003). The mark of a criminal record. *American Journal of Sociology, 108*(5), 937–975.
Pager, D. (2007). *Marked: Race, crime, and finding work in an era of mass incarceration*. Chicago: University of Chicago Press.

Pager, D., Western, B., & Bonikowski, B. (2009). Discrimination in a low-wage labor market: A field experiment. *American Sociological Review, 74*(5), 777–799.

Petersilia, J. (2003). *When prisoners come home: Parole and prisoner reentry*. New York: Oxford University Press.

Pettit, B., & Western, B. (2004). Mass imprisonment and the life course: Race and class inequality in U.S. incarceration. *American Sociological Review, 69*(2), 151–169.

Pew Center on the States. (2008). *One in 100: Behind bars in America 2008*. Washington, DC: Pew Charitable Trusts. Retrieved from http://www.pewtrusts.org/~/media/legacy/uploadedfiles/wwwpewtrustsorg/reports/sentencing_and_corrections/onein100pdf.pdf.

Pew Center on the States. (2009). *One in 31: The long reach of American corrections*. Washington, DC: Pew Charitable Trusts. Retrieved from http://www.convictcriminology.org/pdf/pew/onein31.pdf.

Raphael, S., & Stoll, M. A. (2009). Why are so many Americans in prison? In S. Raphael & M. A. Stoll (Eds.), *Do prisons make us safer? The benefits and costs of the prison boom* (pp. 27–72). New York: Russell Sage Foundation.

Rios, V. M. (2011). *Punished: Policing the lives of black and Latino boys*. New York: New York University Press.

Roman, C. G., & Travis, J. (2006). Where will I sleep tomorrow? Housing, homelessness, and the returning prisoner. *Housing Policy Debate, 17*(2), 389–418.

Royster, D. (2003). *Race and the invisible hand: How white networks exclude black men from blue collar jobs*. Berkeley: University of California Press.

Sampson, R. D., & Laub, J. H. (1993). *Crime in the making: Pathways and turning points through life*. Cambridge, MA: Harvard University Press.

Sampson, R. D., Laub, J. H., & Wimer, C. (2006). Does marriage reduce crime? A counterfactual approach to within-individual causal effects. *Criminology, 44*(3), 465–508.

Statistics Canada. (2015, April 23). *Household living arrangements*. Retrieved August 2015, from http://www.statcan.gc.ca/eng/concepts/definitions/hla

Steele, F. (2008). Multilevel models for longitudinal data. *Journal of the Royal Statistical Society: Series A (Statistics in Society), 171*(1), 5–19.

Travis, J. (2005). *But they all come back: Facing the challenges of prisoner reentry*. Washington, DC: Urban Institute Press.

Turney, K. (2014a). The intergenerational consequences of mass incarceration: Implications for children's co-residence and contact with grandparents. *Social Forces, 93*(1), 299–327.

Turney, K. (2014b). Stress proliferation across generations? Examining the relationship between parental incarceration and childhood health. *Journal of Health and Social Behavior, 55*(3), 302–319.

Turney, K. (2014c). The consequences of paternal incarceration for maternal neglect and harsh parenting. *Social Forces, 92*(4), 1607–1636.

Turney, K. (2015a). Liminal men: Incarceration and relationship dissolution. *Social Problems, 62*(4), 499–528.

Turney, K. (2015b). Paternal incarceration and children's food insecurity: A consideration of variation and mechanisms. *Social Service Review, 89*(2), 335–367.

Turney, K., & Haskins, A. R. (2014). Falling behind? Children's early grade retention after paternal incarceration. *Sociology of Education, 87*(4), 241–258.

Turney, K., & Wildeman, C. (2013). Redefining relationships: Explaining the countervailing consequences of paternal incarceration for parenting. *American Sociological Review, 78*(6), 949–979.

Umberson, D., Chen, M. D., House, J. S., Hopkins, K., & Slaten, E. (1996). The effect of social relationships on psychological well-being: Are men and women really so different? *American Sociological Review, 61*, 837–857.

Vera Institute of Justice, Center on Sentencing and Corrections. (2015). *Public housing for people with criminal histories* (Fact Sheet). Retrieved from http://www.vera.org/sites/default/files/resources/downloads/public-housing-criminal-histories-fact-sheet.pdf

Visher, C. A., & Travis, J. (2003). Transitions from prison to community: Understanding individual pathways. *Annual Review of Sociology, 29*, 89–113.
Wacquant, L. (2001). Deadly symbiosis: When ghetto and prison meet and mesh. *Punishment & Society, 3*(1), 95–133.
Wakefield, S., & Uggen, C. (2010). Incarceration and stratification. *Annual Review of Sociology, 36*, 387–406.
Wakefield, S., & Wildeman, C. (2013). *Children of the prison boom: Mass incarceration and the future of American inequality*. New York: Oxford University Press.
Warr, M. (1998). Life-course transitions and desistance from crime. *Criminology, 36*(2), 183–216.
West, H. C., Sabol, W. J., & Greenman, S. J. (2010). *Prisoners in 2009* (NCJ 231675). Washington, DC: Bureau of Justice Statistics.
Western, B. (2006). *Punishment and inequality in America*. New York: Russell Sage Foundation.
Wildeman, C., Schnittker, J., & Turney, K. (2012). Despair by association? The mental health of mothers with children by recently incarcerated fathers. *American Sociological Review, 77*(2), 216–243.
Wildeman, C., & Turney, K. (2014). Positive, negative, or null? The effects of maternal incarceration on children's behavioral problems. *Demography, 51*(3), 1041–1068.
Wyse, J. J. B., Harding, D. J., & Morenoff, J. D. (2014). Romantic relationships and criminal desistance: Processes and pathways. *Sociological Forum, 29*(2), 365–385.

# Exploring the Challenges Former Prisoners Face Finding Work

**Sandra Susan Smith**

## Introduction

"Families, Prisoner Reentry, and Reintegration" (Harding et al., Chap. 5), from here on referred to as "Families," is centrally concerned with how families both enhance and hinder former prisoners' community reintegration. Using a mixed-methods analytic approach, Harding and collaborators illustrate that the material assistance, informal social control, and emotional support that families provide enable former prisoners to achieve housing stability, to desist from crime, and, most important for my response, to find work. As an illustration, relatives may provide former prisoners with transportation to facilitate job search and help former prisoners to complete job applications. Better-off families go a step further by leveraging their social networks for valuable job information and influence and also by investing in former prisoner's education and training. The objective here is to increase former prisoners' access to stable jobs that pay a living wage and offer opportunities for advancement. Thus relatives' efforts, when successful, can militate against the many challenges former prisoners face when trying to secure employment. To the extent though that families lack the material resources to share, fail to implement effective informal controls, and cause their formerly incarcerated relatives undue stress, they do little to help former prisoners confront challenges associated with finding work and may actually contribute to former prisoners' reduced odds of successful reintegration.

"Families" speaks powerfully to the role that the family plays in shaping former prisoners' life chances immediately post-release. It is at its best when illustrating the ways in which its male subjects attempt to reconcile their identities as good men in a context where they cannot easily fulfill the breadwinner role. The authors'

S.S. Smith (✉)
Department of Sociology, University of California Berkeley, Berkeley, CA, USA
e-mail: sandra.smith@berkeley.edu



L. Burton et al. (eds.), *Boys and Men in African American Families*, National Symposium on Family Issues 7, DOI 10.1007/978-3-319-43847-4_9

focus on men's turn to caregiving as a substitute for breadwinning alone makes the study an extremely important contribution to this area of research and is consistent with findings reported elsewhere that highlight how changes in structural opportunities and constraints can fundamentally alter the roles that men and women play within the family. For its effects on men, one can go as far back as Bakke (1940) and as recently as Sherman (2009).

In some ways though, "Families" struggles to deepen our understanding of the challenges the formerly incarcerated face upon exit from jail or prison and of families' responses to these challenges. Harding and colleagues note on several occasions that multiple challenges exist, but they do not draw from their own unique dataset to develop our understanding about what these challenges are. Instead, relying on research from the early 2000s, they locate former prisoners' work challenges primarily in employer discrimination (Pager, 2003; Pager & Quillian, 2005) and deficient access to job-relevant social capital (Royster, 2003). From these foci, two pictures emerge. The first is that former prisoners struggle mightily to get jobs, *despite their best efforts to find work*, because employers are disinclined to hire them. The authors allude as well to the importance of labor market conditions, but focus less attention on this factor. The second is that because formerly incarcerated job seekers generally lack access to social capital—either because many of their ties erode during imprisonment (Lopoo & Western, 2005; Harding et al., chapter "Families, Prisoner Reentry, and Reintegration,") or because their disadvantaged neighborhood contexts make connections to job-relevant social capital unlikely (Wilson, 1987, 1996; Sullivan, 1989)—they do not learn about the job opportunities that do exist and have no one to influence the job-matching process on their behalf. If they did have such access, the authors intimate, *these personal contacts would certainly do so*. These oft-mentioned structural constraints and, importantly, their related assumptions, are the starting point from which the authors discuss the family's role in former prisoners' efforts to gain a foothold in the labor market.

While employer discrimination and deficient access to job-relevant social capital certainly do affect former prisoners' odds of securing jobs, more recent research calls into question the assumptions that are often drawn from these key insights specifically about former prisoners' search efforts and their ability to mobilize social resources when needed. In what follows I tackle each unquestioned assumption and, in the process, complicate both our understanding of the labor market challenges prisoners face and also the family's role in facilitating and hindering their reintegration, given these challenges.

## Searching for Work with a Criminal Record

The first underlying and unquestioned assumption embedded in "Families" is that, despite former prisoners' efforts to find work, they struggle with employment in good part because employers are disinclined to hire them. Frequent references to Pager's work underlie this assumption. That most employers would hesitate to extend a job offer to ex-offenders, especially black ex-offenders, is beyond dispute. Findings from employer surveys indicate that two-thirds of employers would not knowingly hire ex-offenders; over 40 % indicate that they probably would not or definitely would not; and fewer than 6 % report that they *definitely would* (Holzer, Raphael, & Stoll, 2007). These figures are likely over-estimates, as Pager and Quillian (2005) report that many employers who say that they are willing to hire ex-offenders are no more likely to do so than employers who report being unwilling.

As a growing body of research indicates, however, many former prisoners do not engage in a job search at all, and so it would be difficult to attribute their employment difficulties directly to employer discrimination. Using the National Longitudinal Study of Youth 1997 (NLSY97) panel to estimate the effect of incarceration on employment, for instance, Apel and Sweeten (2010) report that former prisoners had a likelihood of formal employment that was roughly 10 probability points reduced compared to their non-incarcerated convicted counterparts (.79 vs .89). Importantly, they note, "the higher presence of nonemployment [among the formerly incarcerated] stems almost exclusively from labor force nonparticipation rather than unemployment" (Apel & Sweeten, 2010, p. 465). The difference in their employment probabilities, then, was not attributable to former prisoners' unsuccessful efforts at search but instead to their lack of engagement in the search process at all.

Using the same dataset, Nora Broege and I (Smith & Broege, 2015) build on Apel and Sweeten's work by investigating whether and how penal contact and penal disposition alter search patterns and thus search success. Focusing solely on men, who still comprise the vast majority of those who have had contact with the penal system, we also show that penal contact is associated with significant reductions in the odds of searching for work. This was the case across race and ethnicity and regardless of penal disposition—black, Latino, and white arrestees, non-incarcerated criminals, and the formerly incarcerated all saw significantly reduced odds of searching, relative to those who had not yet had (but eventually did have) penal contact, with larger effect sizes for non-incarcerated and incarcerated ex-offenders. We also find that among searchers, those who had penal contact used fewer methods to search, and one of the methods they were less likely to use after penal contact was personal contacts. Further, we show, ex-offender's reduced engagement in a job search helped to explain gaps in search success between pre- and post-penal contact job seekers.

To explain our results, we point to penal interventions and speculate that they are key mechanisms underlying the changes in search patterns that follow penal contact. Although the penal system in some ways facilitates search, for instance by providing institutional supports to former prisoners for search activity (Petersilia & Turner, 1993; Lynch & Sabol, 2001; Pettit & Lyons, 2007; Sabol, 2007; Harris, Evans, & Beckett, 2010; Raphael, 2010), we highlight three ways that penal interventions also create major disincentives to search. First, they can do so by overwhelming former prisoners with criminal justice financial obligations. The vast majority of probationers and parolees are required to abide by multiple conditions to remain free from further sanction (Travis & Petersilia, 2001; Rainville & Reaves, 2003; Siegel & Senna, 2007), including the requirement to pay supervision fees, fines, court costs, and/or restitution to victims, and these obligations can be quite daunting. Amounts vary somewhat by state, but as an example, analysis of data from Washington State revealed court assessments ranging from a minimum of $500 (mandatory for all felony convictions) to a maximum of $256,257; the median amount assessed per felon was $5254; the mean $11,471 (Harris et al., 2010). Most former prisoners simply could not afford to fulfill their obligations in the short term, and given the accumulation of interest on court-imposed sanctions, fulfillment over the long term is also unlikely. Even small monthly payments could reduce take-home pay substantially—between 11 and 15 %, according to Harris and colleagues (2010)—and would make it extremely difficult to meet other needs and obligations, such as buying groceries and paying rent.

Importantly, these liabilities can create major disincentives to find work and keep it. Harris and colleagues (2010) report that 80 % of their respondents found their legal debt obligations to be "unduly burdensome," and their heightened financial stress actually had the unintended consequence of *reducing* commitment to work and related search effort. Despite the possibility that they might be sanctioned with jail time for nonpayment, some of their respondents chose not to work, relying on state benefits and/or further involvement with crime instead. Thus, in the form of heavy monetary sanctions, penal interventions can worsen before-search options to the point of eroding commitments to work and to an engaged job search.

Second, because of government intervention, employment opportunities for offenders are substantially limited. The reasons for this are by now well known: state and federal governments severely restrict access to government employment and government-regulated private occupations (Dale, 1976; May, 1995; Olivares, Burton, & Cullen, 1996; Petersilia, 2003; Bushway & Sweeten, 2007), and employers fear that they might be found liable for negligent hiring if "marked" employees act criminally on the job (Bushway & Sweeten, 2007; Glynn, 1998; Connerley, Arvey, & Bernardy, 2001). These substantial demand-side employment barriers have clear implications for job search—offenders would have to search with much greater effort and intensity to find work than their equally qualified non-offender counterparts (Pager, 2003), a point about which many offenders are well aware (Harding, 2003; Visher & Kachnowski, 2007). With high search costs and poor quality employment opportunities awaiting ex-offenders, the odds of an acceptable outcome are very low, especially in the short run, and employment in general may seem unobtainable (McCall, 1970). Such perceptions have been associated with reduced search effort and withdrawal from search entirely (Kanfer, Wanberg, & Kantrowitz, 2001). Indeed, Apel and Sweeten (2010) speculate that former prisoners' greater labor force detachment, relative to their non-incarcerated ex-offending counterparts, might be rooted in discouragement borne from the anticipation of stigma that diminishes the quality and quantity of employment possibilities.

Third, a growing body of research suggests that some penal interventions actually erode the time and flexibility needed for active and engaged job search. While on probation and parole, former prisoners must contend with a series of obligations and burdens associated with their penal status (Kohler-Hausmann, 2013). Contingent on offense, these include community service, drug testing, and drug or alcohol treatment, including treatment at inpatient facilities. A significant minority of probationers also have their movements monitored or otherwise restricted (Bonczar, 1997). Although most of these obligations would not likely prevent convicts and former prisoners from searching for work, especially since for many of them job search is a condition of community supervision, they represent competing demands, and possibly demands of greater priority, that could affect how much intensity and effort post-contact job seekers are able to expend during the process.

Although just speculation at this point, it seems likely that penal interventions, such as monetary sanctions, employment restrictions, and constraints on opportunities to search, raise the costs while significantly lowering the benefits associated with search. In the process, penal interventions produce former prisoners too discouraged to engage in search with any level of effort or intensity, relative to pre-contact search, if they search at all. Thus, although employer discrimination certainly makes finding work very difficult for former prisoners, many are not even searching for work, and those who are searching are less likely to rely on their personal contacts for job information and influence. The multiple barriers they face are no doubt at issue here, but future research should investigate the extent to which this is so. Furthermore, how families make sense of the barriers former prisoners face and how families understand former prisoners' responses to these challenges is another set of questions worthy of investigation, as the answers to these questions will provide further insight into when, under what circumstances, and how relatives participate in former prisoners' reintegration process, and to what effect.

## Social Capital Mobilization for the Formerly Incarcerated

A second underlying and unquestioned assumption in "Families" is that formerly incarcerated job seekers generally lack access to job-relevant social capital, but if these ties existed, their contacts would provide the help that former prisoners need to get hired and to get ahead. To some extent this makes sense. Few doubt that competitive advantage comes with having personal contacts who can intervene in the job-matching process on job seekers' behalf. Searching for work through friends, relatives, and acquaintances appears to be far more efficient than using most other methods of job search (Granovetter, 1995; Burt, 1992). Generally it takes little effort, time, or money to inform our friends, relatives, and acquaintances that we are willing to consider new opportunities, and, in the process, to potentially mobilize them as important sources for job information and influence. The benefits associated with this relatively "costless" search method can be huge; job seekers who do so tend to have more successful searches. In part, because personal contacts screen job seekers for "desirability," provide useful information about hiring to job seekers at optimal times, and vouch for job seekers' capabilities, their referrals are more likely than non-referrals to receive interview requests, to be offered employment, and to accept those offers (Holzer, 1987a, 1987b; Wielgosz & Carpenter, 1987; Blau & Robins, 1990; Burt, 1992). Referrals' search duration also tends to be significantly shorter (Holzer, 1987a, 1987b; Wielgosz & Carpenter, 1987; Blau & Robins, 1990). Further, finding work through personal contacts increases the likelihood of *keeping* the job, since job contacts often help referrals to learn the job and to become acclimated to the work environment fairly quickly after being hired (Fernandez & Weinberg, 1997; Neckerman & Fernandez, 2003). There is little wonder why searching for work through one's network of personal relations is so pervasive, exceeding 80 % among some populations, including Latinos and the poor (see, for instance, Corcoran, Datcher, & Duncan, 1980; Holzer, 1987a, 1987b; Granovetter, 1995; Green, Tigges, & Diaz, 1999; Falcon & Melendez, 2001; DiTomaso, 2013).

Indeed, the evidence seems compelling that access to networks of job contacts can make the difference between finding work immediately post-release and languishing in a state of joblessness to the point of discouragement (Nelson, Deess, & Allen, 1999; Visher & Kachnowski, 2007; Cobbina, 2009). Several studies, for instance, highlight the central role that networks play in matching former prisoners to jobs post-release. Researchers from the Vera Institute of Justice, for instance, conducted a study of former prisoners' reintegration experiences up to 1 month post-incarceration (Nelson et al., 1999). Of the 49 former prisoners they followed, roughly one-third (18) found work within the first month of release. Twelve of these quick transitioners had been hired even before release from prison—eight were rehired by their former employers and four found new jobs through the help of family members and friends. Finding work quickly seemed to hinge on having connections.

Given results like these, the tendency is to imagine that those who do not find work immediately post-release lack access to job-relevant social capital. Recent work on the conditions that facilitate social capital mobilization, however, suggests that access, while necessary, is hardly sufficient to ensure the provision of aid (Smith, 2005; Marin, 2012). In particular, my research on job-finding among the black poor revealed that even when jobholders had information and could influence the hiring process on behalf of their job-seeking friends, relatives, and acquaintances, they often chose not to. They perceived many in their network of relations to be too needy, too unmotivated, and/or too tainted by spoiled personal and work reputations to be trusted to act appropriately on the job, and thus to be trusted with their own work reputations (Smith, 2005, 2007, 2010). Negative perceptions informed their decisions to help.

The implications from this small but growing body of research is that even when former prisoners have access to job-relevant social capital, there is a good chance that many will be unable to mobilize it because of the mark of the criminal record. Previous research indicates that in general the public views ex-offenders quite negatively. Stereotypes of offenders, shared by diverse populations (Shoemaker & South, 1978), are that they are outsiders from lower-class communities, are unattractive, and are also prone to violence (Simmons, 1965; Saladin, Saper, & Breen, 1988; Roberts, 1992, 1997). It is also often assumed that those convicted of crime have several priors and are very likely to commit new crimes in the future (Roberts, 1997). These concerns about former prisoners' trustworthiness and fears about their risk of reoffending would likely animate the thoughts of many potential job contacts, affecting their decisions to refer. Most would be uncomfortable having former prisoners as co-workers, and like employers, the majority would be unwilling to hire them (Simmons, 1965; Kutchinsky, 1968; Conklin, 1975). This makes sense. After all, the stigma that informs employers' views or perceptions of former prisoners no doubt also shapes to some extent at least how potential job contacts perceive them as well. As with employers, potential job contacts would likely want assurances that ex-offenders' risk of reoffending is negligible before putting their own names on the line. Thus, negative perceptions of job seekers would likely affect potential job contacts' willingness to help, shape the circumstances under which they help, and affect how they help.

In a recent study I show just that (Smith, 2015). Drawing from a small, nonrandom sample of 61 working- and middle-class black jobholders employed at one large public sector employer, I investigate the conditions under which they would be and have been willing to provide job-matching assistance to formerly incarcerated friends, family members, and acquaintances. A central objective of the study was to identify the factors that potential job contacts privileged when making decisions to make such referrals; an objective was also to make sense of the ways that those factors informed jobholders' decisions about whom to help, when to help, and how best to help.

When asked what they thought about helping someone who had been incarcerated, it will come as no surprise that jobholders' responses fell into three categories—generally yes, maybe, and generally no. These responses spoke to jobholders' general inclination, not absolutes. For each of these categories, former prisoners' presumed ability and willingness to change—to give up the life they were assumed to be a part of and instead embrace a worker identity in which only employment in the formal wage economy mattered—was central to what role jobholders saw for themselves during the job-matching process. Among those who were generally open to helping, former prisoners were viewed not only as capable of change but also as deserving of, and entitled to, a second chance to show what they were capable of. Help, they argued, was necessary to facilitate movement away from criminal involvement and so should be offered wherever possible. This was a moral imperative. For the majority of black jobholders, however, the willingness to help was contingent. These jobholders wanted to know what crimes former prisoners had committed, because they were categorically against helping those who had been convicted of violent crimes or theft. In both cases, they reasoned, convictions had meaning for the type of person former prisoners were and would likely always be. Change for them was not possible and so help would not be forthcoming. For those who were not categorically dismissed, contingents required evidence of change, of personal transformation. Only then would contingents assess the risk of reoffending as negligible, offer information, and attempt to influence the hiring process on their behalf. Finally, a small number of jobholders were almost categorically against helping, perceiving change to be just short of impossible. Impossibility was either associated with rigid institutional structures, which disallowed such job seekers access to jobs (employers will not hire), or with formerly incarcerated job seekers, who from job contacts' prior experiences had generally proven them to be incorrigible (they would not likely ever change their ways).

Among those who were strongly inclined to help, help was seen as a necessary pre-condition for change; you give former prisoners a second chance by taking a chance on them. Among contingents, help came only after former prisoners proved their desire to transform or had provided evidence that they had been transformed. Contingents also argued for second chances, but for the most part what they had to offer was the reward for initiating change, not the means through which transformation would be achieved. Those strongly disinclined to help perceived the odds that change would happen to be so low as to make any discussion of second chances moot. In "Families," we do not learn about the frames that motivate former prisoners' relatives to help or not, although such frames, even if not specifically about change, likely inform whether and how relatives engage the job-matching process on behalf of their formerly incarcerated sons, husbands, brothers, and the like. Indeed, in "Families" we are given no reason to suspect that help might not be forthcoming for any reason except that relatives are not structurally well-placed to offer it. This is an important limitation that possibly yields an overly simplistic view of the employment challenges that former prisoners face. Importantly, too, it obscures how families understand the challenges that former prisoners face and what these understandings mean for the efforts, or lack thereof, that families make on former prisoners' behalf, efforts that can either mitigate these challenges or reinforce them.

## Discussion and Conclusion

"Families" is a part of a larger body of research, which has grown exponentially over the past two decades and continues to expand at a remarkable rate, about the factors that shape former prisoners' process of reintegration. The study is at its best when illustrating the ways in which its male subjects attempt to reconcile their identities as good men in a context where they are unable, due to the challenges they face finding decent jobs and holding on to them, to fulfill the breadwinner role. Alone the focus on men's embrace of caregiving as a substitute for breadwinning makes this an extremely important contribution to this area of research.

"Families" does not build much on our understanding about the actual employment challenges former prisoners face though. Because the authors do not engage the growing body of research linking former prisoners' employment problems to disengagement from search, resulting from a whole host of challenges structural in nature, these issues largely go unexamined, as do the family's responses to them. The more important shortcoming, however, is that the authors seek to make sense of the ways in which the family helps and hinders without directly studying the families involved in the process. No interviews were conducted with the relatives, friends, or acquaintances whose patterns of behaviors informed the direction that former prisoners' reintegration would take. No observations were made of former prisoners' interactions with those in their families and communities. What this means is that our understanding of family's role is necessarily limited. Thus, not only are we not privy to the extent and nature of employment challenges former prisoners face, we also know little about how family members understand these challenges, and how their understandings shape their involvement in former prisoners' reintegration. This would seem to be the next step—studying from the perspective of those receiving former prisoners how they make sense of the reintegration process and what this means about their efforts to assist, or not assist, the formerly incarcerated to whom they are attached.

## References

Apel, R., & Sweeten, S. (2010). The impact of incarceration on employment during the transition to adulthood. *Social Forces, 57*(3), 448–479.

Bakke, E. W. (1940). *Citizens without work: A study of the effects of unemployment upon the workers' social relations and practices*. New Haven, CT: Yale University Press.

Blau, D. M., & Robins, P. K. (1990). Job search outcomes for the employed and unemployed. *Journal of Political Economy, 98*(3), 637–655.

Bonczar, T. P. (1997). *Characteristics of adults on probation, 1995*. Bureau of Justice Statistics: Special Report, U.S. Department of Justice.

Burt, R. S. (1992). *Structural holes: The social structure of competition*. Cambridge, MA: Harvard University Press.

Bushway, S. D., & Sweeten, G. (2007). Abolish lifetime bans for ex-felons. *Criminology and Public Policy, 6*(4), 697–706.

Cobbina, J. E. (2009). *From prison to home: Women's pathways in and out of crime*. Washington, DC: National Institute of Justice. http://www.ncjrs.gov/pdffiles1/nij/grants/226812.pdf.

Conklin, J. (1975). *The impact of crime*. New York: Macmillan.

Connerley, M. L., Arvey, R. D., & Bernardy, C. J. (2001). Criminal background checks for prospective and current employees: Current practices among municipal agencies. *Public Personnel Management, 20*(2), 173–183.

Corcoran, M., Datcher, L., & Duncan, G. J. (1980). Information and influence networks in labor markets. In G. J. Duncan & J. N. Morgan (Eds.), *Five thousand American families: Patterns of economic progress* (Vol. 8, pp. 1–38). Ann Arbor, MI: Institute for Social Research.

Dale, M. W. (1976). Barriers to the rehabilitation of ex-offenders. *Crime and Delinquency, 22*(3), 322–337.

DiTomaso, N. (2013). *The American non-dilemma: Racial inequality without racism*. New York: Russell Sage Foundation.

Falcon, L. M., & Melendez, E. (2001). Racial and ethnic differences in job searching in urban centers. In A. O'Connor, C. Tilly, & L. Bob (Eds.), *Urban inequality: Evidence from four cities* (pp. 341–371). New York: Russell Sage Foundation.

Fernandez, R., & Weinberg, N. (1997). Sifting and sorting: Personal contacts and hiring in a retail bank. *American Sociological Review, 62*(6), 883–902.

Glynn, T. P. (1998). The limited viability of negligent supervision, retention, hiring, and infliction of emotional distress claims in employment discrimination cases in Minnesota. *William Mitchell Law Review, 24*(3), 581–633.

Granovetter, M. S. (1995). *Getting a job: A study of contacts and careers* (2nd ed.). Chicago: University of Chicago Press.

Green, G. P., Tigges, L. M., & Diaz, D. (1999). Racial and ethnic differences in job-search strategies in Atlanta, Boston, and Los Angeles. *Social Science Quarterly, 80*(2), 263–278.

Harding, D. J. (2003). Jean Valjean's dilemma: The management of ex-convict identity in the search for employment. *Deviant Behavior, 24*, 571–595.

Harris, A., Evans, H., & Beckett, K. (2010). Drawing blood from stones: Legal debt and social inequality in the contemporary United States. *American Journal of Sociology, 115*(6), 1753–1799.

Holzer, H. J. (1987a). Informal job search and black youth unemployment. *American Economic Review, 77*(3), 446–452.

Holzer, H. J. (1987b). Job search by employed and unemployed youth. *Industrial and Labor Relations Review, 40*(4), 601–611.

Holzer, H. J., Raphael, S., & Stoll, M. A. (2007). The effect of an applicant's criminal history on employer hiring decisions and screening practices: Evidence from Los Angeles. In S. Bushway, M. A. Stoll, & D. F. Weiman (Eds.), *Barriers to reentry? The labor market for released prisoners in post-industrial America* (pp. 117–150). New York: Russell Sage Foundation.

Kanfer, R., Wanberg, C. R., & Kantrowitz, T. M. (2001). Job search and employment: A personality-motivational analysis and meta-analytic review. *Journal of Applied Psychology, 86*(5), 837–855.

Kohler-Hausmann, I. (2013). Misdemeanor justice: Control without conviction. *American Journal of Sociology, 119*(2), 351–393.
Kutchinsky, B. (1968). Knowledge and attitudes regarding legal phenomena in Denmark. In N. Christie (Ed.), *Aspects of social control in welfare states* (Scandinavian Studies in Criminology, Vol. 2, pp. 125–159). London: Tavistock.
Lopoo, L. M., & Western, B. (2005). Incarceration and the formation and stability of marital unions. *Journal of Marriage and the Family, 67*(3), 721–734.
Lynch, J. P., & Sabol, W. J. (2001). *Prisoner reentry in perspective*. Washington, DC: Urban Institute Press.
Marin, A. (2012). Don't mention it: Why people don't share job information, when they do, and why it matters. *Social Networks, 34*(2), 181–192.
May, B. E. (1995). The character component of occupational licensing laws: A continuing barrier to the ex-felon's employment opportunities. *North Dakota Law Review, 71*(1), 187–210.
McCall, J. J. (1970). Economics of information and job search. *Quarterly Journal of Economics, 84*(1), 113–136.
Neckerman, K., & Fernandez, R. (2003). Keeping a job: Network hiring and turnover in a retail bank. *Research in the Sociology of Organizations, 20*, 299–318.
Nelson, M., Deess, P., & Allen, C. (1999). *The first month out: Post-incarceration experiences in New York City*. New York: Vera Institute of Justice. http://www.vera.org/pubs/first-month-out-post-incarceration-experiences-new-york-city.
Olivares, K. M., Burton, V. S., Jr., & Cullen, F. T. (1996). The collateral consequences of a felony conviction: A national study of state legal codes 10 years later. *Federal Probation, 60*(3), 10–17.
Pager, D. (2003). The mark of a criminal record. *American Journal of Sociology, 108*(5), 937–975.
Pager, D., & Quillian, L. (2005). Walking the talk? What employers say versus what they do. *American Sociological Review, 70*(3), 355–380.
Petersilia, J. (2003). *When prisoners come home: Parole and prisoner reentry*. New York: Oxford University Press.
Petersilia, J., & Turner, S. (1993, May). *Evaluating intensive supervision probation/parole: Results of a nationwide experiment*. National Institute of Justice, Research in Brief, Washington, DC: U.S. Department of Justice. http://cebcp.org/wp-content/CRIM781/EvaluatingISP.pdf
Pettit, B., & Lyons, C. J. (2007). Status and the stigma of incarceration: The labor-market effects of incarceration, by race, class, and criminal involvement. In S. Bushway, M. A. Stoll, & D. F. Weiman (Eds.), *Barriers to reentry? The labor market for released prisoners in post-industrial America* (pp. 203–226). New York: Russell Sage Foundation.
Rainville, G., & Reaves, R. (2003). *Felony defendants in large urban counties, 2000*. Washington, DC: Bureau of Justice Statistics.
Raphael, S. (2010, April). *Improving employment prospects for former prison inmates: Challenges and policy* (NBER Working Paper No. 15874). Washington, DC: National Bureau of Economic Research. http://www.nber.org/papers/w15874
Roberts, J. V. (1992). Public opinion, crime, and criminal justice. *Crime and Justice, 16*, 99–180.
Roberts, J. V. (1997). The role of criminal record in the sentencing process. *Crime and Justice, 22*, 303–362.
Royster, D. (2003). *Race and the invisible hand: How white networks exclude black men from blue-collar jobs*. Berkeley: University of California Press.
Sabol, W. J. (2007). Local labor-market conditions and post-prison employment experiences of offenders released from Ohio State Prisons. In S. Bushway, M. A. Stoll, & D. F. Weiman (Eds.), *Barriers to reentry? The labor market for released prisoners in post-industrial America* (pp. 257–303). New York: Russell Sage Foundation.
Saladin, M., Saper, Z., & Breen, L. (1988). Perceived attractiveness and attributions of criminality: What is beautiful is not criminal. *Canadian Journal of Criminology, 30*(3), 251–259.
Sherman, J. (2009). *Those who work, those who don't: Poverty, morality, and family in rural America*. Minneapolis, MN: University of Minnesota Press.
Shoemaker, D. J., & South, D. R. (1978). Nonverbal images of criminality and deviance: Existence and consequence. *Criminal Justice Review, 3*(1), 65–80.

Siegel, L., & Senna, J. (2007). *Essentials of criminal justice*. Belmont, CA: Thomson Wadsworth.
Simmons, J. (1965). Public stereotypes of deviants. *Social Problems, 13*(2), 223–232.
Smith, S. S. (2005). "Don't put my name on it": Social capital activation and job-finding assistance among the black urban poor. *American Journal of Sociology, 111*(1), 1–57.
Smith, S. S. (2007). *Lone pursuit: Distrust and defensive individualism among the black poor*. New York: Russell Sage Foundation.
Smith, S. S. (2010). A test of sincerity: How black and Latino blue collar workers make decisions about making referrals. *ANNALS of the American Academy of Political and Social Science, 629*(1), 30–52.
Smith, S. S. (2015). *'Change frames' and social capital mobilization for formerly incarcerated job seekers* (Working Paper). Berkeley: Department of Sociology, University of California-Berkeley.
Smith, S. S., & Broege, N. (2015). *Searching for work with a criminal record* (Working Paper). Berkeley: Department of Sociology, University of California-Berkeley.
Sullivan, M. L. (1989). *Getting paid: Youth, crime and work in the inner city*. Ithaca, NY: Cornell University Press.
Travis, J., & Petersilia, J. (2001). Reentry reconsidered: A new look at an old question. *Crime and Delinquency, 47*(3), 291–313.
Visher, C. A., & Kachnowski, V. (2007). Finding work on the outside: Results from the "Returning Home" project in Chicago. In S. Bushway, M. A. Stoll, & D. F. Weiman (Eds.), *Barriers to reentry? The labor market for released prisoners in post-industrial America* (pp. 80–113). New York: Russell Sage Foundation.
Wielgosz, J. B., & Carpenter, S. (1987). The effectiveness of alternative methods of searching for jobs and finding them: An exploratory analysis of the data bearing upon the ways of coping with joblessness. *American Journal of Economics and Sociology, 46*(2), 151–164.
Wilson, W. J. (1987). *The truly disadvantaged: The inner city, the underclass, and public policy*. Chicago: University of Chicago Press.
Wilson, W. J. (1996). *When work disappears: The world of the new urban poor*. New York: Alfred A. Knopf.

# Safe Spaces for Vulnerability: New Perspectives on African Americans Who Struggle To Be Good Fathers

**Alford Young, Jr.**

The last three decades has been a period of intensely critical focus on African American males in social science research (Anderson, 2009; Mincy, 2006; National Urban League, 2007; Young, 2004). The attention given to this population grew out of increasing public concern, if not wholesale anxiety, about who these men are and how they navigate their everyday lives in urban communities that are framed in public discourse as riddled with malaise and danger. This period of heightened concern commenced with the introduction of the term *underclass* in the lexicon of social science research on inequality (Anderson, 1990, 1999; Auletta, 1982; Venkatesh, 2000; Wilson, 1987; Young, 2004). Among other consequences, the emergence of the term gave rise to the notion that these men were a menace to society. As a plethora of studies throughout the past three decades has demonstrated, the presence of African American males was seen as contributing to the sense of threat and danger immanent in their communities and neighborhoods (Anderson, 1990, 1999; Auletta, 1982; Billson, 1996; Hunter & Davis, 1994; Liebow, 1967; Macleod, 2009; Majors & Billson, 1992; Rainwater, 1970; Sullivan, 1989; Tolleson, 1997; Venkatesh, 2000, 2006; Williams & Kornblum, 1985; Wilson, 1987, 1992, 1993, 1996; Young, 2004).

During the last three decades, the public representation of low-income urban-based African American males, as both subjected to and instigators of a range of problems in America, was crystallized. In assessments of their social character and social experiences, a social problems paradigm reigned supreme as the interpretive lens applied to them. That paradigm circumscribed virtually all aspects of African American males' lives, including personal and public health, family relations, and community well-being (Murry, Chap. 2). A lingering effect of this imagery has been the idea that African American males need to be detained, controlled, and/or regu-

A. Young, Jr. (✉)
Departments of Sociology and Afro-American and African Studies, University of Michigan, Ann Arbor, MI, USA
e-mail: ayoun@umich.edu



L. Burton et al. (eds.), *Boys and Men in African American Families*, National Symposium on Family Issues 7, DOI 10.1007/978-3-319-43847-4_10

lated for the betterment and well-being of themselves and others. Consequently, even if low-income African American men did not fully embrace nor reflect this depiction, those who inhabit urban spaces necessarily had to adapt styles of interaction and public engagement that provided measures of security and stability in communities that at that time became ravaged by the proliferation of narcotics, such as crack, and increasing rates of crime (Anderson, 1990; Harding, 2010; Rios, 2011). Scholars began documenting patterns of behavior resulting from adherence to the so-called *code of the streets* (Anderson, 1990), which were the inherent rules of negotiating interaction in the public spaces of low-income communities, and to the *cool pose*, which refers to the personal demeanor maintained by black males which promoted confidence while warding off threat in these spaces (Majors & Billson, 1992). These concepts refer to cultural styles of interaction management and expression put forth by black men in order to survive and endure their social environments. In essence, the streets themselves became a part of the problem because public space in low-income communities was seen as insecure and unpredictable terrain upon which to engage one's everyday life experiences.

Despite the intensity of this critical acclaim, the past few decades has involved much debate about constructive rather than punitive intervention on the behalf of black males. Alongside employment, education, physical and mental health and well-being, fatherhood and family remained one of several areas of crucial focus for black males (Hamer, 2001; Mincy, 2006; Nelson, 2004; Roy, 2005, 2006). In order to advance the conversation about African American fathers and family involvement, I suggest that scholars, social service providers, policy makers, and others who critically engage this topic must attend to two concepts that highlight under-treated dimensions of African American male social conduct, especially as it relates to their functioning as fathers. These are *vulnerability* and *safe space*. What follows is a brief explication of the meaning of each term as each pertains to the case of African American fathers and why and how the terms deserve more attention and more thorough incorporation into the discourse on improving the prospects for African American fatherhood.

## Vulnerability and African American Males

Since the propagation of the term underclass, discussions of African American male vulnerability has most often been made in reference to how much they have been subjected to regulation and containment by legal authorities. Otherwise, the association of African American males with the term has been in reference to how much their presence makes others in public space feel vulnerable. I suggest another vantage point for applying the term to the case of African American men. The turn here is to consider vulnerability as an individual's existing in a state of confusion, anxiety, and insecurity in social contexts where public expressions of such dispositions actually may result in exacerbating rather than remedying those feelings. While this state of being is applicable to African American men in general, the case made here pertains to African American fathers in particular. Harding and colleagues (Chap. 8) focus on African American fathers who are ex-offenders. This is a sub-category of African American men who, given their stigmatized identity, may be regarded as the most likely to produce feelings of vulnerability in others. However, Harding and colleagues actually invite broad and deep thinking about African American fathers as highly vulnerable people.

Harding and colleagues (Chap. 8) explore the family re-connection experiences and challenges for formerly incarcerated men. The direction taken in their chapter is to examine the views and experiences of men who are struggling to establish consistency and security as fathers, either as wage-earners or as providers of emotional and social support for their children and partners. Among other objectives, the authors deliver a portrait of formerly incarcerated men as vulnerable due to their inability to establish themselves as the kind of fathers they desire to be. Hence, they require the involvement of various supportive individuals and mechanisms to endure in their social worlds. The authors demonstrate that these men are vulnerable because they are insecure about their prospects for finding the kind of work they desire and they cannot establish themselves as central providers of material needs and interests for their children and partners. Accordingly, the story Harding and colleagues tell is about African American men who maintain highly stigmatized and threatening public identities ut ho are actually acutely vulnerable in most aspects of their lives post- incarceration.

## Safe Spaces

The vulnerability that formerly incarcerated fathers experience calls attention to the second key concept presented here: *safe spaces*. This concept refers to the physical or institutional space that allows for individuals to express confusion, anxiety, or insecurity (i.e., vulnerability) in ways that are met with advice and counsel that may minimize if not eradicate these states of being. In short, safe spaces are sites that allow for positive growth and development by providing opportunities to publicly express and possibly gain support in addressing one's vulnerabilities. It is crucial to note, however, that the very kinds of low-income urban communities that the men in the Harding et al. chapter reside in are comprised of *unsafe spaces*. Most importantly, low-income urban communities lack safety not just in terms of physical well-being (much of which was alluded to earlier) but in terms of emotional and psychological well-being as well.

Sociologist Lee Rainwater (1970) was one of the first social scientist to draw attention to turbulent and unsafe space as a primary characteristic of low-income urban communities. He did so by extrapolating on what he described as the anomic street culture of urban America, which resulted from economic disinvestment and physical decay in the urban communities populated by disadvantaged marginalized people. As he saw it, residents of these communities experienced little collective trust and security as a result of living and interacting with each other amidst despair and blight. In his portrayal, the streets were the structural contexts whereby violence, threats, challenges, and insecurities were managed, disguised, or otherwise surfaced as causal factors for at least some of the profligate public behaviors that ultimately emerged in people's lives.

Rainwater's notion foreshadowed the ways in which the streets would surface in the latter third of the twentieth century as sites of concern and consternation in the vision of low-income, urban-based African American men. More recent scholarship on socio-economic disadvantage in urban communities revitalized and amplified the idea that there is little safe public space for African Americans in the inner cities of America (Anderson, 1989, 1990; Bourgois, 1995; Venkatesh, 2000; Young, 2004). Accordingly, a consequence of the debate about the existence of an entrenched underclass in urban America was the forwarding of a lucid portrait of the urban terrain itself, as especially dangerous, hostile, and uninviting.

A conundrum confronting African American men and others who inhabit impoverished communities is that while the streets became less safe throughout the latter half of the twentieth century, there has been no alternative site for them to engage in important and self-affirming activities of everyday social life that may minimize or counter the effects of vulnerability. They live in social environments that do not easily foster healthy emotional or physical development. Indeed, the social spaces that such men occupy often demand that they maintain aggressive dispositions so that they can manage the challenges that these communities present to their social, emotional, and physical well-being. Moreover, they lack access to social spaces and institutions that allow young men to pose and resolve questions, concerns, inadequacies, or fears about being fathers (and this could be extended to various matters pertaining to healthy male development).

A part of the contemporary situation for urban-based, low-income fathers, then, is the absence of public or institutionalized spaces for constructively working out and resolving tensions, perceived inadequacies, and self-misunderstandings about being fathers. Fatherhood, a social role riddled with challenges and anxiety, is one such area whereby the absence of safe space exacerbates the difficulties of such men learning to operationalize this role. An implicit point made by Harding and colleagues (Chap. 8), and one made evident by a litany of studies of the experiences of African American men, is that the social environments of such communities serve to inhibit the capacity of men to express themselves as vulnerable (Anderson, 1990; Rainwater, 1970; Young, 2004).

Aside from the evidence presented by Harding and colleagues, consider, for instance, the kind of male bravado that unfolds on public basketball courts, in barbershops, or on street corners as men go about promoting their public selves. When the needs and demands for professing bravado, intensity, and assertiveness while engaging public spaces in low-income communities are overwhelming, there becomes less space for such men to express and reconcile the kinds of doubts, anxieties, and insecurities that come with entering the role of father, especially from positions of extreme socioeconomic disadvantage. A part of the contemporary situation for urban-based, low-income fathers then, is the absence of public or institutionalized spaces for constructively working out and resolving tensions, perceived inadequacies, and self-misunderstandings about being fathers.

## Expressing Vulnerability and Finding Safe Space

An example of the ways in which the vulnerabilities of fatherhood intersect with the absence of safe space was made evident to me in the course of field research for a study resulting in a report entitled *Voices of Young Fathers: The Partners for Fragile Families Demonstration Project* (Holcomb & Young, 2007). This study, sponsored by the Office of Child Support Enforcement (OCSE) at the U.S. Department of Health and Human Services (HHS) and the Ford Foundation (and other foundation support) was a product of the Partners for Fragile Families (PFF) demonstration project. The PFF demonstration operated from 2000 to 2003 in 13 projects located in nine states. It focused on promoting the voluntary establishment of paternity; connecting young fathers with the child support system and encouraging the payment of child support; improving parenting and relationship skills of young fathers; helping young fathers secure and retain employment; and strengthening family ties, commitments, and other types of father involvement when parents do not live together. The HHS sponsored a national evaluation of PFF to examine the design and implementation of these projects. As part of this multi-component evaluation, a report of ethnographic case studies of a small number of PFF participants from two demonstration sites—the Father Friendly Initiative in Boston and the Fathers Resource Program in Indianapolis—was produced. The fieldwork for this part of the endeavor consisted of approximately four annual interviews and on-site visits for a 3 year-period with African American and Latino fathers in two U.S. cities. The case explored here was drawn from that report.

In the course of my fieldwork I encountered a gentleman who I refer to here as Antwon. At 26 years of age during my first encounter with him, Antwon was an only child and was raised by his mother, aunt and grandmother in Kokomo, Indiana. His father paid child support but was only minimally involved in his life, making contact with him a little more than once a year throughout his childhood. A number of adults in Antwon's household, including his mother, were substance abusers at various points during his childhood, and he too became a substance abuser at a very young age. He ultimately moved to Indianapolis, where his mother also relocated following successful substance abuse treatment. In commenting about the reason for his move to Indianapolis, Antwon said, "I was tired of going to jail." Antwon never completed high school, but he did receive a GED in 1998.

At the start of my interaction with him, Antwon was unemployed and lived in Indianapolis with his mother, her boyfriend, his cousin, and his uncle. He was the father of two children: a 3 year old boy by one partner and a 1 year old daughter by another partner. The mother of his daughter, who was his partner at the time of the study, was finishing her degree in a nursing program. Antwon had near-daily visitation with his son, and provided full care for him several days a week. He took care of his daughter consistently.

During one visit to his home I noticed that Antwon was unpacking and organizing hair care products on the kitchen table. He seemed quite attentive to these materials, so much so that I was motivated to inquire about them. He explained to me that he was going to do his daughter's hair later in the day after we finished talking. I was intrigued by the image appearing before me, a man bearing tattoos and gold fixtures in his mouth who was wholly preoccupied with preparing to care for his daughter's hair. He told me in prior conversation how uninvolved many of his friends were with their children, so I wondered how much they may have known about his investment in caring for his daughter's hair. Although I already imagined what his answer would be, I asked him whether he talked to his friends about how he cared for his daughter's hair. "Oh no," he replied. I don't talk about this out here (in the streets)."

As the conversation ensued, Antwon told me where and when he had conversations about his daughter's hair care. These conversations took place among a small group of fathers in the fatherhood training program that was the focus of this study that brought me to him for the research interviews. I soon was made to understand that aside from the formal training that the participants received about fathering and family living there were multiple opportunities for the men to share personal experiences and lessons learned about fatherhood. They also found this opportunity to provide safe space for discussing the challenges, concerns, and anxieties they encountered as they strove to fulfill that role. As Antwon explained to me, for him and a few of the other fathers of daughters, the program (and really the protective walls of the facility where it was housed and the supportive culture that was cultivated within them) allowed him to share with these men his own initial ignorance and ultimately enduring anxieties about caring for a daughter. Antwon explained that these fathers began having regular conversations about how they could be more responsive to their daughters' needs and what they needed to learn in order to do so. He explained to me how he believed that this kind of learning could not have occurred in the public spaces that he frequented, but only in the safe confines of the facility that provided fatherhood training services for him. Ultimately, it was in the safe space of this formal institution that he and other fathers began sharing their intrigue, interests, and concerns over how to be better involved in their daughter's lives. The program then served as the safe space for them to recognize, articulate, and act upon an interest that could not have surfaced so easily in the other social spaces that they frequented.

## Vulnerability and Safe Space Extended: Policy-Relevant Thinking and New Portraits of African American Masculinity

Antwon's story contains elements consistent with those told by Harding and colleagues (Chap. 8) about African American ex-offenders struggling with fatherhood. Antwon and many of these fathers were in dire need of advice, counsel, and access to resources that they do not always realize they need or that they have little to no way of finding for themselves. Essentially, they are men who cannot act on what they believe to be their sense of proper manhood, much less fatherhood. Aside from stable employment, and in some cases secure housing, many are in need of intervention to effectively manage the cultural and emotional challenges of fatherhood.

Many urban-based, low-income African American fathers find little support in formal organizational spaces such as social support agencies or the legal system, where they (wrongly or rightly) perceive their interests to be suppressed by the attention given to women and children (Edin & Nelson, 2013; Hamer, 2001; Waller, 2002). The fathers have not only endured consistent social exposure to struggling as well as inattentive fathers in their communities, but also lack the means to express and resolve challenges to their capacity to serve as effective fathers because they recognize no formal or institutional outlets to do so. This panoply of concerns comprises the backdrop for modern fathering in the kind of urban, low-income communities inhabited by African Americans. To make the case more fully, I now employ the concepts of vulnerability and safe spaces as guideposts for working through three specific areas of concern that Harding et al. (Chap. 8) draws attention to about African American fathers who, because they are ex-offenders, struggle with the traditional provider role. Each issue is relevant to the situation of low-income African American fathers more generally.

The first issue is whether African American fathers experience role strain when they can provide only social or emotional support to their children given their lack of employment, and what might this mean for their self-definitions of manhood? The situation is especially concerning for men who never or rarely grasped the maternal provider role throughout their adult lives. Unlike majority families and households throughout and beyond the twentieth century, African American families and households have included adult women who have been gainfully employed (Jones, 2010). Hence, fatherhood for African American men has always occurred in familial contexts (including those in which such men were raised and those in which they have participated in as fathers) that included women in occupational sectors. Harding and colleagues argue that the fathers in their study accepted, if not encouraged, that the mothers of their children be employed, but the effects of the state of vulnerability for men who were raised with women who worked remains underexplored. The women in the lives of these men have worked, and in doing so have had to sustain themselves and many other family members (children and adults) throughout their lives. Hence, further exploration of the possibilities and effects of role strain for African American fathers must take into account the important caveat that such fathers have often been reared among and continue to interact with women who have been fully immersed into the role of material provider. Essentially, these men may not only suffer from role strain, but do so in social contexts where intimate others have consistently, if not successfully, assumed that role. This condition leaves much to explore in regard to African American fathers and role strain concerning service as material providers.

A second issue pertains to the father's capacity to provide emotional support. The Harding et al. chapter argues that both the fathers and the women in the fathers' lives rely upon other women for emotional support. Given the struggle that African American men face in trying to express and manage the kind of emotions that may reveal vulnerability, it is not surprising that they do not rely on other men for this kind of support. Hence, the findings of Harding and his colleagues call for renewed thinking about gender relations for African American men and fathers in particular. It may be the case that these fathers require more consistent and more formally structure programmatic intervention in order to adapt to providing and receiving emotional support from other males. This effort must also take into account that many such fathers, including all of those in the study conducted by Harding and colleagues have encountered highly emotionally challenging and emotionally suppressive institutions (i.e., jails and prisons). The effects of these encounters must be more fully documented and interrogated in order to better ascertain what they might reveal about the prospects for other African American fathers to better embrace their emotional selves.

Both of these issues require broader conversation about the constitution of healthy contemporary African American masculinity. Much has been said in scholarship about what such masculinity should consist of or reflect (Collins, 2005; Hooks, 2004; Hunter & Davis, 1994). However, the circumstances posed in relation to the two issues raised here indicate that considerable effort must be put into charting practical pathways toward that healthy masculinity for African American fathers.

Finally, a third issue concerns the social effects of the return home for African American fathers who are ex-offenders. Not surprisingly, these men are returning to socially turbulent communities and neighborhoods; that is, to spaces that are unsafe in each of the myriad ways acknowledged in earlier parts of this chapter. Accordingly, a question that merits further attention is how might policy makers, social scientists, and other interested parties think more fully about the consequences of reengaging unsafe spaces? Harding and colleagues (Chap. 8), and others who have explored the ex-offender re-entry process, have made it clear that available employment prospects and social support for accessing them are crucial resources for success (Bushway, Stoll, & Weiman, 2007; Raphael, 2011; Travis, 2005; Visher, La Vigne, & Travis, 2004; Western, 2007). Yet, aside from the material resources necessary for societal re-entry, more can be done to uncover the emotional and psychological turmoil resulting from the return to unsafe spaces and its accompanying phenomena of hyper-surveillance, drug-testing requirements, and other social and personal control and regulation efforts (all of which bear upon one's capacity to feel psychologically safe in public space despite what may be deemed as necessary action in the re-entry process).

## Conclusion

Many low-income African American fathers experience a large vacancy of exposure to and involvement with other men who performed the fatherhood role as it is traditionally construed. Coupled with this vacancy is their immersion into a social world where particular pressures are put upon them to protect themselves physically and emotionally as they engage their everyday lives. This leaves little to no room for such fathers to find spaces to express insecurity, weakness, ignorance, or confusion about very many aspects of their lives, either as fathers or simply as men.

The importance of finding themselves in safe spaces for discussing, questioning, and reconsidering the idea and practice of fatherhood is counteracted by their living in spaces that are replete with the kinds of dangers, threats, and turbulence that have been well-documented in social scientific research on the contemporary urban community. Such space often demands that the young men who inhabit it take care to present and preserve public images of themselves as secure, vigilant, and truculent. The emotional consequence of maintaining these dispositions is that such men do not find value in, and therefore do not easily embrace, insecurity, hesitancy, and timidity as parts of their public persona. However, the very experience of coming into fatherhood is riddled with such emotional dynamics.

Without having the social space to approach, consider, and resolve or manage the tensions associated with fatherhood (and when living in communities and households where there is limited, if any, access to the material resources that are associated with successfully engaging that role), there is amble opportunity for these men to react toward their partners, children, or other people in ways that further threaten their capacity to function as responsible fathers. Hence, the opportunity to talk about and act on their concerns, anxieties, and insecurities concerning fatherhood, and especially with other men of the same status and condition, is the first of many steps that can lead toward some amelioration of the problem of struggling disadvantaged African American fathers. Furthermore, and as made evident by the men discussed in the Harding et al. chapter, re-framing African American fathers who also happen to be ex-offenders as vulnerable men helps to reconstitute a vision of African American men and African American masculinity for scholars, policy makers, and a concerned public. More practically, the call is to re-think these men as not simply formerly troubled or potentially troubling individuals who need to make amends to their children and other family members, but as individuals who must be given the opportunity to learn to how to effectively contribute to and draw from their families in order to become the healthy and proactive individuals that they and others in their lives desire that they become.

## References

Anderson, E. (1989). Sex codes and family life among poor inner-city youths. *Annals of the American Academy of Political and Social Science, 501*, 59–78.

Anderson, E. (1990). *Streetwise: Race, class, and change in an urban community*. Chicago: University of Chicago Press.

Anderson, E. (1999). *Code of the streets*. New York: W.W. Norton.

Anderson, E. (Ed.). (2009). *Against the wall: Poor, young, black, and male*. Philadelphia: University of Pennsylvania Press.

Auletta, K. (1982). *The underclass*. New York: Random House.

Billson, J. M. (1996). *Pathways to manhood: Young black males struggle for identity*. Piscataway, NJ: Transaction.

Bourgois, P. (1995). *In search of respect: Selling crack in El Barrio*. New York: Cambridge University Press.

Bushway, S., Stoll, M. A., & Weiman, D. F. (Eds.). (2007). *Barriers to reentry? The labor market for released prisoners in post-industrial America*. New York: Russell Sage Foundation.

Collins, P. H. (2005). *Black sexual politics: African Americans, gender, and the new racism*. New York: Routledge.

Edin, K., & Nelson, T. (2013). *Doing the best I can: Fatherhood in the inner city*. Berkeley: University of California Press.
Hamer, J. (2001). *What it means to be daddy: Fatherhood for black men living away from their children*. New York: Columbia University Press.
Harding, D. J. (2010). *Living the drama: Community, conflict, and culture among inner-city boys*. Chicago: University of Chicago Press.
Holcomb, P. A., & Young, A., Jr. (2007). *Voices of young fathers: The Partners for Fragile Families Demonstration Project*. Prepared for the U.S. Department of Health and Human Services, Office of the Assistant Secretary for Planning and Evaluation. https://aspe.hhs.gov/execsum/voices-young-fathers-partners-fragile-families-demonstration-projects
Hooks, B. (2004). *We real cool: Black men and masculinity*. New York: Routledge.
Hunter, A., & Davis, J. (1994). Hidden voices of black men: The meaning, structure, and complexity of manhood. *Journal of Black Studies, 25*(1), 20–40.
Jones, J. (2010). *Labor of love, labor of sorrow: Black women, work and the family from slavery to the present*. New York: Basic Books.
Liebow, E. (1967). *Tally's corner: A study of Negro streetcorner men*. Boston, MA: Little, Brown.
Macleod, J. (2009). *Ain't no makin' it: Aspirations and attainment in a low-income neighborhood*. Boulder, CO: Westview Press.
Majors, R., & Billson, J. M. (1992). *Cool pose: The dilemmas of black manhood in America*. New York: Lexington Books.
Mincy, R. (2006). *Black males left behind*. Washington, DC: Urban Institute Press.
National Urban League. (2007). *The state of black America: Portrait of the Black Male*. New York: Beckham Publication Group.
Nelson, T. J. (2004). Low-income fathers. *Annual Review of Sociology, 30*, 427–451.
Rainwater, L. (1970). *Behind ghetto walls: Black families in a federal slum*. Chicago: Aldine.
Raphael, S. (2011). Incarceration and prisoner reentry in the United States. *Annals of the American Academy of Political and Social Science, 635*(1), 192–215.
Rios, V. M. (2011). *Punished: Policing the lives of black and Latino boys*. New York: New York University Press.
Roy, K. M. (2005). Transitions on the margins of work and family for low-income African American fathers. *Journal of Family and Economic Issues, 26*(1), 77–100.
Roy, K. M. (2006). Father stories: A life course examination of paternal identity among low-income African American men. *Journal of Family Issues, 27*(1), 31–54.
Sullivan, M. L. (1989). *Getting paid: Youth crime and work in the inner city*. Ithaca, NY: Cornell University Press.
Tolleson, J. (1997). Death and transformation: The reparative power of violence in the lives of young black inner-city gang members. *Smith College Studies in Social Work, 67*(3), 415–431.
Travis, J. (2005). *But they all come back: Facing the challenges of prisoner reentry*. Washington, DC: Urban Institute Press.
Venkatesh, S. A. (2000). *American project: The rise and fall of a modern ghetto*. Cambridge, MA: Harvard University Press.
Venkatesh, S. A. (2006). *Off the books: The underground economy of the urban poor*. Cambridge, MA: Harvard University Press.
Visher, C., La Vigne, N. G., & Travis, J. (2004). *Returning home: Understanding the challenges of prisoner reentry*. Washington, DC: Urban Institute Justice Policy Center.
Waller, M. (2002). *My baby's father: Unmarried parents and paternal responsibility*. Ithaca, NY: Cornell University Press.
Western, B. (2007). *Punishment and inequality in America*. New York: Russell Sage Foundation.
Williams, T., & Kornblum, W. (1985). *Growing up poor*. Boston, MA: Lexington Books.
Wilson, W. J. (1987). *The truly disadvantaged: The inner-city, the underclass, and public policy*. Chicago: University of Chicago Press.
Wilson, W. J. (1992). The plight of the inner-city black male. *Proceedings of the American Philosophical Society, 136*(3), 320–325.

Wilson, W. J. (Ed.). (1993). *The ghetto underclass: Social science perspectives*. Newbury Park, CA: Sage.
Wilson, W. J. (1996). *When work disappears: The world of the new urban poor*. New York: Alfred A. Knopf.
Young, A., Jr. (2004). *The minds of marginalized black men: Making sense of mobility, opportunity, and future life chances*. Princeton, NJ: Princeton University Press.

# On Audre and Malcolm's Advice

**Marcus Anthony Hunter**

## Introduction

In "Families, Prisoner Reentry and Integration," Harding and colleagues (Chap. 8) powerfully illustrate that families of those incarcerated "do time together" (Comfort, 2008) and have a key role in the successful reintegration of a convicted loved one. As they show, families are also significant in successfully combatting recidivism. We learn that the individuals who are able to thrive and survive post-incarceration rely on a network of positive support from those whom they perceive comprise their *family*.

Importantly, Harding and colleagues expand the definition of *family* to allow for the consideration of help, support, and encouragement from those not usually deemed family: fictive kin, romantic interests, coworkers, and other former felons. What results is an analysis rich with insight into how and why reentry programs can facilitate or frustrate broader patterns of recidivism and reintegration of those formerly imprisoned. The intersection of race, incarceration, and family, then, also informs a broader geography of experience and policy outcomes across the United States.

For my part, I will expound on Harding and colleague's incisive research by discussing two paths for building on the analysis they provide. To do so, I will rely on insights from Audre Lorde and Malcolm X (el Hajj Malik El Shabazz). The first path focuses on the experiences of black LGBTs. Building on Lorde's insights, I consider new research pathways emergent from the black LGBT experience and the additional problems that incarceration brings. The second path, borne from Malcolm X's insights in his famous speech "The Ballot or the Bullet," follows his emphasis on the omnipresence of 'The South' as a national system of repression and oppression

M.A. Hunter (✉)
Department of Sociology and Department of African American Studies,
UCLA, Los Angeles, CA, USA
e-mail: hunter@soc.ucla.edu



L. Burton et al. (eds.), *Boys and Men in African American Families*, National Symposium on Family Issues 7, DOI 10.1007/978-3-319-43847-4_11

for racial minorities. Each path offers a springboard to think about the analysis Harding and colleagues provide while underscoring the importance of intersectionality and geography for patterns of imprisonment in the United States. Both Lorde's and X's assertions also give voice to those whom our research often miss and illustrate fruitful pathways provided by Harding and colleagues' generative analysis. Taken together, both paths allow for an expanded discussion of the notion of family, especially among racial and sexual minority populations.

## Whose Family Counts? Two Paths Forward

First, Harding and colleagues (Chap. 8) illustrate that family matters in the prisoner reentry process, especially positive family support. Harding and colleagues offer an expanded definition of family that includes extended family and romantic partners. Here, I would add the significant role of fictive kin (e.g. Stack, 1974) as family, especially for those who are LGBT and black. Often excommunicated from their families upon the revelation of their sexual orientation, faux-cousins, sisters, mothers, fathers, and brothers play a similar role in sustaining and maintaining the mental and economic livelihood of black LGBT Americans (Hawkeswood, 1996; Hunter, 2010a; Mogul, Ritchie, & Whitlock, 2011).

The inclusion of fictive kin in the familial support framework not only helps to capture the influential roles these relationships can play in the lives of people in general, and those incarcerated more specially, it also disrupts the normative ways of understanding and measuring who counts as family. Here, the insights of Lorde (1984) are especially generative:

> For the master's tools will never dismantle the master's house. They may allow us to temporarily beat him at his own game but they will never enable us to bring about real change… Racism and homophobia are real conditions of all our lives in this place and time (pp. 112–114).

Lorde's observation reminds us about those we miss in our research, noting the critical limitations and possibilities of our tools for imagination, measurement and freedom.

Lorde's prescience also points to the limits of models and theories that rely only on dominant and master narratives about marginalized and oppressed peoples. Normative tools of measurement can be a great limit. Including the influence of 'chosen families'—familial support networks of the individual's own making in spite of a lack blood ties—is one way of developing the new tools of which Lorde speaks.

For example, when black transgender Americans are incarcerated, many are forced to serve their time based upon a gender designation not of their choosing (Richie, 2012). Of course this makes for additional stressors and may likely increase the importance of familial support. Where cisgender Americans may have this support from their biological families, oftentimes the opposite is true for those who are transgender; thus making fictive family members as important, if not more important, in overall successful reintegration of formerly incarcerated transgender Americans.

Research has illustrated that there is a vibrant black LGBT population living under equally, if not more, dire constraints relative to their heterosexual counterparts (Richie, 2012). Black LGBT individuals convicted of crimes are incarcerated alongside their heterosexual counterparts, often without proper adjustments to account for the needs of black transgender inmates (Richie, 2012). It is often the case that the gender indicated on birth certificates dictates where the inmate is assigned, leaving many black transgender prisoners misplaced and vulnerable to the gender practices and constraints of the facilities in which they serve their time.

Furthermore, Lorde's provocation illustrates that systemic shifts require intersectional methodological frameworks. That is, the impact of race, class, sexual orientation, and socio-economic status shapes the experience and outcomes of individuals and is also critically reflected in the composition of familial networks. Black LGBT Americans' familial networks are often predominantly comprised of other members of the black LGBT community. Intersectional analyses anticipate this reality and as a result, must be sensitive to the experiences of those impacted by both racism and homophobia. Oppression and prejudice are reinforced by structures and institutions like prisons, rendering the black LGBT experience[1] especially potent for helping to identify and eliminate the mechanisms of inequality deeply embedded in systems of justice and incarceration.

Despite the overlapping oppressions of racism and homophobia, in our research and models we often miss the key experiences of transmen and transwomen (of all backgrounds) because our working conceptions of incarceration and punishment are heteronormative and gendered. Alongside Harding and colleagues' intervention in expanding what and who counts as family, we must also apply Lorde's (1984) advice and continue to develop richer understandings of who comprises America's prison population and who their families of choice are. This intersectionally-informed analytic gaze offers real promise as the experiences of black LGBTs have important similarities and contrasts with the broader black and LGBT populations (see Collins, 2004; Hawkeswood, 1996; Hunter, 2013a, 2013b; Moore, 2011).

U.S. Census data indicates that black LGBT Americans are more likely to be poorer and underemployed relative to most every demographic group. Black LGBTs tend to have higher dropout rates and are just as likely to look to alternative means to economically thrive and survive (Williams Institute, 2014). Not unlike their black heterosexual counterparts, black LGBT Americans tend to reside in predominantly black neighborhoods with high levels of unemployment, poverty and poor educational facilities. As a result, black LGBTs run the risk of being unsuccessful in reentering society after serving time in prison.

Considered within the context of the black LGBT experience, the problems of reentry and integration highlight critical questions about the key levers of family

[1] To be sure, black sexualities are varied in their expressions and have been a key subject for study by researchers. It is clear that the role of sex and sexual orientation in organizing human life is huge and critically important for explaining and apprehending the social world. How black Americans think about themselves and their bodies has been shown to have a real impact on their actions and attitudes toward other black people, sexual partners, and familial arrangements.

and family support identified by Harding et al. (Chap. 8): How do incarcerated black LGBTs articulate and construct family? What are the impacts of the gendered organization of imprisonment on the support black transgender inmates receive from carceral institutions and family? When black LGBTs reintegrate, what are the obstacles and what types of familial support prove most significant?

While we know that LGBT men and women are not immune from mass incarceration, emphasis on their treatment, support, and reentry would help better identify latent and explicit mechanisms of oppression and inequality impacting America's prison population. Questions examining the experiences of black LGBT inmates and former felons would provide a powerful intersectional lens that would identify critical gaps in the reentry and probation programs that contribute to high rates of recidivism and programmatic failures. Black feminism and black LGBT scholarship remind us that some of the best and most profound strategies to correct systems and patterns of inequality and oppression are within the voices and experiences of minorities (see Anzaldua, 1987, 1990; Battle & Bennett, 2005; Carbado, 1999; Cohen, 1999, 2005; Collins, 1989, 1990; Combahee River Collective, 1983; Crenshaw, 1989, 1991; Davis, 1981; Glenn, 1985; Hooks, 1984; Hull, Scott, & Smith, 1982; Johnson & Henderson, 2005; King, 1995; Mohanty, 1988; Moraga, 1983; Moraga & Anzuldua, 1984; Sandoval, 1991; Smith, 1983; Spelman, 1988).

As Harding and colleagues illustrate, the expansion of our understanding of normative concepts such as family can go a long way toward enriching our analysis, policy prescriptions, and appreciation of the full problem. Scholars have shown that of course, African Americans who are not heterosexual have unique perspectives about how to define family.

The second path I propose for building on the Harding et al. (Chap. 8) analysis is to renew focus and emphasis on 'The South,' not only as a region of the U.S. but as shorthand for the pervasive impact of America's racialized penal system. Harding and colleagues implicitly illustrate that incarceration, prisoner reentry, and recidivism play a critical geographic role—confining and dictating the spatial mobility of families, individuals, and communities. To expand here, a scene from Detroit in the spring of 1964 is especially poignant. Before a packed audience at the King Solomon Baptist Church, in a speech titled "The Ballot or the Bullet," Malcolm X explicitly amplified this point:

> So we're trapped, trapped, double-trapped, triple-trapped. Anywhere we go, we find that we're trapped. And every kind of solution that someone comes up with is just another trap.... If you black, you were born in jail, in the North as well as the South. Stop talking about the South... Long as you south of the Canadian border, you're south. (Malcolm X, 1964, para 12, 34)

As Malcolm X made clear for the audience, the black American experience can be understood not by the ideas of freedom characterized by the common distinction of North vs. South. Rather, as Malcolm X's Canadian border comment suggests, the U.S. is comprised of multiple iterations of "The South"—regional areas with distinct yet overlapping and similar patterns of racism, white domination, and oppression alongside black strivings and aspirations for a better and more equal society.

Incarceration in this way is not only affecting most all black communities, but also reveals that race and poverty trump any assumed regional or state-level differences in policy and political persuasion.

We find this fact especially poignant in Harding and colleagues' research (Chap. 8). Mass incarceration and reentry impact the places where inmates' families live and work. Census data indicates that the vast majority of black Americans, especially those identifying as LGBT, live in cities or near-urban areas. We also know that much of this trend is due to the *The Great Migration* (1910–1970) reshaping the landscape of urban America.

Moving individually and in large groups, black Americans, gay and straight, traveled throughout the urban landscape to find new neighborhoods, homes, and refuge from the discrimination they endured in much of the rural South. In many cases, romantic interests were significant in drawing black men and women from rural to urban America. Following lovers, husbands, and wives, black Americans sought to establish new lives in some of America's most vibrant cities (Hunter & Robinson, 2016; Wilkerson, 2010). Across the U.S., this movement led to the establishment of black urban neighborhoods and a range of nightlife practices and venues that provided a space to express their sexual desires (Hunter, 2010b; May, 2014; Robinson, 2014).

As a result, the intersection of place, race and sexuality provide a key window into persisting inequalities such as mass incarceration. From delayed marriage to single motherhood to absentee fatherhood, the link between place and black American sexuality has been used by researchers to show the continued impact of enduring white-black health and economic disparities over time. Malcolm X's geographic sentiment, then, draws our attention to how events like America's prison boom impact black mobility and residential patterns. If family and family support are essential to successful prisoner reentry, then incarceration of one makes many people stay put. Staying put and not moving is a commitment of families supporting incarcerated individuals, which means the prison boom impacts the freedoms of more than the convicted (Comfort, 2008; Wakefield & Wildeman, 2013).

The continued high levels of imprisonment of black and brown people alongside the difficulties of reentry Harding and colleagues detail are sobering indicators that Malcolm X's geographic insight is spot on. In most every state, black and brown people are disproportionately represented in America's prisons. Taken together, Harding et al. (Chap. 8), Lorde (1984), and Malcolm X (1964) all point to the continued importance of innovative and intersectional scholarship that uncovers and seeks to eliminate critical inequalities and gaps in our systems of justice and punishment. Our best answers and solutions reside in the perspectives and experiences of the marginalized and oppressed, and the intersections of place, race and sexuality are pregnant with possibility.

## References

Anzaldua, G. (1987). *Borderlands/la frontera: The new mestiza*. San Francisco, CA: Aunt Lute Books.
Anzaldua, G. (1990). *Making face, making soul/haciendo caras: Creative and critical perspectives by feminists of color*. San Francisco, CA: Aunt Lute Books.
Battle, J. J., & Bennett, N. D. A. (2005). Striving for place: Black lesbian, gay, bisexual, and transgender (LGBT) people. In A. Hornsby Jr. (Ed.), *A companion to African American history* (pp. 412–446). Malden, MA: Blackwell.
Carbado, D. (Ed.). (1999). *Black men on race, gender, and sexuality*. New York, NY: New York University Press.
Cohen, C. J. (1999). *Boundaries of blackness: AIDS and the breakdown of black politics*. Chicago, IL: University of Chicago Press.
Cohen, C. J. (2005). Punks, bulldaggers, and welfare queens: The radical potential of queer politics? In E. P. Johnson & M. G. Henderson (Eds.), *Black queer studies: A critical anthology* (pp. 21–51). Durham, NC: Duke University Press.
Collins, P. H. (1989). *Toward a new vision: Race, class, and gender as categories of analysis and connection*. Memphis, TN: Center for Research on Women, University of Memphis.
Collins, P. H. (1990). *Black feminist thought: Knowledge, consciousness, and the politics of empowerment*. New York, NY: Routledge.
Collins, P. H. (2004). *Black sexual politics: African Americans, gender, and the new racism*. New York, NY: Routledge.
Combahee River Collective. (1983). The Combahee River collective statement. In B. Smith (Ed.), *Home girls: A black feminist anthology* (pp. 264–274). New York, NY: Kitchen Table/Women of Color Press.
Comfort, M. (2008). *Doing time together: Love and family in the shadow of the prison*. Chicago, IL: University of Chicago Press.
Crenshaw, K. (1989). Demarginalizing the intersection of race and sex: A black feminist critique of antidiscrimination doctrine, feminist theory, and antiracist politics. *University of Chicago Legal Forum, 140*, 139–167. http://chicagounbound.uchicago.edu/cgi/viewcontent.cgi?article=1052&context=uclf.
Crenshaw, K. (1991). Mapping the margins: Intersectionality, identity politics, and violence against women of color. *Stanford Law Review, 43*, 124–179.
Davis, A. Y. (1981). *Women, race, and class*. New York, NY: Random House.
Glenn, E. N. (1985). Racial ethnic women's labor: The intersection of race, gender and class oppression. *Review of Radical Political Economics, 17*(3), 86–108.
Hawkeswood, W. G. (1996). *One of the children: Gay black men in Harlem*. Berkeley, CA: University of California Press.
Hooks, B. (1984). *Feminist theory: From margin to center*. Cambridge, MA: South End Press.
Hull, G. T., Scott, P. B., & Smith, B. (Eds.). (1982). *All the women are white, all the blacks are men, but some of us are brave: Black women's studies*. New York, NY: Feminist Press.
Hunter, M. A. (2010a). All the gays are white and all the blacks are straight: Black gay men, identity, and community. *Sexuality Research and Social Policy, 7*(2), 81–92.
Hunter, M. A. (2010b). The nightly round: Space, social capital, and urban black nightlife. *City and Community, 9*(2), 165–186.
Hunter, M. A. (2013a). *Black citymakers: How the Philadelphia Negro changed urban America*. Oxford: Oxford University Press.
Hunter, M. A. (2013b). Race and the same-sex marriage divide. *Contexts, 12*(3), 74–76.
Hunter, M. A., & Robinson, Z. F. (2016). The sociology of urban black America. *Annual Review of Sociology, 42*(1).
Johnson, E. P., & Henderson, M. G. (Eds.). (2005). *Black queer studies: A critical anthology*. Durham, NC: Duke University Press.

King, D. K. (1995). Multiple jeopardy, multiple consciousness: The context of black feminist ideology. In B. Guy-Sheftall (Ed.), *Words of fire: An anthology of African-American feminist thought* (pp. 294–318). New York, NY: New Press.
Lorde, A. (1984). *Sister outsider: Essays and speeches*. Berkeley, CA: Crossing Press.
Malcolm X. (1964). *The ballot or the bullet*. http://www.digitalhistory.uh.edu/disp_textbook.cfm?smtid=3&psid=3624. Accessed April 2015.
May, R. A. B. (2014). *Urban nightlife: Entertaining race, class, and culture in public space*. New Brunswick, NJ: Rutgers University Press.
Mogul, J. L., Ritchie, A. J., & Whitlock, K. (2011). *Queer (in) justice: The criminalization of LGBT people in the United States* (Vol. 5). Boston, MA: Beacon.
Mohanty, C. T. (1988). Under western eyes: Feminist scholarship and colonial discourses. *Feminist Review, 10*, 61–88.
Moore, M. (2011). *Invisible families: Gay identities, relationships, and motherhood among black women*. Berkeley, CA: University of California Press.
Moraga, C. (1983). *Loving in the war years*. Cambridge, MA: South End Press.
Moraga, C., & Anzuldua, G. (Eds.). (1984). *This bridge called my back: Writings by radical women of color* (2nd ed.). New York, NY: Kitchen Table Press.
Richie, B. (2012). *Arrested justice: Black women, violence, and America's prison nation*. New York, NY: New York University Press.
Robinson, Z. F. (2014). *This ain't Chicago: Race, class, and regional identity in the post-soul south*. Chapel Hill, NC: The University of North Carolina Press.
Sandoval, C. (1991). US third world feminism: The theory and method of oppositional consciousness in the postmodern world. *Genders, 10*, 1–24.
Smith, B. (Ed.). (1983). *Home girls: A black feminist anthology*. New York, NY: Kitchen Table/Women of Color Press.
Spelman, E. V. (1988). *Inessential woman: Problems of exclusion in feminist thought*. Boston, MA: Beacon.
Stack, C. (1974). *All our kin*. New York, NY: Basic Books.
Wakefield, S., & Wildeman, C. (2013). *Children of the prison boom: Mass incarceration and the future of American inequality*. Oxford: Oxford University Press.
Wilkerson, I. (2010). *The warmth of other suns: The epic story of America's great migration*. New York, NY: Vintage Books.
Williams Institute. (2014). *LGBT Demographics: Comparisons among population-based surveys*. http://williamsinstitute.law.ucla.edu/research/census-lgbt-demographics-studies/lgbt-demogs-sep-2014/. Accessed November 2015.

# Part IV
# Family Influences on the Health of African American Men

# Family Influences on African American Men's Health: Family-Based Interventions

**Cleopatra Howard Caldwell, Julie Ober Allen, and Shervin Assari**

Recent attention to men's health confirms previous findings that African American men continue to suffer from numerous poor health outcomes when compared to men of other racial and ethnic groups and to women (CDC, 2011; Miniño, 2013; Warner & Hayward, 2006). Evidence shows that disparities in life expectancy, chronic illness mortality and morbidity, and death by homicide persist for African American men compared to other men. Specifically, African American men are 37 % more likely than white men to develop lung cancer, and they are at highest risk of dying from a wide range of causes including heart disease, cancer, chronic liver disease, AIDS, and homicide (Bonhomme, 2004; Xanthos, Treadwell, & Holden, 2010). Compared to white men, African American men are 60 % more likely to die from strokes, 30 % more likely to die from heart disease, and they have a higher mortality rate from diabetes. Remarkably, African American men have the highest rates of hypertension and prostate cancer in the world (CDC, 2011).

African American men are often disadvantaged due to economic, environmental, and psychosocial stressors, such as structural marginalization, discrimination, and negative stereotypes within society, which also place them at risk for depression (Assari, Smith, Caldwell, & Zimmerman, 2015; Bonhomme, 2007; Schwing, Wong, & Fann, 2013; Watkins, Green, Rivers, & Rowell, 2006). Although depression is less prevalent than for other groups, African American men who are depressed have

---

C.H. Caldwell (✉)
Department of Health Behavior and Health Education, University of Michigan, Ann Arbor, MI, USA
e-mail: cleoc@umich.edu

J.O. Allen
Department of Health Behavior and Health Education, University of Michigan School of Public Health, Ann Arbor, MI, USA

S. Assari
Department of Psychiatry and Center for Research on Ethnicity, Culture and Health, University of Michigan, Ann Arbor, MI, USA



L. Burton et al. (eds.), *Boys and Men in African American Families*, National Symposium on Family Issues 7, DOI 10.1007/978-3-319-43847-4_12

significant health comorbidities such as stroke, cardiovascular disease, and diabetes (Oliffe & Phillips, 2008; Wagner, Abbott, Heapy, & Yong, 2009). In addition, depression is a risk factor for suicide (Oliffe & Phillips, 2008) and substance abuse (Rowell, Green, Guidry, & Eddy, 2008). Racial and ethnic disparities in rates of depression show that African Americans have lower or comparable rates of depression as whites. African American men, however, are least likely to seek treatment for depression and their symptoms persist when compared to other racial and ethnic groups (Neighbors et al., 2007; Williams, Neighbors, & Jackson, 2003).

Access to treatment for African American men is often hindered by beliefs that illness is a weakness and they are socialized to disassociate themselves from their emotions by being self-reliant from an early age (Harvey & Alston, 2011; Warner & Hayward, 2006). Consequently, negative health beliefs and behaviors are established early in life. Health beliefs and behaviors, however, may be altered as men encounter role transitions and life demands (Warner & Hayward, 2006). Because African American men are least likely to seek necessary treatments, high racial and ethnic health disparities among men will persist, especially when socioeconomic status is considered within and across groups. The resulting premature illness and death for African American men have implications for the women and children in their lives (Bonhomme, 2007). Thus, health is often a family affair; therefore, it is vital to consider family influences on the physical and mental health of African American men in efforts to develop appropriate health care utilization initiatives, health promotion interventions, and policies designed to reduce disparities in men's health.

The purpose of this chapter is to review empirical evidence of the influence of family relationships on African American men's physical and mental health, highlighting findings from the Fathers and Sons Program as one family-based approach to address the health and well-being of African American men. We offer an integrative theoretical framework which guides our research on parenting and men's health as a model for future research and practice in this area. We also suggest directions for future research and family-based policies that may be beneficial for family involvement as a way to improve the health and well-being of African American men.

## Empirical Evidence of Family Influences

Families can play a protective role for African American men's health by providing access to social support, relationships and home environments that facilitate healthy living, motivation to adopt and maintain healthy behaviors, and opportunities to fulfill key social roles. Multiple sources of stress are often central in the lived experiences of African American men; however, some of the most positive and meaningful aspects of their lives are roles and responsibilities associated with family life (Edin & Nelson, 2013; Griffith, Gunter, & Allen, 2011). African American men often experience barriers to achieving valued male social roles, such as family provider, involved father, and protective husband. These limitations place African American men at increased risk for experiencing gender role strain, which refers to how challenges with fulfilling family roles and negotiating conflicting norms about valued social roles can be a source of stress, influence coping abilities or result in health behaviors that can be hazardous to men's health such as substance abuse and depression (Bowman, 1989, 2006; Griffith, Gunter, et al., 2011; Sobolewski & King, 2005).

The significance of social roles in health has been articulated by African American men through qualitative research with focus groups which illuminates their voices. When asked to define "being healthy," African American men in a focus group study by Ravenell, Johnson, and Whitaker (2006) defined health as being able to fulfill social roles such as holding a job, providing for family, protecting and teaching their children, and belonging to a social network. Family, friends, and social groups were found to be important to maintaining healthy behaviors. Social relationships with family and friends characterized by stress and violence were viewed as having a negative effect on health, while supportive relationships were viewed as having an overall positive effect on their health. Similarly, a focus group study of young African American men by Grande, Sherman, and Shaw-Ridley (2013) demonstrated the importance of learning to navigate life and relationships through interactions with older generations of men. These interactions also affected how the young men viewed health, health care utilization and health behaviors. Collectively, these studies speak to the significance of social relationships in the very definition of health for African American men.

## *Marital Relationships and African American Men's Health*

Wives often assume responsibility for their husbands' health, including promoting healthy eating, physical activity, and health seeking behaviors (Allen, Griffith, & Gaines, 2013; Griffith, Ellis, & Allen, 2012; Markey, Gomel, & Markey, 2008; Umberson, 1992). Studies have found that more African American men than women identified their spouse or partner as critical in providing support for healthy eating (38 % vs. 18 %), increased physical activity (35 % vs. 21 %), and colorectal cancer screening (26 % vs. 15 %) (Thrasher, Campbell, & Oates, 2004). Wives' active engagement in addressing their husbands' health was often heightened when men were diagnosed with chronic illnesses (Berg & Upchurch, 2007). Wives' efforts to protect and improve their husbands' health have been described as expressions of nurturing and caring (Charles & Kerr, 1988; DeVault, 1994). African American men often appreciate and expect their wives' involvement in managing their health (Allen et al., 2013; Rook, August, Stephens, & Franks, 2011). Wives attempt to influence their husbands' health behaviors in a myriad of ways with varied levels of success (Helgeson, Novak, Lepore, & Eton, 2004; Kelsey, Earp, & Kirkley, 1997; Lewis, Butterfield, Darbes, & Johnston-Brooks, 2004; Umberson, 1992). The results of a focus group study by Lewis et al. (2004) found over 30 distinct strategies that wives used to improve their spouses' health behaviors, ranging from providing social support and education to reasoning, nagging, modeling, and changing the home environment.

This research suggests that among married men, wives can provide a stable and assessable resource for influencing the health and health behaviors of their husbands. Unfortunately, intervention efforts rarely consider including wives as a critical component of health interventions for men, especially for African American men.

## *Family Relationships and the Health Behaviors of African American Men*

Many African American men are not married and rely on family members other than wives for assistance with their health. Understanding the influence of family relationships beyond wives is essential in addressing the health of African American men. Prior studies have shown that among men who had ever sought help for mental health problems, African Americans were significantly more likely than whites to have discussed their problems with relatives prior to seeking professional health (Griffith, Allen, &Gunder et al., 2011; Sussman, Robins, & Earls, 1987; Woodward, Taylor, & Chatters, 2011). This is especially true for the health seeking behaviors of African American men. Health experiences and habits of immediate and extended family have influenced whether African American men sought, trusted, and complied with medical care (Griffith, Ellis, et al., 2012). A critical ingredient in motivating positive health behaviors was whether or not the health information received was from a trusted resource. This study demonstrated that trusted resources for health information included medical professionals and the media; however, family members were the most trusted resource to provide health information to motivate behavior change among African American men.

Consistent with the findings discussed thus far, a study of prostate cancer screening by Jones, Steeves, and Williams (2009) found that most African American men identified that having a family member involved in their decision to seek prostate cancer screening was important to them because they trusted their relatives and believed that their family members wanted their health to be good. Similarly, Brittain, Loveland-Cherry, Northouse, Caldwell, and Taylor (2012) found that family support and colorectal cancer beliefs were correlated for both African American men and women; however, the relationship between family support and decisions to seek and receive screenings was only correlated for men. Across studies, African American men listed their spouse or a female family member as their main source of support for receiving cancer tests. Most African American men specified that their initial screening happened because they expressed symptomatic concerns to important women in their social networks. Subsequently, the women in their lives suggested that they schedule a doctor's appointment (Jernigan, Trauth, Neal-Ferguson, & Cartier-Ulrich, 2001). These findings suggest that female family members are especially facilitative for getting African American men into health care services, even when it is men who initially recognize symptoms of illness.

Female influences on the mental health of African American men are also evident in the empirical literature. For example, a longitudinal study of family and neighborhood influences on the depressive symptoms of African American youth transitioning into adulthood examined changes in perceived parental support, neighborhood fear, and depressive symptoms among male and female youth (Assari et al., 2015). Changes in perceived maternal support resulting in less support over time were predictive of depressive symptoms for young African American males, but not for young females. Maternal influences on the mental health of African American males, therefore, represent another vital family relationship that should be assessed in discussions of the health of African American men. Mothers are an especially influential resource for African American men, especially single men who may have less diverse social networks. Programs and policies concerned with reducing health disparities among men should consider the role that females can play in supporting more positive outcomes for African American men

## Barriers to Medical Services Utilization Among African American Men

Underutilization of health care services persists among African American men with the key explanations offered being a lack of health awareness and information, inadequate access to services, poor relationships with medical professionals, racial discrimination, fear of serious illness, different cultural and linguistic needs, masculine role identity, and medical mistrust (Allen, Kennedy, Wilson-Glover, & Gilligan, 2007; Griffith, Passmore, Smith, & Wenzel, 2012; Halbert et al., 2009; Hammond, 2010; Ravenell et al., 2006). Mistrust of the health care system has been a persistent major concern among African American men (Boulware, Cooper, Ratner, La Veist, & Powe, 2003; Griffith, Passmore, et al., 2012; Halbert et al., 2009; Hammond, Matthews, Mohottige, Agyemang, & Corbie-Smith, 2010).

A conceptual model of medical mistrust which incorporates the four psychosocial factors of background characteristics, masculine role identity and socialization, recent health care/socioenvironmental experiences (including discrimination), and health care outcome expectations, was offered by Hammond et al. (2010). In general, the model was supported with empirical evidence which showed a positive association between African American men with traditional masculine values and mistrust in the health care system, while better quality interactions with physicians was linked to less medical mistrust. The authors did not find support for their hypotheses that parental socialization to the health care system and having less medical mistrust were associated with underutilization of health care services. The results suggest that more proximal individual beliefs and experiences may be more influential for establishing a sense of trust in the health care system for African American men than are parental socialization influences. These findings suggest that social roles and recent experiences of African American men within the health care system are important points for intervention. Overcoming medical mistrust is critical for African Americans in general, and African American men specifically, to interact effectively with health care professionals and benefit from medical services (Boulware et al., 2003; LaVeist, Nickerson, & Bowie, 2000).

## Fatherhood and African American Men's Health

Studies among men of the transition to fatherhood show that the demands of fatherhood were often associated with positive health outcomes, including less substance use among at-risk African American men (Kerr, Capaldi, Owen, Wiesner, & Pears, 2011). Changing trends in family life in recent decades indicate that two out of five births nationally are to unmarried mothers, with more than two-thirds of African American children born to unmarried mothers (Hamilton, Martin, & Ventura, 2006). Consequently, a large number of African American fathers live apart from their biological children (i.e., nonresident fathers). Recent research, however, shows an increase in father involvement with their children among nonresident fathers, especially for nonresident African American fathers who often remain involved in their children's lives independent of romantic relationships with their children's mothers (Amato, Meyers, & Emery, 2009; Edin, Tach, & Mincy, 2009; King & Sobolewski, 2006; Tach, Mincy, & Edin, 2010).

Studies concerned with the consequences of having a nonresident father and youth problem behaviors have proliferated, with researchers and governmental officials calling for ecologically-based efforts to prevent youth risky behaviors at multiple levels of influence (i.e., individuals, families, schools, communities, and policies; Thornton, Craft, Dahlberg, Lynch, & Baer, 2002). Ecological models posit bidirectional influences between parents and children, suggesting that involvement with children can influence parents as well (Bronfenbrenner, 1994). Thus, being a father has the potential to influence the physical and mental health of African American fathers, regardless of residential status and across socioeconomic statuses.

Recently, Edin and Nelson (2013) found that fatherhood was one of the most valued social roles in life among low income African American men. The salience of the father role has been linked to men's health in prior research (Flynn & Lemay, 1999). Researchers have found that African American men, who have historically faced more challenges in fulfilling the traditional provider dimension of the fatherhood role, fulfilled child rearing and household responsibilities more often than white fathers (Bove & Sobal, 2006; Sobal, 2005). Some studies have suggested that fathers who are poor or members of racially marginalized groups may be more involved with their children than other fathers (Danziger & Radin, 1990; King, Harris, & Heard, 2004; Stier & Tienda, 1993). Thus, the benefits of fatherhood as a psychosocial context for improving men's health are important to consider in assessing the influence of family relationships on African American men's physical and mental health.

In a comprehensive review of the mental health of African American men in social work journals, Watkins, Hawkins, and Mitchell (2015) reviewed 22 studies which were classified in four areas: psychosocial factors, sexual orientation, mental health care and the role of clinicians, and fatherhood. The focus on fatherhood and mental health among African American men was the second largest area of research (n=6 articles) after mental health care and the role of clinicians (n=7 articles). Most fatherhood studies in this review identified demographic and psychosocial correlates of depression or depressive symptoms among African American fathers, including being single, younger, less educated, limited partner support, and in a poor quality of relationship with the mother of their children. The relational aspect of fatherhood was a consistent correlate in most studies of depression, which highlighted having a wife, partner support, and children as being associated with more positive mental health outcomes for African American men.

## Parenting and Men's Health

Despite the public health significance of problems such as substance abuse and depression among African American men, few evidence-based interventions have been developed specifically for men, and even fewer have focused on their role as fathers as a health promotion strategy. Research informed by identity and social identity theories suggest that social roles and social identities provide purpose, meaning and behavioral guidance in an individual's life, with implications for positive health behaviors and mental health (Oliffe & Phillips, 2008). The salience of the father role and the significance of masculine ideologies have been linked to men's health in prior research (Bonhomme, 2007; Caldwell, Rafferty, Reischl, De Loney, & Brooks, 2010). Garfield, Clark-Kauffman, and Davis (2006) suggest that "illuminating the psychosocial fabric of men's lives may reveal critical links between fatherhood and men's health" (p. 2368). Understanding the benefits and burdens of fatherhood as a psychosocial context for health will provide clinicians, interventionists, and policy makers with additional information for addressing health disparities among men.

### *The Fathers and Sons Program*

As an example of the potential of fatherhood as a context for men's health, we briefly describe the background for the Fathers and Sons Program which was initially funded by the CDC. The Fathers and Sons Program was originally designed to strengthen relationships between nonresident African American fathers and their preadolescent sons as a way to prevent risky health behaviors (i.e., substance use, early sexual initiation, and violent behavior) among African American boys. It was developed using a community-based participatory research (CBPR) approach to increase its relevance and appeal to the intended audiences. The final program curriculum was theoretically-based, culturally relevant, and gender specific. Critical to the success of the intervention was enhancing the parenting skills and behaviors of nonresident African American fathers. Evaluation results indicated that improvement in fathers' communication-based parenting was associated with improvements in their sons' intentions to avoid violence and an actual reduction in their aggressive behaviors (Caldwell et al., 2010; Caldwell et al., 2014). Additionally, we found that the intervention program was promising for promoting positive health behaviors and well-being among nonresident African American fathers (Caldwell et al., 2010; Caldwell, Bell, Brooks, Ward, & Jennings, 2011).

In the next two sections we describe findings from the original CDC funded Fathers and Sons Program in Flint that highlight health and mental health outcomes for fathers using a quasi-experimental design, followed by a discussion of an emerging theoretical model that guides the implementation of a new study of Parenting and Men's Health recently funded by the National Institute of Child Health and Human Development (NICHD), National Institutes of Health. As a more in-depth follow-up to the original study, the new intervention study is a randomized controlled trial designed to assess the role of fathering among nonresident African American fathers in reducing depression and substance abuse, and increasing the use of mental health services. The guiding theoretical model builds on findings from the original study which demonstrated links between parenting and men's health and well-being. Although the expanded theoretical model incorporates influences on outcomes for African American boys, we limit our discussion in this chapter to a model of change for correlates and underlying mechanisms relevant to nonresident African American fathers.

## *Findings from the Fathers and Sons Program*

Results from the Fathers and Sons Program indicated that strengthening paternal competence and skills may be beneficial in promoting men's health, as evidenced by reductions in depressive symptoms and drinking behaviors among nonresident African American fathers who had a good relationship with their preadolescent sons (Caldwell, Antonakos, Tsuchiya, Assari, & De Loney, 2013). We determined that severe depressive symptoms among fathers at baseline were associated with less contact, closeness, monitoring, and high conflict with their sons (Davis, Caldwell, Clark, & Davis, 2009). Fathers who monitored their sons' behavior, however, reported fewer depressive symptoms (Caldwell et al., 2011).

In addition, we found that 76 % of nonresident African American fathers drank alcohol at baseline, with 27 % drinking several times per week or more. Fathers who drank averaged three drinks on one occasion, and 44 % of these fathers felt a need to reduce their drinking. After the intervention, significantly more intervention fathers requested professional assistance for their drinking than fathers in the comparison group (Caldwell et al., 2010). Further, 47 % of fathers reported moderate to high depressive symptoms at baseline. Having a good relationship with their sons was protective against depressive symptoms and drinking among these fathers, with parenting variables explaining additional variance in both outcomes beyond masculine ideologies, perceived discrimination, co-parenting behaviors and socio-demographic controls (Caldwell et al., 2013).

We also found that the moderating effect of a particular masculine ideology on co-parenting and depressive symptoms for fathers was in the opposite direction than we expected. That is, fathers with positive co-parenting relationships with their sons' mother and who had high levels of interconnected masculinity (i.e., reflective of social justice or fighting for the rights of others) reported more depressive symptoms. Perhaps fatherhood social norms operationalized in efforts to effectively co-parent may result in oppositional or competing social norms with being a good citizen concerned with the rights of others. Such a conflict may result in depressive symptoms for these fathers who often lack control over engaging with their children independent of mothers. Addressing both parenting and social justice needs would be especially challenging if these fathers were unable or unwilling to meet society's expectations for fatherhood (e.g., provider role) given their nonresidential status (Sobolewski & King, 2005). The complexity of their family relationships and their sense of social obligations as African American men require more research to better understand how social roles and social identities may combine to influence mental health outcomes for nonresident African American fathers.

## An Integrative Theoretical Model of Parenting and Men's Health

Figure 1 provides the theoretical model that guides the implementation of the current Fathers and Sons Program being conducted in Chicago, which is designed to influence the health behaviors and mental health of nonresident African American fathers. It represents an expansion of our original model which was concerned with explaining the prevention of youth risky behaviors among African American boys by enhancing the parenting behaviors of their nonresident fathers (Caldwell et al., 2004). Figure 1 indicates that specific paternal behaviors and the quality of father-son relationships are interpersonal mediators between the Fathers and Sons Program and intrapersonal mediators and outcomes for fathers as noted by Paths A, B, and C. Path D reflects how fathers' parenting influences mediate the intervention effects on their sons' outcomes. Path E shows how fathers' social identities and other factors may modify intervention effects on the interpersonal mediators. Path F indicates that fathers' and sons' outcomes may influence each other.

Although the current model reflects the role of the intervention program in improving fathers' parenting behaviors (Path A), we relied on an integration of identity and social identity theories to explain positive health behaviors and mental health among fathers as reflected in the expanded model in Fig. 1. Identity theory posits that individuals define who they are by the roles they assume (Connell & Messerschmidt, 2005; Hammond, Caldwell, Brooks, & Bell, 2011). Each role (e.g., father, husband) represents separate identities that have meanings and expectations for behaviors. A hierarchy of role identities is formed based on salience (importance) and reflexivity (what individuals think others think) of the role.

Nonresident fathers must be motivated to stay connected to their children when they do not live with them. They must negotiate with their children's mother to be involved in their lives. This can be a source of stress for fathers or it can energize them. Some studies have found that multiple role identities reduced depression and distress (Courtenay, 2003), while others have found that identity conflict, role imbalance, and diminished relationship quality were associated with more depression (Courtenay, 2000; Fox & Bruce, 2001; Mullen, Watson, Swift, & Black, 2007). As

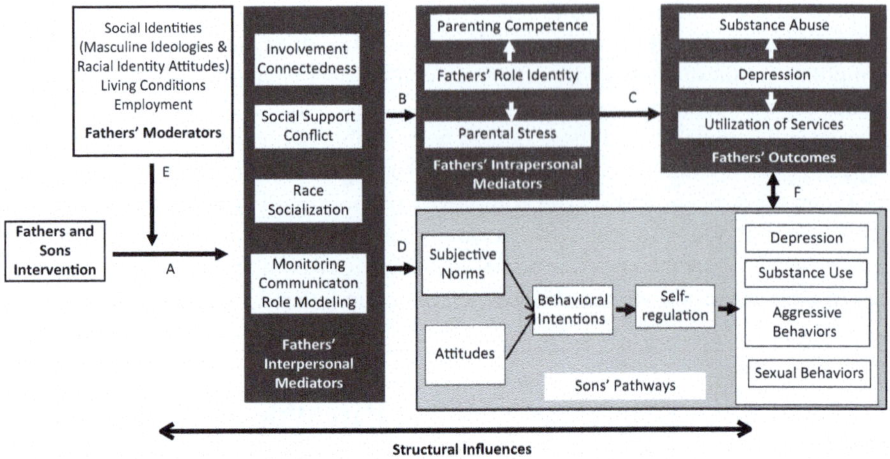


**Fig. 1** Theoretical model of mediators and moderators of the *Fathers and Sons Program* on family outcomes

indicated in Fig. 1, we account for both possibilities by considering father role identity as an intrapersonal mediator of parenting behaviors on health behaviors and mental health outcomes (Links B and C), and as a direct influence on these outcomes (Link C). The benefits of parenting for fathers' will depend on their assessment of the salience and reflexivity of the father role over time as their son ages into adolescence (Connell & Messerschmidt, 2005).

Distinct from identity theory, social identity theory assigns meaning to the self through identification with group processes and intergroup relations. Two influential social identities for African American men in the United States are masculine and racial identities (Franklin, 1999; Mullen et al., 2007). Hegemonic masculine ideologies are described as dominant male role norms, with characteristics such as being powerful, in control, physically strong, status seeking, competitive, autonomous, and emotionally detached (Connell & Messerschmidt, 2005). Past research indicates men engage in health behaviors such as drinking, smoking, and using drugs as a means to demonstrate their masculinity (Courtenay, 2003; Mullen et al., 2007). Male role norms often dictate the suppression of pain and the avoidance of asking for help. Conflicting findings are evident regarding hegemonic masculine ideologies and African American men. Research often shows that African American men endorse aspects of traditional masculinity while also embracing interpersonal interactions and emotional expressions, especially regarding family relationships. Being a successful provider is important to their manhood, as well as being emotionally attached to family and fighting for the rights of others (Hammond & Mattis, 2005; Hunter & Davis, 1994).

Experiencing vulnerability in the family provider role and belief in hegemonic masculine ideologies, however, can place African American men at risk for substance abuse, depression, and other mental health problems. Tendencies toward interpersonal competencies in family relations among African American men suggest that connecting them to their children and enhancing their parenting abilities could be important strategies for better physical and mental health. Incorporating father role identity and masculine ideologies with the cultural aspects of the Fathers and Sons Program which emphasize racial socialization and racial identity, is expected to reduce problematic substance use and depression. At the same time, these components of the program are also expected to increase use of substance abuse and mental health services among African American fathers.

## Structural Influences on Parenting and African American Men's Health

Implementation of the integrated theoretical model presented in Fig. 1 must be considered within the context of structural barriers influencing African American men as fathers, as represented by the arrow across the bottom of the figure. The historical experiences of African Americans in the United States are critical to understanding the present realities of African American men within families. The influences of slavery, racism, generational unemployment, and legislative disenfranchisement have impacted many men's ability to successfully assume the fatherhood role within families (Billingsley, 1992). Historically, there have been many barriers to strong African American father-child and family relationships. During slavery few families had a biological father in the home (Akbar, 1991). Enslaved fathers were often sold and never saw their family again. This created fragmented family structures within African American communities that have survived for generations. The implications of these fragmented family structures for the health of African American men have not been the focus of much research.

In modern times, manhood and the ability to provide are inextricable parts of masculine identities in the United States; however, institutionalized racism within the educational and employment systems over time have left many African American men unable to effectively assume the provider role within their families (Aronson, Whitehead, & Baber, 2003; Hunter & Davis, 1994). In their treatment of factors contributing to the meaning of father role/identity, salience, and commitment among nonresident African American fathers, Hammond et al. (2011) articulated the legacy of active father engagement for many African American men who may not be able to fulfill the provider role based on a historical context born of slavery and replicated across time through institutional discrimination and racism. They highlighted research by African American scholars whose findings offered an alternative perspective on African American family life from the mainstream literature of the time. For example, Hammond et al. (2011) noted that:

> McAdoo (1988) determined that African American fathers made demonstrable efforts to establish and maintain emotional connections during a time when they were often explicitly barred from residing with their children or carrying out traditional fatherhood obligations (e.g., protecting and providing). Taken together, these findings suggest that African American fathers strive to make contributions to their children's socio-emotional development even in the face of structural barriers that may prevent them from adequately fulfilling economic provider roles (p. 309).

The need to connect with children may be strong for some men; however, numerous barriers exist to prevent effective paternal involvement. Findings from their own qualitative study highlight the significance of family substance abuse, criminal activity, and violence as risk factors for disengagement from children among nonresident African American fathers (Hammond et al., 2011). Consequently, providing family-based interventions for African American fathers without consideration for the broader historical and social contexts in which they live will have limited success. Multiple levels of intervention often will be necessary to address their ability to parent effectively, especially among nonresident fathers.

## *Neighborhood Violence and African American Men's Health*

Research on neighborhood violence is a promising area for better understanding structural conditions and African American men's health over the life course. Homicide is the leading cause of death for African American youth ages 10–24 (CDC, 2013), and it remains the leading cause of death for African American men through age 34 (CDC, 2011). Recent analyses of national homicide trends from 2002 to 2011 indicated that the peak homicide rate for African American men (100.3/100,000) occurs at age 23. Nationally, homicide has remained a leading cause of death for African Americans ages 10–24 for over two decades (CDC, 2012).

Homicide disproportionately impacts African American men, with the homicide rate for 10–24 year old males (51.5/100,000) exceeding rates for their Hispanic (13.5/100,000) and white (2.9/100,000) male peers. A recent study examining the national prevalence of trauma among youth in the United States found nearly half experienced at least one traumatic event in childhood (Bethell, Newacheck, Haves, & Halfon, 2014). Youth growing up in urban areas were exposed to even higher rates of traumatic events (Bell & Jenkins, 1993), with low income youth reporting a greater likelihood of witnessing stabbings and shootings in their neighborhoods than youth from neighborhoods of higher socioeconomic statuses (Buka, Stichick, Birdthistle, & Earls, 2001).

Studies have consistently found that neighborhood violence and trauma exposures are enduring stressors for African American youth in low income, urban neighborhoods (Jenkins, Wang, & Turner, 2009; Neumann, Barker, Koot, & Maughan, 2010) with implications for adult health. Early traumatic exposures to neighborhood violence place African American men at risk for a number of negative psychosocial outcomes including depression, anxiety, and posttraumatic stress (Bell & Jenkins, 1993; Cooley-Strickland et al., 2009; Fitzpatrick & Boldizar, 1993; Jenkins et al., 2009; Lambert, Ialongo, Boyd, & Cooley, 2005). Physical health and health behaviors are also impacted by exposures to neighborhood violence with adverse outcomes for blood pressure and substance use among young African American men (Ortiz, Richards, Kohl, & Zaddach, 2008; Wilson, Kliewer, & Sica, 2004). The protective effect of family relationships against neighborhood violence for African American males has been examined most often for youth with an eye toward the prevention of violence perpetration. However, there is a need for more research on risk and protective factors associated with neighborhood violence, family social relations, and the physical and mental health of African American adult males.

## Directions for Future Research

In this chapter, we have focused on the direct influences of family members on the physical and mental health of African American men, highlighting the critical role of wives, other female family members, and the significance of fatherhood as a context for men's health. There are a number of areas, however, that warrants further research. For example, our approach to family influences considered only psychosocial and behavioral aspects of what family members do to encourage better health among African American men. More research is required to understand observational influences on the health of men. For example, Harvey and Alston (2011) found that being aware of medical issues for family members appears to be an important motivating factor in African American men's decisions to take care of themselves. It is not clear if closeness in relationships or if specific demographic characteristics matter more than others for reaching the motivational threshold for men to engage in positive health behaviors. More research in this area is needed to better understand these issues.

A better understanding of family influences on men's health in different social contexts is also needed, especially among African American men who are incarcerated, in the military, or otherwise removed from community life. In addition, more research is required on the facilitators that encourage African American men to use health and mental health services earlier in the illness process and for purposes of prevention. Identifying which family members (i.e., wives, children, parents, female relative, etc.) may be most important to include when designing health promotion interventions to more effectively address the physical and mental health needs of African American men is also critical to understand.

Finally, the role of children in men's decision to care for their own health is not clearly understood. More research is needed to determine at which stage of life children may be most influential in motivating men to engage in more positive health behaviors and to have better mental health outcomes. Current research suggests the transition to fatherhood is a critical stage of life for altering health beliefs and behaviors for men. However, this remains an empirical question because most studies examine resident fathers of infants or young children with little attention to these effects at later stages of development either for fathers or their children, regardless of resident status. Understanding racial/ethnic similarities and differences in these experiences will be essential to future intervention, service, and policy development.

## Family-Based Policy Initiatives

Federal policies that effectively include fathers can assist them in overcoming structural barriers to father involvement with their children and can strengthen family relationships. Most federal policies focusing specifically on fathers can be divided into one of two groups: (1) policies with educational or economic outcomes, and (2) policies that affect family relationships (Knox, Cowan, Cowan, & Bildner, 2011). While policies with educational and economic objectives do little to advance the definition of fatherhood beyond the "provider role," these policies do have implications for fathers' family relationships. The converse may also be true; interventions that enhance fathers' family relationships may have important educational and economic benefits for fathers (Knox et al., 2011).

In assessing federal policies with economic and educational outcomes, there are barriers to father involvement that can be physical, emotional, and financial. Prominent financial barriers include making child support payments, and being low income and unemployed. While current policies highlight financial barriers to father involvement through Responsible Fatherhood programs, we discuss financial barriers to father involvement as they relate to the child support enforcement system and the federal tax structure because of their relevance for distancing African American men from their children.

The child support enforcement system has many advantages for children, but there are also barriers to father involvement. Marked disparities within the child support enforcement system exist between low-income and high-income fathers. On average, low-income fathers are ordered to pay a higher percentage of their incomes in child support than are higher earners (Cancian, Meyer, & Han, 2011). Overall, financial barriers to father involvement are greatest for low-income noncustodial fathers. These barriers are often the result of large financial obligations and unemployment, suggesting the need for policies that help ease financial barriers to father involvement. It is clear that such policies would still implicitly label fathers as providers; however, these policies could also complement family-oriented programs such as Responsible Fatherhood programs. New policies should avoid the largely-punitive focus of the child support enforcement system by rewarding fathers for their involvement in their children's lives (Mincy, Klempin, & Schmidt, 2011).

Current social policies associated with child custody, child support, and visitation among unmarried couples undercut the more modern and complex conceptualizations of the fatherhood role among African American men and the potential benefits to their health. Rather than helping, these policies impose additional barriers to African American men participating in and benefiting from their children's lives. Most policies contribute to African American fathers weakening or abandoning their ties with their children and families. Research has shown that this can have negative implications for their physical and mental health. For example, noncustodial fathers are responsible for providing financial support to their children, yet they are not recognized in the same way through tax incentives as custodial fathers. They do not receive the same tax-relief as custodial fathers for their dependent children because the Earned Income Tax Credit specifically targets custodial parents. This results in less income for noncustodial fathers, which increase their chances of not providing full child support payments (Mincy et al., 2011).

Low-income noncustodial fathers who are responsible and pay their child support orders should be rewarded with an Earned Income Tax Credit. While there are many competing proposals regarding the way in which to implement an increased Earned Income Tax Credit specific to noncustodial parents, Mincy et al. (2011) propose the best solution: an expanded childless worker tax credit for all noncustodial parents. The proposed tax credit would resolve administrative barriers related to timely disbursement and would make the tax credit accessible to a larger group of fathers. Fathers without outstanding child support orders would receive the tax credit in full (Mincy et al., 2011). In this manner, the government would reward responsible low-income fathers, offering them tax relief in recognition of their commitment to their children. This tax relief would allow low-income noncustodial fathers to better support themselves and their children.

By implementing systems that reward responsible fatherhood to complement those that enforce child support, policymakers can encourage noncustodial fathers to remain involved with their children and receive potential physical and mental health benefits which father involvement may afford. Such policies and programs are believed to enhance the well-being of African American fathers and their families.

## Conclusion

Family influences on the physical and mental health of African American men are evident in the empirical literature. Wives and other female family members have been examined most extensively and were identified as vital resources for motivating men to engage in more positive health behaviors and health-seeking behaviors. Children as catalysts for men's health motivations have been examined to a lesser extent. Yet, emerging fatherhood research suggests becoming a father and enhancing fatherhood experiences can improve men's health behaviors and mental health. An intergenerational approach to these issues may be especially useful to consider because such findings will contribute to a better understanding of fatherhood as a critical social context for improving African American men's and boy's physical and mental health.

## References

Akbar, N. (1991). *Visions for black men*. Tallahassee, FL: Mind Productions & Associates.

Allen, J. D., Kennedy, M., Wilson-Glover, A., & Gilligan, T. D. (2007). African-American men's perceptions about prostate cancer: Implications for designing educational interventions. *Social Science and Medicine, 64*(11), 2189–2200.

Allen, J. O., Griffith, D. M., & Gaines, H. C. (2013). "She looks out for the meals, period": African American men's perceptions of how their wives influence their eating behavior and dietary health. *Health Psychology, 32*(4), 447–455.

Amato, P. R., Meyers, R. E., & Emery, R. E. (2009). Changes in nonresident father–child contact from 1976–2002. *Family Relations, 58*(1), 41–53.

Aronson, R. E., Whitehead, T. L., & Baber, W. L. (2003). Challenges to masculine transformation among urban low-income African American males. *American Journal of Public Health, 93*(5), 732–741.

Assari, S., Smith, J. R., Caldwell, C. H., & Zimmerman, M. A. (2015). Gender differences in longitudinal links between neighborhood fear, parental support, and depression among African American emerging adults. *Societies, 5*(1), 151–170.

Bell, C. C., & Jenkins, E. J. (1993). Community violence and children on Chicago's southside. *Psychiatry, 56*(1), 46–54.

Berg, C. A., & Upchurch, R. (2007). A developmental-contextual model of couples coping with chronic illness across the life span. *Psychological Bulletin, 133*(6), 920–954.

Bethell, C. D., Newacheck, P., Haves, E., & Halfon, N. (2014). Adverse childhood experiences: Assessing the impact on health and school engagement and the mitigating role of resilience. *Health Affairs, 33*(12), 2106–2115.

Billingsley, A. (1992). *Climbing Jacobs ladder: The enduring legacy of African American families*. New York, NY: Simon & Schuster.

Bonhomme, J. J. (2007). Men' health: Impact on women, children and society. *Journal of Men's Health and Gender, 4*(2), 124–130.

Bonhomme, J. J. E. (2004). The health status of African-American men: Improving our understanding of men's health challenges. *Journal of Men's Health and Gender, 1*(2–3), 142–146.

Boulware, L. E., Cooper, L. A., Ratner, L. E., La Veist, T. A., & Powe, N. R. (2003). Race and trust in the health care system. *Public Health Reports, 118*(4), 358–365.

Bove, C. F., & Sobal, J. (2006). Foodwork in newly married couples: Making family meals. *Food, Culture, and Society, 9*(1), 69–89.

Bowman, P. J. (1989). Research perspectives on Black men: Role strain and adaptation across the adult life cycle. In R. L. Jones (Ed.), *Black adult development and aging* (pp. 117–150). Berkeley, CA: Cobb & Henry Publishers.

Bowman, P. J. (2006). Role strain and adaptation issues in the strength-based model: Diversity, multilevel, and life-span considerations. *Counseling Psychologist, 34*(1), 118–133.

Brittain, K., Loveland-Cherry, C., Northouse, L., Caldwell, C. H., & Taylor, J. Y. (2012). Sociocultural differences and colorectal cancer screening among African American men and women. *Oncology Nursing Forum, 39*(1), 100–107.

Bronfenbrenner, U. (1994). Ecological models of human development. In M. Gauvain & M. Cole (Eds.), *Readings on the development of children* (2nd ed., pp. 37–43). New York, NY: Freeman.

Buka, S. L., Stichick, T. L., Birdthistle, I., & Earls, F. J. (2001). Youth exposure to violence: Prevalence, risks, and consequences. *American Journal of Orthopsychiatry, 71*(3), 298–310.

Caldwell, C. H., Antonakos, C., Assari, S., Kruger, D., De Loney, E. H., & Njai, R. (2014). Pathways to prevention: Improving nonresident African American fathers' parenting skills and behaviors to reduce son's aggression. *Child Development, 85*(1), 308–325.

Caldwell, C. H., Antonakos, C., Tsuchiya, K., Assari, S., & De Loney, E. H. (2013). Masculinity as a moderator of discrimination and parenting on depressive symptoms and drinking behavior among nonresident African American fathers. *Psychology of Men and Masculinity, 14*(1), 47–58.

Caldwell, C. H., Bell, L., Brooks, C. L., Ward, J. D., & Jennings, C. (2011). Engaging nonresident African American fathers in intervention research: What practitioners should know about parental monitoring in nonresident families. *Journal of Research on Social Work Practice, 21*(3), 298–307.

Caldwell, C. H., Rafferty, J., Reischl, T., De Loney, E. H., & Brooks, C. L. (2010). Enhancing parenting skills among nonresident African American fathers as a strategy for preventing youth risky behaviors. *American Journal of Community Psychology, 45*(1–2), 17–35.

Caldwell, C. H., Wright, J. C., Zimmerman, M. A., Walsemann, K. M., Williams, D., & Isichei, P. A. C. (2004). Enhancing adolescent health behaviors through strengthening nonresident father-son relationships: A model for intervention with African American families. *Health Education Research, 19*(6), 644–656.

Cancian, M., Meyer, D. R., & Han, E. (2011). Child support: Responsible fatherhood and the quid pro quo. *Annals of the American Academy of Political and Social Science, 635*(1), 140–162.

Centers for Disease Control and Prevention. (2011). *Health, United States, 2010: With special feature on death and dying*. Hyattsville, MD: National Center for Health Statistics. http://www.cdc.gov/nchs/data/hus/hus10.pdf. Accessed September 2015.

Centers for Disease Control and Prevention. (2012). Youth risk behavior surveillance—United States, 2011. *MMWR Surveillance Summaries, 61*(4), 1–162.

Centers for Disease Control and Prevention. (2013). *Web-based Injury Statistics Query and Reporting System (WISQARS)* [online]. https://wisqars.cdc.gov:8443/nvdrs/nvdrsDisplay.jsp. Accessed May 2016.

Charles, N., & Kerr, M. (1988). *Women, food, and families*. Manchester: Manchester Press.

Connell, R. W., & Messerschmidt, J. W. (2005). Hegemonic masculinity: Rethinking the concept. *Gender and Society, 19*(6), 829–859.

Cooley-Strickland, M., Quille, T. J., Griffin, R. S., Stuart, E. A., Bradshaw, C. P., & Furr-Holden, D. (2009). Community violence and youth: Affect, behavior, substance use, and academics. *Clinical Child and Family Psychology Review, 12*(2), 127–156.

Courtenay, W. H. (2000). Constructions of masculinity and their influence on men's well-being: A theory of gender and health. *Social Science and Medicine, 50*(10), 1385–1401.

Courtenay, W. H. (2003). Key determinants of the health and well-being of men and boys. *International Journal of Men's Health, 2*(1), 1–30.

Danziger, S. K., & Radin, N. (1990). Absent does not equal uninvolved: Predictors of fathering in teen mother families. *Journal of Marriage and Family, 52*(3), 636–642.

Davis, R. N., Caldwell, C. H., Clark, S. J., & Davis, M. M. (2009). Depressive symptoms in nonresident African American fathers and involvement with their sons. *Pediatrics, 124*(6), 1611–1618.

DeVault, M. L. (1994). *Feeding the family: The social organization of caring as gendered work*. Chicago: University of Chicago Press.

Edin, K., & Nelson, T. J. (2013). *Doing the best I can: Fatherhood in the inner city*. Berkeley, CA: University of California Press.

Edin, K., Tach, L., & Mincy, R. (2009). Claiming fatherhood: Race and the dynamics of paternal involvement among unmarried men. *The ANNALS of the American Academy of Political and Social Science, 621*(1), 149–177.

Fitzpatrick, K. M., & Boldizar, J. P. (1993). The prevalence and consequences of exposure to violence among African-American youth. *Journal of the American Academy of Child and Adolescent Psychiatry, 32*(2), 424–430.

Flynn, R. J., & Lemay, R. A. (Eds.). (1999). *A quarter-century of normalization and social role valorization: Evolution and impact*. Ottawa: University of Ottawa Press.

Fox, G. L., & Bruce, C. (2001). Conditional fatherhood: Identity Theory and Parental Investment Theory as alternative sources of explanation of fathering. *Journal of Marriage and Family, 63*(2), 394–403.

Franklin, A. J. (1999). Invisibility syndrome and racial identity development in psychotherapy and counseling in African American men. *The Counseling Psychologist, 27*(2), 761–793.

Garfield, C. F., Clark-Kauffman, E., & Davis, M. M. (2006). Fatherhood as a component of men's health. *Journal of the American Medical Association, 296*(19), 2365–2368.

Grande, S. W., Sherman, L., & Shaw-Ridley, M. (2013). A brotherhood perspective: How African American male relationships may improve trust and utilization of health care. *American Journal of Men's Health, 7*(6), 494–503.

Griffith, D. M., Allen, J. O., & Gunter, K. (2011). Social and cultural factors influence African American men's medical help-seeking. *Research on Social Work Practice, 21*(3), 337–347.

Griffith, D. M., Ellis, K. R., & Allen, J. O. (2012). How does health information influence African American men's health behavior? *American Journal of Men's Health, 6*(2), 156–163.

Griffith, D. M., Gunter, K., & Allen, J. O. (2011). Male gender role strain as a barrier to African American men's physical activity. *Health Education and Behavior, 38*(5), 482–491.

Griffith, K. A., Passmore, S. R., Smith, D., & Wenzel, J. (2012). African Americans with a family history of colorectal cancer: Barriers and facilitators to screening. *Oncology Nursing Forum, 39*(3), 299–306.

Halbert, C. H., Weathers, B., Delmmor, E., Mahler, B., Coyne, J., Thompson, H. S., et al. (2009). Racial differences in medical mistrust among men diagnosed with prostate cancer. *Cancer, 115*(11), 2553–2561.

Hamilton, B. E., Martin, J. A., &Ventura, S. J. (2006). *Births: Preliminary data for 2005*. (Tables 1, 3) Hyattsville, MD: National Center for Health Statistics. http://www.cdc.gov/nchs/data/hestat/prelimbirths05/prelimbirths05.htm. Accessed November 2009.

Hammond, W. P. (2010). Psychosocial correlates of medical mistrust among African American men. *American Journal of Community Psychology, 45*(1-2), 87–106.

Hammond, W. P., Caldwell, C. H., Brooks, C. L., & Bell, L. (2011). Being there in spirit, fire, and mind: Expressive role/identity salience, negotiation, and commitment among nonresidential African American fathers. *Journal of Research on Social Work Practice, 21*(3), 308–318.

Hammond, W. P., Matthews, D., Mohottige, D., Agyemang, A., & Corbie-Smith, G. (2010). Masculinity, medical mistrust, and preventive health services delays among community-dwelling African-American men. *Journal of General Internal Medicine, 25*(12), 1300–1308.

Hammond, W. P., & Mattis, J. S. (2005). Being a man about it: Manhood meaning among African American men. *Psychology of Men and Masculinity, 6*(2), 114–126.

Harvey, I. S., & Alston, R. (2011). Understanding preventive behaviors among mid-Western African-American men: A pilot qualitative study of prostate screening. *Journal of Men's Health, 8*(2), 140–151.

Helgeson, V. S., Novak, S. A., Lepore, S. J., & Eton, D. T. (2004). Spouse social control efforts: Relations to health behavior and well-being among men with prostate cancer. *Journal of Social and Personal Relationships, 21*(1), 53–68.

Hunter, A. G., & Davis, J. E. (1994). Hidden voices of Black men: The meaning, structure, and complexity of manhood. *Journal of Black Studies, 25*(1), 20–40.

Jenkins, E. J., Wang, E., & Turner, L. (2009). Traumatic events involving friends and family members in a sample of African American early adolescents. *The American Journal of Orthopsychiatry, 79*(3), 398–406.

Jernigan, J. C., Trauth, J. M., Neal-Ferguson, D., & Cartier-Ulrich, C. (2001). Factors that influence cancer screening in older African American men and women: Focus group findings. *Family and Community Health, 24*(3), 27–33.

Jones, R. A., Steeves, R., & Williams, I. (2009). How African American men decide whether or not to get prostate cancer screening. *Cancer Nursing, 32*(2), 166–172.

Kelsey, K., Earp, J. L., & Kirkley, B. G. (1997). Is social support beneficial for dietary change? A review of the literature. *Family and Community Health, 20*(3), 70–82.

Kerr, D. C., Capaldi, D. M., Owen, L. D., Wiesner, M., & Pears, K. C. (2011). Changes in at-risk American men's crime and substance use trajectories following fatherhood. *Journal of Marriage and Family, 73*(5), 1101–1116.

King, V., Harris, K. M., & Heard, H. E. (2004). Racial and ethnic diversity in nonresident father involvement. *Journal of Marriage and Family, 66*(1), 1–21.

King, V., & Sobolewski, J. M. (2006). Nonresident fathers' contributions to adolescent well-being. *Journal of Marriage and Family, 68*(3), 537–557.

Knox, V., Cowan, P. A., Cowan, C. P., & Bildner, E. (2011). Policies that strengthen fatherhood and family relationships: What do we know and what do we need to know? *The ANNALS of the American Academy of Political and Social Science, 635*(1), 216–239.

Lambert, S. F., Ialongo, N. S., Boyd, R. C., & Cooley, M. R. (2005). Risk factors for community violence exposure in adolescence. *American Journal of Community Psychology, 36*(1–2), 29–48.

LaVeist, T. A., Nickerson, K. J., & Bowie, J. V. (2000). Attitudes about racism, medical mistrust, and satisfaction with care among African American and white cardiac patients. *Medical Care Research and Review, 57*(1), 146–161.
Lewis, M. A., Butterfield, R. M., Darbes, L. A., & Johnston-Brooks, C. (2004). The conceptualization and assessment of health-related social control. *Journal of Social and Personal Relationships, 21*(5), 669–687.
Markey, C. N., Gomel, J. N., & Markey, P. M. (2008). Romantic relationships and eating regulation: An investigation of partners' attempts to control each other's eating behaviors. *Journal of Health Psychology, 13*(3), 422–432.
McAdoo, J. L. (1988). Changing perspectives on the role of the black father. In P. Bronstein & C. P. Cowan (Eds.), *Fatherhood today: Men's changing role in the family* (pp. 79–92). New York, NY: John Wiley & Sons.
Mincy, R. B., Klempin, S., & Schmidt, H. (2011). Income support policies for low-income men and noncustodial fathers: Tax and transfer programs. *The ANNALS of the American Academy of Political and Social Science, 635*(1), 240–261.
Miniño, A. M. (2013). *Death in the United States, 2011.* (NCHS data brief No. 115). Hyattsville, MD: National Center for Health Statistics. http://www.cdc.gov/nchs/products/databriefs/db115.htm. Accessed May 2016.
Mullen, K., Watson, J., Swift, J., & Black, D. (2007). Young men, masculinity and alcohol. *Drugs: Education, Prevention, and Policy, 14*(2), 151–165.
Neighbors, H. W., Caldwell, C. H., Williams, D. R., Nesse, R., Taylor, R. J., Bullard, M. K., et al. (2007). Race, ethnicity, and the use of services for mental disorders: Results from the National Survey of American Life. *Archives of General Psychiatry, 64*(4), 485–494.
Neumann, A., Barker, E. D., Koot, H. M., & Maughan, B. (2010). The role of contextual risk, impulsivity, and parental knowledge in the development of adolescent antisocial behavior. *Journal of Abnormal Psychology, 119*(3), 534–545.
Oliffe, J. L., & Phillips, M. J. (2008). Men, depression and masculinities: A review and recommendations. *Journal of Men's Health, 5*(3), 194–202.
Ortiz, V., Richards, M., Kohl, K., & Zaddach, C. (2008). Trauma symptoms among urban African American young adolescents: A study of daily experience. *Journal of Child and Adolescent Trauma, 1*(2), 135–152.
Ravenell, J. E., Johnson, W. E., Jr., & Whitaker, E. E. (2006). African-American men's perceptions of health: A focus group study. *Journal of the National Medical Association, 98*(4), 544–550.
Rook, K. S., August, K. J., Stephens, M. A. P., & Franks, M. M. (2011). When does spousal social control provoke negative reactions in the context of chronic illness? The pivotal role of patients' expectations. *Journal of Social and Personal Relationships, 28*(6), 772–789.
Rowell, K. L., Green, B. L., Guidry, J., & Eddy, J. (2008). Factors associated with suicide among African American adult men: A systematic review of the literature. *Journal of Men's Health, 5*(4), 274–281.
Schwing, A. E., Wong, Y. J., & Fann, M. D. (2013). Development and validation of the African American men's gendered racism stress inventory. *Psychology of Men and Masculinity, 14*(1), 16–24.
Sobal, J. (2005). Men, meat, and marriage. Models of masculinity. *Food and Foodways, 13*(1-2), 135–158. doi:10.1080/07409710590915409.
Sobolewski, J. M., & King, V. (2005). The importance of the coparental relationship for nonresident fathers' ties to children. *Journal of Marriage and Family, 67*(5), 1196–1212.
Stier, H., & Tienda, M. (1993). Are men marginal to the family? Insights from Chicago's inner city. In J. Hood (Ed.), *Men, work and family* (pp. 23–44). Newbury Park, CA: Sage.
Sussman, L. K., Robins, L. N., & Earls, F. (1987). Treatment-seeking for depression by black and white Americans. *Social Science and Medicine, 24*(3), 187–196.
Tach, L., Mincy, R., & Edin, K. (2010). Parenting as a "package deal": Relationships, fertility, and nonresident father involvement among unmarried parents. *Demography, 47*(1), 181–204.

Thornton, T. N., Craft, C. A., Dahlberg, L. L., Lynch, B. S., & Baer, K. (2002). *Best practices of youth violence prevention: A sourcebook for community action*. Atlanta, GA: Division of Violence Prevention, National Center for Injury Prevention and Control, Centers for Disease Control and Prevention. http://www.cdc.gov/violenceprevention/pdf/introduction-a.pdf. Accessed May 2016.

Thrasher, J. F., Campbell, M. K., & Oates, V. (2004). Behavior-specific social support for healthy behaviors among African American church members: Applying optimal matching theory. *Health Education and Behavior, 31*(2), 193–205.

Umberson, D. (1992). Gender, marital status and the social control of health behavior. *Social Science and Medicine, 34*(8), 907–917.

Wagner, J. A., Abbott, G. L., Heapy, A., & Yong, L. (2009). Depressive symptoms and diabetes control in African Americans. *Journal of Immigrant and Minority Health, 11*(1), 66–70.

Warner, D. F., & Hayward, M. D. (2006). Early-life origins of the race gap in men's mortality. *Journal of Health and Social Behavior, 47*(3), 209–226.

Watkins, D. C., Green, B. L., Rivers, B. M., & Rowell, K. L. (2006). Depression and black men: Implications for future research. *Journal of Men's Health and Gender, 3*(3), 227–235.

Watkins, D. C., Hawkins, J., & Mitchell, J. A. (2015). The discipline's escalating whisper: Social work and black men's mental health. *Research on Social Work Practice, 25*(2), 240–250.

Wilson, D. K., Kliewer, W., & Sica, D. (2004). The relationship between exposure to violence and blood pressure mechanisms. *Current Hypertension Reports, 6*(4), 321–326.

Williams, D. R., Neighbors, H. W., & Jackson, J. S. (2003). Racial/ethnic discrimination and health: Findings from community studies. *American Journal of Public Health, 93*(2), 200–208.

Woodward, A. T., Taylor, R. J., & Chatters, L. M. (2011). Use of professional and informal support by black men with mental disorders. *Research on Social Work Practice, 21*(3), 328–336.

Xanthos, C., Treadwell, H. M., & Holden, K. B. (2010). Social determinants of health among African-American men. *Journal of Men's Health, 7*(1), 11–19.

# John Henry and the Paradox of Manhood, Fatherhood and Health for African American Fathers

**Derek M. Griffith, Emily K. Cornish, Sydika A. McKissic, and Donnatesa A.L. Dean**

The concept of parenthood has moved from stereotypical images of a wage-earning father and a stay-at-home mother to reflect a far more complex and diverse set of arrangements (Garfield, Clark-Kauffman, & Davis, 2006). While in decades past it was presumed that the father role meant having marital and residential status, particularly among African American men, these assumptions have proven untrue. However, regardless of this change, African American men still prioritize and value their roles and responsibilities as fathers (Caldwell et al., 2004). While African American men's relationships with their children, particularly their sons, may look very different from what is found in traditionally European American living and marital relationships, it is critical to recognize that these men see the role of father as not only a key part of their identities but also a critical component of their responsibilities as men. As we struggle to appreciate the complexity of how men view themselves and their responsibilities as fathers, it is crucial to also consider how these roles and responsibilities affect the health of fathers.

In this chapter, we discuss the relation between fatherhood and health by examining the roots of these concepts in notions of masculinity and manhood. We discuss a variety of theories of how men consider the interrelationship between their identities

D.M. Griffith (✉)
Center for Research on Men's Health and Center for Medicine, Health, and Society, Vanderbilt University, Nashville, TN, USA
e-mail: derek.griffith@vanderbilt.edu

E.K. Cornish
Center for Research on Men's Health, Vanderbilt University, Nashville, TN, USA

S.A. McKissic
Center for Research on Men's Health, Vanderbilt University, Nashville, TN, USA

D.A.L. Dean
Department of Public Health, Brown School of Social Work, Washington University in St. Louis, St. Louis, MO, USA

 
L. Burton et al. (eds.), *Boys and Men in African American Families*, National Symposium on Family Issues 7, DOI 10.1007/978-3-319-43847-4_13

and responsibilities as fathers and the ways that men are defined in society through cultural expectations to fulfill socially important roles. Not surprisingly, there are a number of parallels between these roles, identities, and priorities, and a familiar story—the fable of John Henry.

In the fable of the "steel driving man," John Henry, an African American railroad worker in the late 1800s, was rumored to be one of the strongest men who ever lived (Voice of America, n.d.). According to legend, John Henry's job was to hammer a steel drill into a mountainside to make holes for explosives that would blast away rock in order to construct a railroad tunnel. His prowess as a steel-driver was challenged in a race against a steam-powered hammer to prove that a man could beat a machine. While he won the race, his heart burst from the strain and he died with his hammer in his hand. Over time, the story has been told many different ways. In one iteration of the tale, John Henry is portrayed not just as one of the strongest men in the world, but as a husband and father. Using this version of the fable of John Henry, we illustrate how African American men's ideals of manhood and the desire to teach their sons key values may paradoxically adversely affect their health. In other words, we will use this children's story to answer a few key questions:

1. Why did he race the steam-powered drill to this morbid conclusion?
2. What lesson was he trying to teach his son by completing the Herculean task?
3. What does the legend say about where health fits within men's life priorities?

We ask you to use these questions as the lens through which you view the literature on men's beliefs about health; interdependence theory; racial and gender socialization; role strain and adaptation theory; and masculinity and manhood, before we return to explicitly consider these questions.

## The Goal is to Live a Long and Healthy Life, Right?

In Western societies, health is presumed to be universally valued and a priority in and of itself. Yet, for men, health is an instrumental value because it affords them the opportunity to fulfill socially-important roles and responsibilities (Griffith, Brinkley-Rubinstein, Thorpe, Bruce, & Metzl, 2015). The ways that men think about and internalize notions of masculinity, masculine social norms, and gendered stressors and strains are often implicated in explanations of men's unhealthy and risky behaviors (e.g., reckless driving, interpersonal violence, alcohol and drug abuse, risky sexual behavior, high-risk sports and leisure activities) (Bruce, Roscigno, & McCall, 1998; Courtenay, 2000, 2002; Griffith, Gunter, & Allen, 2011; Peterson, 2009; Robertson, 2007). Substance use and other risky behaviors are often tools that men use to cope with the stressors that the ideals, norms, and goals associated with masculinity create in their lives (Griffith, Gunter, & Watkins, 2012). Some of these behaviors are culturally sanctioned ways of distinguishing among males and between males and females, and may help explain men's willingness to engage in risky and unhealthy behaviors (Courtenay, 2000; Evans, Frank, Oliffe,

& Gregory, 2011). Men will often prefer to risk their physical health and well-being rather than be associated with traits they or others may perceive as feminine (Bruce et al., 1998; Evans et al., 2011; Messerschmidt, 2013). Health promoting behaviors often are associated with femininity, while health-harming behaviors are linked with masculinity, and men's adherence to masculine ideals are thought to help explain the disparity between men's and women's health outcomes (Connell, 1995; Courtenay, 2000; Courtenay & Keeling, 2000; Robertson, 2007; Sabo, 2005).

While some men may define health based on diagnoses of illnesses or biological and physiological processes, Robertson (2006) found that men's definitions of health may be influenced by their perceptions of what it means to be a man. In his qualitative work, Robertson (2006) found that men related their perceptions of health to their general lifestyle and well-being (e.g., drinking and eating in moderation), engagement in healthy behavior (e.g., regular physical activity, adequate sleep) and ability to fulfill socially important roles (e.g., provider, partner, father). Additionally, Ravenell, Johnson, and Whitaker (2006) found that some African American men define health broadly and in relation to other aspects of their lives that have little to do directly with their own individual health. African American men have conceptualized being "healthy" as being able to fulfill social roles, such as holding a job, providing for family, protecting and teaching their children, and belonging to a social network (Ravenell et al., 2006). Prioritizing success in fulfilling key social roles at the expense of one's health is consistent with various theories that link gender and health (Bird & Rieker, 2008; Griffith et al., 2012; Griffith, Ellis, & Allen, 2013; James, Hartnett, & Kalsbeek, 1983; Robertson, 2006, 2007).

## Notions of Fatherhood

Fatherhood is strongly related to three health related factors: men's perceptions of their own health, the desire to improve their health and their efforts to help their children and other family members be optimally healthy (Hosegood, Richter, & Clarke, 2015). While they are often treated as simply a function of men's individual attitudes, beliefs and choices, men's health practices also are products of their social contexts and networks (Creighton & Oliffe, 2010). Fatherhood can be practiced across households and bloodlines. In fact, it's become necessary to expand the definition of modern day fatherhood to include four types of settings within which men are fathers: (1) men living with their dependent, (2) men living apart from their dependent because of a relationship change with the child's mother, (3) men whose children have grown and are independent adults, and (4) men who have become fathers via remarriage (Eggebeen & Knoester, 2001). Interdependence theory (Kelley & Thibaut, 1978; Rusbult & Van Lange, 2003) expands on these fatherhood definitions and highlights how social relationships, such as that of a father and son, can affect behaviors and outcomes. The essence of the theory is that decisions about health behaviors are shaped by the potential implications of their choices for interpersonal relationships (Lewis et al., 2006). Sometimes the implications of the behaviors on relationships can supplant personal preferences as a primary source of motivation (Lewis et al., 2006). While we have found this theory useful for explaining how men understand the critical role that wives play in their eating behaviors (Allen, Griffith, & Gaines, 2013), we consider that this theory may also explain how African American men's roles as fathers may motivate them to make healthier choices that positively influence their health and their son's behaviors and health.

One's attitudes and behaviors, particularly children's, are learned from and modeled on behaviors of people who are important and influential to them, like fathers (Bandura, 2004; Guzzo, 2011). Because fathers recognize that their words and actions influence their sons, men have recognized that in order to become better fathers, they would need to change previous and current patterns of behavior. Men's commitment to their children is a function of the salience of the father role to a man's sense of self, the satisfaction that father role enactment provides, and the perceived assessment of his performance in the role by other influential persons in his life (Fox & Bruce, 2001).

One of the key roles of a father is teaching boys what it means to be a man. While there are separate literatures on racial socialization—the process by which people's sense of racial identity is shaped by families and communities through oppressive and affirming experiences throughout the lifecourse (Stevenson, 1997) and male gender socialization—the process by which men learn the gender and culturally-ascribed behaviors that characterize masculinity in a particular society (Courtenay, 2000; Nicholas, 2000; Pleck, 1981) it is critical to recognize that African American men's health, goals as fathers and definitions of fatherhood are shaped both. Among African American families, cultural socialization is a salient aspect of child rearing, and African American fathers are often tasked with helping to teach their sons cultural values associated with hegemonic masculinity, black manhood, and racial and ethnic identity (Griffith, 2015; Hughes et al., 2006; Jagers & Mock, 1995; Sellers, Smith, Shelton, Rowley, & Chavous, 1998; Stevenson, 1997). It is not only how African American males' interaction with people of their own race, gender, or identity group influences how they see themselves and their group membership, but it is also how these men are treated when interacting with other groups, and how that difference is interpreted.

It is critical to recognize that the experiences of African American men, and the lessons that they are teaching their sons, are at the nexus of them being African American, middle-aged and male (Griffith et al., 2013). Thus, the idea of intersectionality—or the recognition that socially-defined and socially meaningful characteristics are inextricably intertwined and cannot be fully appreciated as factors that operate independently or additively (Cole, 2009; Warner & Brown, 2011)—is essential not only to understanding men's daily lives and health but also the lessons and values men are trying to instill in their sons (Griffith, 2012). Among any given family, society, or culture, there is no singular set of developmental endpoints or tasks that define competent, supportive fathering for all men (Cabrera, Tamis-LeMonda, Bradley, Hofferth, & Lamb, 2000). Fathers play many roles within the family, and each of these roles is associated with a set of ideas, competencies, and action patterns (Cabrera et al., 2000).

## Provider Role Strain in Father's Lives

How men define themselves as men and the gendered roles they play in their families and communities can be a source of stress. *Role strain* is a theoretical framework that describes how social norms and cultural expectations regarding gender-typed behavior and fulfillment of male gender role expectations can function as stressors for men and men's personal and social coping strategies (Bowman, 1989, 2006; Levant & Pollack, 2003). Theories of role strain suggest that there may be systematic, social causes of stress and psychological and physiological aspects of strain that vary by race, socially-meaningful characteristics, and social determinants of health (Griffith et al., 2013; Griffith, Gunter, et al., 2011).

African American men often face significant challenges in seeking to fulfill the role of economic provider for their families. At every level of education, African American men earn less than white men (Isaacs, Sawhill, & Haskins, 2007). Middle-class African Americans have markedly lower levels of wealth than middle-class whites and are less likely to be able to translate similar levels of income into desirable housing and neighborhood conditions (Williams, 2003). Given the challenges African American men face in achieving economic success, those who define their worth as men by this success or conflate it with manhood may face considerable stress (Griffith, 2015; Neal, 2005). Because manhood, historically, has been conflated with economic success in most industrialized nations, it is critical to recognize how central economic success is to gendered stressors in men's lives (Connell, 1995; Summers, 2004).

When men start a family, fatherhood becomes central to their identity. Men's identity also is strongly influenced by the constraints of paid work, the ages of their children, and their relationships with women partners (Williams, Hewison, Stewart, Liles, & Wildman, 2012). According to Cabrera et al. (2000), there are three dimensions of father involvement: accessibility (presence and availability), engagement (direct contact/caregiving), and responsibility (participation in tasks such as arranging childcare, talking with their children's teachers, etc.). These dimensions hold true among both residential and non-residential fathers, for whom financial child support is an important form of paternal responsibility (Cabrera et al., 2000) and often the most visible and stress inducing role they play. While there is an apparent difference in relationship dynamics between resident and non-resident African American fathers and their sons, nonresident fathers are very capable of being knowledgeable about their sons' activities and are willing to provide oversight and fulfill the roles of father and provider, even though they do not live in the same household (Caldwell, Rafferty, Reischl, De Loney, & Brooks, 2010). Particularly during middle-age, African American men's perceived success in fulfilling the roles of father, provider, employee, and community member are fundamental aspects of their identities and a major focus of this phase of life (Bowman, 1989; Hammond & Mattis, 2005). Despite the cultural shifts that have allowed for more flexibility in defining some men by their fulfillment of certain roles and responsibilities, the family provider role continues to be a salient aspect of African American men's identity (Bowman, 1989; Griffith, Metzl, & Gunter, 2011). The ability to fulfill this role also is a key way that men feel that they are defined by others, particularly women in their lives (Ellis, Griffith, Allen, Thorpe, & Bruce, 2015; Griffith et al., 2013).

## Manhood and Gender Roles

Manhood is a relational construct that highlights how age shapes the meaning of masculinity, and the ways men prioritize performing or demonstrating that they are indeed men (not boys, not women) (Griffith, 2015). Manhood implicitly offers a set of characteristics and virtues that men use to demonstrate that they subscribe to and embody key racialized and class-bound values and goals (Griffith, 2012; Hammond & Mattis, 2005; Kimmel, 2006; Summers, 2004). Consequently, one of the most enduring qualities characterizing manhood is not its contents—stereotypical male qualities, behaviors, preferences, or tendencies—but the constant anxiety of its precariousness (Vandello & Bosson, 2013).

While the specific ideals of manhood change over time, the need to prove manhood remains constant (Kimmel, Hearn, & Connell, 2005). The way in which African American men define manhood has been dependent on patriarchal and heterosexist notions of masculinity (Bowleg et al., 2011; Cook, 2013; Hooks, 1992; Mutua, 2006; Neal, 2005), yet these men pay a price for conforming to gender norms (Broom & Tovey, 2009; Brooms, 2015). While it is critical to help men develop more progressive notions of manhood (Mutua, 2006), it is also important to recognize the psychological and social consequences of not being able to marshal the material resources necessary to express normative or hegemonic masculinities (Connell, 1995; Connell & Messerschmidt, 2005; Griffith, 2015).

A man need not engage in all masculine behaviors to be considered a man, but the more masculine behaviors he enacts, the greater the likelihood he will be respected as a man (de Visser & McDonnell, 2013; de Visser, Smith, & McDonnell, 2009; Gough, 2013). Whitehead argues in the Big Man Little Man Complex that African American men are trying to achieve a level of *respectability* through economic success, educational attainment, and social class status (Whitehead, 1997). The opportunities to achieve respectability through economic, social, and educational means, however, are often blocked by structural factors that vary by race and gender (Griffith, Metzl, et al., 2011; Treadwell & Ro, 2003; Wingfield, 2012; Xanthos, Treadwell, & Holden, 2010). African American men's efforts to overcome obstacles to achieving respectability increase their stress levels and psychological strain. These struggles may trigger a behavioral response such as stress-induced eating, decreased physical activity, or increased alcohol consumption that reduces their physiological and psychological experience of stress but increases their risk of chronic disease, morbidity and mortality (Jackson & Knight, 2006; Mezuk et al., 2013). Given the challenges minority men face in achieving success along the respectability dimension, those who define their worth as men by their economic success, or conflate economic success with manhood, may face considerable stress (Neal, 2005; Wingfield, 2012). So while socioeconomic status is inversely related to stress for African American women, efforts by African American men to achieve a higher level of respectability are likely to induce stress (Watkins, Walker, & Griffith, 2010; Williams, 2003; Wingfield, 2012).

Simultaneous with an effort to achieve respectability, African American men use health behaviors to also advance their reputation and demonstrate prowess along the social and cultural dimensions of traditional masculinity—virility, sexual prowess, risk taking, physical strength, hardiness—which may also increase their risk of morbidity and mortality (Whitehead, 1997). What is critical to recognize in this conceptualization of masculinity is that African American men are expected to balance these gendered expectations and achieve success in both respectable and reputational dimensions, which results in different risks for African American men's health (Whitehead, 1997).

## How Does the Literature Help Us Understand John Henry's Story?

Let's begin to reconsider this literature through the lens of John Henry's story. As you may recall, our framing questions from John Henry's story were:

1. Why did he race the steam-powered drill to this morbid conclusion?
2. What lesson was he trying to teach his son, by completing the Herculean task?
3. What does the legend say about where health fits in men's life priorities?

In sum, what we learned from this review is that while some may question the logic and reasoning of John Henry's decision to compete against the steam-powered drill in a race that he won but that also saw his demise, John Henry's actions were consistent with much of the literature on men's health, masculinity, and manhood. John Henry's notions of manhood and health seemed to embody a relational definition of each construct. For example, the notion of treating his body as a tool to achieve professional success was certainly consistent with the story. John Henry clearly defined health by what his body could do, not by clinical or medical definitions of health. While he valued health and was considered one of the strongest men to have ever lived, he prioritized success in his chosen profession or career more than he did his own health. His objective view of the task and his subjective assessment of it being important for him to prove he could complete the task alone highlights how role strain can both be positive and negative.

We might conjecture that John Henry was further motivated to demonstrate to his son that manhood was not just about physical strength but that it also included a strength of character and desire to demonstrate an internal fortitude and drive, more important than any physical pain or signs of ill health that he might have experienced. The concept of John Henryism is the idea that someone would seek to overcome a chronic stressor or barrier in life by simply working harder and longer, and perhaps spending less time and energy thinking through alternative strategies or resources that might be marshalled to help complete the task (James, 1994). Consistent with John Henryism and notions of hegemonic masculinity, John Henry chose to complete this task alone and kept working even after the steam engine had broken down. Self-reliance is certainly a pillar of how men are taught to view key gendered ideals and to demonstrate an ability to be successful with as little help as possible. It was important to *demonstrate* to his son, not just tell him with words, what it means to be a man and how a man should face adversity and life challenges: alone and through hard work.

While John Henry demonstrated positive characteristics of manhood and wanted to teach his son a positive lesson about work ethic and overcoming adversity, he also taught him a very clear lesson about how health fits into that picture. It is important to note the obvious paradox: in trying to demonstrate and teach positive values, his health suffered and he died. Yet, many remember John Henry's story not for its morbid conclusion but for his triumphant victory. While we might laud the positive values he sought to teach his son through his actions, we also have to consider the cost he paid for this success. This paradox raises interesting rhetorical questions: Would we be telling this story over a century later if John Henry enlisted the support of a co-worker or friend? Had he not died in the end, would we still be telling his story? Do we see his story as a triumphant tale of man vs machine or a cautionary tale about health? What do we want young boys to take away from this story? If John Henry lived today, and died providing for his family, would we remember him fondly or view him negatively for not prioritizing his health and therefore not being there to guide his son as he grew up? Regardless of how you answer these questions, the key question to ask yourself is how are my values shaping my responses?

## Conclusion

As we think about the interrelationships between African American men's health and the lessons African American fathers want to teach their sons, it is critical to recognize the contradictions inherent in promoting manhood and health. Though there are efforts to help men diversify what manhood means and there are cultural changes occurring and pushing men to rid themselves of patriarchal and hegemonic notions of masculinity, we must help men honor the foundational role they play in the lives of their sons. This must be done regardless of their residence and relationship with the son's mother, along with being more transparent about how they will balance notions of manhood and health. Unfortunately, many men do not realize that the choice to prioritize health and manhood is not a zero-sum game; it is possible to have both but it may mean rethinking a broad array of other life activities, priorities, and choices. The choice will not be an easy one, given that many structural forces block African American men's opportunities to demonstrate positive aspects of manhood, and many social and environmental factors limit opportunities to be healthy. However, that is why pulling on social and cultural resources becomes a critical strategy for being healthier and being a good father.

## References


Allen, J. O., Griffith, D. M., & Gaines, H. C. (2013). "She looks out for the meals, period": African American men's perceptions of how their wives influence their eating behavior and dietary health. *Health Psychology, 32*(4), 447–455. doi:10.1037/a0028361.

Bandura, A. (2004). Health promotion by social cognitive means. *Health Education and Behavior, 31*(2), 143–164.

Bird, C. E., & Rieker, P. P. (2008). *Gender and health: The effects of constrained choices and social policies*. New York, NY: Cambridge University Press.

Bowleg, L., Teti, M., Massie, J. S., Patel, A., Malebranche, D. J., & Tschann, J. M. (2011). 'What does it take to be a man? What is a real man?': Ideologies of masculinity and HIV sexual risk among black heterosexual men. *Culture, Health and Sexuality, 13*(5), 545–559. doi:10.1080/13691058.2011.556201.

Bowman, P. J. (1989). Research perspectives on black men: Role strain and adaptation across the adult life cycle. In R. L. Jones (Ed.), *Black adult development and aging* (pp. 117–150). Berkeley, CA: Cobb & Henry Publishers.

Bowman, P. J. (2006). Role strain and adaptation issues in the strength-based model: Diversity, multilevel, and life-span considerations. *The Counseling Psychologist, 34*(1), 118–133.

Broom, A., & Tovey, P. (2009). Introduction: Men's health in context. In A. Broom & P. Tovey (Eds.), *Men's health: Body, identity and social context* (pp. 1–8). Chichester: Wiley-Blackwell.

Brooms, D. R. (2015). Looking for Leroy: Illegible black masculinities. *Ethnic and Racial Studies, 38*(3), 471–473.

Bruce, M. A., Roscigno, V. J., & McCall, P. L. (1998). Structure, context, and agency in the reproduction of black-on-black violence. *Theoretical Criminology, 2*(1), 29–55.

Cabrera, N. J., Tamis-LeMonda, C. S., Bradley, R. H., Hofferth, S., & Lamb, M. E. (2000). Fatherhood in the twenty-first century. *Child Development, 71*(1), 127–136.

Caldwell, C. H., Rafferty, J., Reischl, T. M., De Loney, E. H., & Brooks, C. L. (2010). Enhancing parenting skills among nonresident African American fathers as a strategy for preventing youth risky behaviors. *American Journal of Community Psychology, 45*(1-2), 17–35.

Caldwell, C. H., Wright, J. C., Zimmerman, M. A., Walsemann, K. M., Williams, D., & Isichei, P. A. (2004). Enhancing adolescent health behaviors through strengthening non-resident father-son relationships: A model for intervention with African-American families. *Health Education Research, 19*(6), 644–656.

Cole, E. R. (2009). Intersectionality and research in psychology. *American Psychologist, 64*(3), 170–180. doi:10.1037/a0014564.

Connell, R. W. (1995). *Masculinities*. Berkeley, CA: University of California Press.

Connell, R. W., & Messerschmidt, J. W. (2005). Hegemonic masculinity: Rethinking the concept. *Gender and Society, 19*(6), 829–859.

Cook, S. H. (2013). *Psychological distress, sexual risk behavior, and attachment insecurity among young adult black men who have sex with men (YBMSM)*. (Doctoral dissertation). Retrieved from http://gradworks.umi.com/36/00/3600868.html.

Courtenay, W. H. (2000). Constructions of masculinity and their influence on men's well-being: A theory of gender and health. *Social Science and Medicine, 50*(10), 1385–1401.

Courtenay, W. H. (2002). A global perspective on the field of men's health: An editorial. *International Journal of Mens Health, 1*(1), 1–13.

Courtenay, W. H., & Keeling, R. P. (2000). Men, gender, and health: Toward an interdisciplinary approach. *Journal of American College Health, 48*(6), 243–246.

Creighton, G., & Oliffe, J. L. (2010). Theorising masculinities and men's health: A brief history with a view to practice. *Health Sociology Review, 19*(4), 409–418.

de Visser, R. O., & McDonnell, E. J. (2013). "Man points": Masculine capital and young men's health. *Health Psychology, 32*(1), 5–14.

de Visser, R. O., Smith, J. A., & McDonnell, E. J. (2009). 'That's not masculine': Masculine capital and health-related behaviour. *Journal of Health Psychology, 14*(7), 1047–1058. doi:10.1177/1359105309342299.

Eggebeen, D. J., & Knoester, C. (2001). Does fatherhood matter for men? *Journal of Marriage and Family, 63*(2), 381–393.

Ellis, K. R., Griffith, D. M., Allen, J. O., Thorpe, R. J., Jr., & Bruce, M. A. (2015). "If you do nothing about stress, the next thing you know, you're shattered": Perspectives on African American men's stress, coping and health from African American men and key women in their lives. *Social Science and Medicine, 139*, 107–114. doi:10.1016/j.socscimed.2015.06.036.

Evans, J., Frank, B., Oliffe, J. L., & Gregory, D. (2011). Health, illness, men and masculinities (HIMM): A theoretical framework for understanding men and their health. *Journal of Men's Health, 8*(1), 7–15.

Fox, G. L., & Bruce, C. (2001). Conditional fatherhood: Identity theory and parental investment theory as alternative sources of explanation of fathering. *Journal of Marriage and Family, 63*(2), 394–403.

Garfield, C. F., Clark-Kauffman, E., & Davis, M. M. (2006). Fatherhood as a component of men's health. *Journal of the American Medical Association, 296*(19), 2365–2368.

Gough, B. (2013). The psychology of men's health: Maximizing masculine capital. *Health Psychology, 32*(1), 1–4. doi:10.1037/a0030424.

Griffith, D. M. (2012). An intersectional approach to men's health. *Journal of Men's Health, 9*(2), 106–112. doi:10.1016/j.jomh.2012.03.003.

Griffith, D. M. (2015). I AM a man: Manhood, minority men's health and health equity. *Ethnicity and Disease, 25*(3), 287–293.

Griffith, D. M., Brinkley-Rubinstein, L., Thorpe, R. J., Jr., Bruce, M. A., & Metzl, J. M. (2015). The interdependence of African American men's definitions of manhood and health. *Family and Community Health, 38*(4), 284–296.

Griffith, D. M., Ellis, K. R., & Allen, J. O. (2013). Intersectional approach to stress and coping among African American men: Men's and women's perspectives. *American Journal of Men's Health, 7*(4S), 16–27.

Griffith, D. M., Gunter, K., & Allen, J. O. (2011). Male gender role strain as a barrier to African American men's physical activity. *Health Education and Behavior, 38*(5), 482–491. doi:10.1177/1090198110383660.

Griffith, D. M., Gunter, K., & Watkins, D. C. (2012). Measuring masculinity in research on men of color: Findings and future directions. *American Journal of Public Health, 102*(Suppl 2), S187–S194. doi:10.2105/AJPH.2012.300715.

Griffith, D. M., Metzl, J. M., & Gunter, K. (2011). Considering intersections of race and gender in interventions that address U.S. men's health disparities. *Public Health, 125*(7), 417–423. doi:10.1016/j.puhe.2011.04.014.

Guzzo, K. B. (2011). New father's experiences with their own fathers and attitudes toward fathering. *Fathering, 9*(3), 268–290. doi:10.3149/fth.0903.268.

Hammond, W. P., & Mattis, J. S. (2005). Being a man about it: Manhood meaning among African American men. *Psychology of Men and Masculinity, 6*(2), 114–126. doi:10.1037/1524-9220.6.2.114.

Hooks, B. (1992). Representations of whiteness in the black imagination. In *Black looks: Race and representation* (pp. 165–178). Boston, MA: South End Press.

Hosegood, V., Richter, L., & Clarke, L. (2015). " …I should maintain a healthy life now and not just live as I please…": Men's health and fatherhood in rural South Africa. *American Journal of Mens Health*. doi:10.1177/1557988315586440.

Hughes, D., Rodriguez, J., Smith, E. P., Johnson, D. J., Stevenson, H. C., & Spicer, P. (2006). Parents' ethnic-racial socialization practices: A review of research and directions for future study. *Developmental Psychology, 42*(5), 747–770.

Isaacs, J., Sawhill, I., & Haskins, R. (2007). *Getting ahead or losing ground: Economic mobility in America*. Washington, DC: Brookings Institution.

Jackson, J. S., & Knight, K. M. (2006). Race and self-regulatory health behaviors: The role of the stress response and the HPA axis. In K. W. Schaie & L. L. Carstensten (Eds.), *Social structure, aging and self-regulation in the elderly* (pp. 189–240). New York, NY: Springer.

Jagers, R. J., & Mock, L. O. (1995). The communalism scale and collectivistic-individualistic tendencies: Some preliminary findings. *Journal of Black Psychology, 21*(2), 153–167.
James, S. A. (1994). John Henryism and the health of African-Americans. *Culture, Medicine, and Psychiatry, 18*(2), 163–182.
James, S. A., Hartnett, S. A., & Kalsbeek, W. D. (1983). John Henryism and blood pressure differences among black men. *Journal of Behavioral Medicine, 6*(3), 259–278.
Kelley, H. H., & Thibaut, J. W. (1978). *Interpersonal relations: A theory of interdependence*. New York, NY: John Wiley & Sons.
Kimmel, M. S. (2006). *Manhood in America: A cultural history*. New York, NY: Oxford University Press.
Kimmel, M. S., Hearn, J., & Connell, R. W. (2005). *Handbook of studies on men and masculinities*. Thousand Oaks, CA: Sage.
Levant, R. F., & Pollack, W. S. (Eds.). (2003). *A new psychology of men*. New York, NY: Basic Books.
Lewis, M. A., McBride, C. M., Pollak, K. I., Puleo, E., Butterfield, R. M., & Emmons, K. M. (2006). Understanding health behavior change among couples: An interdependence and communal coping approach. *Social Science and Medicine, 62*(6), 1369–1380.
Messerschmidt, J. W. (2013). *Crime as structured action: Doing masculinities, race, class, sexuality, and crime* (2nd ed.). Lanham, MD: Rowman & Littlefield.
Mezuk, B., Abdou, C. M., Hudson, D., Kershaw, K. N., Rafferty, J. A., Lee, H., et al. (2013). "White box" Epidemiology and the social neuroscience of health behaviors: The environmental affordances model. *Society and Mental Health, 3*(2), 79–95. doi:10.1177/2156869313480892.
Mutua, A. D. (Ed.). (2006). *Progressive black masculinities*. New York, NY: Routledge.
Neal, M. A. (2005). *New black man* (10th anniversary edition). New York, NY: Routledge.
Nicholas, D. R. (2000). Men, masculinity, and cancer: Risk-factor behaviors, early detection, and psychosocial adaptation. *Journal of American College Health, 49*(1), 27–33.
Peterson, A. (2009). Future research agenda in men's health. In A. Broom & P. Tovey (Eds.), *Men's health: Body, identity and social context* (pp. 202–213). West Sussex: Wiley-Blackwell.
Pleck, J. H. (1981). *The myth of masculinity*. Cambridge, MA: MIT Press.
Ravenell, J. E., Johnson, W. E., & Whitaker, E. E. (2006). African American men's perceptions of health: A focus group study. *Journal of the National Medical Association, 98*(4), 544–550.
Robertson, S. (2006). 'I've been like a coiled spring this last week': Embodied masculinity and health. *Sociology of Health and Illness, 28*(4), 433–456.
Robertson, S. (2007). *Understanding men and health: Masculinities, identity, and well-being*. Maidenhead: Open University Press.
Rusbult, C. E., & Van Lange, P. A. (2003). Interdependence, interaction, and relationships. *Annual Review of Psychology, 54*(1), 351–375.
Sabo, D. (2005). The study of masculinities and men's health: An overview. In M. Kimmel, J. Hearn, & R. W. Connell (Eds.), *Handbook of studies on men and masculinities* (pp. 326–352). Thousand Oaks, CA: Sage.
Sellers, R., Smith, M. A., Shelton, J. N., Rowley, S. A. J., & Chavous, T. M. (1998). Multidimensional model of racial identity: A reconceptualization of African American racial identity. *Personality and Social Psychology Review, 2*(1), 18–39.
Stevenson, H. C. (1997). Managing anger: Protective, proactive or adaptive racial socialization identity profiles and African-American manhood development. In R. J. Watts & R. J. Jagers (Eds.), *Manhood development in urban African-American communities* (pp. 35–61). Binghamton, NY: Hawthorne Press.
Summers, M. A. (2004). *Manliness and its discontents: The black middle class and the transformation of masculinity, 1900–1930*. Chapel Hill, NC: University of North Carolina Press.
Treadwell, H. M., & Ro, M. (2003). Poverty, race, and the invisible men. *American Journal of Public Health, 93*(5), 705–707.
Vandello, J. A., & Bosson, J. K. (2013). Hard won and easily lost: A review and synthesis of theory and research on precarious manhood. *Psychology of Men and Masculinity, 14*(2), 101–113. doi:10.1037/a0029826.

Voice of America. (n.d.). *Children's Story: 'John Henry'*. American Stories. http://m.learningenglish.voanews.com/a/childrens-story-john-henry-102197079/115888.html. Accessed November 2015.

Warner, D. F., & Brown, T. H. (2011). Understanding how race/ethnicity and gender define age-trajectories of disability: An intersectionality approach. *Social Science and Medicine, 72*(8), 1236–1248. doi:10.1016/j.socscimed.2011.02.034.

Watkins, D. C., Walker, R. L., & Griffith, D. M. (2010). A meta-study of black male mental health and well-being. *Journal of Black Psychology, 36*(3), 303–330.

Whitehead, T. L. (1997). Urban low-income African American men, HIV/AIDS, and gender identity. *Medical Anthropology Quarterly, 11*(4), 411–447.

Williams, D. R. (2003). The health of men: Structured inequalities and opportunities. *American Journal of Public Health, 93*(5), 724–731.

Williams, R., Hewison, A., Stewart, M., Liles, C., & Wildman, S. (2012). 'We are doing our best': African and African-Caribbean fatherhood, health and preventive primary care services, in England. *Health and Social Care in the Community, 20*(2), 216–223. doi:10.1111/j.1365-2524.2011.01037.x.

Wingfield, A. H. (2012). *No more invisible man: Race and gender in men's work*. Philadelphia, PA: Temple University Press.

Xanthos, C., Treadwell, H. M., & Holden, K. B. (2010). Social determinants of health among African American men. *Journal of Mens Health, 7*(1), 11–19.

# They Can't Breathe: Why Neighborhoods Matter for the Health of African American Men and Boys

**Wizdom A. Powell, Tamara Taggart, Jennifer Richmond, Leslie B. Adams, and Andre Brown**

Recent high-profile murders of African-American males (e.g., Michael Brown, Oscar Grant, Eric Garner, Tamir Rice, and Freddie Gray) have instigated unprecedented national interest in the lives and well-being of African American men and boys. The culmination of which is exemplified by recent public discourse about the 1.5 million missing African American men in America (Wolfers, Leonhardt, & Quealy, 2015a, 2015b). Indeed evidence affirms that despite narrowing sex differences in life-expectancy, African American men live shorter lives than individuals from most other racial and ethnic groups (Kochanek, Murphy, Xu, & Arias, 2014). Yet, the term missing implies that African American men are hiding out, featured on a newly erected milk carton campaign, or that a widespread search party has been formed to locate them. African American men are not simply missing. Rather, they are being stolen from families and communities largely by persistent threats to their mortality and other chronic, yet preventable, health conditions. Factors leading to African American men's more abridged life expectancy and premature morbidity from preventable conditions are myriad and complex. Many of the causes are linked to behavioral health outcomes (e.g., substance abuse and addiction). Males have higher substance abuse-related mortality than women on average, with rates generally the highest among African American males (Center for Behavioral Health Statistics and Quality, 2011). A significant portion of the African American male health disadvantage is also attributable to conditions with high substance abuse comorbidity (e.g., heart disease and homicide) (Kochanek, Anderson, & Arias, 2015). However, African American men are not uniquely hard-wired to take behavioral health risks, nor is there compelling evidence to suggest that they are

W.A. Powell (✉) • T. Taggart • A. Brown• L.B. Adams • J. Richmond
University of North Carolina, Gillings School of Global Public Health,
Chapel Hill, NC, USA
e-mail: wizdomp@email.unc.edu



L. Burton et al. (eds.), *Boys and Men in African American Families*, National Symposium on Family Issues 7, DOI 10.1007/978-3-319-43847-4_14

genetically predisposed to poorer health outcomes. A more compelling explanation is that disparate health outcomes are potentiated by social ecologic exposures. Such exposures can constrain health behavior choices that appear on the surface to be purely volitional or the products of rationality. In other words, the health of African American men and boys is socially determined. Thus, as we consider familial influences on the health and well-being of African American men and boys, it is important to recognize the broader socioenvironmental contexts in which they are embedded.

Neighborhoods are well-cited socioenvironmental contexts for exploring sources of disparate health vulnerability (Clarke et al., 2014; Gee & Payne-Sturges, 2004; Sampson, 2003; Subramanian, Chen, Rehkopf, Waterman, & Krieger, 2005). Neighborhood exposures have been linked to a variety of health outcomes including violence and substance abuse (Brady, 2006; Chuang, Ennett, Bauman, & Foshee, 2005; Lambert, Brown, Phillips, & Ialongo, 2004; Milam, Furr-Holden, & Leaf, 2010; Widome, Sieving, Harpin, & Hearst, 2008). Most of the extant evidence suggests that less optimal neighborhood exposures increase risks for poor health. This chapter briefly synthesizes this now vast body of literature and builds on two important points raised by Caldwell et al. (Chap. 12):

- "Research on neighborhood violence is a promising area for better understanding structural conditions and African American men's health over the life-course." (p. 206)
- "The protective effect of family relationships against neighborhood violence has been most often examined among youth with an eye towards the prevention of violence perpetration. However, there is a need for more research on risk and protective factors, neighborhood violence, family social relations, and the health and mental health of African American adult males." (p. 206)

African American men's vulnerability to neighborhood influences on health is life-course variant and perhaps more pronounced at sensitive developmental stages. Some of the most strikingly disparate health vulnerabilities among African American men present during the transition to adulthood. This more volitional developmental stage is often referred to as emerging adulthood (Arnett, 2014) and is marked by an increased assumption of individual responsibility and more deliberate experimentation with risk-taking behaviors. For example, studies suggest that sexual risk behavior and the use of most substances and alcohol peak during emerging adulthood (Fergus, Zimmerman, & Caldwell, 2007; Johnston, O'Malley, & Bachman, 2003; Schulenberg et al., 2001). Recent national estimates indicate that 18–25 year olds have the highest prevalence of substance dependence and current illicit drug use when compared to both adolescents and older adults (Office of Applied Studies, 2009). Role transitions, relationship instability, declination in social controls, and increased expectations for residential independence that characterize emerging adulthood may also serve as catalysts for engaging in risky behaviors (Arnett, 2000; Dworkin, 2005). Although African American adolescents' rates of substance and alcohol use are typically lower than rates for white adolescents (Bolland et al., 2007), rates begin to increase more steeply during emerging adulthood for African Americans than whites (Office of Applied Studies, 2009). Some researchers suggest that African American emerging adults face unique identity consolidation challenges, explaining the so-called "crossover effects" in substance abuse (Arnett, 2008). More autonomous navigation of social contexts like neighborhoods during emerging adulthood also increase opportunity for exposure to risk-promoting conditions permeating within them (e.g., violence and stress exposure) (Chuang et al., 2005; Dupere, Lacourse, Willms, Leventhal, & Tremblay, 2008). In light of this evidence, we focus on explicating potential pathways between neighborhood conditions and African American emerging adult men's substance abuse.

Our focus on substance abuse is warranted given its high comorbidity with unintentional injury, violence (e.g., homicide), and other chronic conditions linked to premature death among African American men. Understanding how neighborhood conditions increase substance abuse among African American emerging adult males is critical to reducing their risk for long-term addiction and violence engagement, and ensuring optimal familial participation. Also, while we know that neighborhood conditions can catalyze substance abuse, study results are mixed (Allison et al., 1999; Brody et al., 2001; Spencer, McDermott, Burton, & Kochman, 1997) and fail to fully describe the ways that some African American men thrive even in the face of risk-promoting exposures. Exploring psycho-biological mechanisms (i.e., masculine role norms, affect regulation strategies, and stress processes) and protective or resilience-based factors may clarify relationships between neighborhoods, risk-taking, and substance abuse. Largely absent from most investigations of neighborhood health effects are considerations of the strengths that exist even in more disadvantaged contexts. Integrating a consideration of neighborhood strengths might also lead to better understanding of how to cultivate more therapeutic social landscapes (Dunkley, 2009) for African American men and their families.

## Theoretical Frameworks

Our explication of neighborhood effects on African American male risk-taking and substance abuse builds primarily on Phenomenological Variant of Ecological Systems Theory (PVEST) (Spencer, Dupree, & Hartmann, 1997). PVEST frames substance use as a gender-specific coping response to ecologic stressors, strains, and conditions. This theory focuses on identity development and negotiation strategies, providing a useful framework for examining health risk behaviors and outcome as products of ecological exposures. Psycho-biological models of stress, coping, and substance use further suggest that this risk behavior results from complex interactions between neighborhood conditions, stress-affective processes, and biology (e.g., temperament, teratogenic perinatal environments, and androgenic hormones) (Compas, 2006; Dodge & Pettit, 2003; Irwin & Millstein, 1992; Jessor, 1987; Kotchick, Shaffer, Miller, & Forehand, 2001; Udry, 1988). Our conceptual model (see Fig. 1) explicates these hypothesized associations. In subsequent sections, we discuss the empirical evidence-base supporting our central arguments.

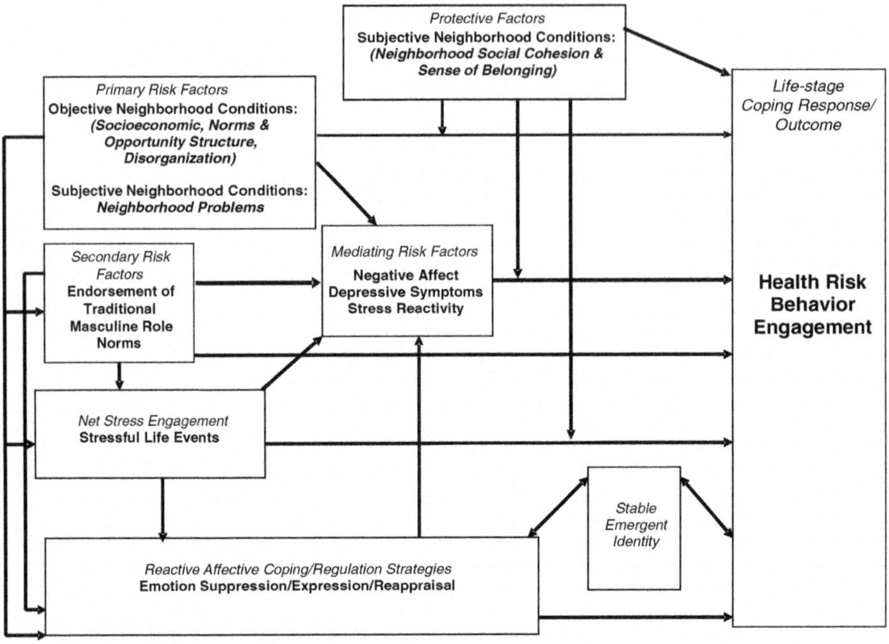


**Fig. 1** Conceptual model linking neighborhoods to health risk-taking among African American emerging adult males

## Neighborhood Effects: Risk-Taking and Substance Abuse

Poor objective neighborhood conditions have been linked to a variety of health risk behaviors among children and adolescents (Browning, Leventhal, & Brooks-Gunn, 2004; Chuang et al., 2005; Dupere et al., 2008; Ku, Sonenstein, & Pleck, 1993; Lambert et al., 2004), but less is known about their impact on risk-taking during emerging adulthood. One review of the literature found that neighborhood effects have most often been examined for youth initiation of sexual activity and childbearing (Leventhal & Brooks-Gunn, 2000). In a study of adolescents aged 12–14 years living in low and high SES neighborhoods, Chuang et al. (2005) found that low SES neighborhoods were independently associated with increased peer and adolescent alcohol use. Higher neighborhood unemployment was associated with increased risk of teenage pregnancy among a nationally representative sample of adolescent males (Ku et al., 1993; Pleck, Sonenstein, & Ku, 1994). Using data from Add Health, Cubbin and colleagues found that four objective dimensions of neighborhood context (socioeconomics, norms and opportunity structures, social disorganization, and racial/ethnic composition) were each independently linked with adolescent sexual initiation (Cubbin, Santelli, Brindis, & Braveman, 2005). Results from this investigation further suggest that the effects of poor neighborhood conditions may be felt more strongly among males than females, who exhibited higher sexual initiation when residing in neighborhoods with higher levels of poverty or more idle youth and lower initiation when residing in more affluent households. Even in light of this compelling evidence, much less is known about mechanisms that may exacerbate or mitigate the negative impacts of neighborhood exposures on African American emerging adult male health.

## Stress-Affective Processes as Mediators and Moderators of Neighborhood Effects

Stressful life events are important links between neighborhood contexts and health (Boardman, 2004; Elliott, 2000). Studies indicate that psychosocial stress negatively impacts health behavior and positive behavior change (House, Strecher, Metzner, & Robbins, 1986; Rod, Grønbæk, Schnohr, Prescott, & Kristensen, 2009; Umberson, Liu, & Reczek, 2008). For example, results from a recent longitudinal study suggest that acutely stressed men and women are less likely to stop smoking, engage in physical activity, or limit alcohol consumption (Rod et al., 2009). Cumulative life adversities are also associated with engagement in health damaging behaviors (Lloyd & Turner, 2008). Experimental study evidence affirms that stress induced under laboratory conditions negatively impacts health behavior by interrupting cognitive ability to process health promoting messages (Millar, 2005). A more recent investigation among young men who have sex with men found that stress experienced in multiple life domains was associated with increased HIV-risk related behaviors (Wong, Kipke, Weiss, & McDavitt, 2010). Daily stress in disadvantaged neighborhoods has been cited as a mechanism of substance abuse risk (Boardman, Finch, Ellison, Williams, & Jackson, 2001; Scheier, Botvin, & Miller, 2000; Stockdale et al., 2007). This finding likely exists because stress proliferation is more likely to occur in violent and otherwise disadvantaged neighborhood contexts. In fact, individuals residing in socioeconomically disadvantaged neighborhoods report more stressful life experiences (Aneshensel & Sucoff, 1996; Cockerham, 1990; Kessler & Neighbors, 1986), which are associated with more behavioral risk-taking (House et al., 1986; Rod et al., 2009; Umberson et al., 2008). Among African American men, evidence suggests that neighborhood violence disrupts social networks and is associated with self-reported post-traumatic stress symptoms (Smith, 2015). African American males also experience a disproportionate amount of race-related trauma and stress (e.g., racial profiling), which can be more pronounced in disadvantaged neighborhoods, but its contribution to substance use has only been minimally considered (Copeland-Linder, Lambert, Chen, & Ialongo, 2011; Gibbons et al., 2007; Gibbons et al., 2010; Rich & Grey, 2005).

A growing scientific consensus suggests that neighborhood conditions alter stress and androgenic hormones and these alterations explain some of the variation in substance use (Boyce, 2007). Cortisol and testosterone are key indicators of stress response shaped by neighborhood conditions (de Wit, Vicini, Childs,

Sayla, & Terner, 2007; Susman, 2006). Adolescents residing in socioeconomically disadvantaged neighborhoods have blunted cortisol and elevated testosterone concentrations. Cortisol is a biomarker of stressful experiences and negative emotions (Gadea, Gómez, González-Bono, Espert, & Salvador, 2005; van Eck, Berkhof, Nicolson, & Sulon, 1996; Van Honk et al., 2003). Elevated cortisol has been associated with more aggressive behavior (de Haan, Gunnar, Tout, Hart, & Stansbury, 1998) as well as greater behavioral inhibition (Kagan, Reznick, & Snidman, 1987; Schmidt et al., 1997). Affective processes are hypothesized to play a role in linking biomarkers of stress reactivity such as cortisol to health outcomes. For example, emotion suppression has been shown to increase sympathetic activation, a marker of stress reactivity (Gross, 1998a) and predicts exaggerated cortisol responses (Lam, Dickerson, Zoccola, & Zaldivar, 2009). Testosterone has also been identified as an important biomarker of risk-taking that may suppress circulating cortisol levels in men (Halpern, Udry, Campbell, & Suchindran, 1993b; Halpern, Udry, Campbell, Suchindran, & Mason, 1994; Halpern, Udry, & Suchindran, 1998). Adolescent boys with higher testosterone levels have more permissive sexual beliefs and are more sexually active than those with lower testosterone levels. Yet, the relationship between testosterone and risk-taking has not been consistent (Halpern et al., 1994). Halpern et al. (1993b) found that higher levels of testosterone predicted sexual ideation and first sexual intercourse transition among adolescent males. Although, these associations were not sustained over time. Greater testosterone levels have also been linked to more aggression by some (Olweus, Mattsson, Schalling, & Low, 1980, 1988) but not all researchers (Halpern, Udry, Campbell, & Suchindran, 1993a), indicating the need for additional investigations.

Largely absent from these investigations is a consideration of social context, which plays a calibrating role in stress reactivity (Boyce, 2007; Boyce & Ellis, 2005). At least one study has found higher levels of salivary cortisol among children residing in impoverished neighborhoods (Fernald & Grantham-McGregor, 1998). Another found higher testosterone levels among male veterans residing in environments with diminished resources (Mazur & Booth, 1998). While school norms were predictive of adolescents' drug use in a study by Allison et al. (1999), neighborhood factors were not. Higher rates of alcohol and cigarette use were found among adolescents residing in more socioeconomically advantaged neighborhoods (Ennett, Flewelling, Lindrooth, & Norton, 1997). Further, few investigations explore these associations among African American emerging adult males in the context of neighborhood exposures even though high testosterone levels among African American males have been hypothesized as strong hormone reactions to stress faced in disadvantaged neighborhoods (Halpern et al., 1994).

Assessing how African American males manage or regulate the negative affect produced by neighborhood and race-related stress exposure is equally important. Affect regulation generally refers to the processes individuals undertake to influence the onset, timing, and expression of emotions (Gross, 1998b). Emotion suppression, or the inhibition of overt emotionally expressive behavior (Gross & Levenson, 1993), is a commonly employed affect regulation strategy among men

(Levant, Hirsch, Celentano, & Cozz, 1992). While, suppressing emotion does not uniformly lead to problematic outcomes (Bonanno, Papa, Lalande, Westphal, & Coifman, 2004), habitual use of this affect regulation strategy is associated with excessive alcohol use among young adults (Magar, Phillips, & Hosie, 2008). In fact, cognition and emotion theorists have hypothesized that individuals who suppress emotions may experience a "post-suppression rebound effect," (Wenzlaff & Wegner, 2000) increasing the salience, memory, and cognitive accessibility of negative emotions (Macrae, Bodenhausen, Milne, & Ford, 1997; Wegner, Schneider, Carter, & White, 1987). Similar effects might also be plausible among males who are more likely to externalize affective experiences (Else-Quest, Hyde, Goldsmith, & Van Hulle, 2006). Indeed, some psychologists have recommended that violent behavior by males be regarded as a consequence of emotion suppression or affect dysregulation (Umberson, Williams, & Anderson, 2002). Although emotion suppression may not uniformly lead to negative outcomes (Bonanno et al., 2004), it can induce more negative affective states, minimize support seeking, and instigate risky behaviors among males. Hence, a critical unanswered question is *does habitual use of emotion suppression amplify stress and hormone impacts on African American male risk-taking, violence propensities, and substance abuse?* In other words, if we want to fully understand associations between poor neighborhood conditions and African American male substance use we need studies that capture the intermediary stress-affective processes driving them.

## Masculine Role Identity, Neighborhoods, Risk-Taking and Substance Abuse

Male risk-taking has been proposed as an attempt by men to recoup threatened aspects of masculine role identity, seen as precarious because it must be constantly earned and proven (Bosson, Vandello, Burnaford, Weaver, & Wasti, 2009). This proposition has been echoed by others who speculate that some risk behaviors (i.e., substance abuse) among young men may be related to difficulties establishing a stable identity (Arnett, 2005). Although there are exceptions (Levant, Wimer, Williams, Smalley, & Noronha, 2009), most research indicates that adolescent and emerging adult males who endorse more traditional masculine role norms are actually more likely to engage in risk behaviors (Mahalik, Lagan, & Morrison, 2006; Pleck et al., 1994; Pleck & O'Donnell, 2001). Men who endorse more traditional masculine role norms are less risk averse (Courtenay, 2000). Stereotypical gender roles are associated with less effective contraceptive use (Fox, 1977) and shape beliefs about sexual experiences (Whitley, 1988). Studies among emerging adult males have found an association between higher levels of masculinity and a greater number of sexual partners (O'Sullivan, Hoffman, Harrison, & Dolezal, 2006), unprotected vaginal sex (Santana, Raj, Decker, La Marche, & Silverman, 2006), and alcohol consumption (de Visser & Smith, 2007).

Stressful life events, particularly those that are race-related, uniquely threaten core aspects of the developing masculine social self by lowering sense of control and restricting agency (Hammond, Fleming, & Villa-Torres, 2016). Race-related stress also creates what theorists refer to as a 'threat-based agonic system' (Kemeny, Gruenewald, & Dickerson, 2004), or rejection-laden contexts that diminish power, control, and dominion. Thus, one reaction to race-related stress is for emerging adult males to engage in risky behaviors and display violence or aggression as a means of recouping manhood (Goff, Di Leone, & Kahn, 2012). Affect regulation strategies are influenced by environmental contexts and governed by sociocultural norms (Raver, 2004). The notion that men do not cry, tell, or complain is a socially reinforced set of normative beliefs that influence affect regulation among males. The pressure to "man-up" by suppressing emotion may be more pronounced during emerging adulthood (Gross & Thompson, 2007) and in neighborhoods with disadvantage and low social cohesion. Sheer existence in such settings can increase the sense of precarious masculinity leading to identity enactments that underscore toughness and emotional control, strategies that may inadvertently increase risk-taking. For example, Stevenson (1997) has shown that anger experience and expression are minimized among adolescent males from urban neighborhoods when they fear being shot or stabbed.

## Advancing Scholarship on Neighborhoods and African American Risk-Taking and Substance Abuse

Augmenting census-based assessments of neighborhood conditions with standardized social observations conducted by trained neighborhood residents has been cited as one way to get more specificity in neighborhood studies (Diez-Roux, 2001; Laraia et al., 2006; Schaefer-McDaniel, Caughy, O'Campo, & Gearey, 2010). Using trained, independent raters, as opposed to study participants also addresses noted "same source biases" that are created when participants provide self-reports on neighborhood conditions and the health behavior of interest (Diez-Roux, 2007; O'Campo, 2003; Schaefer-McDaniel et al., 2010). Contradictory quantitative study results linking neighborhood conditions to risk-taking and substance abuse suggest the need for qualitative and observational studies that focus on the phenomenology of neighborhood settings (O'Campo, 2003 Sullivan, 2001). Ecological momentary assessment (EMA) methods are increasingly used in substance use research (Epstein et al., 2009; Epstein et al., 2014; Epstein, Marrone, Heishman, Schmittner, & Preston, 2010; Epstein & Preston, 2010; Litt, Cooney, & Morse, 1998; Phillips, Epstein, & Preston, 2013; Preston et al., 2009; Shiffman, 2009). EMA can investigate day-to-day substance use and to determine whether high exposure to neighborhood conditions and stress is associated with African American male substance use over time. If we increase understanding of how stress-affective mechanisms naturally unfold in the context of poor neighborhood conditions, then we can design substance use interventions that can modify those mechanisms. While associations between cortisol, testosterone, and risk-taking are fairly, well-documented, findings are mixed. More attention needs to be paid to the dysregulation of such hormones in the face of repeated, race-related stressors among African American males.

Too few studies emphasize potential neighborhood strengths and protective factors. Including protective factors in studies may clarify reasons for mixed results from investigations linking objective neighborhood conditions to health risk behaviors. For example, The Project on Human Development in Chicago Neighborhoods found that neighborhood collective efficacy, or the extent of mutual trust, solidarity, and shared values among neighbors, delayed sexual initiation among adolescent males (Browning, Leventhal, & Brooks-Gunn, 2005). Others have noted less substance and alcohol abuse among adolescents residing in neighborhoods with high social cohesion, an indicator of neighborhood collective efficacy (Duncan, Duncan, & Strycker, 2002). A greater sense of neighborhood belonging has also been associated with more positive health behavior (Edwards & Bromfield, 2009). As a marker of social integration, neighborhood belonging may reduce health risk behavior by minimizing social isolation and subjecting individuals to more social controls (Berkman, Glass, Brissette, & Seeman, 2000). Including assessments of neighborhood strengths and protective factors may illuminate potential public health and policy intervention levers.

## Conclusions

Health inequities among African American men and boys stemming from risk-taking, violence, and substance abuse compromise family functioning and sustainability. When African American men and boys perish prematurely as a consequence of health inequities, there is an economic burden (Thorpe, Richard, Bowie, LaVeist, & Gaskin, 2013), disruption to secure familial livelihoods, and a socioemotional toll exacted on the individuals (often women and girls) they leave behind. African American men and boys are not only inhabiting neighborhoods and other social spaces that impose risks to their physical and psychological safety, they are also embodying those risks in ways that enhance biobehavioral risks for substance abuse. Thus, even as we strive to build stronger families, we have to acknowledge their inability to fully insulate African American men and boys from broader ecologic exposures. At the same time, we must acknowledge that African American men and boys possess untapped strengths and the capacity to thrive in the face of such exposures. Further, African American men define masculinity in ways that emphasize pro-action, redemption, interdependence, and close familial bonds (Hammond & Mattis, 2005). Such definitions imply that African American men may feel less bound by norms that discourage emotional vulnerability, and families may provide 'safe spaces' to disclose stress impacts. To enhance the protective capacities of families and decrease substance abuse risks among African American men, we need more multi-system interventions that focus on improving the noxious socio-structural conditions that suffocate innate potential.

**Acknowledgment** The first author is currently supported by the National Institutes on Drug Abuse (Grant # 1K01 DA032611-01A1) and the National Institute on Minority Health and Health Disparities (Grant # L60 MD010134). The second author is supported by a fellowship from the National Institute of Allergy and Infectious Diseases of the National Institutes of Health (Award Number T32A1007001).

## References

Allison, K., Crawford, I., Leone, P., Trickett, E., Perez-Febles, A., Burton, L., et al. (1999). Adolescent substance use: Preliminary examinations of school and neighborhood context. *American Journal of Community Psychology, 27*(2), 111–141.

Aneshensel, C. S., & Sucoff, C. A. (1996). The neighborhood context of adolescent mental health. *Journal of Health and Social Behavior, 37*(4), 293–310.

Arnett, J. J. (2000). Emerging adulthood: A theory of development from the late teens through the twenties. *American Psychologist, 55*(5), 469–480.

Arnett, J. J. (2005). Developmental context of substance use in emerging adulthood. *Journal of Drug Issues, 35*(2), 235–254.

Arnett, J. J. (2008). A fraught passage: The identity challenges of African American adults. *Human Development, 51*(5–6), 291–293.

Arnett, J. J. (2014). *Emerging adulthood: The winding road from the late teens through the twenties* (2nd ed.). New York, NY: Oxford University Press.

Berkman, L. F., Glass, T., Brissette, I., & Seeman, T. E. (2000). From social integration to health: Durkheim in the new millennium. *Social Science and Medicine, 51*(6), 843–857.

Boardman, J. D. (2004). Stress and physical health: The role of neighborhoods as mediating and moderating mechanisms. *Social Science and Medicine, 58*(12), 2473–2483.

Boardman, J. D., Finch, B. K., Ellison, C. G., Williams, D. R., & Jackson, J. S. (2001). Neighborhood disadvantage, stress, and drug use among adults. *Journal of Health and Social Behavior, 42*(2), 151–165.

Bolland, J., Bryant, C., Lian, B., McCallum, D., Vazsonyi, A., & Barth, J. (2007). Development and risk behavior among African American, Caucasian, and mixed-race adolescents living in high poverty inner-city neighborhoods. *American Journal of Community Psychology, 40*(3), 230–249.

Bonanno, G. A., Papa, A., Lalande, K., Westphal, M., & Coifman, K. (2004). The importance of being flexible: The ability to both enhance and suppress emotional expression predicts long-term adjustment. *Psychological Science, 15*(7), 482–487.

Bosson, J. K., Vandello, J. A., Burnaford, R. M., Weaver, J. R., & Wasti, S. A. (2009). Precarious manhood and displays of physical aggression. *Personality and Social Psychology Bulletin, 35*(5), 623–634. doi:10.1177/0146167208331161.

Boyce, W. T. (2007). A biology of misfortune: Stress reactivity, social context, and the ontogeny of psychopathology early in life. In A. S. Masten (Ed.), *Multilevel dynamics in developmental psychology: Pathways to the future* (pp. 45–82). Mahwah, NJ: Lawrence Erlbaum Associates, Inc.

Boyce, W. T., & Ellis, B. J. (2005). Biological sensitivity to context: I. An evolutionary-developmental theory of the origins and functions of stress reactivity. *Developmental Psychopathology, 17*(2), 271–301.

Brady, S. S. (2006). Lifetime community violence exposure and health risk behavior among young adults in college. *Journal of Adolescent Health, 39*(4), 610–613.

Brody, G., Ge, X., Conger, R., Gibbons, F. X., Murry, V., Gerrard, M., et al. (2001). The influence of neighborhood disadvantage, collective socialization, and parenting on African American children's affiliation with deviant peers. *Child Development, 72*(4), 1231–1246.

Browning, C., Leventhal, T., & Brooks-Gunn, J. (2004). Neighborhood context and racial differences in early adolescent sexual activity. *Demography, 41*(4), 697–720.

Browning, C., Leventhal, T., & Brooks-Gunn, J. (2005). Sexual initiation in early adolescence: The nexus of parental and community control. *American Sociological Review, 70*(5), 758–778.

Center for Behavioral Health Statistics and Quality. (2011). *Results from the 2010 national survey on drug use and health: Summary of national findings*. Rockville, MD: Substance Abuse and Mental Health Services Administration. http://www.samhsa.gov/data/sites/default/files/NSDUHNationalFindingsResults2010-web/2k10ResultsRev/NSDUHresultsRev2010.pdf.

Chuang, Y., Ennett, S., Bauman, K., & Foshee, V. (2005). Neighborhood influences on adolescent cigarette and alcohol use: Mediating effects through parent and peer behaviors. *Journal of Health and Social Behavior, 46*(2), 187–204.

Clarke, P., Morenoff, J., Debbink, M., Golberstein, E., Elliott, M. R., & Lantz, P. M. (2014). Cumulative exposure to neighborhood context: Consequences for health transitions over the adult life course. *Research on Aging, 36*(1), 115–142. doi:10.1177/0164027512470702.

Cockerham, W. C. (1990). A test of the relationship between race, socioeconomic status, and psychological distress. *Social Science and Medicine, 31*(12), 1321–1326. doi:10.1016/0277-9536(90)90071-y.

Compas, B. E. (2006). Psychobiological processes of stress and coping: Implications for resilience in children and adolescents—Comments on the papers of Romeo & McEwen and Fisher et al. *Annals of the New York Academy of Sciences, 1094*(1), 226–234. doi:10.1196/annals.1376.024.

Copeland-Linder, N., Lambert, S., Chen, Y.-F., & Ialongo, N. (2011). Contextual stress and health risk behaviors among African American adolescents. *Journal of Youth and Adolescence, 40*(2), 158–173. doi:10.1007/s10964-010-9520-y.

Courtenay, W. H. (2000). Constructions of masculinity and their influence on men's well-being: A theory of gender and health. *Social Science and Medicine, 50*(10), 1385–1401.

Cubbin, C., Santelli, J., Brindis, C. D., & Braveman, P. (2005). Neighborhood context and sexual behaviors among adolescents: Findings from the National Longitudinal Study of Adolescent Health. *Perspectives on Sexual and Reproductive Health, 37*(3), 125–134.

de Haan, M., Gunnar, M. R., Tout, K., Hart, J., & Stansbury, K. (1998). Familiar and novel contexts yield different associations between cortisol and behavior among 2-year-old children. *Developmental Psychobiology, 33*(1), 93–101.

de Visser, R. O., & Smith, J. A. (2007). Alcohol consumption and masculine identity among young men. *Psychology and Health, 22*(5), 595–614.

de Wit, H., Vicini, L., Childs, E., Sayla, M. A., & Terner, J. (2007). Does stress reactivity or response to amphetamine predict smoking progression in young adults? A preliminary study. *Pharmacology Biochemistry and Behavior, 86*(2), 312–319.

Diez-Roux, A. V. (2001). Investigating neighborhood and area effects on health. *American Journal of Public Health, 91*(11), 1783–1789.

Diez-Roux, A. V. (2007). Neighborhoods and health: Where are we and were do we go from here? *Revue d'Epidémiologie et de Santé Publique, 55*(1), 13–21.

Dodge, K. A., & Pettit, G. S. (2003). A biopsychosocial model of the development of chronic conduct problems in adolescence. *Developmental Psychology, 39*(2), 349–371.

Duncan, S. C., Duncan, T. E., & Strycker, L. A. (2002). A multilevel analysis of neighborhood context and youth alcohol and drug problems. *Prevention Science, 3*(2), 125–133.

Dunkley, C. M. (2009). A therapeutic taskscape: Theorizing place-making, discipline and care at a camp for troubled youth. *Health and Place, 15*(1), 88–96.

Dupere, V., Lacourse, E., Willms, J., Leventhal, T., & Tremblay, R. (2008). Neighborhood poverty and early transition to sexual activity in young adolescents: A developmental ecological approach. *Child Development, 79*(5), 1463–1476.

Dworkin, J. (2005). Risk taking as developmentally appropriate experimentation for college students. *Journal of Adolescent Research, 20*(2), 219–241. doi:10.1177/0743558404273073.

Edwards, B., & Bromfield, L. M. (2009). Neighborhood influences on young children's conduct problems and pro-social behavior: Evidence from an Australian national sample. *Children and Youth Services Review, 31*(3), 317–324.

Elliott, M. (2000). The stress process in neighborhood context. *Health and Place, 6*(4), 287–299.

Else-Quest, N. M., Hyde, J. S., Goldsmith, H. H., & Van Hulle, C. A. (2006). Gender differences in temperament: A meta-analysis. *Psychological Bulletin, 132*(1), 33–72.

Ennett, S. T., Flewelling, R. L., Lindrooth, R. C., & Norton, E. C. (1997). School and neighborhood characteristics associated with school rates of alcohol, cigarette, and marijuana use. *Journal of Health and Social Behavior, 38*(1), 55–71.

Epstein, D. H., Marrone, G. F., Heishman, S. J., Schmittner, J., & Preston, K. L. (2010). Tobacco, cocaine, and heroin: Craving and use during daily life. *Addictive Behaviors, 35*(4), 318–324.

Epstein, D. H., & Preston, K. L. (2010). Daily life hour by hour, with and without cocaine: An ecological momentary assessment study. *Psychopharmacology, 211*(2), 223–232. doi:10.1007/s00213-010-1884-x.

Epstein, D. H., Tyburski, M., Craig, I. M., Phillips, K. A., Jobes, M. L., Vahabzadeh, M., et al. (2014). Real-time tracking of neighborhood surroundings and mood, in urban drug misusers: Application of a new method to study behavior in its geographical context. *Drug and Alcohol Dependence, 134*, 22–29. doi:10.1016/j.drugalcdep.2013.09.007.

Epstein, D. H., Willner-Reid, J., Vahabzadeh, M., Mezghanni, M., Lin, J., & Preston, K. L. (2009). Real-time electronic diary reports of cue exposure and mood in the hours before cocaine and heroin craving and use. *Archives of General Psychiatry, 66*(1), 88–94. doi:10.1001/archgenpsychiatry.2008.509.

Fergus, S., Zimmerman, M. A., & Caldwell, C. H. (2007). Growth trajectories of sexual risk behavior in adolescence and young adulthood. *American Journal of Public Health, 97*(6), 1096–1101. doi:10.2105/ajph.2005.074609.

Fernald, L. C., & Grantham-McGregor, S. M. (1998). Stress response in school-age children who have been growth retarded since early childhood. *American Journal of Clinical Nutrition, 68*(3), 691–698.

Fox, G. L. (1977). Sex-role attitudes as predictors of contraceptive use among unmarried university students. *Sex Roles, 3*(3), 265–283.

Gadea, M., Gómez, C., González-Bono, E., Espert, R., & Salvador, A. (2005). Increased cortisol and decreased right ear advantage (REA) in dichotic listening following a negative mood induction. *Psychoneuroendocrinology, 30*(2), 129–138.

Gee, G. C., & Payne-Sturges, D. C. (2004). Environmental health disparities: A framework integrating psychosocial and environmental concepts. *Environmental Health Perspective, 112*(17), 1645–1653.

Gibbons, F. X., Etcheverry, P. E., Stock, M. L., Gerrard, M., Weng, C.-Y., Kiviniemi, M., et al. (2010). Exploring the link between racial discrimination and substance use: What mediates? What buffers? *Journal of Personality and Social Psychology, 99*(5), 785–801.

Gibbons, F. X., Yeh, H. C., Gerrard, M., Cleveland, M. J., Cutrona, C., Simons, R. L., et al. (2007). Early experience with racial discrimination and conduct disorder as predictors of subsequent drug use: A critical period hypothesis. *Drug and Alcohol Dependence, 88*, S27–S37.

Goff, P. A., Di Leone, B. A. L., & Kahn, K. B. (2012). Racism leads to pushups: How racial discrimination threatens subordinate men's masculinity. *Journal of Experimental Social Psychology, 48*(5), 1111–1116.

Gross, J. J. (1998a). Antecedent- and response-focused emotion regulation: Divergent consequences for experience, expression, and physiology. *Journal of personality and social psychology, 74*(1), 224–237. doi:10.1037/0022-3514.74.1.224.

Gross, J. J. (1998b). The emerging field of emotion regulation: An integrative review. *Review of General Psychology, 2*(3), 271–299.

Gross, J. J., & Levenson, R. W. (1993). Emotional suppression: Physiology, self-report, and expressive behavior. *Journal of Personality and Social Psychology, 64*(6), 970–986.

Gross, J. J., & Thompson, R. A. (2007). Emotion regulation: Conceptual foundations. In J. J. Gross (Ed.), *Handbook of emotion regulation* (pp. 3–24). New York, NY: Guilford Press.

Halpern, C. T., Udry, J. R., Campbell, B., & Suchindran, C. (1993a). Relationships between aggression and pubertal increases in testosterone: A panel analysis of adolescent males. *Social Biology, 40*(1-2), 8–24.

Halpern, C. T., Udry, J. R., Campbell, B., & Suchindran, C. (1993b). Testosterone and pubertal development as predictors of sexual activity: A panel analysis of adolescent males. *Psychosomatic Medicine, 55*(5), 436–447.

Halpern, C. T., Udry, J. R., Campbell, B., Suchindran, C., & Mason, G. A. (1994). Testosterone and religiosity as predictors of sexual attitudes and activity among adolescent males: A biosocial model. *Journal of Biosocial Science, 26*(2), 217–234.

Halpern, C. T., Udry, R., & Suchindran, C. (1998). Monthly measures of salivary testosterone predict sexual activity in adolescent males. *Archives of Sexual Behavior, 27*(5), 445–465.

Hammond, W. P., Fleming, P. J., & Villa-Torres, L. (2016). Everyday racism as a threat to the masculine social self: Framing investigations of African American male health disparities. In Y. J. Wong & S. R. Wester (Eds.), *APA handbook of men and masculinities* (pp. 259–283). Washington, DC: American Psychological Association.

Hammond, W. P., & Mattis, J. S. (2005). Being a man about it: Manhood meaning among African American men. *Psychology of Men and Masculinity, 6*(2), 114–126.

House, J. S., Strecher, V., Metzner, H. L., & Robbins, C. A. (1986). Occupational stress and health among men and women in the Tecumseh Community Health Study. *Journal of Health and Social Behavior, 27*(1), 62–77.

Irwin, C., & Millstein, S. (1992). Risk-taking behaviors and biopsychosocial development during adolescence. In E. J. Susman, L. V. Feagans, & W. J. Ray (Eds.), *Emotion, cognition, health, and development in children and adolescents* (pp. 75–102). London: Psychology Press.

Jessor, R. (1987). Problem-behavior theory, psychosocial development, and adolescent problem drinking. *British Journal of Addiction, 82*(4), 331–342.

Johnston, L. D., O'Malley, P. M., & Bachman, J. G. (2003). *Monitoring the future: National survey results on drug use, 1975–2002. Volume II: College students and adults Ages 19–40* (NIH Publications No. 03-5376). Bethesda, MD: National Institute on Drug Abuse.

Kagan, J., Reznick, J. S., & Snidman, N. (1987). The physiology and psychology of behavioral inhibition in children. *Child Development, 58*(6), 1459–1473.

Kemeny, M. E., Gruenewald, T. L., & Dickerson, S. S. (2004). Shame as the emotional response to threat to the social self: Implications for behavior, physiology, and health. *Psychological Inquiry, 15*(2), 153–160.

Kessler, R. C., & Neighbors, H. W. (1986). A new perspective on the relationships among race, social class, and psychological distress. *Journal of Health and Social Behavior, 27*(2), 107–115.

Kochanek, K. D., Anderson, R., & Arias, E. (2015). *Leading causes of death contributing to decrease in life expectancy gap between black and white populations: United States, 1999–2013* (NCHS Data Brief No. 218). Washington, DC: Centers for Disease Control and Prevention. http://www.cdc.gov/nchs/products/databriefs/db218.htm.

Kochanek, K. D., Murphy, S. L., Xu, J., & Arias, E. (2014). *Mortality in the United States, 2013* (NCHS Data Brief No. 178). Washington, DC: Centers for Disease Control and Prevention. http://www.cdc.gov/nchs/products/databriefs/db178.htm.

Kotchick, B., Shaffer, A., Miller, K., & Forehand, R. (2001). Adolescent sexual risk behavior: A multi-system perspective. *Clinical Psychology Review, 21*(4), 493–519.

Ku, L., Sonenstein, F., & Pleck, J. H. (1993). Neighborhood, family, and work: Influences on the premarital behaviors of adolescent males. *Social Forces, 72*(2), 479–503.

Lam, S., Dickerson, S. S., Zoccola, P. M., & Zaldivar, F. (2009). Emotion regulation and cortisol reactivity to a social-evaluative speech task. *Psychoneuroendocrinology, 34*(9), 1355–1362.

Lambert, S., Brown, T., Phillips, C., & Ialongo, N. (2004). The relationship between perceptions of neighborhood characteristics and substance use among urban African American adolescents. *American Journal of Community Psychology, 34*(3), 205–218.

Laraia, B. A., Messer, L., Kaufman, J. S., Dole, N., Caughy, M., O'Campo, P., et al. (2006). Direct observation of neighborhood attributes in an urban area of the US south: Characterizing the social context of pregnancy. *International Journal of Health Geographics, 5*(1), 11.

Levant, R. F., Hirsch, L. S., Celentano, E., & Cozz, T. M. (1992). The male role: An investigation of contemporary norms. *Journal of Mental Health Counseling, 14*(3), 325–337.

Levant, R. F., Wimer, D., Williams, C., Smalley, K., & Noronha, D. (2009). The relationships between masculinity variables, health risk behaviors and attitudes toward seeking psychological help. *International Journal of Men's Health, 8*(1), 3–21.

Leventhal, T., & Brooks-Gunn, J. (2000). The neighborhoods they live in: The effects of neighborhood residence on child and adolescent outcomes. *Psychological Bulletin, 126*(2), 309–337.

Litt, M. D., Cooney, N. L., & Morse, P. (1998). Ecological momentary assessment (EMA) with treated alcoholics: Methodological problems and potential solutions. *Health Psychology, 17*(1), 48–52.

Lloyd, D. A., & Turner, R. J. (2008). Cumulative lifetime adversities and alcohol dependence in adolescence and young adulthood. *Drug and Alcohol Dependence, 93*(3), 217–226. doi:10.1016/j.drugalcdep.2007.09.012.

Macrae, C. N., Bodenhausen, G. V., Milne, A. B., & Ford, R. L. (1997). On regulation of recollection: The intentional forgetting of stereotypical memories. *Journal of Personality and Social Psychology, 72*(4), 709–719.

Magar, E. C. E., Phillips, L. H., & Hosie, J. A. (2008). Self-regulation and risk-taking. *Personality and Individual Differences, 45*(2), 153–159.

Mahalik, J., Lagan, H., & Morrison, J. (2006). Health behaviors and masculinity in Kenyan and U.S. male college students. *Psychology of Men and Masculinity, 7*(4), 191–202.

Mazur, A., & Booth, A. (1998). Testosterone and dominance in men. *Behavioural and Brain Sciences, 21*(3), 353–363. Discussion 363–397.

Milam, A. J., Furr-Holden, C. D. M., & Leaf, P. (2010). Perceived school and neighborhood safety, neighborhood violence and academic achievement in urban school children. *The Urban Review, 42*(5), 458–467.

Millar, M. (2005). The effects of perceived stress on reactions to messages designed to increase health behaviors. *Journal of Behavioral Medicine, 28*(5), 425–432. doi:10.1007/s10865-005-9009-4.

O'Campo, P. (2003). Invited commentary: Advancing theory and methods for multilevel models of residential neighborhoods and health. *American Journal of Epidemiology, 157*(1), 9–13. doi:10.1093/aje/kwf171.

O'Sullivan, L., Hoffman, S., Harrison, A., & Dolezal, C. (2006). Men, multiple sexual partners, and young adults' sexual relationships: Understanding the role of gender in the study of risk. *Journal of Urban Health, 83*(4), 695–708.

Office of Applied Studies. (2009). *Results from the 2008 national survey on substance abuse and health: National findings*. Rockville, MD: Substance Abuse and Mental Health Services Administration. http://archive.samhsa.gov/data/NSDUH/2k8nsduh/2k8results.pdf.

Olweus, D., Mattsson, A., Schalling, D., & Low, H. (1980). Testosterone, aggression, physical, and personality dimensions in normal adolescent males. *Psychosomatic Medicine, 42*(2), 253–269.

Olweus, D., Mattsson, A., Schalling, D., & Low, H. (1988). Circulating testosterone levels and aggression in adolescent males: A causal analysis. *Psychosomatic Medicine, 50*(3), 261–272.

Phillips, K. A., Epstein, D. H., & Preston, K. L. (2013). Daily temporal patterns of heroin and cocaine use and craving: Relationship with business hours regardless of actual employment status. *Addictive Behaviors, 38*(10), 2485–2491. doi:10.1016/j.addbeh.2013.05.010.

Pleck, J., & O'Donnell, L. (2001). Gender attitudes and health risk behaviors in urban African American and Latino early adolescents. *Maternal and Child Health Journal, 5*(4), 265–272.

Pleck, J. H., Sonenstein, F. L., & Ku, L. C. (1994). Problem behaviors and masculinity ideology among adolescent males. In R. D. Ketterlinus & M. E. Lamb (Eds.), *Adolescent problem behaviors: Issues and research* (pp. 165–186). Hillsdale, MI: Lawrence Erlbaum.

Preston, K. L., Vahabzadeh, M., Schmittner, J., Lin, J.-L., Gorelick, D., & Epstein, D. (2009). Cocaine craving and use during daily life. *Psychopharmacology, 207*(2), 291–301.

Raver, C. C. (2004). Placing emotional self-regulation in sociocultural and socioeconomic contexts. *Child Development, 75*(2), 346–353. doi:10.1111/j.1467-8624.2004.00676.x.

Rich, J. A., & Grey, C. M. (2005). Pathways to recurrent trauma among young black men: Traumatic stress, substance use, and the "code of the street". *American Journal of Public Health, 95*(5), 816–824.

Rod, N. H., Grønbæk, M., Schnohr, P., Prescott, E., & Kristensen, T. S. (2009). Perceived stress as a risk factor for changes in health behaviour and cardiac risk profile: A longitudinal study. *Journal of Internal Medicine, 266*(5), 467–475.

Sampson, R. J. (2003). The neighborhood context of well-being. *Perspectives in Biology and Medicine, 46*(3 Suppl), S53–S64.

Santana, M., Raj, A., Decker, M., La Marche, A., & Silverman, J. (2006). Masculine gender roles associated with increased sexual risk and intimate partner violence perpetration among young adult men. *Journal of Urban Health, 83*(4), 575–585.

Schaefer-McDaniel, N., Caughy, M. O., O'Campo, P., & Gearey, W. (2010). Examining methodological details of neighbourhood observations and the relationship to health: A literature review. *Social Science and Medicine, 70*(2), 277–292. doi:10.1016/j.socscimed.2009.10.018.

Scheier, L. M., Botvin, G. J., & Miller, N. L. (2000). Life events, neighborhood stress, psychosocial functioning, and alcohol use among urban minority youth. *Journal of Child and Adolescent Substance Abuse, 9*(1), 19–50. doi:10.1300/J029v09n01_02.

Schmidt, L. A., Fox, N. A., Rubin, K. H., Sternberg, E. M., Gold, P. W., Smith, C. C., et al. (1997). Behavioral and neuroendocrine responses in shy children. *Developmental Psychobiology, 30*(2), 127–140.

Schulenberg, J., Maggs, J. L., Long, S. W., Sher, K. J., Gotham, H. J., Baer, J. S., et al. (2001). The problem of college drinking: Insights from a developmental perspective. *Alcoholism: Clinical and Experimental Research, 25*(3), 473–477.

Shiffman, S. (2009). Ecological momentary assessment (EMA) in studies of substance use. *Psychological Assessment, 21*(4), 486.

Smith, J. R. (2015). Unequal burdens of loss: Examining the frequency and timing of homicide deaths experienced by young black men across the life course. *American Journal of Public Health, 105*(Suppl 3), S483–S490.

Spencer, M. B., Dupree, D., & Hartmann, T. (1997). A phenomenological variant of ecological systems theory (PVEST): A self-organization perspective in context. *Development and Psychopathology, 9*(4), 817–833.

Spencer, M. B., McDermott, P. A., Burton, L. M., & Kochman, T. J. (1997). An alternative approach to assessing neighborhood effects on early adolescent achievement and problem behavior. In J. Brooks-Gunn, G. J. Duncan, & J. L. Aber (Eds.), *Neighborhood poverty, Volume 2: Policy implications in studying neighborhoods* (pp. 145–163). New York, NY: Russell Sage Foundation.

Stevenson, H. C. (1997). Missed, dissed, and pissed: Making meaning of neighborhood risk, fear and anger management in urban black youth. *Cultural Diversity and Mental Health, 3*(1), 37–52.

Stockdale, S. E., Wells, K. B., Tang, L., Belin, T. R., Zhang, L., & Sherbourne, C. D. (2007). The importance of social context: Neighborhood stressors, stress-buffering mechanisms, and alcohol, drug, and mental health disorders. *Social Science and Medicine, 65*(9), 1867–1881. doi:10.1016/j.socscimed.2007.05.045.

Subramanian, S. V., Chen, J. T., Rehkopf, D. H., Waterman, P. D., & Krieger, N. (2005). Racial disparities in context: A multilevel analysis of neighborhood variations in poverty and excess mortality among black populations in Massachusetts. *American Journal of Public Health, 95*(2), 260–265. doi:10.2105/ajph.2003.034132.

Sullivan, M. L. (2001). Hyperghettos and hypermasculinity: The phenomenology of exclusion. In A. Booth & A. C. Crouter (Eds.), *Does it take a village? Community effects on children, adolescents, and families* (pp. 96–101). Mahwah, NJ: Lawrence Erlbaum Associates, Inc.

Susman, E. J. (2006). Psychobiology of persistent antisocial behavior: Stress, early vulnerabilities and the attenuation hypothesis. *Neuroscience and Biobehavioral Reviews, 30*(3), 376–389.

Thorpe, R. J., Jr., Richard, P., Bowie, J. V., LaVeist, T. A., & Gaskin, D. J. (2013). Economic burden of men's health disparities in the United States. *International Journal of Men's Health, 12*(3), 195.

Udry, J. R. (1988). Biological predispositions and social control in adolescent sexual behavior. *American Sociological Review, 53*(5), 709–722.

Umberson, D., Liu, H., & Reczek, C. (2008). Stress and health behavior over the life course. In H. A. Turner & S. Schieman (Eds.), *Stress processes across the life course, advances in life course research* (Vol. 13, pp. 19–44). Oxford: Elsevier JAI.

Umberson, D., Williams, K., & Anderson, K. (2002). Violent behavior: A measure of emotional upset? *Journal of Health and Social Behavior, 43*(2), 189–206.

van Eck, M., Berkhof, H., Nicolson, N., & Sulon, J. (1996). The effects of perceived stress, traits, mood states, and stressful daily events on salivary cortisol. *Psychosomatic Medicine, 58*(5), 447–458.

Van Honk, J., Kessels, R. P. C., Putman, P., Jager, G., Koppeschaar, H. P. F., & Postma, A. (2003). Attentionally modulated effects of cortisol and mood on memory for emotional faces in healthy young males. *Psychoneuroendocrinology, 28*(7), 941–948.

Wegner, D. M., Schneider, D. J., Carter, S. R., & White, T. L. (1987). Paradoxical effects of thought suppression. *Journal of Personality and Social Psychology, 53*(1), 5–13.

Wenzlaff, R. M., & Wegner, D. M. (2000). Thought suppression. *Annual Review of Psychology, 51*(1), 59–91. doi:10.1146/annurev.psych.51.1.59.

Whitley, B. E. (1988). The relation of gender-role orientation to sexual experience among college students. *Sex Roles, 19*(9), 619–638.

Widome, R., Sieving, R. E., Harpin, S. A., & Hearst, M. O. (2008). Measuring neighborhood connection and the association with violence in young adolescents. *Journal of Adolescent Health, 43*(5), 482–489.

Wolfers, J., Leonhardt, D., & Quealy, K. (2015a, April 20). 1.5 million missing black men. *The New York Times*. http://www.nytimes.com/interactive/2015/04/20/upshot/missing-black-men.html. Accessed November 2015.

Wolfers, J., Leonhardt, D., & Quealy, K. (2015b, April 20). The methodology: 1.5 million missing black men. *The New York Times*. http://www.nytimes.com/2015/04/21/upshot/the-methodology-1-5-million-missing-black-men.html?src=twr. Accessed November 2015.

Wong, C. F., Kipke, M. D., Weiss, G., & McDavitt, B. (2010). The impact of recent stressful experiences on HIV-risk related behaviors. *Journal of Adolescence, 33*(3), 463–475.

# Black Men Love Family and Community

**Trabian Shorters and Truman Hudson, Jr.**

For centuries, the road to success for black men in America, as for many groups, has not been easy. Overcoming tremendous odds, black men have made significant gains in many areas. In the fields of science, sociology, education, architecture, and technology, black men in the U.S. have played an intricate role in the development of the country. Pioneers like George Washington Carver, Elijah McCoy, Garrett Morgan, W.E.B. Du Bois, Ph.D., Carter G. Woodson, Ph.D., Booker T. Washington, Geoffrey Canada, Benjamin Banneker, Vivien Thomas, Charles Drew, M.D., and Benjamin Carson, M.D., are credited with accomplishments such as designing mobile classrooms to educate farmers, improving the lubrication process for steam engines, inventing the traffic signal, leading human rights and social justice movements, pioneering the field of sociology, founding colleges, universities and the wraparound family educational support system, building institutions that have aided in the advancement of mankind, and inventing lifesaving medical procedures. Businessmen and political strategists such as Quincy Jones, Barry Gordy, John Johnson, Kenneth I. Chenault, Reginald F. Lewis, John R. Lewis, Coleman A. Young, and Ralph J. Bunche created pathways for success that have allowed others to engage in the social, political, and economic prosperity of the country.

Like other members of the greater community, black men not only love their families, but they also support important causes and exhibit a deep passion for and commitment to each other, their communities, and their country. Given the research on family and community engagement, black men as a whole have remained steadfast in being fathers, brothers, uncles, and sons who champion the development of their families (Arnold, 2015). Whether through faith, entrepreneurship, the arts, education, sports, or the community, black men love serving as role models,

T. Shorters (✉)
BMe Community, Miami, FL, USA
e-mail: CEO@bmecommunity.org

T. Hudson, Jr.
BMe Community, Detroit, MI, USA



L. Burton et al. (eds.), *Boys and Men in African American Families*, National Symposium on Family Issues 7, DOI 10.1007/978-3-319-43847-4_15

advocates, and mentors (Shorters, 2015). In a study that measured fathers' involvement in their children's lives, Jones and Mosher (2013) contend, when compared to their white and Hispanic counterparts, black fathers led in engagement in their children's lives. More specifically, for children 5–18 years old, black fathers took children to and from activities and helped their children with homework more than white and Hispanic fathers. Based on Jones and Mosher's (2013) research, black fathers spent more time preparing and eating meals with their children who were five years old and younger. As leaders in their families and communities, black men take pride in their formal and informal mentor interactions with others (Lewis, 1993; Moore, 2014; Sobota, 2015).

Unfortunately, data specific to black male's engagement in their families and community are sparse in mainstream media, and even more so in the academy. According to Arnold (2015) "[I]n America, the perception is that the black father doesn't exist. Negative stereotypes of black men persist" (para. 1). From various outlets, the image of black men in general has been tarnished via the constant bombardment of negative images and messages, which are oftentimes reinforced in the dominant discourse (Davey, 2009). As referred to in Smith's (2013) research on black males:

> These negative representations of black males are readily visible and conveyed to the public through the news, film, music videos, reality television, and other programming and forms of media. The typical roles are all too often the black sidekick of a white protagonist, for example, the token black person, the comedic relief, the athlete, the over-sexed ladies' man, the absentee father or, most damaging, the violent black man as drug-dealing criminal and gangster thug (para 2.).

Oftentimes when cases of blacks' successes are highlighted in the media, their accomplishments are viewed in a negative light or as 'different' and atypical. While viewed as different, like others in the black community, much of what black celebrities say and do is racialized in the media (Pepin, 2015). As an example, seven years post winning the 2008 national election, President Barack Obama's successes as a husband, father, scholar, community builder and President of the United States (POTUS) are often downplayed in mainstream media.

## Shaping a New Narrative

Efforts to counter the deficit narrative of blacks in general, and black men specifically, have been met with great trepidation. People from various cultural, social, and racial backgrounds, along with those who represent institutions that value all humans, have spent years challenging the dominant discourse on race. Although various strategies such as the Harlem Renaissance, the Civil Rights Movement, Black Power Movement, and corporate social responsibility campaigns have aided in updating the narrative of black citizens' contributions to American culture, there is still more work to be done.

In an effort to get more black men positively engaged in community, Trabian Shorters and colleagues at The John S. and James L. Knight Foundation (Knight) launched a project that revealed the premise of the deficit narrative to be incorrect.

Black men were positively engaged at a high rate in both Detroit and Philadelphia where the concurrent research by Context Partners took place (Context Partners, 2011). Subsequently Knight learned:

- Black male engagement is not a problem.
- The majority of black men mentor but do not subscribe to the typical practices or guidelines of most mentoring organizations.
- Black men are among the most likely to start businesses.
- Black men are the most likely to serve their country in the military and to support charitable causes.

In addition to these findings, Context Partners' (2011) research unearthed:

- There was a need to update the narrative about black males to more accurately reflect reality.
- Black men are not only serving and leading at high rates in unacknowledged ways, but they are leading on issues that people of all races and genders care about; specifically, youth development, education, economic opportunity, public health & safety, and the environment.

Rooted in the Love Doctrine (Shorters, 2015) and building on its research, Shorters understood that black men were catalysts for change that could galvanize people from varied backgrounds around issues of common interest. With this in mind, BMe Community was developed as a network of leaders and community builders who intentionally identify and share fact-based remarkable stories through an asset narrative lens. In doing so, BMe's asset narrative approach focuses on investing in black men and communities that embrace the ideology that we are better together. With 142 black males leading in communities such as Akron, OH, Baltimore, MD, Detroit, MI, Philadelphia and Pittsburgh, PA, BMe leverages its resources to engage local champions and black males in the work that they do naturally—building communities (Schmitz, 2012). Through more than 35,000 Community Builders in the network whose work is rooted in the servant leader philosophy (Greenleaf & Spears, 2002), BMe has launched and sustained social media campaigns that have engaged well over 1.5 million people in the sharing of asset based discourse germane to black males and their love for family and community.

## Investing in the Future

In their effort to establish identity, black men in America, like many groups, have overcome many challenges (Du Bois, 1903). In doing so, they have remained resolved in being leaders who invest in their families, communities, and country. In their roles as leaders, black men provide support and guidance that empower others to navigate environmental factors that adversely influence individual and collective success (Bronfenbrenner, 2005; Du Bois & Karcher, 2005). In doing so, they develop and engage in meaningful relationships (Canada, 1998; Connor, 2016). From informal activities to formal programs that are supported by partners like 100 Black Men of America, Historical Black Colleges and Universities, Big Brothers/Big Sisters, Boys and Girls Club, POP Warner, Amateur Athletic Union, block clubs, Greek letter organizations, and faith-based organizations, black males lead the country in mentoring and community-building (Context Partners, 2011; Corporation for National and Community Service, 2015). When narrowing the scope, through their combined efforts in BMe's five communities, black men share their social and intellectual capital to inspire and empower well over 400,000 people annually (Benson, 2008). Impact areas from investments, include but are not limited to

- Early Childhood
- Literacy
- High School Completion
- Re-Entry/Violence Reduction
- Workforce/Entrepreneurship
- Health and Wellness.

With a $3.64 million grant from The John S. and James L. Knight Foundation, BMe has leveraged resources from private donors, corporate sponsors, and leading foundations like Open Society Foundation, Campaign for Black Male Achievement, and The Heinz Endowment to lift up the narrative that black males are assets. In standing for a better way, a better message, and a better future, BMe's focus on asset-based narratives exposes more than 2.2 million people annually. Guided by its credo of valuing people, recognizing black men as assets, rejecting narratives that denigrate people, and working together to strengthen communities, BMe provides asset framing techniques and language that connect people with engaged communities. Through the investments of a few, BMe is making demonstrative impacts that will benefit many.

## References

Arnold, A. P. (2015). Dispelling the myths about Black fathers. *CNN*. http://www.cnn.com/2015/07/20/opinions/arnold-black-fathers/. Accessed January 2016.

Benson, P. L. (2008). *Sparks: How parents can help ignite the hidden strengths of teenagers*. San Francisco, CA: Jossey-Bass.

Bronfenbrenner, U. (Ed.). (2005). *Making human beings human: Bioecological perspectives on human development*. Thousand Oaks, CA: Sage Publications.

Canada, G. (1998). *Reaching up for manhood*. Boston, MA: Beacon.

Connor, E. M., Jr. (2016). *My Brother's Keeper: Rebuilding, reconciling, and restoring the lives of boys and men*. Royal Oak, MI: Norbrook Publishing.

Context Partners. (2011). *Knight Black males initiative—Research preview: Initial insights, design principles and what we heard*. Miami, FL: The John S. and James L. Knight Foundation.

Corporation for National and Community Service. (2015). *Mentoring in America: A summary of new research fact sheet*. Corporation for National & Community Service and MENTOR. http://www.nationalservice.gov/sites/default/files/documents/06_0503_mentoring_factsheet.pdf. Accessed January 2016.

Davey, L. (2009). *Strategies for framing racial disparities: A FrameWorks Institute message brief*. Washington, DC: FrameWorks Institute.

Du Bois, D., & Karcher, M. (2005). Youth mentoring: Theory, research, and practice. In D. Du Bois & M. Karcher (Eds.), *The SAGE Program on Applied Developmental Science: Handbook of youth mentoring* (pp. 2–13). Thousand Oaks, CA: Sage. doi:10.4135/9781412976664.n1.

Du Bois, W. E. B. (1903). *Souls of black folk*. Chicago, IL: A.C. McClurg and Company.

Greenleaf, R. K., & Spears, L. C. (2002). *Servant leadership: A journey into the nature of legitimate power and greatness*. Mahwah, NJ: Paulist Press.

Jones, J., & Mosher, W. D. (2013, December 20). *Fathers' involvement with their children: United States 2006–2010*. (National Health Statistics Report Number 71). U.S. Department of Health and Human Services Center for Disease Control. http://www.cdc.gov/nchs/data/nhsr/nhsr071.pdf. Accessed March 2016.

Lewis, D. L. (1993). *W.E.B. Du Bois: Biography of race 1868–1919*. New York, NY: Henry Holt and Company, Inc.

Moore, P. L. (2014). *Personal and professional recollections 1940–2012: Memoir and pictorial essay*. Bloomington, IN: AuthorHouse.

Pepin, J. R. (2015). Nobody's business? White male privilege in media coverage of intimate partner violence. *Sociological Spectrum, 36*(3), 123–141. doi:10.1080/02732173.2015.1108886.

Schmitz, P. (2012). *Everyone leads: Building leadership from the community up*. San Francisco, CA: Jossey-Bass.

Shorters, T. (2015). Trabian Shorters. In B. Jealous & T. Shorters (Eds.), *REACH: 40 Black men speak on living, leading and succeeding* (pp. 172–179). New York, NY: Atria Paperback.

Smith, D. T. (2013, March 14). Images of Black males in popular media. *Huffington Post*. http://www.huffingtonpost.com/darron-t-smith-phd/black-men-media_b_2844990.html. Accessed March 2016.

Sobota, L. (2015, September 12). 100 Black Men mentors encourage youths to aim high. *The Pantagraph*. http://www.pantagraph.com/news/local/black-men-mentors-encourage-youths--to-aim-high/article_597ee510-2d39-5118-aa19-f7f76a97815a.html. Accessed March 2016.

# Part V
# Where Do Family Scholars Go from Here?

# Heterogeneity in Research on African American Boys and Men: Focusing on Resilience, Social Networks, and Community Violence

**Wade C. Jacobsen and Cecily R. Hardaway**

Prior research has made tremendous advancements toward informing policymakers and practitioners of racial biases and consequences of structural conditions that disproportionately affect African American males relative to whites, but there is now a need for broader focus. Indeed, many scholars propose moving beyond simple race dichotomies and placing greater emphasis on within-group diversity, unique strengths and resources, and positive life outcomes (Celious & Oyserman, 2001; Connell, Spencer, & Aber, 1994; Sarkisian & Gerstel, 2004). Astoundingly, 20 % of black men (3 % of white men) served time in prison by their early 30s (Pettit & Western, 2004), but perhaps less known is that 34 % of young black men (38 % of young white men) are enrolled in a college or university (National Center for Education Statistics (NCES), 2013; see also Bennett & Xie, 2003). More than 70 % of black births are to unmarried parents (Martin, Hamilton, Osterman, Curtin, & Mathews, 2015), but black nonresident fathers are often more involved with their children than nonresident fathers of other races (Cabrera, Ryan, Mitchell, Shannon, & Tamis-LeMonda, 2008; King, 1994; King, Harris, & Heard, 2004); they also have more family and more frequent contact in their social networks (Ajrouch, Antonucci, & Janevic, 2001). The majority of blacks live in the South, but 19 million live in other regions of the United States (Rastogi, Johnson, Hoeffel, & Drewery, 2011), and more than 1 in 12 are immigrants, bringing languages and cultural traditions from the Caribbean, Africa, and Central America (Anderson, Lopez, & Rohal, 2015).

---

W.C. Jacobsen (✉)
Department of Sociology and Criminology, The Pennsylvania State University, University Park, PA, USA
e-mail: wcj106@psu.edu

C.R. Hardaway
Department of African American Studies, University of Maryland, College Park, MD, USA



L. Burton et al. (eds.), *Boys and Men in African American Families*, National Symposium on Family Issues 7, DOI 10.1007/978-3-319-43847-4_16

A common theme emerging in literature on black males is adaptive racial socialization, which we define as socialization that promotes racial identity and prosocial behavior while preparing boys and men to navigate stressful racial encounters. Racial socialization plays an important role in resilience because it is associated with positive outcomes like emotional well-being, self-regulation, and academic success (Murry, Block, & Liu, Chap. 2; Stevenson, Chap. 5); it may also help protect against trauma from racial violence (Smith Lee, Chap. 6). Beginning with parents and family, racial socialization occurs in social network contexts of kin, peers, and community (Demo & Hughes, 1990; Miller, 1999; Stanton-Salazar, 1997) and likely varies across family structures, biracial settings, and immigrant status (Thomas, Chap. 3).

Building from the papers presented at the 2015 Family Symposium, the purpose of this final chapter is to highlight three areas in prior research that we believe have potential for advancing understanding of well-being among black men and boys in the US. These include (1) a shift from deficit-focused approaches toward an emphasis on resilience, (2) greater focus on the characteristics and influences of family and other social networks, and (3) a sociocultural perspective on exposure to community violence and associated trauma. We briefly review prior research in these areas and discuss the role adaptive racial socialization plays in each. Based on these findings we provide several specific suggestions for future research.

## Three Promising Areas in Prior Research on African American Boys and Men

### *An Emphasis on Resilience*

In unarguably worthwhile efforts to address black-white gaps in academic achievement, wages, violence, life expectancy, and other outcomes (Harper, Lynch, Burris, & Smith, 2007; Jencks & Phillips, 2011; Light & Ulmer, 2016; Western & Pettit, 2005), prior research on African American boys and men has focused heavily on disadvantages associated with being a black male. However, there is movement within the developmental and clinical literatures to expand the research lens away from a focus on fixing problems toward identifying and nurturing strengths (Garmezy, 1993; Lerner, 2002; Masten, 2001; Seligman & Csikszentmihalyi, 2000). Resilience occurs when individual and environmental strengths translate to good developmental outcomes—emotional well-being, academic achievement, and low delinquency—in spite of serious risk factors such as family dissolution or poverty (Amato & Keith, 1991; Brooks-Gunn & Duncan, 1997). Research suggests resilience is not unusual but arises from "ordinary human adaptive processes [that draw on] resources in the minds, brains, and bodies of children, in their families and relationships, and in their communities" (Masten, 2001, p. 234). Developmental problems emerge when these adaptive systems are impaired and poor environmental conditions remain.

Some resilience research examines how important points in individuals' lives can alter their developmental trajectories. Masten (2001, p. 233) notes that, "… opportunities and choices at crucial junctures play an important role in the life course of resilient individuals." These "crucial junctures" (i.e., finding a mentor, religious conversion, leaving a delinquent peer network) represent what life course theorists call "turning points" and include events or transitions in ties to family, school, employment, and other institutions that substantially, though not necessarily immediately, alter the direction of a person's life (Elder, Johnson, & Crosnoe, 2003). Resilience occurs when turning points counteract the effects of poor socialization or an unfavorable environment and result in positive developmental trajectories. For example, for disadvantaged young men during the World War II era, military service often served as a turning point leading to trajectories of stable employment and family life (Elder, 1986; Sampson & Laub, 1996).

Murry and colleagues (Chap. 2) posit that research on black men and boys should have a similar focus, with more emphasis on resilience and less on deficits (see also Barbarin, 1993). In line with Masten (2001), they argue that strengths necessary for resilience are found in ordinary adaptive processes, such as racial socialization by parents and kin. Adaptive racial socialization may provide resources black boys need to navigate racial discrimination and negative effects of economic disadvantage, family complexity—such as having an unmarried or step parent (Manning, Brown, & Stykes, 2014), and other conditions to which blacks are disproportionately exposed (Hughes et al., 2006; Miller, 1999). For example, several studies of black youth suggest that strong racial identity, confidence in confronting stereotypes, and other indicators of socialization could counteract or buffer the negative effects of perceived racial discrimination and other stressors on academic engagement and achievement (Harper, 2015; Miller & MacIntosh, 1999; Neblett, Philip, Cogburn, & Sellers, 2006; Wong, Eccles, & Sameroff, 2003).

In addition, certain types of institutional involvement may act as turning points that lead to resilience among black males. Whereas criminological research suggests that incarceration is a turning point that sets young men on negative developmental trajectories (Pettit & Western, 2004) by limiting labor market opportunities and increasing housing instability (Geller & Curtis, 2011; Western, 2002), other findings suggest program interventions can foster resilience among reentering ex-offenders. For example, Uggen (2000) found that participation in an employment program served as a turning point toward desistence from crime (See also Uggen & Staff, 2001). In addition, Kirk (2009, 2012), showed that parolees released into a neighborhood other than the one they were living in prior to their incarceration, were less likely to recidivate. Previous chapters suggest that intervention strategies may benefit from greater emphasis on adaptive racial socialization (Stevenson, Chap. 5; Tolan, Chap. 7) or by providing "safe spaces," or supportive environments for formally incarcerated black fathers where they can share experiences in adapting to post-release challenges (Young, Jr., Chap. 10).

Many studies of resilience among black males are of children and adolescents in academic settings, and these tend to focus on short-term rather than later-life outcomes. Thus we know little about long-term effects of adaptive racial socialization or institutional interventions and other potential turning points. A major reason for this research gap is that, as the penal population has grown in recent decades, disproportionately affecting black males (Travis, Western, & Redburn, 2014), large-scale surveys have not adjusted their sampling frames accordingly (Pettit, 2012). Many surveys include household samples, which may not be effective at capturing hard-to-reach adult populations such as those who are institutionalized or homeless—conditions more common among blacks (Lee, Tyler, & Wright, 2010; Lindsey & Paul, 1989). An exception to the lack of studies on resilience among black men may be life course criminological research on turning points. However, much of this research focuses on men already caught up in the criminal justice system (Edin, Nelson, & Paranal, 2004; Uggen, 2000) and thus limits opportunities to examine heterogeneity. Another important exception is the National Black Male College Achievement Study (Harper, 2012), which includes qualitative data from black males attending college in 20 states. These data are informative about strategies black males use to navigate racial stereotypes at predominately white institutions (Harper, 2015), but the absence of a detailed longitudinal component precludes an examination of resilience over the long term.

## *Family and Other Social Networks*

Prior research is informative about roles of family and broader social networks including kin, peers, mentors, and community members in socialization and shaping life course trajectories (Bronfenbrenner, 1974, 1986; Cochran & Brassard, 1979; Elder, 1998; Elder et al., 2003), but among black men and boys, the characteristics and influence of these "linked lives" deserve further attention. Strong or weak, such ties provide social capital, emotional support, and resources that influence a host of outcomes at all stages of the life course (Coleman, 1988; Granovetter, 1973; Wellman & Wortley, 1990). For example, among children and adolescents, family structure, parenting behavior, and sibling interactions can have important consequences for academic success, educational attainment, behavior problems, and other outcomes (Astone & McLanahan, 1991; Lareau, 2003; Manning & Lamb, 2003; McHale, Bissell, & Kim, 2009; McLanahan & Sandefur, 1994; Thornberry, 2009). For young adults, changes in family ties such those associated with marriage or childbearing can be turning points that lead to desistance from criminal involvement (Kreager, Matsueda, & Erosheva, 2010; Laub & Sampson, 2003; Sampson & Laub, 1996; Warr, 1998). Beyond the immediate family, the roles that grandparents and extended kin play as co-residents, primary caregivers, and child care providers have become increasingly relevant, with varying outcomes for parents and children (Dunifon, Ziol-Guest, & Kopko, 2014). For example, intergenerational contact is associated with decreasing parenting stress for black mothers not living in intergenerational households. However, living in an intergenerational household is associated with increasing parenting stress (Greenfield, 2011). In addition, children being raised by grandparents have higher levels of behavioral problems (Pittman, 2007) but lower levels compared to those placed in foster care (Rubin et al., 2008).

Peers in one's school or neighborhood, including friends and romantic relationship partners, also play important roles in child and adolescent development (Crosnoe, 2000; Giordano, 2003). Indeed, in line with Powell et al. (Chap. 14), social network scholars find that school peer behavior is associated with substance use and behavior problems (Haynie, 2001; Kreager & Haynie, 2011; Osgood et al., 2013). Extending even more broadly, individuals of all ages are embedded in networks of teachers, religious leaders, counselors, and informal mentors who have important influences on social mobility and life course trajectories (Dove, 2015). Whereas unstructured socializing in the absence of these authority figures is associated with criminal behavior and substance use (Osgood, Wilson, O'malley, Bachman, & Johnston, 1996), having an adult mentor is associated with lower involvement in risky behaviors (Beier, Rosenfeld, Spitalny, Zansky, & Bontempo, 2000), greater academic achievement, and higher educational attainment (Erickson, McDonald, & Elder, 2009). Throughout adulthood, social support is associated with greater health and cognitive functioning (Seeman, Lusignolo, Albert, & Berkman, 2001; Uchino, 2006). Taken together, these studies suggest that family and other social network contexts are time-varying sources of positive and negative influences that shape behavior and alter trajectories across the life course.

Among black men and boys, less is known about the characteristics and influence of family and other network contexts, largely because they are underrepresented in large-scale studies of social networks. Oliver (1988, p. 626) contends that black urban communities are comprised of dense networks characterized by strong emphasis on kin, including pseudo or fictive kin, that provide mutual support and "respond creatively to the economic marginality imposed on their residents." Other research finds social networks among blacks to be smaller than those of whites or Hispanics but characterized by more family ties and more contact with network members (Ajrouch et al., 2001). In line with these findings, authors of the preceding chapters (Caldwell, Allen, & Assari, Chap. 12; Harding et al., Chap. 8; Murry et al., Chap. 2) argue that networks in which black males are embedded—particularly families—play meaningful roles in black males' lives and can be salient sources of protection against negative outcomes of poverty growing up in a racialized society (Barbarin, 1993).

Parents are primary agents of children's socialization (Maccoby, 1992), and Murry and colleagues (Chap. 2) emphasize parents in reviewing research on adaptive racial socialization (see also Stevenson, Chap. 5). Their review finds parental support and racial socialization associated with greater school readiness, increased academic expectations, improved mental health, and reduced involvement in risky behaviors. Indeed, in terms of substance use, black youth may be less influenced by peer networks and more by parents than their white or Hispanic counterparts (Resnicow, Soler, Braithwaite, Ahluwalia, & Butler, 2000). Parents, and in many cases grandparents and kin, also provide necessities such as food, housing, and financial support, important not only in childhood and adolescence, such as when kinship care meets demands for foster care placement (Scannapieco & Jackson,

1996), but also among adult men experiencing joblessness or other effects of incarceration (Harding et al., Chap. 8; Smith, Chap. 9; Hunter, Chap. 11). Other kin, especially women, are important in helping black men to improve health behaviors and seek medical care (Caldwell et al., Chap. 12; Griffith, Cornish, Sydika, & Dean, Chap. 13). However, as these authors note, the support these families provide depends on the resources they have available and the quality of their relationships. For example, nonresident fathers often want to be involved in their children's lives (Edin & Nelson, 2013; Mincy, Um, & Turpin, 2015), but are limited by poor relationships with their child's mother (Carlson, McLanahan, & Brooks-Gunn, 2008; Turney & Wildeman, 2013).

Fathers and other family members may be especially important for racial socialization among black boys, but so are teachers, counselors, coaches, religious leaders, and other institutional agents within their social networks (Stanton-Salazar, 1997). Anderson (1990) notes the loss of "old heads," that is, adult male role models from black communities who traditionally, had been important for socializing boys in the ways of family life and work. Educators and mentors in other settings may be able to compensate, especially if cultural gaps are met (McKay, Atkins, Hawkins, Brown, & Lynn, 2003; Sleeter, 2001). For example, Stevenson (Chap. 5) suggests ways in which racial socialization may be incorporated into school-based interventions in order to reduce racial disproportionality in school discipline (Skiba, Shure, & Williams, 2012). Furthermore, Griffin, Pérez, Holmes, and Mayo (2010) and Griffin (2012) describe the mutual benefits of mentor relationships between black faculty members and undergraduate students at predominately white colleges where blacks often face stereotypes such as being admitted for race rather than academic ability (Fries-Britt & Griffin, 2007). In addition, Harper (2013) found that racial socialization in peer networks of black male undergraduates was associated with campus engagement and leadership. Racial socialization may be most effective when family members and institutional agents communicate effectively and work together to promote resilience among black boys. It may be that such collaboration engenders greater network density in black communities (Oliver, 1988). However, structural conditions that undermine community cohesion such as family complexity, unemployment, and mass incarceration must also be addressed (Rose & Clear, 1998; Shaw & McKay, 1942; Sykes & Pettit, 2014; Western, 2002).

One reason family contexts are so often neglected in survey research on black males is the lack of black male participation in large-scale datasets. Studies of families often rely on household surveys which underrepresent black males due to factors like incarceration (Pettit, 2012) and housing instability (Lee et al., 2010; Wildeman, 2014). One exception is the Fragile Families and Child Well-being Study (used by Turney & Adams, Chap. 4), a birth cohort study of children (roughly half of whom are black) born in 20 of the largest US cities. Originally aimed at understanding experiences of unmarried parents (especially fathers), couples at baseline were interviewed in hospitals within days of their child's birth—a time when fathers were usually present and willing to be interviewed (Reichman, Teitler, Garfinkel, & McLanahan, 2001). A major source of data on unmarried fathers, the Fragile Families Study has spawned a tremendous body of research over the past

15 years, much of which focuses on racial variation and experiences of blacks relative to white or Hispanic children and fathers (e.g., Edin, Tach, & Mincy, 2009; Martinson, McLanahan, & Brooks-Gunn, 2012). However, the data may not be generalizable beyond urban families and do not allow for moving beyond the "bias toward studying young, unmarried fathers who are primarily from low socioeconomic backgrounds" (Roopnarine, 2004, p. 60). Such limitations underscore the need for longitudinal studies of black fathers, including their relationships with and impacts on their children, as well as the effects of their parental experiences on the men themselves.

## *Community Violence and Trauma*

Most prior research on race and community violence focuses on explaining race and gender gaps in violence perpetration or victimization (Light & Ulmer, 2016; Sampson, Morenoff, & Raudenbush, 2005). Though gender differences have declined in recent years (Sickmund & Puzzanchera, 2014), boys report higher levels of exposure to violence than girls (Ceballo, Dahl, Aretakis, & Ramirez, 2001; Perez-Smith, Albus, & Weist, 2001), perhaps because they engage in riskier behaviors or are monitored by parents less stringently (Albus, Weist, & Perez-Smith, 2004; Lambert, Ialongo, Boyd, & Cooley, 2005). Black-white gaps at the aggregate level are explained by greater levels of socioeconomic disadvantage among blacks (Light & Ulmer, 2016; Sampson et al., 2005), but survey data suggest that regardless of social class, black adolescents are at greater risk of exposure to violence than whites (Crouch, Hanson, Saunders, Kilpatrick, & Resnick, 2000), perhaps because middle-income blacks are more likely than whites to live in or near more disadvantaged neighborhoods (Adelman, 2004; Pattillo-McCoy, 1999).

We know much less about sources of within-group heterogeneity in violence exposure and its implications among black males. Some research examines resilience among black youth exposed to community violence and finds exposure associated with internalizing behavior problems (e.g., anxiety, depression) (Ceballo et al., 2001; Gaylord-Harden, Cunningham, & Zelencik, 2011; Li, Nussbaum, & Richards, 2007). Scholars suggest that families and communities may protect against mental health consequences of exposure to community violence (Horowitz, McKay, & Marshall, 2005; Howard, 1996), but results are somewhat inconsistent across studies. For example, Li et al. (2007) found no evidence of a buffering effect of family support. In contrast, O'Donnell, Schwab-Stone, and Muyeed (2002) found that parental and school support were positively associated with resilience but that peer support was linked to lower resilience. Most research on resilience focuses on short-term outcomes among boys and girls; findings that males are generally at greater risk than females suggests a need for more research on predictors of mental health and other indicators of resilience among black males specifically, and black men especially.

Particularly important will be studies that identify culturally-relevant protective factors, like adaptive racial socialization, that may help black boys and men cope with community violence exposure (Hardaway, Sterrett-Hong, Larkby, & Cornelius, 2016). Smith Lee's (Chap. 6) work begins to fill this gap by recognizing violence exposure as a source of trauma among black males and incorporating trauma-informed approaches into intervention efforts.

## Directions for Future Research on African American Boys and Men

In closing, we offer suggestions for effectively building on the three areas described above. We begin with a brief discussion of the role of intersectionality in conceptualizing heterogeneity among African American boys and men and then provide methodological recommendations. An intersectional approach emphasizes simultaneous experiences across multiple identifying characteristics (Crenshaw, 1994); for example, being a black male and an immigrant (Thomas, Chap. 3) or being a black male and a sexual minority (Hunter, Chap. 11). Two classifications that are broadly relevant among black males but deserve greater attention are gender identity and social class.

Among black males, research focuses more on racial identity than gender identity, but Rogers, Scott, and Way (2015) underscore the role of strong racial and gender identities for positive adjustment among black youth. Gender identity discussions generally focus on masculinity or hyper-masculinity, which previous chapters suggest may negatively influence resilience in terms of physical health or involvement in community violence (Griffith et al., Chap. 13; Powell et al. Chap. 14). Future research should examine how family and other social networks influence gender identity development, but other aspects also deserve attention. For example, in moving beyond narratives of disadvantage and vulnerability, scholars should consider ways in which black men and boys benefit from male privilege (Collins, 2000; Crenshaw, 1994). An intersectional approach allows for the examination of disadvantage and discrimination faced by black males face as well as privileges their male status confers (Adu-Poku, 2001).

With regards to intersectionality of race and social class, future research should examine experiences of black males of various economic strata. Prior research concentrates almost exclusively on the poor, even though most blacks are not poor (McAdoo, 1992; Pattillo-McCoy, 1999). Overall, black males may be disadvantaged relative whites, but social class plays a critical role in structuring life experiences (Day-Vines, Patton, & Baytops, 2003). If prior findings do not generalize across social class, readers may be left with a myopic view of black men and boys. Black males from higher class backgrounds may have greater access to social capital through family and social networks, which may be used a resources for resilience, including in terms of outcomes of exposure to community violence. From an intersectional perspective, social class likely affects experiences and contexts of racism and discrimination, how individuals are impacted, and the power individuals have to respond (Hardaway & McLoyd, 2009).

Beyond the value of new conceptual groundings, understanding of black men and boys will be advanced through methodological rigor and innovations. First, in keeping with the resilience literature's grounding in developmental and life-course perspectives, studies of resilience among black males should employ longitudinal designs. Reliance on cross-sectional studies limits opportunities to examine individual change over the life course and may also result in biased estimates of the effects of risk and adjustment problems. For example, an association between indicators of adaptive racial socialization and academic engagement could be due to unobserved characteristics of children in families and settings where such socialization is more likely to occur, rather than to causal processes (e.g., attending a predominately white school with better resources versus a mostly black school with fewer resources). Studies that examine time-varying covariates of within-individual change can control for observed and unobserved time-stable characteristics (Johnson, 1995). Furthermore, cross-sectional studies of children and youth that do not consider outcomes in adulthood and later life limit understanding of resilience across the life course. Thus, future studies should examine effects of exposure to community violence on long-term mental health outcomes. Such efforts should adopt prospective designs such as panel studies that track cohorts of boys as they transition to adulthood, or retrospective designs based on life-history calendars (Horney, Osgood, & Marshall, 1995) or personal narratives (Roy & Lucas, 2006).

Second, surveys of black males should incorporate methods for collecting data about families and other networks of individuals in hard-to-reach populations. Relying solely on household surveys may exclude institutionalized or otherwise "invisible" black boys and men (Pettit, 2012). Large-scale surveys of incarcerated individuals by the US Department of Justice and other organizations are important for understanding variation among such individuals, but they lack data on family and network ties outside the institution and inmate peers within, as well as how changes in these ties affect adjustment and well-being. One project that is advancing work in this area is the *Prison Inmate Networks Study* (Kreager et al., 2015) which uses a social network perspective (Wasserman & Faust, 1994) to examine changes over time in family relationships and peer ties among incarcerated men (roughly half are black) at a single prison. Two waves of in-prison data have been collected, and because incarceration most often appears to sever men's family ties (Edin et al., 2004; Lopoo & Western, 2005), a qualitative component is underway, which examines relationship experiences following release.

Additional studies that promise new insights about black men involve data collection using new technologies such as smartphones. Smartphones may be an especially effective method of collecting data on social networks of hard-to-reach populations because they are convenient and facilitate the collection of frequent self-reports, an important feature for populations with irregular routines and changing circumstances. One example is the *Newark Smartphone Reentry Project* (Sugie, 2016), which is gathering real-time data (e.g., "Who are you with right now?") over a three-month period from a sample of men on parole. Another is the *mDiary Study of Adolescent Relationships*, a supplement to the age-15 wave of the *Fragile Families Study*. More than 1200 youth in 16 cities participate in biweekly surveys about family, peers, and romantic relationships. As such methods become more feasible, future research should consider their use for collecting data from black men and boys who are recent immigrants, attending predominately white educational institutions, homeless, or in other conditions in which networks play an important role but deserve more attention in the literature.

## Conclusion

Research on African American men and boys continues to focus primarily on black-white differences and black deficits, with little attention to the tremendous variability among black boys and men and the strengths and resources they often display that lead to resilience over the life course (Shorters & Hudson, Jr., Chap. 15). The traditional focus contributes to a narrative that overlooks the agency of black males and discounts the complex ways that other characteristics like social class, masculinity, immigrant status, or family structure interact with racial oppression in their lives. In this concluding chapter, we have suggested three areas that may advance understanding of heterogeneity in research on black male well-being: (1) an emphasis on resilience; (2) greater attention to characteristics and influences of family, kin, and other social networks; and (3) research from a cultural perspective on exposure to community violence. By building in these areas, the research literature may provide a more complete portrayal of the diversity of black male experiences and help to dispel—rather than reinforce—negative stereotypes. In encouraging these steps, we echo other calls for research across the translational spectrum from descriptive studies to intervention research that does not shy away from—but instead explores the complexities and nuances in black male development and well-being (Burton, Burton, & Austin, Chap. 1; Celious & Oyserman, 2001).

## References

Adelman, R. M. (2004). Neighborhood opportunities, race, and class: The black middle class and residential segregation. *City and Community, 3*(1), 43–63.

Adu-Poku, S. (2001). Envisioning (black) male feminism: A cross-cultural perspective. *Journal of Gender Studies, 10*(2), 157–167.

Albus, K. E., Weist, M. D., & Perez-Smith, A. M. (2004). Associations between youth risk behavior and exposure to violence: Implications for the provision of mental health services in urban schools. *Behavior Modification, 28*(4), 548–564.

Ajrouch, K. J., Antonucci, T. C., & Janevic, M. R. (2001). Social networks among blacks and whites: The interaction between race and age. *The Journals of Gerontology Series B: Psychological Sciences and Social Sciences, 56*(2), S112–S118.

Amato, P. R., & Keith, B. (1991). Parental divorce and the well-being of children: A meta-analysis. *Psychological Bulletin, 110*(1), 26–46.

Anderson, E. (1990). *Streetwise: Race, class, and change in an urban community*. Chicago, IL: University of Chicago Press.

Anderson, M., Lopez, M. H., & Rohal, M. (2015). *A rising share of the U.S. black population is foreign born: 9 percent are immigrants; and while most are from the Caribbean, Africans drive recent growth*. Washington, DC: Pew Research Center.

Astone, N. M., & McLanahan, S. S. (1991). Family structure, parental practices and high school completion. *American Sociological Review, 56*(3), 309–320.

Barbarin, O. A. (1993). Coping and resilience: Exploring the inner lives of African American children. *Journal of Black Psychology, 19*(4), 478–492.

Beier, S. R., Rosenfeld, W. D., Spitalny, K. C., Zansky, S. M., & Bontempo, A. N. (2000). The potential role of an adult mentor in influencing high-risk behaviors in adolescents. *Archives of Pediatrics and Adolescent Medicine, 154*(4), 327–331.

Bennett, P. R., & Xie, Y. (2003). Revisiting racial differences in college attendance: The role of historically black colleges and universities. *American Sociological Review, 68*(4), 567–580.

Bronfenbrenner, U. (1974). Developmental research, public policy, and the ecology of childhood. *Child Development, 45*(1), 1–5.

Bronfenbrenner, U. (1986). Ecology of the family as a context for human development: Research perspectives. *Developmental Psychology, 22*(6), 723–742.

Brooks-Gunn, J., & Duncan, G. J. (1997). The effects of poverty on children. *The Future of Children, 7*(2), 55–71.

Cabrera, N. J., Ryan, R. M., Mitchell, S. J., Shannon, J. D., & Tamis-LeMonda, C. S. (2008). Low-income, nonresident father involvement with their toddlers: Variation by fathers' race and ethnicity. *Journal of Family Psychology, 22*(4), 643–647.

Carlson, M. J., McLanahan, S. S., & Brooks-Gunn, J. (2008). Coparenting and nonresident fathers' involvement with young children after a nonmarital birth. *Demography, 45*(2), 461–488.

Ceballo, R., Dahl, T. A., Aretakis, M. T., & Ramirez, C. (2001). Inner-city children's exposure to community violence: How much do parents know? *Journal of Marriage and the Family, 63*(4), 927–940.

Celious, A., & Oyserman, D. (2001). Race from the inside: An emerging heterogeneous race model. *Journal of Social Issues, 57*(1), 149–165.

Cochran, M. M., & Brassard, J. A. (1979). Child development and personal social networks. *Child Development, 50*(3), 601–616.

Coleman, J. S. (1988). Social capital in the creation of human capital. *American Journal of Sociology, 94*, S95–S120.

Collins, P. H. (2000). *Black feminist thought: Knowledge, consciousness, and the politics of empowerment*. New York, NY: Routledge.

Connell, J. P., Spencer, M. B., & Aber, J. L. (1994). Educational risk and resilience in African-American youth: Context, self, action, and outcomes in school. *Child Development, 65*(2), 493–506.

Crenshaw, K. W. (1994). Mapping the margins: Intersectionality, identity politics, and violence against women of color. In M. A. Fineman & R. Mykitiuk (Eds.), *The public nature of private violence* (pp. 93–118). New York, NY: Routledge.

Crosnoe, R. (2000). Friendships in childhood and adolescence: The life course and new directions. *Social Psychology Quarterly, 63*(4), 377–391.

Crouch, J. L., Hanson, R. F., Saunders, B. E., Kilpatrick, D. G., & Resnick, H. S. (2000). Income, race/ethnicity, and exposure to violence in youth: Results from the national survey of adolescents. *Journal of Community Psychology, 28*(6), 625–641.

Day-Vines, N. L., Patton, J., & Baytops, J. (2003). Counseling African American adolescents: The impact of race and middle class status. *Professional School Counseling, 7*(1), 40–51.
Demo, D. H., & Hughes, M. (1990). Socialization and racial identity among black Americans. *Social Psychology Quarterly, 53*(4), 364–374.
Dove, S. (2015). *Black male achievement in the U.S.: Why families matter*. Paper presented at the 23rd Annual National Symposium on Family Issues: Boys and Men in African American Families, University Park, PA.
Dunifon, R. E., Ziol-Guest, K. M., & Kopko, K. (2014). Grandparent coresidence and family well-being implications for research and policy. *The ANNALS of the American Academy of Political and Social Science, 654*(1), 110–126.
Edin, K., & Nelson, T. J. (2013). *Doing the best I can: Fatherhood in the inner city*. Berkeley, CA: University of California Press.
Edin, K., Nelson, T. J., & Paranal, R. (2004). Fatherhood and incarceration as potential turning points in the criminal careers of unskilled men. In M. Patillo, D. Weiman, & B. Western (Eds.), *Imprisoning America: The social effects of mass incarceration* (pp. 46–75). New York, NY: Russell Sage Foundation.
Edin, K., Tach, L., & Mincy, R. (2009). Claiming fatherhood: Race and the dynamics of paternal involvement among unmarried men. *The ANNALS of the American Academy of Political and Social Science, 621*(1), 149–177.
Elder, G. H. (1986). Military times and turning points in men's lives. *Developmental Psychology, 22*(2), 233–245.
Elder, G. H., Jr. (1998). The life course as developmental theory. *Child Development, 69*(1), 1–12.
Elder, G. H., Jr., Johnson, M. K., & Crosnoe, R. (2003). The emergence and development of life course theory. In J. T. Mortimer & M. J. Shanahan (Eds.), *Handbook of the life course* (pp. 3–22). New York, NY: Springer.
Erickson, L. D., McDonald, S., & Elder, G. H., Jr. (2009). Informal mentors and education: Complementary or compensatory resources? *Sociology of Education, 82*(4), 344–367.
Fries-Britt, S., & Griffin, K. (2007). The black box: How high-achieving blacks resist stereotypes about black Americans. *Journal of College Student Development, 48*(5), 509–524.
Garmezy, N. (1993). Children in poverty: Resilience despite risk. *Psychiatry, 56*(1), 127–136.
Gaylord-Harden, N. K., Cunningham, J. A., & Zelencik, B. (2011). Effects of exposure to community violence on internalizing symptoms: Does desensitization to violence occur in African American youth? *Journal of Abnormal Child Psychology, 39*(5), 711–719.
Geller, A., & Curtis, M. A. (2011). A sort of homecoming: Incarceration and the housing security of urban men. *Social Science Research, 40*(4), 1196–1213.
Giordano, P. C. (2003). Relationships in adolescence. *Annual Review of Sociology, 29*(1), 257–281.
Granovetter, M. S. (1973). The strength of weak ties. *American Journal of Sociology, 78*(6), 1360–1380.
Greenfield, E. A. (2011). Grandparent involvement and parenting stress among nonmarried mothers of young children. *Social Service Review, 85*(1), 135–157.
Griffin, K. A. (2012). Learning to mentor: A mixed methods study of the nature and influence of Black professors' socialization into their roles as mentors. *Journal of the Professoriate, 6*(2), 27–58.
Griffin, K. A., Pérez, D., Holmes, A. P., & Mayo, C. E. (2010). Investing in the future: The importance of faculty mentoring in the development of students of color in STEM. *New Directions for Institutional Research, 2010*(148), 95–103.
Hardaway, C. R., & McLoyd, V. C. (2009). Escaping poverty and securing middle class status: How race and socioeconomic status shape mobility prospects for African Americans during the transition to adulthood. *Journal of Youth and Adolescence, 38*(2), 242–256.
Hardaway, C. R., Sterrett-Hong, E., Larkby, C. A., & Cornelius, M. D. (2016). Family resources as protective factors for low-income youth exposed to community violence. *Journal of*

*Youth and Adolescence, 45*(7), 1309–1322. doi:10.1007/s10964-015-0410-1. Advance online publication.
Harper, S. R. (2012). *Black male student success in higher education: A report from the National Black Male College Achievement Study*. Philadelphia, PA: University of Pennsylvania, Center for the Study of Race and Equity in Education.
Harper, S. R. (2013). Am I my brother's teacher? Black undergraduates, racial socialization, and peer pedagogies in predominantly white postsecondary contexts. *Review of Research in Education, 37*(1), 183–211.
Harper, S. R. (2015). Black male college achievers and resistant responses to racist stereotypes at predominantly white colleges and universities. *Harvard Educational Review, 85*(4), 646–674.
Harper, S., Lynch, J., Burris, S., & Smith, G. D. (2007). Trends in the black-white life expectancy gap in the United States, 1983–2003. *Journal of the American Medical Association, 297*(11), 1224–1232.
Haynie, D. L. (2001). Delinquent peers revisited: Does network structure matter? *American Journal of Sociology, 106*(4), 1013–1057.
Horney, J., Osgood, D. W., & Marshall, I. H. (1995). Criminal careers in the short-term: Intra-individual variability in crime and its relation to local life circumstances. *American Sociological Review, 60*(5), 655–673.
Horowitz, K., McKay, M., & Marshall, R. (2005). Community violence and urban families: Experiences, effects, and directions for intervention. *American Journal of Orthopsychiatry, 75*(3), 356–368.
Howard, D. E. (1996). Searching for resilience among African-American youth exposed to community violence: Theoretical issues. *Journal of Adolescent Health, 18*(4), 254–262.
Hughes, D., Rodriguez, J., Smith, E. P., Johnson, D. J., Stevenson, H. C., & Spicer, P. (2006). Parents' ethnic-racial socialization practices: a review of research and directions for future study. *Developmental Psychology, 42*(5), 747.
Jencks, C., & Phillips, M. (2011). *The black-white test score gap*. Washington, DC: Brookings Institution Press.
Johnson, D. R. (1995). Alternative methods for the quantitative analysis of panel data in family research: Pooled time-series models. *Journal of Marriage and the Family, 57*(4), 1065–1077.
King, V. (1994). Variation in the consequences of nonresident father involvement for children's well-being. *Journal of Marriage and the Family, 56*(4), 963–972.
King, V., Harris, K. M., & Heard, H. E. (2004). Racial and ethnic diversity in nonresident father involvement. *Journal of Marriage and the Family, 66*(1), 1–21.
Kirk, D. S. (2009). A natural experiment on residential change and recidivism: Lessons from Hurricane Katrina. *American Sociological Review, 74*(3), 484–505.
Kirk, D. S. (2012). Residential change as a turning point in the life course of crime: Desistance or temporary cessation? *Criminology, 50*(2), 329–358.
Kreager, D. A., & Haynie, D. L. (2011). Dangerous liaisons? Dating and drinking diffusion in adolescent peer networks. *American Sociological Review, 76*(5), 737–763.
Kreager, D. A., Matsueda, R. L., & Erosheva, E. A. (2010). Motherhood and criminal desistance in disadvantaged neighborhoods. *Criminology, 48*(1), 221–258.
Kreager, D. A., Schaefer, D. R., Bouchard, M., Haynie, D. L., Wakefield, S., Young, J., et al. (2015). Toward a criminology of inmate networks. *Justice Quarterly, 33*(6), 1000–1028. doi:10.1080/07418825.2015.1016090. Advance online publication.
Lambert, S. F., Ialongo, N. S., Boyd, R. C., & Cooley, M. R. (2005). Risk factors for community violence exposure in adolescence. *American Journal of Community Psychology, 36*(1), 29–48.
Lareau, A. (2003). *Unequal childhood: The importance of social class in family life*. Berkeley, CA: University of California Press.
Laub, J. H., & Sampson, R. J. (2003). *Shared beginnings, divergent lives: Delinquent boys to age 70*. Cambridge, MA: Harvard University Press.
Lee, B. A., Tyler, K. A., & Wright, J. D. (2010). The new homelessness revisited. *Annual Review of Sociology, 36*, 501–521.

Lerner, R. M. (2002). *Concepts and theories of human development* (3rd ed.). Mahwah, NJ: Erlbaum.

Li, S. T., Nussbaum, K. M., & Richards, M. H. (2007). Risk and protective factors for urban African American youth. *American Journal of Community Psychology, 39*(1), 21–35.

Light, M. T., & Ulmer, J. T. (2016). Explaining the gaps in white, black, and Hispanic violence since 1990 accounting for immigration, incarceration, and inequality. *American Sociological Review, 81*(2), 290–315.

Lindsey, K. P., & Paul, G. L. (1989). Involuntary commitments to public mental institutions: Issues involving the overrepresentation of blacks and assessment of relevant functioning. *Psychological Bulletin, 106*(2), 171–183.

Lopoo, L. M., & Western, B. (2005). Incarceration and the formation and stability of marital unions. *Journal of Marriage and Family, 67*(3), 721–734.

Maccoby, E. E. (1992). The role of parents in the socialization of children: An historical overview. *Developmental Psychology, 28*(6), 1006–1017.

Manning, W. D., Brown, S. L., & Stykes, J. B. (2014). Family complexity among children in the United States. *The ANNALS of the American Academy of Political and Social Science, 654*(1), 48–65.

Manning, W. D., & Lamb, K. A. (2003). Adolescent well-being in cohabiting, married, and single-parent families. *Journal of Marriage and Family, 65*(4), 876–893.

Martin, J. A., Hamilton, B. E., Osterman, M. J. K., Curtin, S. C., & Mathews, T. J. (2015). *Births: Final data for 2013*. Washington, DC: National Vital Statistics System.

Martinson, M. L., McLanahan, S., & Brooks-Gunn, J. (2012). Race/ethnic and nativity disparities in child overweight in the United States and England. *The ANNALS of the American Academy of Political and Social Science, 643*(1), 219–238.

Masten, A. S. (2001). Ordinary magic: Resilience processes in development. *American Psychologist, 56*(3), 227–238.

McAdoo, H. P. (1992). Upward mobility and parenting in middle-income black families. In K. H. Burlew, W. C. Banks, H. P. McAdoo, & D. A. Ya Azibo (Eds.), *African American psychology* (pp. 63–86). Newbury Park, CA: Sage Publications.

McHale, S. M., Bissell, J., & Kim, J.-Y. (2009). Sibling relationship, family, and genetic factors in sibling similarity in sexual risk. *Journal of Family Psychology, 23*(4), 562–572.

McKay, M. M., Atkins, M. S., Hawkins, T., Brown, C., & Lynn, C. J. (2003). Inner-city African American parental involvement in children's schooling: Racial socialization and social support from the parent community. *American Journal of Community Psychology, 32*(1–2), 107–114.

McLanahan, S., & Sandefur, G. (1994). *Growing up with a single parent. What hurts, what helps*. Cambridge, MA: Harvard University Press.

Miller, D. B. (1999). Racial socialization and racial identity: Can they promote resiliency for African American adolescents? *Adolescence, 34*(135), 493–501.

Miller, D. B., & MacIntosh, R. (1999). Promoting resilience in urban African American adolescents: Racial socialization and identity as protective factors. *Social Work Research, 23*(3), 159–169.

Mincy, R., Um, H., & Turpin, J. (2015). Effect of father engagement on child behaviors. In S. M. McHale, V. King, J. Van Hook, & A. Booth (Eds.), *Gender and couple relationships* (pp. 141–159). New York, NY: Springer.

National Center for Education Statistics (NCES). (2013). *Percentage of 18-to 24-year olds enrolled in degree-granting institutions, by level of institution and sex and race/ethnicity of student: 1967 through 2012* (Table 302.60). http://nces.ed.gov/programs/digest/d13/tables/dt13_302.60.asp. Accessed May 2016.

Neblett, E. W., Philip, C. L., Cogburn, C. D., & Sellers, R. M. (2006). African American adolescents' discrimination experiences and academic achievement: Racial socialization as a cultural compensatory and protective factor. *Journal of Black Psychology, 32*(2), 199–218.

O'Donnell, D. A., Schwab-Stone, M. E., & Muyeed, A. Z. (2002). Multidimensional resilience in urban children exposed to community violence. *Child Development, 73*(4), 1265–1282.

Oliver, M. L. (1988). The urban black community as network: Toward a social network perspective. *The Sociological Quarterly, 29*(4), 623–645.

Osgood, D. W., Ragan, D. T., Wallace, L., Gest, S. D., Feinberg, M. E., & Moody, J. (2013). Peers and the emergence of alcohol use: Influence and selection processes in adolescent friendship networks. *Journal of Research on Adolescence, 23*(3), 500–512.

Osgood, D. W., Wilson, J. K., O'malley, P. M., Bachman, J. G., & Johnston, L. D. (1996). Routine activities and individual deviant behavior. *American Sociological Review, 61*, 635–655.

Pattillo-McCoy, M. (1999). *Black picket fences: Privilege and peril among the Black middle class*. Chicago, IL: University of Chicago Press.

Perez-Smith, A. M., Albus, K. E., & Weist, M. D. (2001). Exposure to violence and neighborhood affiliation among inner-city youth. *Journal of Clinical Child Psychology, 30*(4), 464–472.

Pettit, B. (2012). *Invisible men: Mass incarceration and the myth of black progress*. New York, NY: Russell Sage Foundation.

Pettit, B., & Western, B. (2004). Mass imprisonment and the life course: Race and class inequality in US incarceration. *American Sociological Review, 69*(2), 151–169.

Pittman, L. D. (2007). Grandmothers' involvement among young adolescents growing up in poverty. *Journal of Research on Adolescence, 17*(1), 89–116.

Rastogi, S., Johnson, T. D., Hoeffel, E. M., & Drewery, M. P., Jr. (2011). *The black population: 2010*. Washington, DC: United States Census Bureau.

Reichman, N. E., Teitler, J. O., Garfinkel, I., & McLanahan, S. S. (2001). Fragile families: Sample and design. *Children and Youth Services Review, 23*(4), 303–326.

Resnicow, K., Soler, R., Braithwaite, R. L., Ahluwalia, J. S., & Butler, J. (2000). Cultural sensitivity in substance use prevention. *Journal of Community Psychology, 28*(3), 271–290.

Rogers, L. O., Scott, M. A., & Way, N. (2015). Racial and gender identity among black adolescent males: An intersectionality perspective. *Child Development, 86*(2), 407–424.

Roopnarine, J. L. (2004). African American and African Caribbean fathers: Level, quality, and meaning of involvement. In M. E. Lamb (Ed.), *The role of the father in child development* (4th ed., pp. 58–97). Hoboken, NJ: John Wiley & Sons.

Rose, D. R., & Clear, T. R. (1998). Incarceration, social capital, and crime: Implications for social disorganization theory. *Criminology, 36*(3), 441–480.

Roy, K. M., & Lucas, K. (2006). Generativity as second chance: Low-income fathers and transformation of the difficult past. *Research in Human Development, 3*(2–3), 139–159.

Rubin, D. M., Downes, K. J., O'Reilly, A. L. R., Mekonnen, R., Luan, X., & Localio, R. (2008). Impact of kinship care on behavioral well-being for children in out-of-home care. *Archives of Pediatrics and Adolescent Medicine, 162*(6), 550–556.

Sampson, R. J., & Laub, J. H. (1996). Socioeconomic achievement in the life course of disadvantaged men: Military service as a turning point, circa 1940–1965. *American Sociological Review, 61*(3), 347–367.

Sampson, R. J., Morenoff, J. D., & Raudenbush, S. (2005). Social anatomy of racial and ethnic disparities in violence. *American Journal of Public Health, 95*(2), 224–232.

Sarkisian, N., & Gerstel, N. (2004). Kin support among blacks and whites: Race and family organization. *American Sociological Review, 69*(6), 812–837.

Scannapieco, M., & Jackson, S. (1996). Kinship care: The African American response to family preservation. *Social Work, 41*(2), 190–196.

Seeman, T. E., Lusignolo, T. M., Albert, M., & Berkman, L. (2001). Social relationships, social support, and patterns of cognitive aging in healthy, high-functioning older adults: MacArthur Studies of Successful Aging. *Health Psychology, 20*(4), 243–255.

Seligman, M. E. P., & Csikszentmihalyi, M. (2000). Positive psychology: An introduction. *American Psychologist, 55*(1), 5–14.

Shaw, C. R., & McKay, H. D. (1942). *Juvenile delinquency and urban areas*. Chicago, IL: University of Chicago Press.

Sickmund, M., & Puzzanchera, C. (2014). *Juvenile offenders and victims: 2014 national report*. Pittsburgh, PA: National Center for Juvenile Justice.

Skiba, R. J., Shure, L., & Williams, N. (2012). Racial and ethnic disproportionality in suspension and expulsion. In A. L. Noltemeyer & C. S. Mcloughlin (Eds.), *Disproportionality in education and special education* (pp. 89–118). Springfield, IL: Charles C. Thomas Publisher, Ltd.
Sleeter, C. E. (2001). Preparing teachers for culturally diverse schools research and the overwhelming presence of whiteness. *Journal of Teacher Education, 52*(2), 94–106.
Stanton-Salazar, R. (1997). A social capital framework for understanding the socialization of racial minority children and youths. *Harvard Educational Review, 67*(1), 1–41.
Sugie, N. F. (2016). Utilizing smartphones to study disadvantaged and hard-to-reach groups. *Sociological Methods and Research*. Advance online publication. doi:10.1177/0049124115626176.
Sykes, B. L., & Pettit, B. (2014). Mass incarceration, family complexity, and the reproduction of childhood disadvantage. *The ANNALS of the American Academy of Political and Social Science, 654*(1), 127–149.
Thornberry, T. P. (2009). The apple doesn't fall far from the tree (or does it?): Intergenerational patterns of antisocial behavior—The American Society of Criminology 2008 Sutherland address. *Criminology, 47*(2), 297–325.
Travis, J., Western, B., & Redburn, S. (2014). *The growth of incarceration in the United States: Exploring causes and consequences*. Washington, DC: National Academy Press.
Turney, K., & Wildeman, C. (2013). Redefining relationships: Explaining the countervailing consequences of paternal incarceration for parenting. *American Sociological Review, 78*(6), 949–979.
Uchino, B. N. (2006). Social support and health: A review of physiological processes potentially underlying links to disease outcomes. *Journal of Behavioral Medicine, 29*(4), 377–387.
Uggen, C. (2000). Work as a turning point in the life course of criminals: A duration model of age, employment, and recidivism. *American Sociological Review, 65*(4), 529–546.
Uggen, C., & Staff, J. (2001). Work as a turning point for criminal offenders. *Corrections Management Quarterly, 5*(4), 1–16.
Warr, M. (1998). Life-course transitions and desistance from crime. *Criminology, 36*(2), 183–216.
Wasserman, S., & Faust, K. (1994). *Social network analysis: Methods and applications*. Cambridge, UK: Cambridge University Press.
Wellman, B., & Wortley, S. (1990). Different strokes from different folks: Community ties and social support. *American Journal of Sociology, 96*(3), 558–588.
Western, B. (2002). The impact of incarceration on wage mobility and inequality. *American Sociological Review, 96*(3), 526–546.
Western, B., & Pettit, B. (2005). Black-white wage inequality, employment rates, and incarceration. *American Journal of Sociology, 111*(2), 553–578.
Wildeman, C. (2014). Parental incarceration, child homelessness, and the invisible consequences of mass imprisonment. *The ANNALS of the American Academy of Political and Social Science, 651*(1), 74–96.
Wong, C. A., Eccles, J. S., & Sameroff, A. (2003). The influence of ethnic discrimination and ethnic identification on African American adolescents' school and socioemotional adjustment. *Journal of Personality, 71*(6), 1197–1232.

ERRATUM

# Families, Prisoner Reentry, and Reintegration

**David J. Harding, Jeffrey D. Morenoff, Cheyney C. Dobson, Erin B. Lane, Kendra Opatovsky, Ed-Dee G. Williams, and Jessica Wyse**


L. Burton et al. (eds.), *Boys and Men in African American Families*, National Symposium on Family Issues 7, DOI 10.1007/978-3-319-43847-4_8

**DOI 10.1007/978-3-319-43847-4_17**

**Chapter opening page:**

The error is in Chapter 8, page 105: The co-author name should read Erin B. Lane instead of Erin R. Lane.

**Contents:**

In page x, author name has been changed from Erin R. Lane to Erin B. Lane

**Contributors:**

In page xii, author name has been changed from Erin R. Lane to Erin B. Lane

The updated original online version for this chapter can be found at http://dx.doi.org/10.1007/978-3-319-43847-4_8


L. Burton et al. (eds.), *Boys and Men in African American Families*, National Symposium on Family Issues 7, DOI 10.1007/978-3-319-43847-4_17

# Index





L. Burton et al. (eds.), *Boys and Men in African American Families*, National Symposium on Family Issues 7, DOI 10.1007/978-3-319-43847-4

The manufacturer's authorised representative in the EU is Springer Nature Customer Service Centre GmbH, Europaplatz 3, 69115 Heidelberg, Germany. If you have any concerns regarding our products, please contact ProductSafety@springernature.com

Printed and bound by CPI Group (UK) Ltd, Croydon, CR0 4YY
25/09/2026
02222893-0002